D1532466

2016 YOUR NEW ASTROLOGY HOROSCOPES

Chinese & Western
Predictions for 2016
The Year of the
Fire Monkey

BY
SUZANNE WHITE

Who Takes Full Responsibility For All Typos, Grammar Mistakes
And Other Goofs

Thanks Will Schwarz, for your willing assistance and tireless,
dependable quest for the perfectly turned phrase. sw

SUZANNE WHITE'S

ANNUAL NEW ASTROLOGY™ FORECASTS FOR

2016
THE YEAR OF THE FIRE MONKEY
FEBRUARY 8, 2016 THROUGH JAN 27, 2017

COMPLETE MONTH-BY-MONTH PREDICTIONS FOR ALL 24 (12 WESTERN AND 12 CHINESE) ASTROLOGICAL SIGNS

INTRODUCTION

(Please read. Not boring.)

On February 7, 2016, the eccentrically turbulent Wood Sheep year will be over. Long live the merrier, more entertaining and stimulating year of the Fire Monkey.

On February 8, 2016 all the herded Sheep and gamboling Goats will scamper back to their mountain and farmyard retreats, leaving us with an exciting Fire Monkey Year that promises to bring us a boatload of surprises. Some jolly ones. And some not so amusing. But think of it! If ever you had a brainstorm or a wild dream, the Fire Monkey is the go-to guy for results. Of all years, this year you can *do* it. Nothing stumps a Monkey. Monkeys were born to find solutions to our most complex problems. Monkeys don't let any bananas get too ripe on their watch. Directly the fruit turns from green to a golden yellow, Monkeys pounce on it and gobble it down. Do likewise this year. Court your dreams. Seduce yourself into achieving goals and un-sticking yourself from any and all inertia. Rejoice! But watch your back. Monkeys can be devious.

AUTHOR'S NOTE: In Africa (and India), the natives use a technique to catch monkeys. They hollow out one end of a coconut and put peanuts in there (I've also heard bananas...but same concept). The monkey puts his hand in the coconut and when he makes a fist to grab the peanuts, he's trapped. The natives will pull a string attached to the other end of the coconut and capture the monkey. In other words, in order to set ourselves free to forge our own lives - our own way - all we have to do is let go of the peanuts. sw

TABLE OF CONTENTS

WHAT IS THE NEW ASTROLOGY™?

THE NEW ASTROLOGY™ is a revolutionary astrological concept that, some years ago, I dared to invent and write a book about. To create The New Astrology™, I combined the attributes of our 12 Western signs with those of the 12 Chinese signs and I came up with **144 *New* Astrology signs.**

For example, if you are a Sagittarius and were born in 1937,49, 61,73 or 97 then you are a Sagittarius/Ox. You sincerely believe you are never wrong. You like to help others. You are an eloquent fast talker - direct, humanistic, openhanded and strong. It's simple. Take your regular, familiar western astrological sign and match it with the animal sign of the year you were born. **Now you know your NEW ASTROLOGY™ sign**

BUT WHICH IS YOUR CHINESE SIGN?
FIND IT ON THIS CHINESE CALENDAR

NOTE: Capricorn and Aquarius
Find Exact Dates For Your Years On The Calendar Below

THE CHINESE CALENDAR SINCE 1900

Year | Sign | Element | Year begins | Year ends

1900 | Rat | Metal | 1/31/1900 | 2/18/1901

1901 | Ox | Metal | 2/19/1901 | 2/7/1902

1902 | Tiger | Water | 2/8/1902 | 1/28/1903

1903 | Cat | Water | 1/29/1903 | 2/15/1904

1904 | Dragon | Wood | 2/16/1904 | 2/3/1905

1905 | Snake | Wood | 2/4/1905 | 1/24/1906

1906 | Horse | Fire | 1/25/1906 | 2/12/1907

1907 | Goat | Fire | 2/13/1907 | 2/1/1908

1908 | Monkey | Earth | 2/2/1908 | 1/21/1909

1909 | Rooster | Earth | 1/22/1909 | 2/9/1910

1910 | Dog | Metal | 2/10/1910 | 1/29/1911

1911 | Pig | Metal | 1/30/1911 | 2/17/1912

1912 | Rat | Water | 2/18/1912 | 2/5/1913

1913 | Ox | Water | 2/6/1913 | 1/25/1914

1914 | Tiger | Wood | 1/26/1914 | 2/13/1915

1915 | Cat | Wood | 2/14/1915 | 2/2/1916

1916 | Dragon | Fire | 2/3/1916 | 1/22/1917

1917 | Snake | Fire | 1/23/1917 | 2/10/1918

1918 | Horse | Earth | 2/11/1918 | 1/31/1919

1919 | Goat | Earth | 2/1/1919 | 2/19/1920

1920 | Monkey | Metal | 2/20/1920 | 2/7/1921

1921 | Rooster | Metal | 2/8/1921 | 1/27/1922

1922 | Dog | Water | 1/28/1922 | 2/15/1923

1923 | Pig | Water | 2/16/1923 | 2/4/1924

1924 | Rat | Wood | 2/5/1924 | 1/23/1925

1925 | Ox | Wood | 1/24/1925 | 2/12/1926

1926 | Tiger | Fire | 2/13/1926 | 2/1/1927

1927 | Cat | Fire | 2/2/1927 | 1/22/1928

Year | *Sign* | *Element* | *Year begins* | *Year ends*

1928 | Dragon | Earth | 1/23/1928 | 2/9/1929

1929 | Snake | Earth | 2/10/1929 | 1/29/1930

1930 | Horse | Metal | 1/30/1930 | 2/16/1931

1931 | Goat | Metal | 2/17/1931 | 2/5/1932

1932 | Monkey | Water | 2/6/1932 | 1/25/1933

1933 | Rooster | Water | 1/26/1933 | 2/13/1934

1934 | Dog | Wood | 2/14/1934 | 2/3/1935

1935 | Pig | Wood | 2/4/1935 | 1/23/1936

1936 | Rat | Fire | 1/24/1936 | 2/10/1937

1937 | Ox | Fire | 2/11/1937 | 1/30/1938

1938 | Tiger | Earth | 1/31/1938 | 2/18/1939

1939 | Cat | Earth | 2/19/1939 | 2/7/1940

1940 | Dragon | Metal | 2/8/1940 | 1/26/1941

1941 | Snake | Metal | 1/27/1941 | 2/14/1942

1942 | Horse | Water | 2/15/1942 | 2/4/1943

1943 | Goat | Water | 2/5/1943 | 1/24/1944

1944 | Monkey | Wood | 1/25/1944 | 2/12/1945

1945 | Rooster | Wood | 2/13/1945 | 2/1/1946

1946 | Dog | Fire | 2/2/1946 | 1/21/1947

1947 | Pig | Fire | 1/22/1947 | 2/9/1948

1948 | Rat | Earth | 2/10/1948 | 1/28/1949

1949 | Ox | Earth | 1/29/1949 | 2/16/1950

1950 | Tiger | Metal | 2/17/1950 | 2/5/1951

1951 | Cat | Metal | 2/6/1951 | 1/26/1952

1952 | Dragon | Water | 1/27/1952 | 2/13/1953

1953 | Snake | Water | 2/14/1953 | 2/2/1954

1954 | Horse | Wood | 2/3/1954 | 1/23/1955

1955 | Goat | Wood | 1/24/1955 | 2/11/1956

1956 | Monkey | Fire | 2/12/1956 | 1/30/1957

1957 | Rooster | Fire | 1/31/1957 | 2/17/1958

1958 | Dog | Earth | 2/18/1958 | 2/7/1959

1959 | Pig | Earth | 2/8/1959 | 1/27/1960

1960 | Rat | Metal | 1/28/1960 | 2/14/1961

1961 | Ox | Metal | 2/15/1961 | 2/4/1962

1962 | Tiger | Water | 2/5/1962 | 1/24/1963

1963 | Cat | Water | 1/25/1963 | 2/12/1964

1964 | Dragon | Wood | 2/13/1964 | 2/1/1965

Year | *Sign* | *Element* | *Year begins* | *Year ends*

1965 | Snake | Wood | 2/2/1965 | 1/20/1966

1966 | Horse | Fire | 1/21/1966 | 2/8/1967

1967 | Goat | Fire | 2/9/1967 | 1/29/1968

1968 | Monkey | Earth | 1/30/1968 | 2/16/1969

1969 | Rooster | Earth | 2/17/1969 | 2/5/1970

1970 | Dog | Metal | 2/6/1970 | 1/26/1971

1971 | Pig | Metal | 1/27/1971 | 2/14/1972

1972 | Rat | Water | 2/15/1972 | 2/2/1973

1973 | Ox | Water | 2/3/1973 | 1/22/1974

1974 | Tiger | Wood | 1/23/1974 | 2/10/1975

1975 | Cat | Wood | 2/11/1975 | 1/30/1976

1976 | Dragon | Fire | 1/31/1976 | 2/17/1977

1977 | Snake | Fire | 2/18/1977 | 2/6/1978

1978 | Horse | Earth | 2/7/1978 | 1/27/1979

1979 | Goat | Earth | 1/28/1979 | 2/15/1980

1980 | Monkey | Metal | 2/16/1980 | 2/4/1981

1981 | Rooster | Metal | 2/5/1981 | 1/24/1982

1982 | Dog | Water | 1/25/1982 | 2/12/1983

1983 | Pig | Water | 2/13/1983 | 2/1/1984

1984 | Rat | Wood | 2/2/1984 | 2/19/1985

1985 | Ox | Wood | 2/20/1985 | 2/8/1986

1986 | Tiger | Fire | 2/9/1986 | 1/28/1987

1987 | Cat | Fire | 1/29/1987 | 2/16/1988

1988 | Dragon | Earth | 2/17/1988 | 2/5/1989

1989 | Snake | Earth | 2/6/1989 | 1/26/1990

1990 | Horse | Metal | 1/27/1990 | 2/14/1991

1991 | Goat | Metal | 2/15/1991 | 2/3/1992

1992 | Monkey | Water | 2/4/1992 | 1/22/1993

1993 | Rooster | Water | 1/23/1993 | 2/9/1994

1994 | Dog | Wood | 2/10/1994 | 1/30/1995

1995 | Pig | Wood | 1/31/1995 | 2/18/1996

1996 | Rat | Fire | 2/19/1996 | 2/6/1997

1997 | Ox | Fire | 2/7/1997 | 1/27/1998

1998 | Tiger | Earth | 1/28/1998 | 2/15/1999

1999 | Cat | Earth | 2/16/1999 | 2/4/2000

2000 | Dragon | Metal | 2/5/2000 | 1/23/2001

2001 | Snake | Metal | 1/24/2001 | 2/11/2002

2002 | Horse | Water | 2/12/2002 | 1/31/2003

Year | *Sign | Element | Year ends | Year begins*

2003 | Goat | Water | 2/1/2003 | 1/21/2004

2004 | Monkey | Wood | 1/22/2004 | 2/8/2005

2005 | Rooster | Wood | 2/9/2005 | 1/28/2006

2006 | Dog | Fire | 1/29/2006 | 2/17/2007

2007 | Pig | Fire | 2/18/2007 | 2/6/2008

2008 | Rat | Earth | 2/7/2008 | 1/25/2009

2009 | Ox | Earth | 1/26/2009 | 2/13/2010

2010 | Tiger | Metal | 2/14/2010 | 2/2/2011

2011 | Cat | Metal | 2/3/2011 | 1/22/2012

2012 | Dragon | Water | 1/23/2012 | 2/9/2013

2013 | Snake | Water | 2/10/2013 | 1/30/2014

2014 | Horse | Wood | 1/31/2014 | 2/18/2015

2015 | Goat | Wood | 2/19/2015 | 2/7/2016

2016 | Monkey | Fire | 2/8/2016 | 1/27/2017

2017 | Rooster | Fire | 1/28/2017 | 2/15/2018

2018 | Dog | Earth | 2/16/2018 | 2/4/2019

2019 | Pig | Earth | 2/5/2019 | 1/24//2020

READ YOUR NEW ASTROLOGY™ SIGN'S HOROSCOPE FOR 2016

Let's say you followed the instructions above and discovered that you are a Cancer/Tiger. To get the complete Cancer/Tiger Horoscope for any given month of 2016, start by reading the monthly predictions for CANCER. After you have digested your CANCER predictions, take a deep breath and turn to the Chinese Zodiac Signs half of the book. Read the month's predictions for TIGER. Then, switch on your mental blender and whip Cancer and Tiger together. In a wink, the Cancer and Tiger forecasts will merge and you will know what will be going on in your New Astrology™ sign's life for the month ahead.

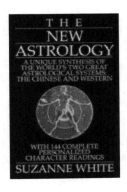

E-Book available at **http://www.suzannewhite.com**

Or from **http://www.Amazon.com**

http://www.Apple.com

http://www.Barnes&Noble.com

http://www.Draft2Digital.com

Handsome (690 page/ 144 New Astrology Signs) Paperback Available from http://www.Amazon.com and all fine booksellers.

MONKEYSHINES

MONKEYS POSSESS THE FOLLOWING CHARACTERISTICS

THEY ARE:

*ACUTELY INTELLIGENT • WITTY • CREATIVE • AFFABLE •
PROBLEM-SOLVERS • INDEPENDENT • SKILLFUL •
ACHIEVERS • ENTHUSIASTIC • LUCID • NIMBLE • PASSIONATE
YOUTHFUL • AGILE • ENTERTAINING*

BUT MONKEYS CAN ALSO BE:

*SCHEMING • VAIN • MANIPULATIVE • OPPORTUNISTIC • PROLIX
• DISINGENUOUS • JUVENILE • UNSCRUPULOUS • NEUROTIC •
DECEITFUL • SHREWD • DESIGNING*

A QUICK LOOK AT THE BASIC MONKEY MAKEUP

When they are not tempted to be naughty, Monkeys are the most affable, capable people ever. They are both perceptive and witty. They are crafty and intelligent. They know how to finagle and wangle. Monkeys also have a Santa Claus side. They distribute gifts, offer presents and bestow charity (and sometimes loans) with abandon. Monkeys are a spot juvenile and, like kids, are often mischievous. And when Monkeys get into mischief, hold your hats! But don't take off your clothes. Not yet anyway.

Monkeys have enormous charm and oodles of redeeming social value. They can manage any enterprise, deftly and with razor-sharp skill, from behind the scenes. Neither power hungry nor glory seeking, Monkeys revel in finding answers to even the most zig-zaggy of questions. And they demand little or no applause or recognition in return. If you want to see who is running any show, sidle on backstage. There, you are very likely to encounter a marvelous merry Monkey.

Monkeys are not always direct. They can be outrageously tricky. They are sly when they need to be. Yet, when the situation calls for cunning, Monkeys smile pretty and dance with the guy who brought them. Monkeys may scheme and plot. But when it comes to dealing directly with any delicate situation, Monkey people are entirely improvisational. Nobody in the whole Chinese Zodiac can beat the Monkey for agility and slip slidin' away. Problem to solve? Decision to make? Need practical advice? Get the Monkey App. Or simply Dial-a- Monkey.

2016 THE FIRE MONKEY YEAR OVERVIEW
2016

The influence of the Fire Monkey in 2016 will cause many of our preconceived notions to hit the fan. It's going to be a scurrying kind of year. Individuals can accomplish great deeds. But extremist group movements will have less and less effect on the world at large. Fire Monkey years are chockablock with wakeup calls for all and sundry. Fire Monkeys have no time for ostriches.

Sweeping global shifts are afoot. Whether it's climate change which brings everything from volcanic eruptions to cyclones, drought, floods and unbearable heat and cold spells. Or it's the prevalence now of religious wars when enemies fight each other over whose God is the best God and whose God doesn't count. These, we know are futile wars. But they exist and will persist and even try to worsen in the Fire Monkey Year. Another planetary niggle in 2016 will be about massive exodus and immigration of desperate refugees from the above-mentioned conflicts. Many war-torn countries today can do nothing for their people who are homeless and frightened and hungry. So these same people (understandably) need to leave their stricken lands and find a place where they can live in safety and peace and try to make a better life for themselves. Trouble is, where can they go? Where will they be welcomed and accepted? Looks like 2016 will be chockablock with trials and tribulations. In other words, 2016 might be the perfect time to **Dial-A -Monkey.**

Because 2016 is a Fire Monkey Year, progress will be accelerated in all the above areas. Wars might not stop being fought and tornadoes and earthquakes may not desist. But the Monkey, you will remember, is the problem solver. The arrival of a Monkey year just at this juncture, is like a sunrise full of hope. Monkeys find solutions to even the most labyrinthine of issues. And they do it in subtle ways that other, less wily and crafty signs, would find impossible. Everybody's life will be somehow altered because of the Monkey's know-how in 2016.

In 2016, alternative energies to dangerous pollutants will suddenly be taken seriously and developed quickly. Populations everywhere will begin calling for reforms to delay the progress of global warming. Detractors and fanatics who have resisted the idea of climate change will be forced to accept that the consequences of their faulty beliefs are grave and they can no longer hide behind reactionary rhetoric. Let's face it. When the underpinnings of their million dollar seaside villas begin eroding and their houses teeter on the brink and threaten to topple into the ocean, even the most conservative climate change dinosaurs will begin to pay attention to what reforms are necessary to save the earth from self destruction.

In 2016, unconventional medical advances and a new respect for naturopathic cures will also thrive. Already we see that scads of people are fed up with allopathic remedies that not only make people sicker, they don't always cure them. Instead they treat the symptoms - not the cause. The Fire Monkey will see to it that this trend changes. In 2016, more and more patients will be drawn to homeopathy, acupuncture, osteopathy, naturopathy, traditional Chinese medicine, Ayurveda and many other nonconformist techniques. Health maintenance and disease prevention products such as food supplements and natural healing methods will begin to be taken seriously. 2016 could be just the right time to invest in the stocks of laboratories which make vitamins, homeopathic remedies, food supplements and the like.

During this Fire Money year more and more countries will be outlawing toxic insecticides and refusing to allow farmers to use genetically modified seeds (GMO's). It's the Monkey's job to clean up what has gotten muddled and soiled through greed. Monkey years are famous for making order out of chaos.

Monkeys are forever seeking novel solutions for all the world's problems. The Monkey, instead of looking at the problem, looks through it, calculates the risks and then begins to pick it apart. This unique method of sorting out predicaments gives the Monkey an edge. Monkeys have few hostile verbal confrontations because their enemies know full well that they are up against a superior Monkey mind.

This is not to say that the Monkey year will always favor your side. If you are a Dragon or a Rat, you might have an easier row to hoe in 2016. Not so the Rooster or the Dog who consider Monkeys scatty and inconsequential. And by comparison to the hardworking Horse or the slog and drudge Ox person, Monkeys look like lightweights. But they are not. Monkeys achieve their goals. But often they don't succeed merely through sheer toil and trudge. Monkeys get what they want by adapting their behavior to the situation and then setting about dismantling it in order to fix it.

On a personal level, everyone will be called upon this year to take stock of the condition of their bodies. Some of us are dealing with extra body weight. Others have developed chronic conditions such as carpal tunnel syndrome, trick knees or tennis elbow. Some people ache in every joint. 2016 will be the perfect year to start a régime and perform at least one detox. Simultaneously hie yourself to a physical therapist who can guide you through exercises to heal even the most painful and debilitating complaints. Too, you should either join a gym, swim 4 times a week, jog or sign up for courses in Pilates, Yoga, Zumba or Cycling. If you can afford it, hire a coach to assist you in building and maintaining muscle. If you're too fat, see a nutrionist and follow their instructions. If all of the above approaches are also above your means, grab a throw rug and switch on an exercise video. Not just Jane Fonda, but myriad other trainers have made excellent videos for those of us who haven't the money, time or inclination to leave the house to work out. The Fire Monkey year urges and even pushes us to find original ways to remain healthy and strong.

Love in the Fire Monkey year? Well... it's iffy. There are some New Astrology™ signs whose love lives will float along without incident this year. Others of you will encounter snag after snag, often having to do with one of the members of the couple evolving and growing in a direction that both frightens and alienates the other. If you are planning to improve your life and/or make huge personal changes this year, don't forget to inform your partner and, if they so desire, take them along for the ride. The more you do together, the closer you will become. This advice however doesn't always work. If a portly couch potato guy suddenly notices his formerly chubby wife slinking around in skintight leotards weighting 30 pounds less, he may freak out. Why didn't she tell him? What has she been up to? How did she get so thin? Ditto the wife who notices her husband choosing colorful spiffy garments and developing sexy new muscles? She wonders: *Is he having an affair? Is he gay? Has he gone mad?* So when you take up a health-improving practice this year, include your sweetheart. Leave them in the dark and you may one day come home to an empty house. No matter how passionate you are about your bodywork and cures for chronic ills, remember to maintain a satisfactory level of passion between the sheets.

The real estate markets will improve in 2016. Low interest bank loans for mortgages will become more available. The banks themselves will show more flexibility with the people they lend money to. In most places, homosexual couples can now be married. This breakthrough alone means that 2016 will see new approaches to fusty old obstacles. As Bob Dylan warned way long ago: *The Times They are a Changin'*. Banks will become more user friendly. You may even see a real human being welcoming you when you visit your bank in 2016. And if you are buying or selling property, don't hesitate to negotiate the price.

Monkeys applaud and encourage the haggler in us.

In the Fire Monkey year you can get ahead, create new concepts, start a business or leave a job. This is a time to be bolder and cleverer than the next guy. But remember that this Fire Monkey year will also be rife with chicanery and deceit. You must play each opportunity deftly. Do not barrel ahead on any project or make any investments that you have not thoroughly researched. Study each situation and pore over complex documents till your eyes are sticking out of your head. Just because 2016 is a leap year doesn't mean you should leap before you take a good hard objective look at all the details.

Nonetheless, forge ahead. Take charge and dare in the Fire Monkey year. But before you rush into any enterprise - be it personal, romantic, professional or social - do your homework. The Monkey encourages the spunky, audacious you. But he or she might also be hanging out on a neighboring branch, waiting for you to show weakness. When you do, the Monkey may swing right on over and snatch your banana.

ALL ABOUT MONKEYS

IN OUR TIME ALL MONKEYS WERE BORN IN THESE YEARS.

1908,1920,1932,1944,1956,1968,1980,1992,2004,2016

NB: Capricorns and Aquarians.... For your exact Chinese Animal Sign, check the dates (they vary) of the Chinese New Year on your birthday on the Chinese calendar above.

By Suzanne White
High Priestess of Chinese and Western Astrologies

THE MONKEY ID CARD

Monkeys can enhance their self-image by surrounding themselves with tangible signs of their identity and making these symbols known to friends and loved ones. A wise Monkey will use them daily to ensure luck, security and a impart feeling of personal worth.

THE MONKEY'S BEST

color is *yellow*

flower is *dandelion*

fragrance is *jasmine*

tree is *sycamore*

flavor is *sweet*

birthstone is *tiger-eye*

lucky number is *10*

THE MONKEY'S FAVORITE

food is *fruit pie*

animal is *tiger*

drink is *lemonade*

spice is *cinnamon*

metal is *gold*

herb is *thyme*

musical instrument is *guitar*

Merry Monkey,

You're a delightful person who never misses a trick and who, despite an undeniable tendency to cunning and chicanery, rarely jumps a red light. Contradictory? Yes, indeed. And more. Monkeys are astute and like to be in on everything. You catch on long before the punch line, but you never laugh till you're good and ready. You're a plotter and a planner. When confronted with a seemingly impervious miasma of human complexity, you, nimble-spirited Monkey, will always find the means to restore order. You are an invaluable aide-de-camp, employee and helpmate. You'd make a super vice-president. Titles and position mean nothing to you as you instinctively recognize that, no matter how high up you are seated, you will still only be sitting on your derriere. Without fanfare you manage to run the show quite deftly from the wings. You refuse to grow old. If you have the funds you will be first to leap on to that old operating table for a face-lift, nose job, hair transplant or all three!

In choosing a partner, treat yourself to a magnificent Dragon, a go-getting Rat or even an impetuous Tiger, who will keep your problem-solving talents busy. The first and last phases of your life will pass smoothly. At around thirty-seven or thirty-eight you may experience a sudden loss of confidence from a major mid-life love crisis. This sinking spell will pass after the age of forty-five.

My advice? It's not enough to be cleverer than the rest. Knowing when to bet and when to pass is the secret of winning at those games you so enjoy. Refine your sense of timing through careful, patient observation. You will live longer and better on less if you learn to save your precious energy (and your money) for the big stakes.

Affectionately, Suzanne White

THE MONKEY CHARACTER

Monkey is Yang. Monkey is the ninth sign of the Chinese horoscope.

Monkeys have the following characteristics:
IMPROVISATION - LEADERSHIP
CUNNING - WIT
STABILITY - ZEAL

Monkey sins may include:
DECEIT - SELF-INVOLVEMENT
RUSE - SILLINESS
LOQUACITY - OPPORTUNISM

There is absolutely nothing wrong with Monkeys. They are stable, upstanding creatures who blaze trails, love children and animals, take trouble with detail, and, one is tempted to say, "See no evil, hear no evil, speak no evil." When they are not tempted to be "naughty," Monkey people are the nicest people you would want to know. Trouble is, Monkeys are a mite childish and, like kids, are often drawn to mischief. And when Monkeys get into mischief, hold your hats!

The thing about Monkeys that charms the pants off almost anybody who encounters them is that they are adorable. Monkeys, even at their most vain and chattery, are irresistibly lovable. They make you laugh and are often informative; they are pleasant to look at as they care enormously about their appearance, and. most of all, Monkeys are nice. They make super, long-lasting friends, fine neighbors and excellent employees. Monkeys are naturally conscientious and always prefer to see a job well done rather than sign their name to a slapdash piece of work.

Take a look at the person who cracks the most jokes at the next party you attend. Does he or she have simian features? Is there anything wiry and agile about his morphology? Moving from audience to audience, the Monkey seeks out his most appreciative public and then proceeds to dazzle with rib-tickling tales of experiences he's had or eccentric people he's known. And if this tactic, that of the charming raconteur, doesn't work, don't put it past the Monkey to unbutton his shirt, put it on backward and clown around that way. If you don't pay attention to a Monkey, trust him to find a way to see that you do.

Most admirable about Monkey people is their ability to solve problems. It is difficult to imagine a dilemma wherein the Monkey cannot take the upper hand, wade through the gory particulars, think up new and exotic ways to get at the pith of the problem and come triumphantly, if somewhat the worse for wear, out the other side.

Monkeys make excellent business people. They are apt at negotiating deals and finding little ways to beat their adversaries at their own game. Monkeys like sports and are usually very fit. If they gain too much weight or notice a paunch forming atop their waistline, Monkeys are the first to go on diets, work out and find a way to solve the fat problem.

Deep inside of Monkeys runs a current of equilibrium. No matter how crazy they go; or how much they overindulge, Monkeys always land on their feet. They about never sink into self-destruction and are gifted with an uncanny ability to stand back from themselves, appraise the results of their follies and pull themselves together. In the pit of their most profound selves lives a little watcher whose job it is to warn the Monkey of danger. If he listens to his watcher and heeds the watcher's advice, the Monkey will never fall apart.

Finally, if you have a Monkey close to you, my advice is, let him swing. He can go out and stay out and carouse and philander. But the essentially good Monkey will always come home to his favorite tree. Monkeys often have lots of children and make exceptional parents, taking original stands where child-rearing is concerned, helping them over hurdles in adolescence and always being able to recall their own childhoods—hence understanding and communicating, endlessly communicating.

THE FIVE KINDS OF MONKEY

Chinese Astrology uses 5 elements: Wood, Fire, Earth, Metal and Water. As a result, there are 5 distinctly different versions of each animal sign. A different type of Monkey comes along every 12 years. The same kind of Monkey only comes along every 60 years.

WHAT KIND OF MONKEY ARE YOU?

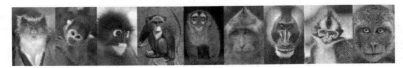

The Wood Monkey 1884, 1944, 2004

1884 Harry Langdon, Walter Huston, Amadeo Modigliani, Eleanor Roosevelt, Harry Truman

1944 Angela Davis, Helmut Berger, Jacqueline Bisset, Françoise Hardy, Brenda Lee, Rod Stewart, Geraldine Chaplin, Joe Cocker, Diana Ross, Sally Kirkland, Tom Selleck, Tim Reade, Danny De Vito, Swoozie Kurtz, Frank Alamo, George Lucas, Julio Iglesias Carl Bernstein, Jill Clayburgh. Stockard Channing, Jerry Springer, Alice Walker, Roger Daltrey, Sly Stone, Dame Kiri Te Kanawa, Helmut Berger, Patti LaBelle, Marvin Hamlisch, Sylvie Vartan, Michael Douglas, Michael Franks, Madeleine Kahn, Barry White, Swoozie Kurtz, Dennis Frantz, Peter Tosh, Rita Mae Brown, Lorne Michaels, Jane Birkin, Stephen Sills, Mia Farrow, Bob Marley, Charlotte Rampling

2004 Leah Gosselin, Joel Gosselin, Alexis Gosselin, Hannah Gosselin, Aaden Gosselin, Collin Gosselin

Belief in the future is the key characteristic of the Wood Monkey's personality. He's always out and about, into everything, doing something. He is forever building and making, plotting and scheming to increase his output, improve his own environment or make the world a more pleasant place to live.

Wood Monkeys are social creatures. They respond brightly to interaction with their peers and are always looking for new ways and places to find different friends, make acquaintances and widen the scope of their social lives. The Wood Monkey is a creative partygoer. He is the smiley one who cuts a smooth path through any chattering company, meeting and greeting folk with a cheery "Hi" and "How d'you do?" as though swinging blithely from tree to tree in a squawking jungle. When it comes to getting along on a purely sociable, superficial level, the Wood Monkey is definitely tops.

The less positive side of the Wood Monkey's high affability quotient is that he often cannot (or does not) maintain long-term, high-quality friendships. Somehow, the good-natured charm that this Monkey exudes in public just doesn't carry enough weight to support and intensify lasting relationships. He suffers from a profound lack of intimacy, wondering why people find him so seductive and alluring and yet cease to be his friend after knowing him only a short time. He is certain his intentions are honorable. He tries to be helpful and generous. Where, then, does the Wood Monkey go wrong?

Perhaps he doesn't try to get to know his friends and cronies well enough. Though he means to be charitable and care about the other fellow's welfare, the Wood Monkey cannot sit still for long. He aims to be of use in the world and he really means to cultivate many friends, but he doesn't take time to sit down and be with friends, to listen to their woes. He hates to wait for things to develop naturally, always thinking he knows better. He's jumpy and talks too much. He's always in a rush and has little compassion for people he considers weaklings. If devoted friendship is what he's after, the communicative Wood Monkey is missing the point. Either he doesn't internalize what he hears or else he never listens in the first place.

The Wood Monkey bridles when he realizes that others cannot always keep pace with his hectic lifestyle. He is compulsively impulsive and is bitingly critical of slow-moving, single-minded types and those who prefer to take life as it comes. Although he reveres efficiency, he fails to see that this slow, methodical approach may be just as efficacious as rapid-fire action.

This type of Monkey is a social climber. A name-dropper. He feels secure when surrounded by people of status who offer him both social rank and means. He is apt to seek lovers from among people he feels are socially superior, as he fears being ostracized if he is not acceptable to equals or betters. This gregarious soul needs lots of outside assurance that he will be included, loved and, above all, allowed to hang around his peers for a good long time.

A fine quality which always saves the day for this impetuous creature is his good nature. This resilient person knows how to be the brunt of jokes and still come up smiling. He gets teased because of his obvious desire to be liked but he's got a strong grip on his own self-image. It is difficult to bruise this amiable fellow's ego.

Wood Monkeys are achievers. They need and want to get ahead. They dream of ending up far above where they started off in life. To accomplish their ambitious ends, Wood Monkeys never stop studying the competition for flaws and strategizing to win in the most socially acceptable fashion.

If the Wood Monkey is really to succeed, he must learn to relax, to slow down and, most of all, to delve deeper into friendships and acquiesce to intimate human love. Unless he can learn to listen for the needs of others, all the chitchat and backslapping in the universe will not get him where he wants to go. If he applies himself, the Wood Monkey can learn to share and exchange his deepest thoughts and ideals rather than just dropping them, like a bunch of hot bananas, in the laps of everyone he meets and continuing on his merry but solitary way.

The Fire Monkey 1896, 1956, 2016

1896 F. Scott Fitzgerald, Virgil Thompson, Howard Hawks, Ira Gershwin, Ethel Waters, George Burns, Wallis Simpson, John Dos Passos

1956 Mel Gibson, Carrie Fisher, Björn Borg, Caroline of Monaco, Timothy Daley, Geena Davis, Eric Roberts, Tom Hanks, Andy Garcia, Kenny G, Joe Montana, Dorothy Hamill, Tony Kushner, Montel Williams, Debby Boone, Michael Feinstein, Bo Derek, Katie Couric, Adam Gopnik, Bill Maher, Martina Navratilova, Kenny G, Montel Williams, Anthony Bourdain, Michele Bachmann, Jerry Hall, Latoya Jackson, Danny Boyle, David Sedaris

Fire Monkeys enjoy being dominant in all their undertakings. Unlike most Monkeys, these types stay very much focused on their personal goals, creating and molding their enterprises as they go along. Fire Monkeys are driving and ambitious. They want results and are not afraid to look for the means to achieve them. The Fire Monkey is a self-starter whose enormous energy, although sometimes inconsistent and uneven, propels him speedily through life.

As the Fire Monkey's mind is fertile—his imagination is crawling with projects and innovative plans—he is doubly blessed. His capacity for hard work, coupled with his gift for invention, should make him a professional wizard. This Monkey will start trends, set a fashion in clothing or food, invent a new literary style or initiate a novel film project. But even with his myriad talents and dynamic personality, if he isn't careful, he may exhaust himself before he is halfway to his goal.

Although Fire Monkeys have all the punch, drive and authority necessary for high achievement, they also crave the baser thrills of "having a good time". Over-indulgence in gambling, late nights in clubs, and making whoopee may drain their strength, indeed may take precedence over their initial high-flown ambitions. Though not excessive by nature, Fire Monkeys are driven by the promise of excitement. They also have a dangerous taste for perversion. Some accuse them of being downright corrupt. If not curbed, Fire Monkeys can easily overload their systems and ruin their lives.

Fire Monkeys are deeply passionate, driven people. They respond to every experience with lightning speed and emotion. They struggle bravely with the complexities of getting things done and seem almost inspired by setbacks - stimulated by adversity. To the agile-minded Fire Monkey nothing is impossible. He looks for and finds solutions to the thorniest problems. He's wily and wiry, flexible and sharp. The Fire Monkey is always willing to take a chance or jump on a new bandwagon.

Though supple of spirit and freewheeling, Fire Monkeys enjoy controlling others. You will often find them drawn to or living with partners of lesser willpower who need them for sustenance or who look to them for emotional stability. Fire Monkeys may choose their lovers because of their own need to dominate someone less forceful. Yet the tables often turn on this would-be dominator and, through an odd system of emotional blackmail and unavoidable entanglement, the Fire Monkey dominator becomes the one dominated by the mate he imagined was the weakling.

Fire Monkeys are born cynics, too. In youth, they carry a disarming air of candor, but as they mature, they grow wiser, less credulous and sometimes even embittered. They have a hard time trusting anyone, especially their colleagues and associates. Little by little, they lose their respect for morality and begin to wear a jaundiced, knowing smile. Raw ambition is not much of a cushion against disappointment, but once he has lost his youthful charm and earnest beliefs, ambition is frequently all this Monkey has left.

The Fire Monkey doesn't take kindly to being made to look a fool. He is jealous in both his love and work lives. He is competitive and can be vindictive, vengeful even. Speculation is his favorite game. He may take on many partners, form corporations or assemble groups for projects, but no matter how equitable the terms of any agreement, the Fire Monkey will always insist on remaining the boss.

This Monkey is far and away the most power-hungry of all Monkeys, yet he may not always be the most visible. Much of his real pith remains buried or hovers in the wings. Outwardly, the Fire Monkey is scornful of callow dreams and loudly dismisses ideals as corny, puerile and vapid. But the tough Fire Monkey longs for a better world, too, and would go to even greater lengths than all other Monkeys if only he believed that his wonderful dream could come true.

The Earth Monkey 1908, 1968

1908 Bette Davis, James Stewart, Rex Harrison, Herbert von Karajan, Victor Borge, Fred MacMurray, Jacques Tati, Henri Cartier-Bresson, Michael Redgrave, Douglas Fairbanks Jr, David Lean, Joshua Logan, Carole Lombard, Robert Morley, Eddie Albert, Salvador Allende, Balthus, Simone de Beauvoir, Robert Cummings, Lew Ayres, John Kenneth Galbraith, Alistair Cooke, Amy Vanderbilt, William Saroyan, Milton Berle

1968 Molly Ringwald, Lisa Marie Presley, Celine Dion, Lucy Lawless, Patricia Arquette, Sandrine Kiberlain, Ashley Judd, Carnie Wilson, Kylie Minogue, Rachel Griffiths, Billy Crudup, Will Ferrell, Stephanie Seymour, Gillian Anderson, Halle Berry, Monica Bellucci, Will Smith, Naomi Watts, Thom Yorke, Parker Posey, Owen Wilson, Carla Bruni, Lucy Liu, Marilyn Manson

This Monkey is calmer, more sentimental and deep thinking than most. Altruism is well developed in his character and he is markedly less devil-may-care than his fellows. He truly ponders both the past and future of mankind and attempts to comprehend the shape of things to come. Earth Monkeys love all types of people and can assume the problems of others as if they were their own.

The Earth element endows the Monkey with solid natural wisdom and insight. Because he is so perceptive, he is painfully aware of certain dark truths about life at an early age. He may speak out in family or school situations, shocking adults with unnaturally astute comments. Although silence is not his strong suit, study is. He will be capable of reaching lofty social positions through education. In China, the Earth Monkey is known as the teacher Monkey. Not only is he learned, but he is also able to impart knowledge and exercise devotion in the pursuit of a professorial career. His students will be faithful admirers. They will adore his jaunty manner and are instructed and amused by the Earth Monkey's imaginative presentation of inherently difficult or dull material.

This Monkey's best attribute lies in his ability to interact with his peers: people like him immediately. He is affable and jolly, optimistic and inspirational. He's bright and witty, and so smart and intuitive that he seems to see around corners. Better yet, the Earth Monkey knows how to make us laugh. He won't waste time on gloomy reruns of his bad childhood or tedious school exploits. He is fun, spontaneous and full of life. He is strong without being overpowering and yet he remains a serious, even ponderous, thinker.

The biggest flaw in the Earth Monkey's character is his desire for perfection. This hail-fellow-well-met seems to be so easy-going and fun-loving that we sometimes wonder if he can truly be taken seriously-- but this Monkey is worse than serious—he's nit-picking—perfection-crazed. He longs for a home that runs like a well-oiled machine, a family to be nothing but proud of, a place for everything and everything in its place.

But the family life of the average Earth Monkey is never nirvana. His need for order in the essentially disorderly atmosphere of home and kids leads to trouble for him and his poor, subjugated offspring. Either the kids and spouse become terrorized by all the maniacal fussing, or as time goes by, the meticulous Earth Monkey parent becomes a subject of family ridicule and has to take refuge in the basement or is forced out of the nest.

This Monkey is fatally attracted to the opposite sex. An imaginative lover, he cannot resist the urge to play at love. He adores the intrigue, the chase, the seduction. Extra-marital affairs are common in the life of this extra-sensual Monkey. Usually, fear of scandal (the specter of imperfection again) prevents him from confessing his peccadilloes to a passing newspaper reporter. He hates to recognize his own mistakes, yet is quick to point out those of his family. Live-in loving with the Earth Monkey is not for amateurs: it takes more than patience – even a spirit of masochistic self-abnegation. Yet this Monkey is kind and can be reached through a large, tender guilt window. If reminded of how difficult he is, the Earth Monkey will rally. Underneath his difficult, superficial nature, he is devoted to those he loves and can always be counted on to provide and maintain order.

The Earth Monkey is blessed with good health and a sturdy constitution. He will live to a ripe age. With his innate talents for study and concentration, he could work in scientific research, law enforcement or history.

Because of his ability to go it alone, he can pursue a career in the arts as an independent filmmaker, a literary scholar, a painter or sculptor.

If an Earth Monkey could improve one aspect of his character, it should definitely be his perfection seeking. He could and should partake of some of life's Earth Monkeys need to cool out their fuddy-duddy side, break down personal barriers which prevent them from enjoying a relaxed lifestyle, and rid themselves of the need to show off their brilliant achievements in public. Developing the spiritual side of this neurotically driven perfectionist is a sure way to loosen those inhibitions for something more lofty than clandestine extracurricular sex.

The Metal Monkey 1860, 1920, 1980

1860 Gustav Mahler, Annie Oakley

1920 Pope John Paul II, Gaston Le Notre, Roger Angell, Howard Cosell, Federico Fellini, Charlie Parker, Roberta Peters, Dirk Bogarde, Gene Tierney, Montgomery Clift, Ravi Shankar, Mickey Rooney, Clive Donner, Tony Randall, Viveca Lindfors, Maureen O' Hara, Anatole Broyard, Walter Matthau, Ricardo Montalban, Carol Channing, Arthur Hailey, Isaac Stern, Eileen Farrell, Tony Randall, Lana Turner, Peggy Lee, Bella Abzug, David Brinkley, Amalia Rodrigues, Bob Waterfield, Ray Bradbury, Timothy Leary, Mario Puzo, Johnny Desmond, Virginia Mayo, Stan Musial, Dave Brubeck, David Susskind, Mario Lanza

1980 Venus Williams, Jessica Simpson, Macaulay Culkin, Martina Hingis, Ashanti, Gisele Bundchen, Christina Aguilera, Alicia Keys, Elijah Wood, Justin Timberlake

The thinking side of this Monkey aids him in being a creative, self-made person. He usually prefers to make his way alone, working happily at a job which takes him into lofty realms.

This autonomous person will encounter miles of obstacles along the road to finding his independent niche. But find it he will—or die! This is the fighter Monkey. When in doubt, he confronts issues, battles with demons, fiercely attacks adversaries. He often wins by means of persuasion, reason and logic. But, if the issue warrants it, he is unafraid to put up his fists and trounce his opponent. The Metal Monkey's muscle is not like the stormy, fiery bravura of a Dragon. Nor can he match the Ox or Rooster for perseverance and endurance. The Metal Monkey comes on wiry and hostile. He simply annihilates challengers through might of mind and twist of spirit. Then he drops the cadavers in the ditch and moves ahead, as feisty as ever, to challenge the next contender. He's tough—but he's *nice* tough.

The Metal Monkey's personal life is never a romantic novel. He's bent on achieving a major place in his career, making his mark on society and forcing his creative ideas through the fusty system to make time for a family or emotional space. As a major difference maker, he must have unusual ideas. He is neither obedient to norms nor blatantly revolutionary, but he needs the thrill of achievement, advancement, and position. He wants to be where the action is, and if his entourage doesn't understand, then that's *their* problem.

It is of course possible for this person to marry and maintain a semblance of family life. Metal Monkeys are usually financially secure and make good providers but may not be disposed to spending much time at home. This person needs an independent, loving and patient mate, unafraid to take responsibility for home, family and marriage alone.

Metal Monkeys have sociable, gregarious personalities. They talk a lot and (although they are Monkeys) are often able to learn foreign languages. They enjoy travel and are quite apt to expatriate early in adulthood, moving away to start again in a new place to slake their thirst for self-sovereignty. The Metal Monkey hates criticism, does not wish to be compared to siblings and/or cousins, and deplores the existence of relatives who insist on loading his kitbag with unwanted advice. The Metal Monkey wants to be separate, officially unallied - an individual. He makes his own way and refuses to credit his frequent successes and financial gains to anyone else.

The Metal Monkey is intelligent. He is argumentative and yet has a charming, winning manner. The close relative who has to live with this seductive person knows just how cranky and picky he can be, and resents all the extra hugging and kudos that the Metal Monkey receives from his multiple admirers. For the Metal Monkey, family situations are often tense and fraught with hatred. Metal Monkeys are the sort of people who try to wrench the family home away from sisters and brothers to turn it into an old folks' home which, of course, bears Metal Monkey's illustrious name.

The Metal Monkey can be melancholy. If this person, (who would perform amateur open-heart surgery on friend or foe to get where he wants to go) does not succeed, he may go under. All that push and shove and strategizing is so depleting and the stakes so all-or-nothing that the fatigued Metal Monkey sometimes can't drag himself up to begin all over again. His sin lies in his puffed-up self-image - his pride. He can take setbacks as long as he comes out of them victorious. Too many losses and he skulks away, dejected and hopeless. I sometimes wonder how many down-and-outs are Metal Monkeys who gave up?

When and if despair sets in, the Metal Monkey may blame his failures on his upbringing, his family, friends or associates who were jealous of him and tried to do him down. This "poor me" attitude is that of an non evolved character who cannot accept his own shortcomings, who will not assume responsibility for breakdowns in communication, and who can only see himself as a victim. Truly, this attitude is dead-ended.

The remedy for despondency in Metal Monkeys is directive group therapy. Although I don't often recommend it, I see the Metal Monkey as so blind to his own errors and so unwilling from an early age to consult with or take advice from elders or peers that he cannot help but benefit from a group experience. Metal Monkeys do not realize that they cannot always be right. They need to learn early on to take hints from those around them.

This Monkey makes an excellent salesman or TV talk-show host, newscaster or disc jockey. He is so articulate and nimble-minded that he could sell fur coats to bears. Whatever the verbal challenge that arises, he meets it with equanimity and a smooth-talking manner. He makes strangers feel comfortable. He exudes confidence and competence even when he hasn't a clue what he's about.

Finally, don't expect anything but the best from the genius side of this person. Leonardo da Vinci was a Metal Monkey, as is Pope John Paul. These Monkeys are hugely individualistic. This is a sign of achievement and versatility. Metal Monkeys can learn how to do almost anything.

But if Metal Monkeys undergo too many failures their mental and physical health will give out. They are born afflicted with more pride than resilience. The breaking-up of this brittle surface can destroy their sunny demeanor and they may fast begin to crumble into oblivion.

The Water Monkey 1872, 1932, 1992

1872 Bertrand Russell, Aubrey Beardsley, Piet Mondrian, Calvin Coolidge, Emily Post

1932 Elizabeth Taylor, Melvin van Peebles, Sylvia Plath, Halston, François Truffaut, Omar Sharif, Gene Shallit, Anthony Perkins, Joel Grey, Meir Kahan, Angie Dickinson, Debbie Reynolds, Little Richard, Milos Forman, Max Gallo, Emmanuel de la Taille, Anouk Aimee, Michel Legrand, Ted Kennedy, Jean Cacharel, Ellen Burstyn, Louis Malle, John Updike, Gay Talese, Peter O' Toole, Johnny Cash, Milos

Forman, Elaine May, Mario Cuomo, Athol Fugard, Eydie Gorme, Melvin Van Peebles, Glenn Gould, Dick Gregory, Petula Clark, Shel Silverstein, Ellen Burstyn

1992 Miley Cyrus, Grace Phipps, Josh Hutcherson, Dylan Sprouse, Cole Sprouse

A sublime combination of cooperation and genius, the Water Monkey is a peach! Ask around. Everybody agrees. He is one of the world's most spirited people.

Although Water Monkeys can always be counted on to defend their own piece of pie, they are sharing people, willing to lend a hand, or distribute whatever bounty they have. Water Monkeys are never slapdash friends who tramp through your living room, grab a pear or an apple and scoot out by the back door without leaving more than a lingering trace of patchouli. They take friendship and love seriously. Not that they go over the top about how much they love you, but from the moment they decide to pull a friend on board their ship, their affection is true, their willingness to be there when the other person needs a hand is ever ready and their loyalty unswerving.

Water Monkeys are clever and witty without being cynical. There is a sweetness to their affability and they are always seeking to assist others in realizing their dreams. They have an innate ability to care deeply without being maudlin. They do not mind relinquishing the spotlight in favor of someone they admire, and except for a basic need to maintain a modicum of security, they are squanderously generous with everything from hospitality to money, kudos and affection.

The Water Monkey has an elfin or sprightly quality. A whimsical energy pervades everything he does. He is forever sending out vibes of ironic gaiety, which couples neatly with his natural tenderness towards others. Look at the teasing cartoons of Sempé, the lyrical films of Milos Forman or the mordant yet humane works of François Truffaut. There's something both socially worthy and sardonic about the way Water Monkeys look at life. They're cutting and caring at the same time. They don't mind pointing out the foibles of friends and relatives but they wouldn't hurt them for the world, because they care so ardently about their happiness.

Water Monkeys don't always fare as well as their friends. They tend to be needlessly neurotic. They are easily beset by worry and become flummoxed when little things go wrong—they may grow anxious when the hall porter forgets to say good morning. Perhaps the porter is having a bad day and forgot to greet him - but it will trouble the Water Monkey, who may not be able to let himself, or you, forget it for weeks. The insignificant scene is inflated out of all proportion and the Water Monkey suffers. It is always he who apologizes and makes it up.

Water Monkeys are ingenious problem-hunters—and solvers. They do not want to hear the word "impossible". For a Water Monkey, getting through a thicket of thorns means thinking your way round it-- and the Water Monkey makes an excellent mediator, troubleshooter or organizer. He is a great motivator—he can spend his life urging, scolding, monitoring, finding and fixing flaws, and be contentedly fulfilled with that secondary role.

The Water Monkey is never a prim Donna or an egomaniac. The innovative talents of this warm, loving person would not suit end to-end talk show appearances. The Water Monkey's ego is trapped in the clever mind of a giving soul. Even Elizabeth Taylor, with her astounding beauty, has never become a siren like Zsa Zsa Gabor or a delectably simpering Marilyn Monroe. She's always married to some giant ego of a man whom she's trying to cure of alcoholism (and maybe getting caught up herself) or helping to combat prejudice about AIDS. Liz Taylor is a failure as a prima Donna because she simply wasn't born selfish enough.

Gloom and depression can sink the Water Monkey's buoyant spirit. If his petty neuroses or others' demands close in on him and he's made to feel guilty, his high spirits may crash. The idea of being wrong jangles his nerves, and as he blames himself for much that goes wrong anyway, he is ill equipped to defend himself against accusations. Water Monkeys are easy targets for manipulative folk who ruthlessly play on their sympathies.

There is something of the merry meddler in the Water Monkey. Sometimes he becomes intrusive. Water Monkeys enjoy gossip, which contributes to their reputation as sociable mates and excellent companions. But once in a while, they spill someone else's beans when they might better opt for the "speak no evil" position.

Water Monkeys are wildly sexy. They adore cavorting in the act of love. They glory in all the imaginative ways to play the oldest human game. Unfortunately, they are rarely cool-headed in their choice of lovers and cannot resist taking up with complex and difficult characters. Perhaps it is natural for the problem-solver to take on problem people. Water Monkeys always find implacable monster mates with testy tempers and precarious emotional infrastructures. People whom you or I might joyfully throw out of the house Water Monkeys adopt as house pets. They are irresistibly attracted to living out perplexing scenarios in the hope that they will get to play a key role in untying the most defiant knots.

2016

MONTH BY MONTH WESTERN SIGNS FUTURES

FORECASTS FOR ALL 12 WESTERN ZODIAC SIGNS

YOUR MONTHLY FORECASTS FOR THE FIRE MONKEY YEAR 2016

ARIES

Author's Note... Mercury Retrograde

Sometimes planets appear to be zooming backward through the zodiac. Of course this backward motion is only an illusion. The planet has not turned tail. But it appears to have. Astrologers call this apparent reversing: **"retrograde"**.

Any planet can be retrograde. But only Mercury's retrogrades cause communications to break down. Mercury has its retrograde period for a few weeks 3 or 4 times each year. Whilst Mercury is retrograde, we humans are encouraged to take stock, make plans and discuss different approaches to a variety of subjects. But because information is often muddled, promises broken and electronic devices on the blink during Mercury retrograde, we must remain flexible and open-minded. Advice? Always allow extra time for travel. Schedule changes are common. Do not sign any contracts or cement agreements during Mercury retrograde. Make no irreversible promises. Watch out for con artists. Make no final decisions, binding engagements or major purchases during a Mercury retrograde. You are allowed to have tantrums or rail against your fate. But Mercury will continue to be retrograde till it decides to go direct again.

Mercury Retrogrades
2016

January 5 thru January 25
April 28 thru May 22
August 30 thru September 22
December 19 thru January 8 2017

OVERVIEW OF 2016 THE YEAR OF THE MONKEY FOR ARIES

Dynamic Aries.

Last year saw you exiting a period of low self-confidence. By now, you should be well on your way to deciding for yourself what's in store for 2016. But let me give you a few hints. In 2016 the travel bug will once again bite you. And when this voyager urge comes upon you, you don't just take a drive to a nearby city or set out to visit your Aunt Mary. You organize ahead, Plan and find the best rates for flights and trains and rickshaws and hotels. You make certain everything is in order weeks or even months before you leave. You will be heading to exotic lands in 2016.

On one of your trips you will very likely fall in love. Nobody will be more surprised than you. Could it be that garrulous Gemini gentleman sitting next to you on the plane or perhaps it will be the attractive lady who was dining alone in the restaurant in Bangkok every evening. You strike up a conversation and, although you are speaking to a perfect stranger, it's as though you have known each other all your lives. This encounter could very well be just a fling. Or (and I advise you do some research about the person's personal life) because of the intense feeling of instant friendship, it could become both serious and long term.

But the end of 2016, all Aries will have swerved their lives in a new direction. You may have changed jobs or spouses or had a child or moved to a new city or retired to the country to raise sheep. Whatever it is, by December, you will be the master or mistress of your own destiny. Work conscientiously toward that goal from January 2016 onward. sw

ARIES - January 2016

The beginning of the western New Year bodes a time for your most dynamic self to extend into all areas of your life. Engaging in new activities - taking a personal enrichment workshop, learning how to concoct a special new kind of exotic cuisine or simply deciding to get serious about your exercise routine etc. Establishing discipline with a new class or ongoing endeavor will help structure the whole year ahead. It is far from a piece of cake to keep resolutions. But this coming Monkey year will demand that all Aries be focused on progress and quick on their feet.

Mid January 2016 you will be attracted to all things romantically delicious. You are being tempted and influenced by the sirens of love and voluptuousness. Be careful. Watch that Aries tendency to be impulsive. Your natural inclination to surrender to dangerous *liaisons* is at its peak. At this time, you are mesmerized by the possibility of multiple indulgences. Keep your sense of humor and your wits about you whilst you ride out this intoxicating wave. Examine your motives. If a love affair ignites now, make sure to think ahead to where it may lead. Any new crush could be posing as long term and, for multiple good reasons, turn out to be nothing more than a disappointing fling. Do some digging. Find out all about the person and their past before you fall hopelessly in love. Otherwise the last laugh may be on you.

You are about to live out very expansive 2016. In order to benefit from the bustle of the Monkey's frenetic energy, you should think long and hard about where you want to be in your personal development when this new Chinese year is done. Will you drop everything and escape to a desert island or cabin in the woods? Or will you return to the ranks of the "nine to fivers" whence you so cleverly emerged in one piece in 2015. Either way, you learned a great deal about yourself last year. Now it's time to put all that new self-knowledge into practice.

ARIES - February 2016

Sedate and steadying planetary transits promise to bring you consistent income and better budgeting early this month. Your optimistic attitude and self-respect opens doors for your growth in business and career. Moonlighting at a secondary job for a while will help you reap benefits. So don't hesitate if you spot an opportunity. This activity could add an extra feather to your cap and put you in line for a future promotion. A friend cum lover steps up to fulfill your needs and goes out of his or her way around the 8th to the 12th. And that's much to be grateful for. A simple soul at your workplace may also try to reach out to you for help in some matter. You may have formed a negative impression about this colleague earlier. Do not judge this person by his or her appearance.

Around the 14th, a sensual, desire-oriented moon reflects evening activities geared for fun and romance. This Valentine's Day promises to be special. Relationships exude warmth and love. Spiritualism, joy in family interactions, a sense of commitment to the community and to society will be the major themes over the next one week. There may also be some very important paperwork or legal issue needing your attention. Do not try to avoid or postpone it or you will pay a heavy price.

A close friend divulged some sensitive but spicy information some time back. He or she swore you to secrecy. Be careful and preserve the confidentiality. Someone is likely to tempt you to spill the beans around the 24th of this month. Do not give in. Your plate is overflowing with events and activities by this month's end. Superiors and colleagues appreciate your innovative initiatives at work place. Several lucrative property deals may suddenly fall into your lap now. Investment in properties providing rental income is favored. But be patient while making decisions. Negotiations may take slightly longer than usual. But the end result will be worth the wait. You are likely to have solid returns in the future from whatever you invest in now.

ARIES - March 2016

Early march promises to light up your life with excessive physical energy. Your aura glitters and you feel extra special. If you have been one of those nerdy, workaholic types, this phase could develop a healthy appetite for sex within you. Your partner is also more than willing. While you are at it, why not use the power of yoga? Poses like butterfly and mountain climber have shown great results in heightening sexual energy and experience. Surprising news around the 8th or the 9th may force you to ponder some of your past decisions. Or it could generate new ideas that you have never considered before. This changed thought pattern is likely to make a serious contribution to your life in surprising and different ways.

From the 12th to the 16th is a good time to dream and dream big. Some of you may start getting ideas of going into your own business. Get ready to seize opportunities that come your way now. Planets are in a supportive mode for Aries. Both the 17th and 18th could be hectic days at work. Make sure that you fully understand all the instructions given you before you execute tasks. Don't neglect important projects that need your immediate attention. Colleagues will compliment you on your abilities. Finances will be smooth now.

A neighbor may have some important and useful information to share around the 21st. It could benefit you financially. So keep in touch with them. The 23rd and the 27th are favorable for scheduling business meetings, conferences and arranging or attending job interviews. Negotiating better conditions or wages at your workplace will also prove fruitful if done during the mornings on these days. Those of you looking out for home and electrical appliances are likely to come across very good deals now. A close friend may prove problematic around the month's end by whining and winging about trivial matters. Even if you are not inclined to, there may be no other choice than to deal with his or her issues. Offer them whatever support you possibly can muster as this friend already has or is likely to be very helpful to you in future.

ARIES - April 2016

Personal distractions could divert your attention from daily duties early in April from the 4th to the 7th. Morning blues at your workplace are likely to strike many of you. However you may not have the opportunity to give in to these feelings, as others could be relying on your organizational skills and expertise. You may be a bit withdrawn, but try not to be grouchy. When addressed, a polite reply is always imperative. Around the same time, you also realize that it may be next to impossible to please everyone in the family. Kids may be demanding especially around the 7th and the 8th. Don't expect everything to fall into place without your insistence. If you are unable to satisfy the needs of every individual, then at least try to please your partner. Things improve by the 11th of this month.

April 14th to the 20th is a good time to explore the outdoors and plan an adventure trip. Set aside some time to plan things properly. Go somewhere you have never been before. For maximum enjoyment, travel light - both in terms of luggage and company. Ideally, you and a partner or just one or two friends will ensure a pleasurable holiday. Focus on trying new things - Scuba diving, whale watching, running rapids, hiking in dense forests and/or riding horseback. Experimentation is key to learning. Try to attempt the new in everything from foods to the activities you practice. You will come home a happier and wiser person.

Communication with influential people is on the cards from the 23rd to the 27th. Business people, medical industry professionals and those involved in sports get a taste of fame and success. You are likely to be in the limelight without much effort on your part. This phase is also favorable for getting publicity through media communication if you are involved in humanitarian work or politics. Planet Mercury goes retrograde on the 28th of the month. Mercury rules communications, debts and diseases for you. So these areas are likely to be impacted over the next few weeks. State your points clearly. Have a checkup. Pay bills on time.

ARIES - May 2016

Mercury is retrograde till the 22nd May. Intervention in disputes among colleagues or family members may be necessary early in this month. Step lightly to avoid personality conflicts or inflaming an already tense situation. This is likely to be a time of crossed wires and miscommunications. General chaos may also ensue in your personal life. Try to keep calm amid the commotion. By the 22nd, most of the issues will have been sorted out. In the interim, do not lash out at anyone for being late or making blunders. Avoid uttering anything or signing any documents that could have permanent consequences. Any minor surgeries are better avoided during this phase. Your know-it-all attitude could cause an argument at work or home with your partner around the 6th. You may need to concede that you don't have all the answers.

A brilliantly conceived gift from a family member, lover or close friend could light you up around the 12th. Not only does this person know your tastes intimately. He or she has impeccable timing. You may have been in a state of gloom lately for a variety of reasons. And this present will inject some joy into your melancholy. Distant relatives or friends could also be coming to pay a visit between the 12th and the 15th. You probably have not seen them for years. You may not have even met them at all. But make their stay a pleasant one. They will certainly repay the favor.

The 20th to the 24th brings into focus a certain economic issue. Did you recently rush into a financial commitment? If so, you may be better off paying an early cancellation penalty than impoverishing yourself in an attempt to see the obligation through. Last week of this month will bring in sudden influx of some funds from an unexpected source. Also a friend or acquaintance that you had loaned money to in his time of severe financial distress long ago turns up suddenly and returns the full amount plus interest. If you have the chance to do so, invest the amount in a sure thing. Real estate?

ARIES - June 2016

Your self-confidence is high early this month. This is the time for you to finish off as many pending work projects as you possibly can. Your aim and judgment should be particularly sharp this month. So go ahead and make the most of it. You will be thankful in the months ahead when you have more pressing issues on your plate. Also you will have a little money that came in last month. So around the 7th to the 15th is just the right time for some home improvement in the kitchen and bathroom. If you have invested all the loot and are short of liquid cash, rather than making half-hearted improvements to both, concentrate on upgrading one and leave the other till early next year. Whichever room you work on, think elegant and simple. Just choose one or two basic colors and classic designs. Simple of course does not necessarily mean cheap.

There is likely to be a minor altercation with a close friend around the 19th. He or she will act in a way that leaves you flabbergasted and disenchanted. You might let the person know how you feel. But be gentle. Take advantage of some social event over the next few days to bring up the subject in a good-humored manner. Then just forgive and forget the incident and move on. An artistic streak around the 22nd pushes you to resurrect your easel and palette now and start painting. Or you may drag out your old guitar and strum a few chords. Under the current planetary influence, you can safely take your skills further than you ever have.

Small disputes and tensions within the family and within your office team may test your patience between the 27th and the 30th. You might find yourself catapulted into the uncomfortable realm of office politics. This is likely to be instigated by an incompetent colleague who is unhappy with his/her job. Your boss too may not be his or her usual friendly self. Handle everything with kid gloves. Don't let choppy waters in career matters put a damper on your enthusiasm. You will gain traction by end of the month. Everything will return to normal. Your professional goals will be reaffirmed and back on track.

ARIES - July 2016

Come July and the winds of change start blowing. Some of you Aries may start looking for new jobs. If you are seeking opportunities for further advancement at your existing workplace, then between the 4th and the 9th is the right time to make bold and confident moves. The stars also warn that your confidence is in the danger of spilling over into over-confidence and even into the arrogance zone. The bitterness and frustration within you could lead to an unnecessary argument with someone in a position of authority from the 7th to the 10th. Walking out of a meeting in a huff will give you a sense of power and self-righteousness. But it will spoil an important relationship with a senior colleague who wishes you well. Burning bridges has never worked for anyone and never will.

Diplomacy and tact will help you to showcase your efforts at work - talents that may have gone unnoticed earlier. You might just have to change your tactics and "sell yourself" better. You will feel like promoting your ideas openly and think more about augmenting your skills. Between the 14th and the 19th, there will be a focus on wealth, taxes, debts, legacies and shared property. You may be looking at wills. Many of you are likely to gain a lot from an unexpected inheritance. A visit from a close friend or a sibling is likely around this time. This person has and will always be a big source of comfort and support for you. If you need sound advice on any matter, you can trust him or her.

Physical relationships will become intense during the last ten days of this month. You exude sexuality and people will notice it now. A new romantic interest enters your life around the 23rd or 24th of July. This person is likely to be of the Libra sun sign. Conversation on general topics will go deeper and reveal a subtle underlying chemistry. After a couple of meetings, there will be a whopper of a physical attraction between you and this person. You may find yourselves skipping dinner reservations in favor of sexual romps.

ARIES - August 2016

The health of one of your parents or perhaps another older relative is likely to be a cause of concern around the 6th. It could be early dementia. You are likely to have to face facts and search for an assisted living facility. Or perhaps the older person can move in with another family member. Or if the family has the means, they can hire trained aides to come in 24/7. All the family members affected by this decision will have to hold a meeting to deliberate. People tend to be highly emotional about this kind of transition. So there may be disagreements. And tempers could flare. Use your skills of diplomacy to try to bring everyone to a consensus. Balancing pros and cons of different options will be necessary. It will take a few days to reach a sensible conclusion.

Mid August will find you in a sudden difficult- to- dispel black mood. Your partner and friends will remark on how glum you seem. Part of the mood swing problem may stem from lack of sleep. Sleep deprivation affects one's state of mind. Even if you get eight hours of snooze time regularly, the effects of stress can leave you exhausted. Try going to bed earlier at night. Go for that early morning swim. Water will be therapeutic and refreshing. This time also gives you a few opportunities to serve others who need your help and support. You may be approached by a friend who needs a shoulder to cry on. Your child may need your help with some hefty school project. Or you may participate actively in a local charity. Give and share whatever you can – time, money other resources. Mercury is retrograde from the 30th of this month. There is a risk of losing objects during this time. Do not leave any belongings lying on your car seat where they may attract thieves. Change the PIN codes on your debit and credit cards. Keep cash reserve on hand in case any payments to you are delayed. This is a time to look for lost objects. Be prepared to find some random items you don't remember buying or never bought at all.

ARIES - September 2016

Mercury is retrograde during the first twenty-one days of this month. Best laid plans as well as appliances, electronics and love affairs often go awry during Mercury retrograde. In case you have plans to supplement or boost income through an additional weekend job, you may face hurdles. Don't give up though. Maintain your patience. Any legal documentation or decisions are best postponed till the 21st. This is a good space in which to negotiate. However refrain from signing binding agreements. The 3rd to the 8th September are days that provide you a rich source of fresh concepts that help you to make a sale or a powerful presentation to a big fish. You colleagues are likely to go green with envy. Turn a blind eye to them. A minor partnership alliance of some kind comes up at workplace after the 9th. Someone with skills you do not possess will prove invaluable to you. Prepare to do your part to make this alliance fruitful. You will be surprised at the dividends it pays in the future.

Pleasure and fun activities with children are highlighted in mid-September. You can become a hero to the little ones when you treat them to the circus or even buy them an ice cream cone. Use the occasion to bond with them as well as having some fun. Reading stories and making yourself available to assist with homework will score you big points and create a lifetime of fond memories. Be open to a super treat this month. Someone will ask to take you out on the town. Enjoy this little indulgence. At least that dime gets to stay in your piggy bank.

Be vigilant about people using manipulation or trickery to keep you in their company from the 23rd to the 29th. This intrusive behavior could come from a lonely relative who uses guilt trips and innuendos to compel you to visit and stay longer than is good for you. Or the manipulation may be emanating from a friend who wants to keep you on the phone for hours on end to fill the void after a difficult breakup. Decide beforehand what your time boundaries will be and stick to them no matter the implied consequences.

ARIES - October 2016

A little feeling of boredom and restlessness may pervade your mind early this month. Monotonous work will frustrate even those who don't mind routine activities. On top of this, you may also feel as if you are walking a tightrope between commitments. On one side is your romantic partner who would like to see more of you. On the other is an ailing family member who has come to depend on you. The truth is that neither side needs as much of your time as they think. Allay their respective paranoias by assuring both that you will always be there if and when their need becomes urgent. Remind them that in between times, you too may need some closeness and understanding too. If insomnia is a problem, pay more attention to your sleep hygiene. Read and watch television away from your bed. Consume warm herb teas before sleeping. Prepare for bed. Play soothing music. Do some deep breathing. Read a not-too-gripping novel. Once in bed, keep your bedroom as dark as possible. If your schedule requires you to sleep during daylight hours, consider blackout blinds. Your sleep pattern returns to normal after the 10th. And you will swan through your days with grace and aplomb.

After the 15th of July will be an excellent time to network and communicate with a well-known person or group of famous people whom you admire and would like to get to know. The chances of them responding positively are higher than they will be at any other time. Send an email or, better still, write a real letter on real paper and post it. The energy around you is warm and positive and many people will notice this. Staying abreast of the latest news is essential. Broaden your attention to include newspapers and blogs that you may have overlooked until now.

The 23rd till month's end sees you splurging on luxurious items. Self-restraint is crucial now where finances are concerned. A reckless indulgence or two can erode your resources. If you want leisure travel, try a local vacation and let the tropical seaside holiday wait until next year. Meanwhile, focusing on what is going well in your life will keep your spirits high and your cash outlay within safe limits.

ARIES - November 2016

You will have a brief window to sell some property for a very decent price between the 3rd and the 9th. This opportunity may not come by for several months after this. So if you need funds-Sell, sell, sell! Get ready to display your nurturing spirit for the first half of this month. Could be a child who needs your care. Or it could also be a friend, brother or sister. These new demands can be emotionally draining as well as exhausting. The level of attention this person requires will absorb a maximum amount of time and energy. Not that you will complain for a minute. You realize how much they depend on and appreciate your efforts. Do not drink and drive this month around the 11th or 12th. There is a strong possibility you will be stopped by a traffic cop. You could end up with a nasty fine and/or a suspended license. It would be best to not touch a drop if you are planning on getting behind the wheel.

There may be sudden unexpected expenditures between the 14th and the 23rd due to kitchen or bathroom plumbing problems in your home. Don't let this household glitch dampen your spirit. Why not spend the extra money and buy those fancy new bathroom fittings you have been contemplating. You may have been vowing to change them now for a long time. Besides, that small bathroom leak upstairs is irritating the downstairs neighbor. Plumbers don't come cheap. But if you do your utmost to put things to right, the repairs won't bother you again for quite some time.

The last few days of this month offer a good time to set aside any mutual differences with your better half. A few romantic evening walks will blow away any cobwebs in your relationship. Initially some old wounds and grievances may surface. But just be at your diplomatic best. And by the end of it, all the thorny issues will dissolve. Both of you will feel more emotionally connected and physically rejuvenated.

ARIES - December 2016

This is a month of changes. You and your partner may be managing the logistics of a major life change in early December. You could be preparing for a happy event like childbirth in the family. Or your attention may be on fine-tuning the specifics of some type of ending such as moving house. Even if this is a positive transition, you may find managing things rather stressful. The two of you will have to confer and agree on many details. Your digestion and sleep are likely to be disturbed during this phase. So watch what you eat. Especially avoid late-night snacking. Maintain your sense of equilibrium through physical movement classes (yoga, Pilates, tai chi) as well as meditation. It is also wise to put away your work at least an hour before bedtime.

This Christmas promises to be extra bright and cheerful. The holiday season will also feature a happy announcement and celebration. Your family may be expecting a new member – either birth or adoption. Alternately, there could be a windfall gain of some kind. Partying, socializing, meeting old buddies, visiting family, decorations and Christmas festivities at home, cozy dinners and gift shopping are going to take up your time during the last ten days of this month. The financial situation will improve further during this holiday season.

Mercury takes another of its three-week retrograde journeys this month. It will run from December 19th through the 31st. During this period, you may experience minor problems related to travel plans, missed messages, crossed wires, and just plain glitches. Not disasters. Just small mix-ups and snags. Unless you can get things done before the 19th do postpone important commitments, legal documents and major purchases. Any contracts entered into during this phase normally need changes and alterations later.

ARIES - January 2017

Mercury retrograde continues till the 8th of January. Local travel might prove to be a nightmare for most of you during this phase. Whatever is happening around the city, no matter whether you drive or jump on a bus, train, subway or helicopter, your daily commute is going to encounter snags. If at all possible, arrange with your employer to work from home for a few days. You will be much more productive that way. You should be exhibiting an extraordinary gift of gab between 6th to the 13th. Motivating and sweeping people off their feet are going to be a breeze.

Persuading a reluctant partner to do almost anything you want is child's play. Do not abuse your power, because the situation will reverse in a few months and the scale between the two of you will want to be balanced again. Another downside is that you may attract unwanted attention of which you are not aware. Someone whom you don't particularly fancy at your place of work is likely to try and make advances. Be discreet in turning them down.

You are due for a period of heightened activity between the 12th and the 20th. This busyness is likely to be focused in one particular facet of your life. It may be your creative side, which flourishes. Or you could become a champion around the office due to your intensive efforts at beating out the competition. Maybe you will break the club point record for your basketball team. Regardless of where you excel, you will lap up and enjoy all the extra attention. It's time to soak up the sunshine of admiring fans. Go for it!

Your health may need some attention in the last of week of January. During this phase, refuse to try new foods you've never tasted lest you fall ill with indigestion. Start nursing any health issues involving the head at this time. Migraines and dizziness may be prevalent now. You could be prone to a rolling cough and on-and-off headaches that may last the duration of the month. Keep relief medicines handy and do more exercise than usual. If you can't get to the gym or engage in sports activities, try taking walks - even on sidewalks in town. Keep the body agile and the blood coursing through your veins.

YOUR MONTHLY FORECASTS FOR THE FIRE MONKEY YEAR

2016

TAURUS

Author's Note... Mercury Retrograde

Sometimes planets appear to be zooming backward through the zodiac. Of course this backward motion is only an illusion. The planet has not turned tail. But it appears to have. Astrologers call this apparent reversing: **"retrograde"**.

Any planet can be retrograde. But only Mercury's retrogrades cause communications to break down. Mercury has its retrograde period for a few weeks 3 or 4 times each year. Whilst Mercury is retrograde, we humans are encouraged to take stock, make plans and discuss different approaches to a variety of subjects. But because information is often muddled, promises broken and electronic devices on the blink during Mercury retrograde, we must remain flexible and open-minded. Advice? Always allow extra time for travel. Schedule changes are common. Do not sign any contracts or cement agreements during Mercury retrograde. Make no irreversible promises. Watch out for con artists. Make no final decisions, binding engagements or major purchases during a Mercury retrograde. You are allowed to have tantrums or rail against your fate. But Mercury will continue to be retrograde till it decides to go direct again.

Mercury Retrogrades
2016

January 5 thru January 25
April 28 thru May 22
August 30 thru September 22
December 19 thru January 8 2017

OVERVIEW OF 2016 THE YEAR OF THE MONKEY FOR TAURUS

Steadfast Taurus,

You aced your way through an eventful - not tragic - but at times frantic 2015 Year of the Sheep. In the beginning of the Monkey year, you can kick back a bit and rest on your 2015 laurels. By the middle of 2016 however, a few gray clouds may roll into your romantic picture. There has been precious little passion going on in your life of late. You keep longing for some magical person to appear out of the blue and become your hot companion. I hate to break it to you Taurus, but fresh new love is not going to come sashaying into your bedroom with its clothes off this year. Oh no. In the Fire Monkey year, locating love and enjoying its various joys and sorrows will be entirely up to you. Yes. Use the Internet. Yes. Join groups. Yes. Talk to people you find attractive - anywhere. Just communicate and you will see positive results.

Taurean health looks promising, as does fitness in 2016 for Taureans. But there will be worries and anxiety about the health of some family members or good friends. You will want to DO something about these ills. Unfortunately, all you will be able to do is be there for these people. Visit them. Read to them. Take them thoughtful gifts. Encourage them to be brave and to fight their condition. If they are far away, ring them all the time to check in. They count on your concern to help them get better.

The above-mentioned tribulations may cause you to become more aware of your own mortality. 2016 therefore, will be a time of emotional growth and soul searching. All that is metaphysical and philosophical will become interesting to you again. sw

TAURUS - January 2016

You are back from the holiday break with loving memories. Interest in spiritual matters may come to the fore again now. You rekindle a desire to read and learn more about the metaphysical and divine. Mercury takes another of its three-week retrograde journeys this month. It will run from January 5th through the 25th. During this period you may experience minor glitches: muddled travel plans, missed messages, crossed wires, and just plain glitches. Not disasters. Just mix-ups and snags. Unless you can get things done before the 25th, postpone important commitments, legal documents and major purchases until a day or so after Mercury goes direct. Contracts entered into during this phase normally need changes and alterations later.

Your attention scatters from the 12th to the 19th of the month. There is likely to be a slight fogginess in your perceptions. You may be at risk of making errors at work. Tasks that require focused thinking will become more challenging. With the ongoing retrograde Mercury phase, we need to keep Murphy's Law in mind – "Anything that can go wrong will go wrong". Don't be alarmed. Blame your passing brain fog on Mercury. A minor driving mishap is also possible now. Ensure that your vehicle insurance papers are up to date. Be careful while drafting official emails and confirm the addresses carefully before sending out anything confidential. Do not escalate any issue without grasping the full scope of the matter. A slight misunderstanding can snowball into a big controversy. Express yourself after the 19th, when your thinking becomes clearer.

Your partner may have some good news or an interesting notion that he or she wants to share with you around the 26th. The news may be about a tempting job offer or a dazzling business opportunity. There could be more hard work and traveling involved for them. But there is much more money and improvement in status too. Offer them your creative input and ensure that you are supportive of his or her plans. Your partner's career may be about to take off to another level now and you will be proud of it.

TAURUS - February 2016

Thanks to Venus and Mars, your sixth house of health and wellness is activated between the 3rd and the 12th of February. What does that mean? Enthusiasm to exercise is at an all-time high. One piece of advice? Don't bite off more than you can chew. If your first run is a marathon or your first weight session is 200 kilos, a muscle strain or cramp will have you hobbling all month. For the time being, take baby steps. Besides, if you truly want to reach optimal health, exercise will not be enough. Are you smoking a pack a day? Drinking your weight in vodka every weekend? Were you once "Customer of the Month" at McDonald's? Replace any lingering bad habits with healthy new ones. Swapping the Marlboros, the Budweisers or that juicy double cheese-burger (with extra cheese) for a check-in at the yoga and aerobics class will do wonders for your body, mind and spirit. The more gentle exercise you do, the less you will crave poisons.

Have the perfect squeeze waiting for you at home? If so, snuggle up with them during the second week of the month. Why not set the stage for a romantic home-prepared dinner? Spray fresh bed sheets with their favorite perfume. Scatter rose petals on the duvet. Fill the room with scented candles. Play delicate melodies on the sound system. Hoping for a baby? If you pull out all the stops, this could be the ideal time to start one. Still a lone ranger? Don't be glum. During this period, bold overtures are likely to be returned. Search for a different pool of sin-gles. You could be in for a cross-cultural romance. As you cruise out-side your normal flight patterns, listen for sexy accents. Keep an eye out for any exotic arrivals to the neighborhood. Alternate your com-mute to involve a foreign coffee shop. If you step out of your comfort zone, you will be amazed at the various kinds of handsome or ravishing strangers you will meet.

Toward the end of the month, pleasure and recreational activities are beckoning. Indulge in some artistic hobbies. Painting, photography, music lessons—all are now within the realm of possibility. If your sweetie suddenly decides to attend an international film festival, tag along. After catching a live performance, some of you may even be inspired to join an amateur theatre group. Taureans tend to resolutely cling to the inside of the box. Outside that box is better for you at this time.

TAURUS - March 2016

As March begins, take some time to think about the future. Where do you see yourself ten years from now? What do you need to do to get there? How can you invest those spare funds to assure yourself a comfortable retirement? Look into low-interest business loans. Start raising seed capital for that health food truck venture. If you don't try now, you'll never know whether you could have succeeded! While you are busy with these mental exercises, someone in your circle may clue you in to an investment opportunity around the 7th or 8th. The source might be a bit of an oddball. But do not let that discourage you. Investigate their tip. Consult the family and your significant other. Still intrigued? Pledge your allegiance. Just remember—do not invest so much capital that your day-to-day lifestyle suffers. The promise of future riches is not worth eating magarine-coated noodles five nights in a row.

Unfortunately, accidents happen. Toward the middle of the month, your partner or a youngster in his or her family is likely to be involved in a minor fender-bender. Don't nag. But do remind them to be more attentive behind the wheel. Better still, for the time being, offer your services as chauffeur. Wait for them to get over the shock. Experiencing an accident can turn people into paranoid drivers. To be on the safe side, make sure that all vehicle insurance is renewed and all inspections are up-to-date. Surprisingly, either the other motorist or one of their passengers might be a family acquaintance. Small world!

The last week of the month sees some upheaval in your life. Has company relocation been bandied about during meetings? Perhaps you will be transferred out of the blue to another department or to a distant neighborhood. Or maybe the end of a relationship will inspire a cross-country move. Regardless, adjusting to the strange surroundings will be a shock to the system. Minor valuables or cherished items may get lost in transit. You could lose your temper after dropping a couch on your foot. Take heart! The change of address is the harbinger of better times ahead. Remember to store important local numbers in your cell phone. In other words, save the digits for your new office and the closest late-night pizza delivery service.

TAURUS - April 2016

During the first ten days of April, family matters are in the spotlight. An elderly female relative looms large. Did you have a nasty argument with an aunt or grandmother awhile back? If you need to clear the air, a no-holds-barred chat on the 3rd or 4th could put your relationship back on track. Married couples may end up arguing over money or property issues. Are you in the midst of a divorce or a breakup? Try to avoid falling down the bottomless rabbit hole of tussling over assets. Everything will be resolved about three or four months from now. Until then, rein in your anger. Unkind words now will only come back to bite you later on.

Have you recently developed an interest in distant cultures? If so, the middle of the month presents a prime opportunity to advance your worldly knowledge. How about enrolling in a language immersion course in Spanish or German? If you are fascinated by Eastern traditions, how about studying Japanese or Mandarin? Few activities are healthier for the brain than learning a foreign tongue. The improvement in your problem-solving abilities will astound you. However, this foray into other cultures need not be limited to language. You could take up Ikebana flower arrangements or classical French cooking. Go ahead. Plunge in. The process will be a transformative experience for you.

After the 24th, you will have an opportunity to contribute to a good cause. Perhaps you'll be appointed to with recruit donations for a fundraising marathon. Or you could have the chance to spend time with an elderly friend who is in a retirement home. This octogenarian might have been your guardian angel during tough times. When you visit, remember to bring flowers and a thoughtful gift. Laugh over old photos. Gossip about the latest happenings over mugs of tea or coffee. You could also catch a funny movie together. As April comes to an end, empty that overstuffed closet. Sift through the unwanted toys and clothes. Donate the leftovers to charity. Mercury, the celestial messenger, enters his first retrograde of the year on the 28th. Get ready to deal with crossed wires and mystifying interactions.

TAURUS - May 2016

Until the 22nd, Mercury remains in retrograde. Be cautious wherever travel, technology or communication are involved. Waiting until the eleventh hour to print that boarding pass? Bad idea. Take care of it now. Presenting an important PowerPoint slideshow at work? Double-check that you actually saved it to that USB key. In addition, censor yourself when using corporate email systems. That image which superimposed your boss's head onto a donkey's body is another bad idea. During Mercury retrograde, due to a glitch in the system, that jokey email might just get cod to the entire company. Venting your ire about overbearing supervisors is safest done through your personal account. The positive side of this phase? It is a great time to revise or revamp existing projects. Why not give your website or social media profiles a makeover? The extra polish may help you land the next great job.

Between the 17th and the 22nd, schedule reunions with old pals or colleagues. A former contact may tip you off to an investment opportunity or a hot date. And don't be afraid to branch out from your tried-and-true crew. Befriend someone who isn't quite like the rest of the herd. Perhaps a person of a different sexual orientation could use a buddy. Speaking of reunions, you may accidentally offend an acquaintance with a stray remark on the 19th. Avoid telling a dirty joke or dropping a sarcastic jibe about their appearance. Now especially, you must resist hurting other people's feelings. For the time being, deliberate before speaking your mind. Religion or race are probably not suitable topics for a wisecrack. Err on the side of caution.

Is loose change burning a hole in your wallet or purse? During the fourth week of May, you are sorely tempted to embark on a shopping spree. Before you whip out the MasterCard and snap up whatever swanky new gadget you suddenly can't live without, remember your monthly household budget. Can you actually afford this glorified trinket? Hunt for bargains. Can you find a similar product at a lower price? If you do give in to that *why not?* impulse, by the time June rolls around you may find yourself borrowing money to pay the utility bills.

TAURUS - June 2016

The first ten days of June present a favorable period for real estate transactions. Having trouble locating a buyer for that fixer-upper? Add a mystical touch to the house. Contact a nearby Feng Shui practitioner for suggestions. After incorporating the changes and additions, put the property back on the market. Prospective clients will be pounding on your door in no time! Speaking of real estate, why not give your own home a makeover? Perhaps you've outgrown that tired décor. Repaint, renovate and repair. A few calculated touches could turn your abode into the sophisticated haven you crave.

Have young ones at home? From the 14th to the 20th, spoil the kids, grandkids or little cousins. Fun-filled bonding time is just what the doctor ordered. Raid the local crafts store. Colorful clay and messy finger-paints would make for a splendid intergenerational arts and crafts day. Not a parent yourself? Still want some tiny tot time? There is hope for you yet! Offer to baby-sit for a harried mom who never gets a night out. While she enjoys a sexy date or reunion with the girls, bake cookies with her little ones. Watch silly movies. Indulge in pint-sized hugs and cuddles. You with leave feeling ten years younger!

Give yourself a pat on your back. Over the past few weeks, you've been hitting the gym regularly. Impressive! Unfortunately, exercise is only part of the equation. Poor dietary choices are preventing you from achieving peak health. If changing over to nutritious foods has been an uphill battle, take heart! Motivation to eat vegetables and cook fiber-filled beans will return by the 25th. But before you detox your body, you must detox your pantry. Ditch salty snacks and frozen dinners. Make sure the junk food finds its way to the trash can. Keep only dietician-approved ingredients such as whole grains, fruits, seeds, nuts, veggies, and organic dairy. Say NO to processed crap. Get rid of cheesy leftovers. Foodstuffs lose nutrients over time; heating and reheating also affects their quality. Still hounded by cravings for pizza or cheeseburgers? Try drinking chamomile tea to dull those pangs. It can't hurt - even temporarily - to turn to vegetarian selections around now.

TAURUS - July 2016

As July ignites, you may be forced to take on the burden of someone else's financial mess. A close relative is facing a sudden medical emergency. They may not approach you directly for help. But consider it your duty to step in. Offer whatever aid you can. Keep in mind; this could entail dipping into your savings. Are you willing to sacrifice that holiday you've been planning? Are you ready to go without sprucing your wardrobe for a couple of months? The rest of the family may not be on board with your decision. They caution that this humanitarian gesture will leave you broke and destitute. Your challenge? Tune out their disapproval. Play the Good Samaritan. Let compassion, not criticism from detractors, guide your choices.

Between the 13th and the 20th, a painful situation will arrive at its long-overdue conclusion. Are you stuck in a stale romance? Has a workplace alliance gone sour? Whether you are dealing with a lover, friend or business associate, maintaining this connection no longer serves any purpose. It is no longer a question of either side making sacrifices. There is no common ground to find! Deep in your heart of hearts, you know you outgrew this relationship many moons ago. Sentimentality is the only thing keeping the two of you together. During the third week of the month, a minor argument will be the straw that breaks the camel's back. The resulting formal separation will lift a burden off your heart. The good news? The parting will be amicable. The bad news? Now you need to hunt for a new partner.

As July comes to a close, some fabulous news on the professional or business front is coming your way. Do you head your own company? A rival's withdrawal from the industry or a technological breakthrough in your labs may soon have you jumping for joy. These glad tidings ensure that you will be raking in profits for the foreseeable future. For my otherwise employed Bulls? A sudden promotion or contract restructuring may grant you the tasty benefits you've been dreaming of. Enjoy using the office daycare facilities or taking advantage of that flextime clause!

TAURUS - August 2016

Is your house filled with outgrown baby toys? Apartment cluttered with moldy books? Use the first week of August to purge your living space.

Clean out that overstuffed attic or dusty basement. Ask your partner to lend a helping hand. As you scrub or organize, sort out the junk you no longer need. But don't scrap it just yet! Instead, host a yard sale. That way, you can recoup at least some return on your original investments. Around the 12th, enough is enough. A minor but nagging health issue has become too pesky to ignore. Are you suffering from a hormonal problem? Have you been postponing dental work? Stop dilly-dallying. If you fail to schedule that appointment now, the issue could snowball into something worse.

Toward the middle of the month, kiss your peace of mind goodbye. Money-related arguments and power struggles have you pulling your hair out. Did you come into an inheritance a while back? Perhaps a sibling or cousin is unhappy with the distribution of funds. If this case gets dragged into court, resolving it will be an expensive nightmare. Try to reach an amicable settlement before that point. Some of you may simply be haggling with a lover over whose turn it is to pay for dinner. Is tension hanging in the air even after you call for a truce? Iron out any differences of opinion between the sheets.

Normally, you are quite practical. But news of a friend's unexpected religious conversion has you contemplating your own spirituality. Fortunately, August's final week offers you some serious me-time. Let your mind wander to heavenly topics. Ever tried meditating or chanting? If you give either a shot now, you might gain a fresh perspective on previously indecipherable situations. Refuse all social invitations. Take lengthy strolls along the countryside. Get in touch with your higher self. Have any weird phobias been interfering with your life of late? If a fear of spiders or odd-numbered stairs has you feeling like a fool, book yourself a past-life regression or hypnosis session to release inharmonious energies. On the 30th, Mercury returns to his retrograde orbit. Watch out for some clumsy moments during the next three weeks or so.

TAURUS - September 2016

With Mercury doing backstrokes until the 21st, be wary of the company you keep. As much as you love camaraderie, a snake in the grass is slithering unseen through your social circle. Around the 5th, a "friend" may stop responding to texts. Or maybe a buddy will stand you up on a lunch date. Although their actions are no big deal on the surface, something feels wrong. Perhaps your gut is trying to tell you that this person isn't playing for Team Taurus. Probe discreetly. If you uncover a plot to stab you in the back, cease communication immediately. Do not trust this character with any personal secrets or confidential work-place information. If you maintain your distance, you can nip any machinations in the bud.

Between the 8th and the 15th, watch out for phishing scams and identity theft. Someone may hijack your email or social media account and begin to spam your contacts with virus-laden messages. If any booby-trapped files reach your colleagues? A public relations disaster could result. To protect yourself, update all passwords to include scrambles of letters and numbers. In addition, be careful when paying with plastic. Perhaps an ATM will gobble up your card. Or you will forget your wallet in a truck stop. Don't bother retracing your steps. That credit card is gone forever. Call the bank and cancel it.

Toward the end of the month, is your eye on a swanky new luxury ride? Traipse over to the bank. They will be more than willing to grant you a loan with a reasonable interest rate. As a matter of fact, borrowing cash in general will be a breeze for the time being. Perfect strangers will trust you with their life savings. You should also be able to pay off any outstanding debts. Alas, the reverse is not true. Does an unemployed friend need a bailout? Is an alcoholic cousin begging for some cash? Ignore their pleas. No matter how fiercely their impassioned words tug at your heartstrings. If you lend any money, you will have a hard time recouping it. The ensuing awkwardness may strain a treasured relation-ship. Better to be called a cheapskate than to lose a friend!

TAURUS - October 2016

Around the 5th, planetary alignments increase the likelihood of accidents and possible bone fractures. Minor surgery and a short stay at the hospital cannot be ruled out. Be careful while climbing stairs or crossing busy intersections. Furthermore, avoid all activities with a high potential for injury. Planning an expert-level rock climbing expe-dition? Embarking on your first ever skydive? Postpone such extreme sports until a later date. If you must bike or rollerblade to work, strap on knee and elbow pads in conjunction with that ugly helmet. Do not fret too much, though. If you take the proper precautions, a shiny bruise or inexpensive fender bender will be the worst you have to deal with.

Toward the middle of October, an old romantic wound may start throbbing again. Has an ex begun to resurface in a series of unsettling dreams? This blast from the past will remind you of how bitterly that relationship ended. In fact, you may not be able to prevent yourself from replaying old fights word-for-word in your mind. How can you deal with the resulting rage? You could lash out at this person in person.

Or badmouth them via Facebook or a personal blog. But negative karma is the last thing you need. Instead, wish them well. Send loving thoughts. Pray for their troubled soul. Remember—"to err is human; to forgive, divine." As always, the choice is yours. But if you select the forgiving option, you will experience a sense of emotional release by the 20th.

Perhaps it's all the "Food Tourism" television shows you've been watching. Or maybe it's that snotty coworker's exotic vacation stories. But during the last week of the month, itchy feet are making it impossible to concentrate. Are you surreptitiously surfing discount hotel websites from your cubicle? Does wanderlust have you daydreaming about trekking through distant mountains? Well, I hate to be the bearer of bad news, but you aren't going anywhere for at least a couple of weeks. If that realization makes you despondent, think about all the money that will accumulate in your bank accounts in the meantime. Once you actually manage to escape the office, those savings will help you afford the trip of a lifetime.

TAURUS - November 2016

Early November shows you tending to a houseguest. Maybe a cousin from across the nation will develop a stinging pain in his or her back while crashing at your pad. Or is a university-bound sibling or nephew laid up on your couch with a mysterious lack of energy? Unfortunately, ordinary medical channels are unable to provide an answer for these maladies. Instead of merely trying a different doctor, make an appointment with an acupuncturist or acupressurist. Healers trained in Traditional Chinese Medicine know how to use the pulse to diagnose problems in various organs of the body. They can sometimes detect anomalies that Western MDs miss. During the second week of the month, expect chaos on the home front. Are pipes leaking in the bathroom? Electrical outlets sparking in the kitchen? Stop putting off those plumbing or electrical repairs. Phone the local handyman. A partner may also decide to leave town for a business trip around now. Guess who that leaves to pick the kids up from football practice and keep the house stocked with groceries? Worry not! You will manage to balance your many duties. By mid-October, peace and quiet should be restored to your hectic life.

By the 15th, your attention is diverted to the work front. A manager's tantrums are interfering with your concentration. But before you report his or her improper behavior, think about the reasons behind their foul mood. Does that superior see the writing on the wall? Is their department getting phased out? Are they about to get laid off? Keep your complaints to yourself. This issue should iron itself out by the 22nd. Harmony will once again reign in the office without your even lifting a finger.

Is an acquaintance continuously boasting about the fat pile of money they made playing the financial markets? This character is always urging you to invest. Around the 28th, they may offer to manage your trading account for a small commission. Do not take the bait! This is a gambler's bluff. His or her original profits were greatly exaggerated. Besides, whatever winnings he or she has are soon to evaporate. Continue to plug along at that humdrum day job. At this point, get-rich-quick schemes will bring you nothing but heartache and regret.

TAURUS - December 2016

As December begins, you may find yourself happily acquiescing to a long-term commitment. Have you been thinking of moving in with that boy/girlfriend? Deliberating on whether you should exchange rings with an amour? Perhaps you will finally sign a contract with a new business partner. Don't have a honey to discuss marriage with? No corporate mergers to arrange? Look around you. A neighbor or friend of a friend is searching halfheartedly for a romantic companion. Although it will not lead to anything serious, make a move. The holiday season will be much more enjoyable with someone to warm your bed.

Toward the middle of the month, you continue to brim with love and optimism. Why not spread those positive vibes to your less-fortunate brethren? Wrap strangers in warm hugs. Surprise a homeless person with a brand new down jacket. Make a colleague's day when they are least expecting it. After all, what goes around comes around. That's what the law of karma is all about, isn't it? Well, around the 17th, you are in for a pleasant surprise. You have always assumed that a certain relative or schoolmate dislikes you. But now? This person confesses to being your secret admirer! Not only will the idea flatter you, but this new pal may also extend you an invitation (and free tickets) to a musical or sporting event.

Bolt the front door. Tug the blankets over your head. On the 19th, Mercury turns into his final retrograde of the year. Until the end of the month, his obfuscating influence spells trouble in the workplace. Computers crashing mysteriously? Ill-timed network outages interfering with teleconferences? There is nothing to do but shrug and wait for the lights to turn back on. In spite of your reputation for punctuality, you may have trouble delivering on deadline during this phase. To avoid being reprimanded, finish all long-term assignments before the 19th. Holiday celebrations should be joyful. The only hiccup? A small flare-up with your dad. Is he criticizing your budgeting (or lack thereof)? Could he be pressuring you to seek a better job? Before dismissing his opinions, listen to what the old man has to say. He has a point. In fact, his advice will come in handy sooner rather than later.

TAURUS - January 2017

Unfortunately, Mercury remains in retrograde until the 8th. Look on the bright side! These periods often bring back characters from the past. On the job hunt? Reconnect with former colleagues or employers. Is success still eluding you? Re-draft your resume. Do you have expe-rience relevant to the field to which you're applying? Put it in bold text. Consider speaking with a recruiter or career coach. Chances are, you could use some additional training or education to make you stand out from the crowd. During the second week of the month, focus on beauty, aesthetics and personality development. No one has ever accused you of being a fashion plate. So seek a salesperson's advice on what to wear. Select an outfit that is both fashionable and office-appropriate. Enroll in a local Toastmasters workshop to improve your leadership skills. Feel like ironing out those wrinkles? This could be the perfect time for Botox treatments or non-invasive plastic surgery.

Normally, there is no one more grounded in reality than you. But during the middle of January, you find yourself unable to prevent sentimentality from creeping into your psyche. Assuage your nostalgia by enjoying home-cooked meals with childhood friends, meandering conversations with elderly relatives and quality time with loved ones. Visit your alma mater. Get in touch with university buddies. Visit a favorite adolescent-era haunt. Flip through old diaries, yearbooks or photo albums. Research early family history. Make the most of these uncommon emotions. Reflecting on where you came from can only strengthen the trajectory of where you're going.

Around the 24th, your partner is unusually quiet. Do they suspect that you have a soft spot for a mutual friend? Are they wondering whether you are having a fling with an administrative assistant? It is your responsibility to reassure your lover that their fears are baseless. Squelch this rumor immediately. Otherwise, their suspicions may begin to undermine the foundation of your relationship. Challenge that anxious squeeze to a game of badminton or volleyball. The increase in heart rate and forced interaction will chase their blues away. Avoid activities that stifle conversation (like watching movies). The silence will only make them dwell on their worries again. As long as you aren't actually having an affair, your romantic situation should return to normal by the 29th.

YOUR MONTHLY FORECASTS FOR THE FIRE MONKEY YEAR

2016

GEMINI

Author's Note... Mercury Retrograde

Sometimes planets appear to be zooming backward through the zodiac. Of course this backward motion is only an illusion. The planet has not turned tail. But it appears to have. Astrologers call this apparent reversing: **"retrograde"**.

Any planet can be retrograde. But only Mercury's retrogrades cause communications to break down. Mercury has its retrograde period for a few weeks 3 or 4 times each year. Whilst Mercury is retrograde, we humans are encouraged to take stock, make plans and discuss different approaches to a variety of subjects. But because information is often muddled, promises broken and electronic devices on the blink during Mercury retrograde, we must remain flexible and open-minded. Advice? Always allow extra time for travel. Schedule changes are common. Do not sign any contracts or cement agreements during Mercury retrograde. Make no irreversible promises. Watch out for con artists. Make no final decisions, binding engagements or major purchases during a Mercury retrograde. You are allowed to have tantrums or rail against your fate. But Mercury will continue to be retrograde till it decides to go direct again.

Mercury Retrogrades
2016

January 5 thru January 25
April 28 thru May 22
August 30 thru September 22
December 19 thru January 8 2017

OVERVIEW OF 2016 THE YEAR OF THE MONKEY FOR GEMINI

Gregarious Gemini,

By the beginning of the Monkey year, you will probably be engaged to your newfound 2015 love interest. Remember. Take it slow. Marriage is a lifelong commitment and you are a Gemini. You like to be mobile and have your fingers in all kinds of different pies. Make sure your intended partner cannot only put up with your love of impermanence, but will also tolerate your burning desire for communication on any and all topics at all times. Be certain to analyze and work through any potential conflicts over long-term goals before you sign on the dotted line. In 2016, you will be favored in the areas of health and fitness. As hard as you have been working at building your health picture over the past year, tiptop shape has been eluding you. In 2016 your luck will shift and you will feel the old energy returning. You'll be eager to get back into the work world and be able to show your superiors just how much you have grown. In choosing colleagues and/or associates to work with, make a point of joining forces with people who are more experienced than you.

Monkeys and Geminis always get along. In fact, you are very alike. Monkeys, like yourself, are all over the place sticking their noses in everybody's business and excelling at the art of communication. This year will be salutary for your social life. Making new friends will become a priority. Also, meeting the family and cronies of your lover will occupy a sweet part of the year for you. If you feel up it, mid year you might do well to resume a vigorous sport and get back onto a wholesome diet. In short, the Fire Monkey year will bring you closure on many of the complex issues which beleaguered you last year and the year before. sw

GEMINI - January 2016

Keep a watchful eye on your bank balance early this month. With detail-oriented Mercury turning retrograde from Jan 5th until Jan 25, money issues could get wonky. The backspin could easily thrust you into a cash crunch. Do not spend capriciously. If you have a larger purchase to make, try to hold off till March. Use Mercury retrograde's investigative energies to shop and find the best possible deal - perhaps one with a low-interest payment plan. Beware the retail therapy monster too. Splurging will only bring a temporary high. Take the usual Mercury retro precautions about backing up data, putting off signing contracts, etc. If surgery is advised, schedule it for after Mercury goes direct again on January 26th.

There could be some issues related to outstanding debt or shared property between the 12th and the 19th. If you have hungry creditors, be prepared to deal with collection calls this month. If you own property jointly with anyone else - an ex-spouse, a business partner, a sibling or parent - you may all be in a tizzy about how to handle that property. Any assets you acquired through inheritance may also be subjects of heated discussion. In any case, as you know, contractual documents should never be concretized during Mercury retrograde. It's a super time for contemplating tactics and planning strategies. Not for signing on the dotted line.

Have you been planning to take up a new hobby? Planets suggest you are going to engage in a new and unusual activity from the 23rd to the 27th. This novel pastime could be anything from learning to play an obscure musical instrument to enrolling yourself in some little-known martial arts classes that are not offered anywhere else in the world. Go ahead and permit yourself to invest some time and money in this arcane interest. At month's end, you may find yourself at odds with a charity group regarding their misuse of funds. You can either withdraw your support completely or blow the whistle and draw public attention to the organization's having fiddled the accounts. Lawsuits can get messy - especially when your opponent has scads more loot than you. I would think twice before whistling. But of course the final decision is up to you.

GEMINI - February 2016

February begins with a flurry of activity in your relationships, both personal and business. In a nutshell, if you already have a significant other, you crave one-on-one time with him or her. If you are single, you could be engaged in a series of intense workplace negotiations. Use those famous Gemini networking skills to win the day for your team.

Table for two, Gemini? The 4th and the 6th are ideal dates for romantic candlelight dinners. You are likely to remain starry-eyed (and forgetful) with romantic passion for the next couple of weeks, so book those reservations now. All eyes will be on you on the 10th. Why is this day special? A long-term project has culminated. Perhaps you will present your research findings or give a rousing speech at an annual company banquet. Credit for your labors is coming. Get ready for the spotlight. A thunderous round of applause or a hefty bonus will only add to your sense of satisfaction.

The party continues! The middle of the month presents a superb opportunity for all artists to get their work into the public eye. Record a demo. Exhibit those artsy photographs. Bombard a publisher with writing samples—or cut out the middleman and start a blog. As a matter of fact, this is an auspicious time to launch an online business. The web could provide a forum to showcase your immense talents to a wider (possibly global) audience. But take baby steps. In other words, don't fizzle out like a shaken-up soda can. Reinforce your ambitious dreams with a concrete plan. If you've bitten off more than you can chew, spit something out. Pick one idea or focal point to concentrate on. Then build on that foundation.

Around the 27th or 28th, you are likely to hear from an ex. Perhaps an email from this former flame will pop up unexpectedly in your inbox. Or you could run into each other at a mutual friend's party. Try as you might to play it cool, your heart is a-flutter. Is there some unresolved baggage or residual chemistry between the two of you? You will always have a soft spot for this old squeeze. But that chapter of your life is over. Smile, chitchat awhile and move on.

GEMINI - March 2016

Time to tidy up! Early in March sees you on a mission to whip your surroundings (and yourself) into shape. Grab the broom and the vacuum cleaner. Spare no closet or filing cabinet your cleansing wrath. While you are at it, work toward streamlining your daily routines. Proper time management will make your life easier, reduce stress, increase vitality and improve your sleep. If you've fallen off the fitness wagon, extend this newfound focus to your eating and exercise habits. Do your arteries really need those burgers and fries? Wouldn't your system be served best by a ginger-infused green juice or a smoothie? Stock up on vitamins and incorporate all the major food groups into your diet. In particular, boost your protein intake. That will help you sustain a high energy level all day long.

During the middle of the month, you truly have the Midas touch. You have long dreamed of landing a date with a certain fetching possibility, and he or she (out of the blue) phones you up. You fret over dwindling bank accounts then all of sudden you trip over a pile of loose cash in the street. You are drooling over an exotic piece of jewelry in a storefront window, and someone gifts it to you. At work, even the most difficult of tasks turns out to be a breeze. In other words, Lady Luck is not merely smiling upon you. She is hugging and kissing you like a long-lost lover. I wouldn't be surprised if you start feeling invincible after a few days. But do not get too cocky. This fortuitous phase will be over in a matter of weeks.

A family gathering toward the end of the month is the perfect opportunity to unleash the child within you. Stay up all night nattering. Rehash decades-old debates. Who needs to dress in Grandma's fancy jewelry? Who gets to inherit Grandpa's smoking pipes? A quarrel between two female family members may arise. Perhaps over a loudmouth in-law or black sheep nephew. Let them fight it out. Do not pick a side. Once you hear each person's side of the story, play the part of the wise mediator and offer a satisfactory solution.

GEMINI - April 2016

If March had you dancing on cloud nine, the beginning of April brings you down to earth with a thud. Bills, deadlines and all things tedious have your stomach in knots. But worry not, Gemini. Take this opportunity to review your financial matters. Is some belt-tightening is in order? Dial back on impulse purchases. If you're dying to splurge on an expensive gadget but your income is unreliable, just tell yourself "No" with a capital N. Luckily, there is some light at the end of the tunnel. On or around the 7th, you could receive a job offer from an old client or employer. Coupled with some astute penny-pinching, this influx of cash will help you maintain your lifestyle. You will still be able to afford the occasional sushi and sake night. During this upswing phase, use the concept of building your nest egg as motivation to save when you are tempted to swipe that credit card.

The second week of April sees you in your full mercurial element. You kissed the Blarney stone and just about cannot shut up. You are even more prolix than usual. Ideas are bubbling up nonstop. At this point, you could sell a golden hairbrush to a bald man. Naturally, this is a great time for business negotiations and pitches. In addition to being impressed with your innovative ideas, people are going to be struck by how you speak. However, watch a tendency to take constructive criticism personally. On the 14th, a lively debate could quickly morph into a feud. A few snappy remarks could send a sensitive colleague rushing off to a corner to stifle their tears. Be conscious of a strident tone of voice - especially when speaking with less confident coworkers. Since Mars' active nature is influencing your horoscope after the 19th, indulge your athletic side. Lasso a few friends. Start up a game of tennis, racquetball or five-a-side soccer. Form a mixed basketball team or join an ultimate Frisbee tournament. But whatever you do, don't allow the competitive juices to flow too freely. Just let your hair down and have fun getting sweaty together with buds. Make sure no one's feelings get hurt. In addition, your ruling planet, the infamous Mercury, goes retrograde on the 28th. Brace yourself. That period will provide plenty of drama.

GEMINI - May 2016

For the first three weeks of the month, Mercury has you pinned between a rock and a hard place. From the 2nd to the 12th, the friendly neighborhood devil perched on your left shoulder grabs your attention. The angel on your right? He seems to have taken a vacation. You derive a strange sadistic pleasure now in stirring the pot and creating hassles for others. Perhaps you will play two competing clients or two chest-puffing suitors against each other. Or you may be tempted to broadcast a close friend's clandestine secret. This chicanery may give you a cheap thrill. But be warned! During this phase, any machinations on your part are likely to backfire. And no amount of apologizing will protect you from the fallout.

As the littlest planet's disrupting influence lingers on, be extra careful with your hygiene. You risk catching a cold. Avoid those who have a habit of standing too close while talking. Keep the natural antibacterial hand gel ready. Between the 15th and the 22nd be especially vigilant about what you eat. Pay a visit to the local health food store. Line your shelves with Vitamin C-rich mangoes, strawberries and grapefruit to boost your immunity.

Shakespeare had it right with that famous line from *Hamlet*: "Neither a borrower, nor a lender be." On or around the 25th, a close relative is likely to solicit some substantial financial assistance from you. Perhaps the aunt who took you on childhood vacations will come round and guilt you about needing money. Or maybe a down-on-their-luck sibling or cousin will ask for a loan. You know full well that said person is a moocher. If you open your checkbook now, you may not be reimbursed for years. In fact, you'll be lucky if this unreliable character even pays you back at all! My advice? Slip into your dancing shoes. Trip the light fantastic out of there. Elude these requests. Bob and weave. Duck and hide. Be out of town. Switch off your phone or pretend you lost it. Draw the curtains. Lower the shades. Dim the lights so the house looks abandoned. Report that you have gone scaling the Himalayas on a spiritual voyage. With a little luck and foresight, you should be able to escape this testy period with your bank account intact.

GEMINI - June 2016

As June takes the reins from May, it might be time to readjust your workout routine. Is inadequate exposure to sunlight turning your skin the color of library paste? Are you growing bedsores because it's been so long since you shifted from the sofa to the road? Join a gym. But keep it simple. Don't fall for a swanky place thirty kilometers away from home. Such a commute will sap your mojo after a few weeks. Also, when it comes to motivating yourself to get your heart rate pumping, two bodies are better than one. Find a workout partner or hire a personal trainer. If you can rope in your squeeze to accompany you - even better. Thanks to an impulse from the planet Venus, dancing is also likely to take your fancy. Go out on a limb and try a Zumba, hip hop or tap class. Any and all vigorous gyrating will make exercising that much more enjoyable.

The middle of this month has an optimistic aura about it. An opportunity to travel approaches. Has someone offered to pay you to trek through the Andes and write about the experience? Is your company sending you to a business summit or training session abroad? Perhaps you will embark on your own ad hoc spiritual pilgrimage and expand your mind as never before. Bold enterprises will find success around now. If you've been pondering going back to school for a higher degree, this is the perfect moment. Or you could launch that start-up you've been dreaming about. Fortune favors the brave. So take some risks. Follow your hunches. Adventure awaits!

Watch out for a mini-crisis involving a child or pet on the 22nd. The poor thing might sustain a minor injury or suffer from a bout of food poisoning. This incident will give you one heck of a fright. But within three days, the little one or the pup should be bounding around the house like nothing ever happened. During the last week of the month, it's time to test-run any new significant others. If you have not already introduced them, see how your sweetie deals with your friends or family. Present him or her to everyone during a dinner outing on the 25th or the 26th. If everything goes swimmingly, they are a keeper. But if tension from friends chokes the life out of the party, it might be wise to reconsider this romantic choice.

GEMINI - July 2016

Early July couples good news with bad. Perhaps an exciting, well-compensated work assignment will materialize. Unfortunately, the gig will also demand long hours and the sacrifice of precious shuteye. Or a stunning lovebird could flit into your bedroom. Problem is, he or she used to date your best friend. Talk about a conflict of interest! In the workplace, dissension in the ranks is likely on or around the 11th. Maybe a competitive colleague is bad-mouthing you to the boss. You feel like a pressure cooker of pent-up tension. But worrying will accomplish nothing. Seek a Zen-like calm when it comes to personal and business difficulties. Admittedly, such mental relaxation is difficult for most Geminis. But at least give it a running start.

Between the 15th and the 22nd, burnout and exhaustion dog you. The current amount of turmoil in your personal life is unsustainable. Feeling some nasty gas bubbling up from your stomach? Symptoms of hypertension and acid reflux could be the last straw. Go easy on yourself, my just-can't-sit-still Gemini. You cannot put out everyone else's fires. Do have a pal who always calls with a sob story, begging for an ear to vent into? Make an excuse. You have something boiling over and must hang right up. No worries. The sob storyteller can snare someone else into listening to this current episode. You need to be mindful of whom you let into your sphere. Some people are "energy vampires." Whether you realize it or not, you waste valuable strength dealing with their dramas. The worst part is that they often masquerade as your closest comrades. Graciously distance yourself from such toxic characters. Focus instead on the people who can help boost your flagging spirit in this journey through life. As painful as it may be to cut ties with an overly self-centered friend, their absence will help you sleep better in the long run.

Take solace. Get yourself some "me" time after the 25th. Relax and unwind. Cancel all non-urgent meetings. Switch off your mobile phone. Devote some time to art, photography or theatre. Listening to soothing chants or a "Sounds of the Ocean" album can also help quiet the mind. On the 27th and the 28th, investigate a Feng-Shui overhaul of your home space. De-clutter and light some candles or burn some sage. This process will freshen the atmosphere and remove blocked chi energy.

GEMINI - August 2016

During the first week of August, you could face a health scare. Perhaps a routine visit to the doctor will turn up an unexplained lump or a suspicious mole, requiring more complex tests. Or nagging joint pain may have you limping around the house. Avoid the grin-and-bear-it technique. There is no use ignoring this problem. But neither should you assume the worst. Especially avoid internet-based self-diagnosis. Many health websites are designed to awaken the users' latent hypochondriac tendencies, incite panic and encourage them to buy medicines. Listen only to a reliable health professional. If you don't trust your current doctor, ask for references from friends. Physicians, like every other type of professional from mechanics to lawyers, come in a range of styles and competence levels. Choose someone you like and who likes you back. Make friends with your doctors. Invite them to dinner. Friends don't want their friends to die.

Thanks to the Sun, your third house of communication is afire again this month from the 10th to the 19th. Use that Gemini smooth-talk to get ahead in the workplace. You should be able to generate ideas to help your company break into parallel industries or launch groundbreaking product lines. Colleagues will be knocking on your cabin, begging for your brilliant advice. Oblige them willingly. Grade their proposals. Critique their strategies. Becoming the resident sage will only solidify your reputation as indispensable to the business. And that should place you next in line for a promotion.

During the last ten days of August, you are agonizing over a personal decision. Should you take the plunge and relocate to another city? Should you make a copy of the house keys and move in with that girlfriend or boyfriend? Whatever it is that you are mulling over, keep it to yourself. Running life-altering plans past parents or other relatives will only provoke a negative reaction. Many friends and family members have their own agendas and will answer subjectively. Let's face it. Mom and Dad do not want to have to hop on a plane to see you every holiday. Don't allow jealous or clingy family members or pals to emotionally blackmail you into abandoning your plans. You do have some time to re-consider. Mercury retrograde looms on the 30th, you will need to put major moves and decisions on the back burner for the next three weeks.

GEMINI - September 2016

Even though September begins with Mercury sailing backwards across the sky, you can still twist this retrograde to your advantage. Maybe an old contact will email you out of the blue with an intriguing opportunity for some freelance work. Or perhaps you can resurrect a former cash-generating skill. Were you once an expert writer? Maybe an acquaintance could use your help with some ghostwriting. Or you could tap your web design talents and build a colleague's site. Property-related matters will be fortuitous. If you are seeking to purchase a new home, you may find the perfect sun-drenched abode on or around the 12th. Or perhaps a buyer will finally materialize for that old house of yours that's been wilting on the market for months. However, wait until the littlest planet reverts to his natural orbit on the 21st before you sign on the dotted line. If you finalize a contract before then, you may miss a clause in the fine print that you will regret agreeing to later.

The middle of this month gives you a dose of Murphy's Law: anything that can go wrong, will. A short-distance picnic trip or general outing with friends goes awry when the car engine fizzles out halfway to the destination. The weather doesn't cooperate either. Sulking faces and bad moods will make this "fun" excursion more trouble than it's worth. Petty arguments also abound in your romantic relationships. Thank-fully, your spirit is buoyed by children on the home front. The kids—whether yours or a relative's—surprise and delight you with some of their performances in sports, theater or academics.

Around the 28th or 29th of September, the day you've been praying for since God-knows-when will finally come to pass. Perhaps you will belatedly rediscover the lost book that was your favorite as a teenager. Maybe you will hit the jackpot at the horse races. Or a favorite singer or instrumentalist might be giving a concert in your city for the first time. This event may seem like a trifle to others. But for you, it's a dream come true. Pay no mind to those scoffing at your jubilation. This is your moment. Revel in the satisfaction of a small victory.

GEMINI - October 2016

The first two weeks of October see you feeling flirtatious. Sex is on your mind. But it comes with a rotating cast of supporting actors. Stability can rapidly bore someone of your versatility. Your sign's motto might be "variety is the spice of life." Enjoy your freedom! You are dripping charm like never before, and everyone around is taking notice. The line between love and friendship could blur a bit. Don't hesitate to take risks. Now is not the time to be a dignified lady or gentleman. If your current relationship is boring your socks off, flirt a bit. This planetary gift of increased sensuality will also heighten your sense of intuition—very helpful in both the love and creativity depart-ments. As you experiment and meet new kinds of people, use those elevated instincts to determine what truly thrills them. Nothing is as stimulating as having a partner who does exactly what you always dreamed of without being asked.

Between the 12th and the 21st, an elderly relative may face severe health issues. Their immediate care will probably fall to you. If his or her condition becomes critical, make the tough choices. Move this aunt, parent or longtime friend to a place where they can be better looked after. Don't allow their doctors to over-medicate. Trust your judgment. A tricky family member may try to twist the current medical issue into a question of money. If they try to bully you, bully them back.

The end of the month ushers in a moment of spiritual awakening for you. Perhaps a New Age book will inspire you to research a non-traditional avenue of prayer or worship. Use that extra sensitivity to seek out and practice the path that's right for you. That choice could come down to pure and simple meditation, energy work (Reiki, for instance) or one of the esoteric Yoga branches, like the Kundalini. Late October is also an advantageous time to root out the deeper issues skulking about in your psyche. Visiting a past life regression therapist or specialized psychiatrist could help you attain some much-needed inner peace.

GEMINI - November 2016

In early November, torrents of positive energy rain from the heavens. As a consequence, you are full of "ready to take on this world" verve. Signing up for daily hot yoga classes? Committing to run a marathon in three weeks? Don't let enthusiasm trump good sense. Avoid piling more onto your plate than you can handle. "Let me get back to you on that!" would be a far smarter answer than a knee-jerk "Yes!" On the 5th or the 6th, an acquaintance may call in a favor. Maybe they set you up with a hot date a couple of months ago or loaned you a small chunk of change. But if they are asking you to co-sign a mortgage or to borrow your life savings, politely pass on the request. Your original debt was not so steep as to warrant that much of return favor.

Opportunities for career advancement abound between the 9th and the 17th. During this phase, try your hardest to grasp that next rung on the corporate ladder. If you show your true mettle on a crucial venture now, a promotion is possible. Is there an opportunity to join a group project or attach your name to a burgeoning startup? Do not hesitate to throw your hat in the ring. The endeavor's future is uncertain now, but it looks like it will grow to be a bonny feather in your cap over the next six months. If you are still wary of committing to this enterprise, pick a highly successful mentor's brain. Chances are, they faced a similar choice on their rise to the top. Listen closely to their advice. A wizened elder's tips can be invaluable.

During the last week of the month, you are likely to be put in charge of a group of youngsters. Perhaps as a chaperone on a class trip. Or as a babysitter for some distant cousins. Spoil them a little. You and the children will get along much better if you allow them some leeway. Carve out time for good old-fashioned fun—the kind where you get a little mud on your clothes. Bring on the art projects, housecleaning, sewing lessons and football games! For those who are trying to pop out a baby of your own, late November presents an increased likelihood of getting pregnant.

GEMINI - December 2016

The first week of December brings you closer to a family member. Perhaps you have been bickering with your parents of late. Arguments over in-laws, not calling home enough—the usual suspects. But now? That is water under the bridge. Let bygones be bygones. While those personal relationships are healing, a creative mood takes hold of you from the 7th to the 15th. Feel like going on a home redecorating spree? Let your innate good taste guide you. Glance around your humble abode. If anything from a creepy painting to some outdated bedroom furniture triggers a negative reaction, trash it. Are eyesores such as stained coffee tables or fingerprint-laden walls cringing you out? A fresh layer of polish or a dazzling new coat of paint should do the trick. A pro tip? Use pastel shades of green in the accents. That will really make the centerpiece of the room pop.

Unfortunately, Mercury is in retrograde from the 19th until the 31st of December. Get ready for blown light bulbs, malfunctioning word processors and unintelligible voicemail messages. Not to mention a wild office rumor. Before you lock yourself inside your bedroom and throw away the key, take a deep breath. That workplace gossip? Entirely fabricated. The CEO is not really selling off assets as if he or she knows something you do not. The boss did not sleep with the janitor. There is a heap of misinformation swirling about. Plaster a grin on your face. A chipper attitude will keep you chugging along amidst the pandemonium.

Planning a cozy, peaceful winter vacation? Well, kiss that dream goodbye. The holidays will see you pulled asunder by conflicting desires. Half of you craves intimacy. But the other half thirsts for boozy wigged out adventure. If you give in to the latter urge, remember one thing: everything in moderation. Binge-drinking eggnog at the company Christmas party may not be the world's greatest idea. Nor is replacing the mistletoe with an empty vodka bottle. Maintain strict control over your alcohol consumption. And if you do get a little too tipsy, phone a cab. Or bum a ride from a sober fellow partygoer.

GEMINI - January 2017

Mercury refuses to relinquish his grip on your sanity until the 8th of January. Until then, ensure that all credit card numbers and online banking passwords are secure. In fact, why not reset those login codes that you've been using for the last decade? While you're at it, back up your personal files on an external hard drive or pay-per-month storage site. Retrogrades are notorious for online glitches. When it comes to your digital security, an ounce of prevention is worth a pound of cure. On the other hand, your love life is going superbly right now. You are almost ready to take that next big step. Putting a ring on it? Making the relationship Facebook-official? Before you get your hopes up, be prepared for a final snag. For whatever reason, you are not well liked by your partner's family. They do not trust your intentions. If you are truly serious about this squeeze, you need to get this unspoken issue out into the open. After the 8th, bring up the topic during a dinner or gathering. Pledge your undying allegiance to the person they are protecting. With the support of your significant other, that in-lawiciness should thaw faster than a glacier in Barbados.

Around the middle of the month, an opportunity for an entrepreneurial venture with a close friend presents itself. Is a buddy starting up his own brewery? Is a childhood neighbor looking for a partner in their restaurant business? Dive in. Take the plunge. This is no fool's errand. In fact, if you combine your talents, this project may be the beginning of a mutually beneficial long-term partnership.

Around the 27th, you may suddenly realize that you've outgrown a spiritual group or charitable cause that had been close to your heart for many years. Perhaps a new documentary will reveal that those contributions aren't really going to the poor kids that the pamphlet advertised. Or maybe your church or congregation is attracting members with different values than you hold dear. Whatever the case may be, withdraw gracefully. Never waste energy on people or missions that no longer enhance your life.

YOUR MONTHLY FORECASTS FOR THE FIRE MONKEY YEAR

2016

CANCER

Author's Note... Mercury Retrograde

Sometimes planets appear to be zooming backward through the zodiac. Of course this backward motion is only an illusion. The planet has not turned tail. But it appears to have. Astrologers call this apparent reversing: **"retrograde"**.

Any planet can be retrograde. But only Mercury's retrogrades cause communications to break down. Mercury has its retrograde period for a few weeks 3 or 4 times each year. Whilst Mercury is retrograde, we humans are encouraged to take stock, make plans and discuss different approaches to a variety of subjects. But because information is often muddled, promises broken and electronic devices on the blink during Mercury retrograde, we must remain flexible and open-minded. Advice? Always allow extra time for travel. Schedule changes are common. Do not sign any contracts or cement agreements during Mercury retrograde. Make no irreversible promises. Watch out for con artists. Make no final decisions, binding engagements or major purchases during a Mercury retrograde. You are allowed to have tantrums or rail against your fate. But Mercury will continue to be retrograde till it decides to go direct again.

Mercury Retrogrades
2016

January 5 thru January 25
April 28 thru May 22
August 30 thru September 22
December 19 thru January 8 2017

OVERVIEW OF 2016 THE YEAR OF THE MONKEY FOR CANCER

Creative Cancer,

2016 will bring you closer to many of the goals you have been secretly guarding because you feared others might find them trite or frivolous. This is the year you have been waiting for to break out of the mold that society has created for you. I am not suggesting divorce or revolution; but there are certain projects you have always wanted to devote yourself to, but didn't dare.

Last year, you downsized. You offloaded excessive possessions and even lost weight. This year, you are in shape, both emotionally and physically, and ready to regain the kind of confidence you felt as a younger person - before you were saddled with responsibility and labels. You may at first feel, in this Fire Monkey year, that your love life lacks a certain passion. You long to rekindle the flame that set you two on the path of togetherness in the first place. By the middle of the year, you will be surprised to note that your partner (lover or spouse) is suitably turned on by the new you. They always knew who you really were underneath the masks you have often felt compelled to wear for the sake everything from your profession to your family life. As soon as they see that you are breaking out and being the real you, the flame will rekindle itself.

You are in for some exciting personal adventures in 2016. Last year brought you significant emotional issues and some health matters that had to be worked out. You got through. But just barely. The Monkey year will offer you the strength and wisdom to revisit the past without fear. When you begin to turn over some of those heavy rocks that were blocking your path, your life will take on a whole new glow. Bye bye aches and pains. Hello fine fettle. sw

CANCER - January 2016

Yippee! Your challenging period appears to be over. As we take stock of the year, you had meteoric changes, and then some tough months. In January, events plateau. Finally, you can take some time to breathe. Enjoy the fruits of your efforts. If you earned a lot of money this year, spend some of it. Take the family on a vacation. No family? No problem. Organize a camping or foreign country trip with friends. Change of venue creates new challenges for all. How do we operate this weird camping stove? Who knows how to pitch a tent? Does anybody know the German word for hot water? Should you report your lost passport to the police? Being out of one's usual water is a fabulous way to bolster old bonds and even create some new ones.

By the way, this is an optimum moment to investigate a place you've never been before. Research nearby natural attractions you have always been intrigued with. Often, we neglect to visit the sites closest to us. It seems almost too easy. Besides, Cancers can get very stuck in their ways. Break out of the cycle. Explore. Go with a pal. Or travel solo. Either way you will be thrilled by the wonders you can find right on your doorstep.

Work seems to level off again. You feel as though you're going nowhere. Treading water. Tread away! Just keep your longer-term goals in mind. Maybe you aren't working at your dream job or maximum speed right now. But you may be doing something that will lead to that ideal job? Or, if your dream job is to have no job at all, think seriously about starting your own business or pursuing artistic goals you have always set aside in favor of the race for a kind of success you never wanted in the first place.

CANCER - February 2016

As the month begins, you may have a chance to boost your finances. For instance, if you have a cushy hospital job, perhaps you will pick up a lucrative weekend post at a wellness center. In this vein, do not be surprised if you receive an opportunity for some freelance work or to earn a nice chunk of change from a side project. For many of you, this may be also a wakeup call to quit micro managing and put your eyes on the larger prize. I know you've had enough of toiling away at that 9-to-5 job. So how about investigating affiliate marketing or residual income, such as royalties from sales or downloads? Your financial genius is alive and well this month, so leave no stone unturned. But hang on a minute! Are you saving enough for the future? Watch out for a tendency to splurge on the 7th and the week thereafter. If you do insist on a shopping spree, make sure to keep all receipts. Once your retail therapy fever ends, there are going to be a lot of returns.

The third week of February would be a good time to work on home repairs or renovation projects. Especially if you are thinking about selling a few months down the line. As you plan that new porch or garden, watch out for a sudden rift or minor misunderstanding with an elderly female relative. Probably over your infrequent visits or questionable romantic choices. My advice? Calmly listen to her point of view. Don't reject any well-meaning advice. Take some time to reflect. Then decide whether to come home more often or to dump that ill-chosen love interest.

After the 25th, buck up and assume more responsibility in the household. Start tracking your expenses. Get into the habit of scrubbing the kitchen clean after cooking. Make the crucial transition out of your free spirit phase. This maturation will boost your confidence and set a good example for the younger members in your family. Over the next few weeks, your relatives should start noticing and appreciating this welcome change in your habits.

CANCER - March 2016

The first half of March is all about service to others. During the first week, you could find yourself getting pressed into service for a hospitalized relative or elderly neighbor. Be the Good Samaritan. Deliver that chicken soup. Water their flowers. Provide all the tender loving care they need. Do not shrink from sacrificing your personal time. Remember: no good deed goes unnoticed. What goes around comes around.

The week of the 10th is somewhat emotionally disturbing. Problems seem to spring up from all directions. At home and at work. You may find it difficult to shake off a crabby mood. The remedy? Spending time with kids. No matter how much abuse you absorbed in the office during the day, make time to play, read to or talk with children. If you are not a proud papa or mama, volunteer to take someone else's progeny on an outing. Perhaps your grandchildren (or nieces or nephews), the offspring of a friend, or some underprivileged kids would like to check out a local museum or catch the latest action movie. Be both materially and emotionally generous. Buy them treats, but also offer non-judgmental, non-condescending, undivided attention. Turn off your cell phone. Listen closely to what the little ones have to say. Bing more playful will serve to evaporate any accumulated stress.

After the 22nd, a new development in your love life captures all your

81

attention. Could this be a case of friends becoming lovers? You might find yourself looking at an old university buddy with a decidedly more amorous eye. Or maybe a colleague or confidant will put the moves on you. He or she might show up for an innocent coffee date and suddenly start being overtly flirtatious. It may seem exciting to suddenly have a "friend with benefits." But think carefully before you jump into the bed with this character. Getting involved "casually" could turn out to be stickier than you were hoping for. Someone (read: *you*) might start dreaming of your shared future, while the other assumes the relationship to be only a frivolous fling. Ask yourself: is a sexy romp between the sheets worth the possible loss of a friend?

CANCER - April 2016

Jackpot! Early April sees you involved with inheritance or other lucrative legal matters. Perhaps you will receive a chunk of money from a wealthy benefactor. Or a windfall could come from an even more unexpected source. That elderly neighbor you used to play chess with? Maybe he or she will bequeath you their apartment. If you are feeling motivated to write or revise your own will, set up a retirement fund or make a savvy investment, take the opportunity to do so now. For those who work in the non-profit sector, this is also an excellent time to apply for a loan or grant.

From the 9th to the 15th, connect with your humanitarian and volunteering spirit. Why not get involved with a noble cause? If protecting the environment is what floats your boat, many green organizations are looking for help spreading their message or maintaining web pages. If you like working with kids, perhaps you could create an after school performance workshop for the local youth. If you have the event-planning bug, you could help a charity organize their fundraising gala. The message for these few days is "get involved".

By the 21st, you are ready to commit to a regular fitness regimen. But you don't know where to start. So why not enlist a little help from the experts? Hire a gym instructor or a boot camp-style trainer to help you stick to a set schedule. If you can't afford a trainer, see if he or she can work out some sort of barter arrangement. You walk their dog and they keep you in shape sort of thing. But keep it simple. If you are prospecting for a gym, don't base your selection on the amenities, VIP ambiance or premium membership rates. All that glitters is not necessarily efficient. When it comes to your health, trust the tried and true, not the flashy and fleeting. It's more important to find out if the staff members are helpful and friendly. Also, avoid joining a club that's not in your neighborhood. If you need to travel 10 miles just to jog on the treadmill, motivating yourself will be a drag. And take care toward the end of the month. Mercury goes retrograde on the 28th. Steel yourself to deal with his signal scrambling effects during the next three weeks.

CANCER - May 2016

Unfortunately for put planetary peace of mind, Mercury remains in retrograde until May 22nd. So during these early weeks of May, be cautious while using credit cards or doing online banking. In particular, be on the lookout for identity theft. You don't want to wake up one morning to discover that someone has charged hundreds of dollars of high-end purchases to your Master Card. If your passwords are worn out, change them. Shred all financial papers. Make sure to use a secure web browser. No matter how promising a deal with a lover or business partner looks, you would be wise to think twice before making a firm commitment as during this testy period, not all is as it seems. Hold off on finalizing any investments or popping the question until the littlest planet has reverted to its normal orbit.

Disturbing news regarding your residence is likely to arrive on or around the 12th. You have forged many a memory here. Passionate nights, idyllic afternoons. However, your landlord might be selling the premises. Or perhaps a developer is tearing up all the local land. While moving out of your cherished abode may be traumatic, you will soon see the silver lining. An even better place will become available. Or else you will realize that this is the perfect time to explore home ownership and snap up a piece of attractive property. If you decide to go the ownership route, beware of the retrograde delays. Clarify possible points of contention before you sign on the dotted line. Best to wait until the fourth week of the month to make things official. Luck it on your side now. You might even have a new address before the end of May.

Solo Crabs are likely to discover romance while getting healthy this month. Maybe you will bump into a stunning potential lover at a fruit juice bar (as opposed to the usual wine bar). Or you might catch a charmer checking you out at a smoking cessation hypnosis clinic. Don't be surprised. If you started working out last month, the increased activity has elevated your spirit and begun to show on your physique. It is natural for others to be drawn to your healthy and glowing aura. The relationship you develop now is genuine and might be here to stay. Just be prepared to fight a slight tendency to be hyper critical of this squeeze. Give them the benefit of the doubt.

CANCER - June 2016

Slaving away at a routine 9 to 5 job? Unhappy with your position or income? You cannot wait around for other people to recognize your excellence. If you think you deserve an improvement in title, salary or perks, then boldly state your case in June. Unleash a round of shameless self-promotion between the 3rd and the 12th. Hand the powers-that-be concrete evidence that you've increased their productivity, profits and prestige. Put together a PowerPoint or PDF and share it during a performance review. Spell it out for them. There should be no doubt left in their minds as to what an asset you are to the team. If you can pull this off, your efforts will strike a harmonious chord with the movers and shakers. It looks like another job opening or a dream client will become available during this phase. Fasten your seatbelt! You may be blasting off to the stratosphere of job satisfaction sooner than you anticipated.

Being a watery sign, you are often highly intuitive. Like a sponge, you unconsciously absorb the moods and energies of people around you. During the week after the 15th, you are especially sensitive to strong vibes—both negative and positive. These are the days when it's best to stay tucked inside your cozy shell. Snuggle up under the covers. If you can, work from home. Focus on a detailed project that needs your attention. During this phase, be selective about your companions. Schedule quality one-on-one time with only the closest of friends. If you want to catch up with someone, opt for a quiet dinner. Avoid guzzling alcohol. Conserving social energy is your best bet to survive this period unscathed.

Between the 25th and the 29th, the green-eyed monster threatens to emerge. Much to your partner's discomfort, you are becoming overly possessive. You might end up in arguments with your lover over familiar refrains. "Why can't we have sex more often?" "Why should I share my savings with you if you don't spend any time with me?" "Why should I buy all the groceries? You never help me with the cooking!" Sound familiar? Clearly, tensions are running high. Be assertive with your needs. But do not let your frustrations boil over into complaints. A more satisfying solution? Let off some steam between the sheets!

CANCER - July 2016

Structure and routine are not among your favorite concepts. But between the 2nd and the 9th, your emotional Cancer nature needs to take a seat on the sidelines. Efficiency is the name of the game. So what are you waiting for? Get your entire life in working order. From your workout habits to your office filing system. Clean up the way you organize your clothes in the closet —restructure everything. In particular, concentrate on home improvements. Beat a path to the discount store. Purchase tall, stackable plastic bins to store items in closets. Some flat containers will keep those movies and video games under the sofa and out of the way. And how about an inexpensive plastic piggy bank to stash all the loose change jangling around inside that top dresser drawer? This tidying exercise may consume a couple of hours. But the increased coordination in your life will be worth the trouble.

From the 12th to the 17th, you have the opportunity to right a wrong. A few years ago, you let your petty dislike of someone get in the way of good judgment. This person simply grated on your touchy nerves. Probably with an offhand comment about your parents or a dismissal of your career accomplishments. After you reacted so strongly, this character was ostracized from your close-knit group of friends. Being so harsh was probably a mistake. Now the alignment of the planets brings the two of you into contact again, giving you a chance to atone for your error. Perhaps he or she is interviewing for a position at your company. Or they're searching for an apartment in your neighborhood. Do not pass up this chance to revive a relationship. If you do the person a favor now, you may indeed erase some of your soiled karma.

The focus shifts to the workplace after the 25th. A new project might drop onto your desk. Seemingly out of nowhere. Unfortunately, deadline pressure and general stress may lead to a few sleepless nights. On top of everything, you may clash with an authority figure on the 28th. Probably because you feel constricted by dumb rules and protocols. But before you jeopardize your job security by losing your cool, take ten slow breaths. Things should settle down on their own by the weekend.

CANCER - August 2016

This month ushers in sudden changes for you and your family. During the first week, an unexpected offer to relocate to another city has you intrigued. Did a more highly paid long-distance job just become available? Perhaps you didn't see this one coming, but in reality, the situation has been brewing since November. On the other hand, your partner could be the one receiving a juicy work opportunity. Regardless of who bags the offer, this change of scenery could be too enticing to refuse. If it's your lover's long distance opportunity and he or she is set to skip town, don't despair. You should be able to hone in on employment in the same area. If you are a student, a very promising educational program could materialize between the 3rd and the 10th. It offers a degree or track perfectly tailored to your unique interests. For some of you, there could also be an invitation to travel overseas and participate in an international project. An experience abroad will alter your perspective forever. Don't pass it up.

An allergy may give you hell mid-August. You may have eaten something you didn't know you were allergic to. Or a particular tree or unfamiliar plant might cause a skin rash or a slight swelling in your throat. Ring your doctor. Perhaps a simple pill can alleviate the symptoms. If allopathic meds don't help, try ayurvedic or homeopathic remedies. Such natural cures have fewer side effects than do chemical compounds. Do act decisively. If you don't do anything about this flare-up, the discomfort could persist for weeks.

The final ten days of August are chockablock with socializing. Could be a class reunion is coming up. Or you will be invited to an old friend's luxury wedding or anniversary party. Do enjoy reminiscing about bygone days with old mates. But be ready for a pair of "frenemies" making disparaging remarks about your income level or choice of attire. Resist the urge to retaliate by uttering a sassy riposte. If you stoop to their level, things could snowball into proper fight. And definitely take it easy with any alcoholic drinks. If you drink, don't drive. There is a high risk of automobile accidents between the 24th and the 28th. Brace yourself for another Mercury retrograde which begins on the 30th.

CANCER - September 2016

As September begins, a hot-and-heavy attraction to a no-good charmer has you clenching the armrests a bit more insistently than usual. Their looks and gift of gab are captivating. But this person is not completely trustworthy. He or she may be hiding some skeletons in their closet. Unless you want your heart trampled, proceed with caution. If you end up in bed with this character, remember that Mercury is obfuscating all systems of communication until the 22nd. Resist the urge to snap any nude selfies as they may "accidentally" be shared and find a much larger audience than intended.

The past few weeks have seen you burning the midnight oil in your quest for career success. Slow the pace. On the 13th, expect to feel unusually tired and lethargic. These low energy levels may persist for the next week or so. During this phase, insomnia will probably have you tossing and turning all night long. Whenever you do actually manage to grab a few winks. Your slumber may be invaded by disturbing, vivid dreams. The solution? Banish electronics from your sleeping area. If you can't bear to part with the laptop or smartphone at your bedside, at least cover the appliances with a piece of fabric. You will be surprised at how much better you will sleep without them flashing or buzzing or ringing or lighting up. Incidentally, when was the last time you tended your secret garden of inner calm? Take time now to enjoy a bubbling bathtub, scented candles, soothing music. Get back to caring for yourself. Set aside some "me" days in the middle of the month. Remind your brain that it is not a 24-hour conduit to the stresses of the outside world. Concentrate on nurturing and intentional relaxation.

Is that the pitter-patter of tiny feet lurking around your humble abode in late September? There is a chance that an infant is entering your life. Maybe a sibling will become a parent. Or you might be entrusted with babysitting a child for a stretch. Who knows? An addition to your own immediate family could even be in the works. Whatever the nature of your baby bond, the truth is that you are a natural with kids. Your motherly, doting personality makes you a perfect caretaker. So fret not! Kick back and enjoy yourself.

CANCER - October 2016

Why will the first ten days of October be so intriguing? In spite of being occupied with numerous activities in your daily life, a silent spiritual awakening is slowly taking hold over you. Maybe an illuminating book will inspire you. Or perhaps a heart-to-heart with a family elder will engender a transformation. You may feel like reconnecting with your childhood religion or studying a new one. Why not read up on Eastern mysticism? Try meditation or chanting. Or join a local prayer circle. If you are already a believer in religious philosophies, be on the lookout this month for even more profound epiphanies than usual.

Brace yourself for some monetary setbacks between the 9th and the 17th. Unexpected losses and unforeseen expenses threaten to drain your bank account. Avoid any form of betting or gambling. In particular, be vigilant on the 15th. Swindlers abound. Unfortunately, the hustle may come from a familiar face. Perhaps a friend of a friend wooed you into spending where you ought not to have. Or you may be tempted by an "act fast, or lose your chance" financial proposition. Distance yourself from all schemes as hastily (and discreetly) as possible. By the same token, if you are on the street, in a railway station or airport, do not give in to desperate requests for money from strangers. Most times those pleas are nothing more than ruse.

Feeling bored during your spare time of late? After the 23rd, take up a hobby. You Crabs adore being carried away by music, dance, poetry, or gardening or any other hobbies ruled by Venus. If you have a green thumb, check out a few books on plant cultivation from the local library. If beautiful language is what piques your interest, search for nearby literature readings. If you fancy taking up jazz dancing or want to learn to play the tuba, sign up for a weekend class. Your initial dabbles into this new pastime may only be moderately successful. But your passion is so strong that your beginner's awkward dabbles will leave you hungering to improve. Stick with it. Practice. Practice. Invest time and money in furthering your self-enhancement. Over the next few years, this side interest or new discipline will cause you to grow in many thrilling ways.

CANCER - November 2016

Cancers are all about emotion. Period. Colleagues, friends or lovers— once you've got one wrapped in your claws, it is not easy for you to relinquish your grip. But you must learn to draw the line somewhere. In early November, you may be forced to "eclipse" someone from your life. Could be a jilted lover or an increasingly flaky friend. Or perhaps you will need to cut ties with a former mentor. This episode will leave you brain-scrambled for a bit. Deep down, you sense that this fracture is for the best. Especially since the person you are leaving behind doesn't really respect the person you've grown to be. Remember: personal happiness and self-esteem are more important than mere loyalty for its own sake. Just because someone was the right companion for you in 1999 doesn't mean you are bound to them for life. Unhealthy dependencies are easy to fall into and often very difficult to undo.

A small financial risk you took a few months ago has ripened and is ripe for the picking. Around the 16th, a stock market investment or gambling trip should pay off big time. It feels good to be on top, doesn't it? But don't get too cocky and push your luck. You are unlikely to be blessed with such fortune again until the middle of next year. Invest any profits in a plain vanilla un-sexy mutual fund or pension plan. Even if it means lower yields, stability is the best option for your money right now.

Between the 23rd and the 28th, planning an important event will suck you in like a black hole. Perhaps a friend or relative will ask you to help organize their wedding. Maybe you will be elected director of a fine arts performance or be asked to stage a musical children's play. Or you could even be put in charge of the opening ceremonies for a local art gallery. At first, you will be flattered. And pleased by this distraction from your usual *ennui*. But halfway through setting up the project, you may be overwhelmed by the sheer volume of responsibility you have undertaken. Once the party or concert or exhibition is over, get some undisturbed rest. Even if it entails taking a sleeping pill. Sleep is the great healer. The requisite eight hours of uninterrupted sleep will your whole system.

CANCER - December 2016

Finally, the festive season has arrived. But alas! Minor accidents or health issues are likely to plague you from the 2nd to the 9th. Fortunately, they are not too serious. Still, poor timing may see you beset will multiple nagging problems at once. For instance, you may recover from a head cold only to sprain your wrist lifting weights. Or you may sign on for dental work, then have an allergic reaction to the dentist's antibiotics. Perhaps you will even discover a serious digestion issue the same week that you contract strep throat. When it rains, it pours! Recreate as accurately as possible the relaxing, home-sick-from-school days you enjoyed as a child. Stay in your pajamas all day. Read in bed. Indulged in light escapist literature only. Dust off a classic comedy to watch. And if you boost your immune system with fresh fruit juice, you will be back on your feet in no time.

If you need to travel this month, try to get home safely before the 19th which is the beginning of our next Mercury retrograde. That infamous cosmic cycle has been known to disarrange even the most carefully plotted itineraries. Incidentally, if you can afford to take the time off now, the days just previous to the 19th could be a good time to visit your family. Even better than Christmas Day. However, if you insist on taking a trip after the 19th, do not overbook yourself. It may seem like a good idea now to visit your mom for two days, the old man for two hours and your honey's family for a weekend. But will those folks you threaten to visit appreciate being pre-scheduled according your plan? Perhaps they have an agenda of their own to organize. Cut back on how many people you want to pop in on this season. Your goal is to have fun - not to ruffle your relatives' feathers. Before you firm up any destinations, check with the folks you want to spend time with. Then make your travel plans.

The holidays will be joyous and nostalgic, making you crave a stronger connection with loved ones both past and present. Spend some time reminiscing with family members or old friends about the good old days. Also, you may have noticed, there is an inextricable link between our taste buds and our memories. Now's the time to gorge on a little childhood comfort food. Chow down on a home-style hamburger with "the works" or butter up a few oven-baked biscuits. These homemade treats will bring back delicious memories. Home and family, especially mothers or mother figures (like yourself), are in the spotlight until December 31st. Spend time caring or being cared by or caring for your near and dear.

CANCER - January 2017

Mercury's retrograde visit lingers until the 8th. In January's early stages, take extra precautions with your health. For those who suffered from flu or respiratory ailments last month, your immune system may still not be up to snuff. Before you go sprinting to the over-the-counter medicine aisle, try do-it-yourself remedies. Practice deep breathing. Get back on a regular workout regimen. Eat lots of greens, moderate amounts of protein and take an extra does of Vitamin D. Fruit helps too. Some of you may feel the inclination to take up a martial art like kickboxing, karate or jiu-jitsu around this time. But I advise you save the extreme sports for the spring. For now, keep calisthenics in mild mode. Restorative exercises and gentle massages will be most beneficial. Since a healthy mind also depends on your physical surroundings, this is a great time to de-clutter, tidy up and do some harmonizing Feng Shui in your dwelling.

After the 9th, release your inner social butterfly. For the next week or so, meet as many new faces as possible. Everyone has a story. Listen to them all. This interest in others will help you both personally and professionally. Connect with a wide range of people. Go ahead. Mix and mingle. Come out of your shell and test your networking skills. Don't forget to carry business cards. Or you might even download a contact-sharing app onto your smartphone. Forging alliances is pointless if no one remembers your name.

Between the 19th and the 27th, you have a chance to progress on the career front. If an opportunity for a group project comes your way now, sign up! This undertaking could snowball into a once-in-a-lifetime adventure over the next six months. Some of you might feel like switching career paths. Or simply taking a sabbatical. Tap a trusted mentor for guidance. Someone who has "been there, done that" will be invaluable to your own ascent up the ladder. Don't be afraid or too proud to ask key questions. A seasoned person with long years of experience will offer you valuable tips on where to focus your attention when. And—just as important—they can advise you on which bad habits (and seedy people) to avoid.

YOUR MONTHLY FORECASTS FOR THE FIRE MONKEY YEAR

2016

LEO

Author's Note... Mercury Retrograde

Sometimes planets appear to be zooming backward through the zodiac. Of course this backward motion is only an illusion. The planet has not turned tail. But it appears to have. Astrologers call this apparent reversing: **"retrograde"**.

Any planet can be retrograde. But only Mercury's retrogrades cause communications to break down. Mercury has its retrograde period for a few weeks 3 or 4 times each year. Whilst Mercury is retrograde, we humans are encouraged to take stock, make plans and discuss different approaches to a variety of subjects. But because information is often muddled, promises broken and electronic devices on the blink during Mercury retrograde, we must remain flexible and open-minded. Advice? Always allow extra time for travel. Schedule changes are common. Do not sign any contracts or cement agreements during Mercury retrograde. Make no irreversible promises. Watch out for con artists. Make no final decisions, binding engagements or major purchases during a Mercury retrograde. You are allowed to have tantrums or rail against your fate. But Mercury will continue to be retrograde till it decides to go direct again.

Mercury Retrogrades
2016

January 5 thru January 25
April 28 thru May 22
August 30 thru September 22
December 19 thru January 8 2017

OVERVIEW OF 2016 THE YEAR OF THE MONKEY
FOR LEO

Loyal Leo,

For Leos, the Fire Monkey year 2016 will be a period wherein you are obliged to use strategy. You like to be direct and are not fond of slaloming around in dicey terrain. But this year - especially in the first part of the year, you'll be confronted with some baffling family matters, which disarm you and set your emotional teeth on edge. I mention using strategy as should you enter into a head-on collision with the offending next of kin, you will invite long-term strife - not only for yourself, but also for some more fragile members of your clan. So bob and weave. Think ahead. Create a savvy plan of battle before you deal with the issue at hand. Find out the New Astrology™ sign of the agitator before you launch any defensive action. If their sign warns of ruthlessness or greed, manage your own game plan accordingly.

Last year you opened a new era in your life. You made some major life-altering decisions and they served you well. The Fire Monkey year will test those choices. Will you, brave Leo, have the courage of your convictions? Will you be able to slay the Dragons who might very well test your mettle by deriding or mocking you for taking steps to live your life as you see fit? My guess is you are up to it. But watch for potential detractors. Peek behind every scene. In short, don't get lazy.

Your health could be more tonic in this year of general commotion. But despite a dip in your energy level mid year, you will still be able to monkey around enough to get into some bona fide leonine mischief. Notwithstanding the hectic planetary aspects influencing your love life, it appears your sex drive will peak about September. Enjoy! sw

LEO - January 2016

Avoid entering into political discussions with your friends in the first two weeks of January. If you do, you may end a friendship. This is a time of deep divides between personal philosophies. Some of your acquaintances have starkly different beliefs than you. The very tenets of their propos may surprise you. If you value their continued companionship, avoid politics. Governmental issues inspire a particular kind of inability to reason. Politics are the reason the expression "hot under the collar" was invented.

Social media is the most volatile arena. Remember that someone is always watching what you post. Unless you are up for a pitched battle, avoid writing incendiary comments on Twitter, Facebook or Instagram. If you like scrapping about such matters, go for it. You will be judged. But maybe you don't much care what others think. Leos are often stronger than their adversaries. But they are not always stealthier.

This will be a transitional month for you. If you are a single Leo, you may be waking from a long period of social hibernation. You may feel rusty. Even talking to the opposite sex may seem awkward after so many nights in front of the computer. Fear not, oh timid Don Juan/-Juanita. This shrinking violet sensation is temporary. Early as next month, your fluttery nerves will be a distant memory. There is true passion on the near horizon for you.

You should enter a period of familial bliss following the holidays. After a time of focusing on yourself, your parents in particular will be ecstatic at having you around more often. Plus which, it feels good to be missed. But it also feels good to be appreciated. Bask in their love. Try to give as much as you take.

During the last week of the month, set aside time to meditate on your gains from the year. You should have preserved your list of goals from October. Give it a good look. Do not be demoralized if you didn't accomplish everything on your lineup! Even checking off one item is a victory. Revel in what you have done. And never stop pushing for what you desire.

LEO -February 2016

During the first two weeks of February, you have the potential to form alliances and solidify existing relationships. Craft a win-win corporate merger. Ask a flirty crush if they want to spend more time with you. Make sure to focus on the personal aspect. Only link up with characters or companies which share your values. If you can finesse that, both parties will end up satisfied with the arrangement. On the 6th, Lady Luck is on your side. Why not throw a posh dinner party? Show off those cooking skills you've been polishing for the last couple of months. Hosting such an event will give you the perfect opportunity to catch up and network with close friends and/or potential business partners. Whilst schmoozing, pull your shoulders back. Maintain eye contact. Emanate self-confidence. That way you are likely to attract a powerful person. This attraction could lead to a juicy job opportunity. Or even to an auspicious power-couple union. Do be sure to record names and numbers before your guests depart. Otherwise, the power person in question might just evaporate without a trace.

Toward the third week of February, a lull at work will give you more free time to concentrate on your love life. A stalled romantic relationship could pick up steam. Have you recently broken up with a lover? Called off an engagement? Go ahead. Stick your toe dating scene waters. You may well enjoy what you find. If you are seeking to enhance a flagging passion, remember that this year Valentine's Day falls on a Sunday. Pull out all the stops. Splurge on a champagne brunch with your sweetie. Surprise him or her by reserving a swanky hotel room for a midday tryst. Scatter flower petals on the bed. Play their favorite tunes on the sound system. Your romantic tactics will pay off - in spades!

By the 20th, the party is over. The spotlight is on your domestic life. Long-brewing family issues require your attention. Has a sibling been taking care of your ailing mother or father? Well, now he or she has landed a day job and it's your turn to pick up the slack. Or maybe a spouse is demanding you spend more quality time with the kids. Adjust your schedule to accommodate these increased responsibilities. If you are take up the burden graciously, by the end of the month, life will settle into a tranquil rhythm.

LEO - March 2016

As March begins, Mars' influence leaves you susceptible to small accidents and injuries. Are you being clumsy? Or are these mishaps (falling off stepladders and tripping over your own feet) a normal part of your existence? The way I look at it, from the 5th to the 10th, you may be tempted to behave impulsively and find yourself in a pickle. Try to nip any devil-may-care desires in the bud. And be careful with fire and heat. Don't be blasé about leaving candles burning in the bedroom all night. If you are leaving the house to run an errand, think. *Did I leave the water boiling on the stove? Is the iron still plugged in? Did I turn off the oven? Do I have the keys?* During this phase, keep a first-aid kit handy. If not treated, small cuts and bruises from household objects can turn into major health issues.

During the third week of March, you may feel spaced out. *Where were you? Why did you walk into the kitchen again?* Try as you might, concentration does not come easily. Because of that, you risk glossing over certain critical facets of your work. Minimize that Excel spread-sheet. Close that instruction manual. Put detail-oriented tasks on hold. If your attention is scattered like dead leaves in a windstorm, there's no future in muscling through a workday. What you are yearning for is some unstructured leisure time. Why not cash in a personal day and stroll through a museum? Or take a hike in a nearby forest or woods? You will return inspired and prepared to tackle even the most tedious of tasks.

Toward the end of March, you may feel that some instinct making your gooey romantic side has decided to bubble over. It's the Venus effect! Your lovey-dovey behavior is a pleasant surprise for your sweetheart. Embrace the moment. Buy that *boo* a thoughtful gift. Light some scented candles. Rent a fall-in-love movie. Offer an unsolicited back-rub. The extra thought and effort you expend will pay off in sultry, unexpected ways. By the 25th, move "management of personal finances" to the top of your to-do list. How about rolling your loans into a mortgage or consolidating debt in some savvy new manner? Pen-cil in time with a trusted financial advisor. Check your credit rating. Sketch out a five-year plan to eliminate all debt. Scrutinize those bank statements for inconsistencies. Have you missed any bill payments lately? Leos are not built to handle the mental pressure that comes with owing money. If you can tighten your belt, thereby staving off col-lection agencies and bill collectors, you will sleep better at night.

LEO - April 2016

During the first two weeks of April, restlessness leaves you dissatisfied with the status quo. Sick of gabbing with strangers in the same bars or restaurants every weekend? Tired of seeing the same faces at work every single day? Do you catch yourself clicking into holiday sight-seeing blogs? Sounds as though you've been bitten by the travel bug! Check discount websites like Kayak or Expedia for once-in-a-lifetime deals. Coupled Leos might plan an exotic getaway together. Cairo, Copenhagen, Copacabana—think outside the box for a foreign desti-nation to quench your wanderlust and quell the boredom. If you're single and ready to mingle, there is a strong possibility of an exciting vacation romance. Perhaps even with that someone in the adjoining airplane seat. If time and budget constraints prevent you from actually leaving the country, get your kicks locally. Sign up for a foreign language course. Take along your significant other. To wax exotic, attend a basic Mandarin class, then explore your city's Chinatown.

Are you an expert in your field? Underpaid in your current position? Feel like expanding your career horizons? Well, between the 12th and the 18th, don't be shy about self-promoting. Buy advertising space on an Internet search engine or nearby billboard. Spread the word that you are accepting freelance consultant gigs. If you can improve your personal PR, you may land an opportunity to teach a workshop or publish your insights on a prestigious blog. Go ahead. Claim the limelight! There is no reason not to become the go-to guru in your industry.

The month could end with a stunning triumph. If anyone deserves an executive promotion or a big payday, it's you. If you've been pondering quitting your job or cashing in those leftover sick days, tough it out for a few more weeks. As long as you keep on keeping on, professional recognition should happen in the very near future. On the 25th or 26th, you are set to cross paths with a very influential figure. Someone with deep roots in your field. Pick their brains. If you can grab and hold this person's attention, you could forge a powerful new partnership. But move quickly. Our first Mercury retrograde of the year starts on the 28th and won't wind down until the 22nd of next month. Family bonds, financial assets and business relationships will become a lot more treacherous to navigate during that phase.

LEO - May 2016

As May begins, Mercury is still befuddling every move. Botched plans, deleted phone numbers, trusted friends suddenly refusing to speak with you. Try not to take anything personally. Until the retrograde ends on the 22nd, forces beyond our control are erecting roadblocks. Around the 3rd of the month, a family spat over ancestral property ownership threatens to spiral into a long-term feud. Is a grandfather's will unclear as to who inherits the yacht? Has a drug-addled cousin staked a claim to a decades-old cabin? As relatives align themselves with one side or another, take up the mantle of mediator. Waste no time bringing the two factions together for a peace summit. Don't let either party walk out and slam the door. No matter how ugly the arguments become, talking things through is always better than not talking at all. With your steady *Leo-the-Leader* hand steering the discussion, it may be possible to nip what could become an extended battle in the bud.

The middle of the month presents an ideal opportunity to get serious about your health. Have you been eagerly accepting party invites lately, no matter how exhausted you are? Are you always eager to spend your off-days helping friends move couches and tables? Take a hard look at your work/life balance. A propensity of commitments is wearing you out. It could be time to shut off the cell and apply some restorative treatment. Meditation or an ayurvedic detox would fit the bill nicely. If you can quiet body and soul for even a short period of time, the stress will wash away like a sand castle during high tide.

After the 21st, forget about office conundrums and family squabbles. Go out enjoy some more-than-platonic amusement. Have sparks been flying between you and a colleague? Perhaps someone in your inner circle could set you up with a blind date. Plus, if you can squelch your resistance long enough to give it a try, online dating is always an option. You won't be trash-talking Match.com after seeing the invitations piling up in your inbox. Whatever your methods, avoid getting too serious with any one person right now. There's nothing wrong with playing the field. Take time to ponder. Table any weighty talks about the future. Just kick back and have fun. And if one of your companions starts to pressure you about "where this relationship is going", hand them a pink slip and go back to hanging out with your friends!

LEO - June 2016

Early in June, watch out for workplace treachery. Long ago, during a similar planetary cycle, a Leo friend of mine caught a colleague downloading sensitive data from his computer after stealing his ID and passwords. Do not let this happen to you. Without being paranoid, do be more conscious of your surroundings. Is a superior taking notes on employee work habits to determine who survives the next round of layoffs? Is a cubicle buddy angling to gobble your job? Trust no one. On the 2nd or 3rd, any snake in the grass should reveal him/herself. Perhaps the culprit will be a coworker who has been too quick to agree to all your ideas of late. Don't hesitate to be a bit suspicious. You knew all the time that said person was never on your team in the first place. Cut them out of the loop. With a little caution and foresight, you can head their machinations off at the pass.

Have you been the shoulder-to-cry-on for all the whining and moaning of friends and family of late? Mid month, more of the same comes sniveling along. Brace yourself before opening personal emails. Treat voicemails like live grenades. Everyone you've ever met seems to have some pressing issue to talk to you about. But not all stories of sick pets or spousal spats are created equal. Your task? Filter the gold from the brass. There are only so many hours in the day you can spend weighing in on someone else's drama. If hopeless cases insist on monopolizing your time with their repetitious tales of woe, explain gently but firmly that a professional therapist might be better suited to their needs.

It appears the stork will be paying someone a visit around the 25th. Whether the big bird will be landing on your windowsill or on that of a loved one is up in the air. Regardless, this birth will be a joyous occasion for all involved. In the meantime, baby-proof your humble abode. Exposed wiring? Duct tape should cover that up nicely. Not-quite-spotless floors? A round of sweeping or vacuuming will make those surfaces much safer for tiny hands. Take steps to make your home safe so you can feel comfortable babysitting (or raising!) a tender infant.

LEO - July 2016

Due to your lofty nature, you have an innate distaste for authority. This month, your tendency to buck the system could land you in the hot seat. Is a boss demanding that you log eight hours on a Saturday? Is a pushy coworker requesting that you bring him or her a cup of coffee every morning? This person's condescending words and manner make your blood boil. Do not lose your cool. Instead, use this as an opportunity to test your willpower. When authority kicks you in the shins, take a deep breath and count to ten. As you slowly exhale, smile and do as you are bid. If you do blow your stack, you risk damaging your reputation with senior management. Such a haughty attitude will land you in the unem-ployment line sooner rather than later.

Holy Guacamole! The middle of July sees you fully ensconced in glutton mode. Jumbo cheeseburger and a large cola for lunch? Why not! Six course meals with red wine and exotic fondues for dinner? Dust off that splatter bib. Feel free to indulge yourself. But keep a basic count of the calories you've ingested. Not mention which belt loop you are using. After the 21st, you can start pulling out of your dive into Fatty Food Lake. Reintroduce a daily dose of fruits and veggies into your diet. Swap those *pommes frites* for baked sweet potatoes (sans butter please). Substitute a tasty glass of all-natural tomato juice for that bottle of booze. If you can overcome nasty and debilitating eating habits, your weight and general health should stabilize without too much hair tearing.

Toward the last week of July, coupled Leos must navigate a brier patch of bickering. Money, jealousy, intimacy—all may be hot-button issues.

Are you the aggrieved party? Want to avoid World War III? Then listen closely. "I've been feeling neglected lately" is a much more reasonable starting point than "You don't love me anymore!" Have a rational conversation with your partner before waxing emotional. Put yourself in his or her shoes. Is a perfectionist boss keeping your squeeze late at the office each night? Is a significant other from a troubled family worried about bailing a sibling out of jail? With issues of the heart, there is always more than meets the eye. Be conscious of that fact and adjust your manner accordingly.

LEO - August 2016

Toward the beginning of August, a lavish dinner invitation awaits you. This is no mere leisure meal. The host or emcee has an enticing offer for you. Perhaps a juicy marketing gig has just opened up. Or maybe this person wants you to head the accounting department for a ground-breaking startup. For your own sake, take it easy on the champagne during this meal. Although promises of future riches or a much-improved resume may sound tempting, all is not as it seems. This project may not be utterly legitimate. Is "marketing gig" code for "door-to-door salesman?" Is that fascinating new company staffed by illegal immigrants? Do some research. Poke your nose into their books and ask for serious references - the names and emails of clients they have worked with successfully. A simple Internet query may help too. If you find the slightest hint of anything inappropriate, decline the proposal

Low bank balance alert! No, that ATM warning is not a typo. Nor did your financial institution make a miscalculation. Your bank account really is getting low on funds. During the second week of the month, that realization is going to hit you like a mini tsunami and worry you sick. Could you have been a wee bit irresponsible with your spending recently? Have you racked up some fancy dinners in expensive restaurants? Been splurging on Prada shoes or Louis Vuitton luggage? I know you think that money is made for buying things? But for now, rein in the expenses. No more catered dinner parties or lunches on the town. Bring your own plastic-wrapped food from home. Cancel any unnecessary or trashy magazine subscriptions. Quit scanning fashion websites for temporary discounts. If you can manage a month or two of economizing, you should be able to pull out of the bank balance doldrums.

Unfortunately, the end of August brings tidings of a loved one's critical illness. This friend or relative's misfortune is likely to bring out a never-before-seen side of them. Perhaps a hardcore materialist will find God. Or a lifelong Christian will lose his or her faith. Visit them at the hospital or their place of residence. Stuff a book or two about spirituality or mental fortitude into your jacket or purse. And most of all, Listen. And curb your tendency to yammer platitudes at them about how chipper they will feel when they get better. Leave them with some profound reading material. But don't dwell on your own particular methods of self-realization. Your friend or relative will be better equipped to handle their struggle without any preaching from you. So keep it light. In other news, Mercury goes retrograde again on the 30th. Prepare for the usual impaired communications.

LEO- September 2016

Mercury remains in retrograde for the first three weeks of September (ends on the 22nd). If you need to sign a contract during this period, peruse the fine print as though your life depends on it. Have a knowledgeable friend run a second pair of eyes over the text. If lawyers are involved, make sure yours is not asleep at the wheel. Looking into finalizing a mortgage or moving into a new apartment? If possible, delay etching in stone any and all finite plans until after the 22nd. Otherwise, you risk missing an important detail that changes the whole flavor of the agreement. Now, before you resign yourself to a few weeks of mayhem, there are some positive aspects to this phase. Are any high school or university reunions coming up on the calendar? If so, focus your energy on reconnecting with successful old contacts and colleagues. Is the former class clown heading an oil conglomerate? Did an ex start his or her own travel agency? Perhaps he or she has a job opening. Or knows of a person who does. If you chat with enough buddies from yesteryear, someone is bound to pass along some valuable insider info.

Beware of a charming moocher on the 18th. This character may take the form of a wily businessperson. Or a seductive suitor. They will attempt to trick you into joining them in some hopeless venture. Could be a capitalist begging you to invest in something that sounds suspiciously like a pyramid scheme. Is that seductive character from your French class swearing up and down that he or she can't live without you - even as they're palming your credit card? Tempting though they may seem, you must tune out this person's honeyed words. They are talking BS, don't have a real plan and secretly wish you would organize (and pay for) everything.

Between the 22nd and the 28th, your love life could get a bit complicated. Is your sweetheart back in contact with a past lover? Perhaps you recently entered a relationship with a dark, mysterious type. Are you positive they aren't already taken? Do some sleuthing. But exercise judgment. If you discover some innocent online flirting, there's no need to overreact. After all, you are not exactly as pure as the driven snow yourself. But if a significant other is actually cheating on you, make plans to free yourself from their delicious clutches ASAP.

LEO - October 2016

Why so serious? As October begins, you will be fighting an urge to sulk. Every time you log in to Facebook or catch up with friends, you see only promotions and exotic vacations and engagement rings. Yet, you remain stuck in the mud. Why wait around for someone to rescue you? The squeaky wheel gets the grease, as they say. Toot your own horn. Make it known to senior management that you are intelligent, hard working and deserving of a raise (or an engagement ring). Here is an anecdote to bring my point to life. A Leo client of mine was an accountant at a humongous British firm. For months, he slaved away from dawn till dusk with naught to show for his labors. But finally, he came up with a creative way to draw attention to himself. He would wait until his boss was about to leave for the evening, then quickly fire a request to the printer that sat near the exit. Each night, as his superior strode toward the elevator, he would see this fellow retrieving documents from the machine, obviously busting his butt. Before long, the underappreciated employee asked for and received a substantial salary hike. Moral of the story? Sometimes strategy is the only way to get ahead in this world.

Healthy mind, healthy body! The middle two weeks of the month could see you achieve a breakthrough in your physical health. Personal motivation is at an all-time high. Join a gym. Hire a trainer. Basically, any blood-pumping activity that pushes you beyond your comfort zone is welcome. That is not an invitation to start rock climbing without a harness every day before work. Remember: when it comes to sustaining great habits, slow and steady wins the race. Want to lose twenty kilos? Trim six notches off your belt loop? Set a three-month goal of five kilos or two notches. If you ratchet up the intensity of your workouts in bite-sized increments, you can achieve fitness levels that you would never have dreamed of previously.

Between the 26th and the 30th, try to sneak away from any nagging responsibilities to connect with your loved ones. Children will be a source of joy. A powerful but nurturing female (possibly an aunt or mother figure) could have words of advice about love or money. Take notes. Counsel this valuable comes around all too rarely.

LEO - November 2016

Early in November, a little drama may unfold concerning a younger person of the opposite sex. Do you have a friend who comes to you for intimate advice? A junior colleague who looks to you for career guidance? You are an essential part of this person's support system. But that's all. In your mind, yours is a purely platonic relationship. Out of nowhere, they confess their undying affection for you. This inexperienced youngster does not seem to realize how impossible acting on that impulse would be. For one thing, there's the age difference. Plus which, you are almost certainly already involved with someone else. You know what you must do. Gently break their heart. Advise them of the truth. Explain that you are (and forever will be) only a mentor and well-wisher in their life.

A chance brush with fame on the 14th or 15th promises to leave you in a jubilant mood. Perhaps you will unexpectedly encounter a celebrity in a restaurant or bar. Or maybe you yourself will weasel your way to a certain level of notoriety. An appearance on the local news or in a viral video is not out of the question. Do make sure not to leave the house with un-brushed hair or wrinkled clothes during those two days. Later that week, a low-grade water disaster in the kitchen or bath might necessitate an emergency call to the plumber. Expenses, expenses! Ask around. Does anyone in your circle know of a jack-of-all-trades who will dash to your rescue in return for freshly baked cookies and a cup of coffee? If so, save the number. Nothing is more valuable than a reliable (cheap and available) handyman.

Toward the end of the month, vivid nightmares leave you wide awake in bed. Try some hot milk. The concoction should be soothing enough to help you get some shuteye. When the following morning arrives, think about the root cause of your restlessness. As we sleep, our brains relive and categorize all the important activities that happened that day. That is where dreams come from. So alter your nightly routine. As you lie in bed, consciously process the day's events before you drift off. That exercise should eliminate the need for your subconscious to work so hard while you snooze. You will be surprised how rapidly your insomnia problems evaporate.

LEO - December 2016

In the early days of December, you face risk of loss or damage to your assets. In fact, a break-in is possible on the 3rd or 4th. Be extra careful about bolting doors and securing windows. Does your angry ex still have a set of keys to your house? Change the locks. Even if there is no crazy former flame in the picture, it would still be prudent to update all your locks. Pay especially close attention to any means of entry to the basement, attic or backdoor. If you have the cash, burglar-proof your humble abode. Invest in a home security system. Electronic alarms, while annoying when they start blaring accidentally, do dissuade potential thieves. Toward the 12th, someone in your immediate or extended family may be hurt in a vehicular mishap. Don't worry! The accident will not be fatal. But make sure your car insurance is all paid up.

It's your favorite time of the year (again)—Mercury retrograde! Starting on the 19th, expect to face logistical havoc. Watch out for identity theft. Be extra careful when shopping online or forking over your credit card number. Sure, PayPal and Xoom are considered secure methods of payment, but right now, you have every reason to be cautious. Better to be safe than sorry! During this period, be prepared to repeat yourself. If an elderly parent or fresh-faced employee or a cocky youngster does not understand a request the first time around, tell them again - and again. The message will eventually sink in.

While others are wiling away the time beneath the mistletoe, you are feeling industrious. Ready to roll up your sleeves and start that business takeover? Might it not be a better idea to fine-tune your strategy first? Mercury retrogrades are all about planning and review, not execution. Postpone huge monetary investments. Delay any drastic career switches. Ever hear of the book *Rich Dad, Poor Dad*? Buy it. Read it. Live it. It lists methods of making your money work harder for you. Have you investigated putting your funds into high-performance, low-risk investments or retirement accounts? Outline a personal get-rich-slowly plot while the littlest planet is still impeding communications. Next month, put your newfound knowledge into practice.

LEO - January 2017

Until the 8th of January, Mercury remains in retrograde orbit. Ordinarily, your authoritative nature is useful whenever leadership skills are necessary. But during the first week of the month, dial back the intensity. Trying to motivate colleagues or employees with a rousing speech? Experimenting with the "tough love" technique with an unruly teenager? Choose your language more delicately. The atmosphere is ripe for misunderstanding. A coworker or friend is likely to interpret your words as more hurtful than you intended. Also, avoid buying any big-ticket items right now. How pressing is your need for a glittering sports car? Or a fancy new laptop? Sleep on the decision for a week before reaching for that credit card, wallet or purse. Wait until after the 8th to start spending again.

During the second week of January, you are destined for a Eureka moment. This epiphany could take many forms. It's all about listening for co-incidence. Keep your ears peeled for a letter, email, text, or seemingly casual conversation that strikes a chord and makes your heart jump with joy. Perhaps you have been pondering a return to school. Maybe a stranger at the bus stop will tip you off to an institution with the exact program you've been seeking. Or a self-help book could inspire you to change careers or jettison that toxic relationship. In a nutshell, follow your instincts. If taking a six-month sabbatical to learn Kundalini Yoga with a Tibetan Master seems to be your calling, give it a shot. Whatever you dabble in now could well remain the passion of a lifetime.

Is your house prepared to receive guests? Are you? Well, ready or not, here they come. Toward the end of January, half the family may show up on your doorstep. The logistics make no sense. Where will Grandma sleep? Can the teenage cousins be trusted to share a bed? Whose allergies preclude them from crashing on the dusty floor? Draw up a plan. But when the hordes arrive, you can throw it straight in the trashcan. These pushy loved ones have no interest in following your orders. They will insist on selecting their own sleeping digs. Prepare for a convivial week of household mess.

YOUR MONTHLY FORECASTS FOR THE FIRE MONKEY YEAR

2016

VIRGO

Author's Note... Mercury Retrograde

Sometimes planets appear to be zooming backward through the zodiac. Of course this backward motion is only an illusion. The planet has not turned tail. But it appears to have. Astrologers call this apparent reversing: **"retrograde"**.

Any planet can be retrograde. But only Mercury's retrogrades cause communications to break down. Mercury has its retrograde period for a few weeks 3 or 4 times each year. Whilst Mercury is retrograde, we humans are encouraged to take stock, make plans and discuss different approaches to a variety of subjects. But because information is often muddled, promises broken and electronic devices on the blink during Mercury retrograde, we must remain flexible and open-minded. Advice? Always allow extra time for travel. Schedule changes are common. Do not sign any contracts or cement agreements during Mercury retrograde. Make no irreversible promises. Watch out for con artists. Make no final decisions, binding engagements or major purchases during a Mercury retrograde. You are allowed to have tantrums or rail against your fate. But Mercury will continue to be retrograde till it decides to go direct again.

Mercury Retrogrades
2016

January 5 thru January 25
April 28 thru May 22
August 30 thru September 22
December 19 thru January 8 2017

OVERVIEW OF 2016 THE YEAR OF THE MONKEY FOR VIRGO

Vigilant Virgo,

In late 2015, your romantic sector caught on fire. Many changes came about because of those sizzling passions and you gained a concomitant understanding of what it is in love that you really crave. You are a calculating person who likes to pay attention to details. The advent of true romance in your love life may have clouded the picture so that instead of being able to see the road ahead with clarity, you got all mired in emotion. When you feel fuzzy-brained and addled because of overflowing sentiment, you lose your footing and wonder where the real you went. By June of 2016 you should be out of the woods and settled into a steady love pattern which better suits your need for order.

Professionally, the Fire Monkey year will offer you myriad opportunities to exhibit your intellectual talents. You will be much appreciated for your ability to see a situation for what it is rather than for what others wish it were. When this happens you are often called upon to lay down the law. You are not naturally given to being authoritarian. But when you must speak up and clear they for logic, you can do a fabulous job.

In July and August watch your step. You could be in for a fall (literally and figuratively). Hidden obstacles crop up in the weirdest places. Somebody leaves an errant shoe in your path or a child's toy underfoot catches you unawares. Too, many of the glitches you feared might appear in your career path really were there. Just keep your eyes peeled and remain your vigilant self. All in all, the Monkey year will not burden you unduly - except for the messy parts. Read your horoscopes for every month so as not to miss a trick. sw

VIRGO - January 2016

January wraps up the Sheep year with a flourish. Expect the unexpected. A family member may soon present you with an expensive gift. It may not be exactly to your taste, but treasure it anyway. It is, after all, the thought that counts - especially with blood relations. If you do not want to wear the old-fashioned gold watch or outrageous-looking earrings from the forties, bear up and wear them at family gatherings. Your gesture will let the other person witness your appreciation for their gift in something stronger than words.

In the midst of basking in your year's triumphs, beware of gossip and rumors creeping up in your place of work. Be extremely conscious of the difference between work friends and real friends. You may spend forty hours a week with someone, but that does not mean you really "know" them. After all, they are paid to hang out with you. It's part of their job to be "friendly". By all means, remain courteous and convivial, but do not take it personally if your "friend" tries to sabotage you to advance their own career.

As the Chinese year comes to a close, reflect on what has transpired. Take note of your struggles and what you did to overcome them. What worked? What did not? Find a place to write this all down. Don't let your list of achievements and mishaps be forgotten. With a list, next year, or further down the line, you will have a reference guide to return to. You can relive how you overcame a certain obstacle the first time around. Hence avoid making the same mistake twice.

Take a look around you. Which family members stuck by you in times of crisis this year? Which friends made it through the fire unscathed? Related, but more painful: which loved ones failed to stand by you? The ones that remained on your team should stay. The others you can consign to a kind of emotional purgatory. At least, now you know who your friends truly are. Give them a hug. A group hug. We are social animals. And your personal social animals in particular have been and will continue to be a vital part of your journey.

VIRGO -February 2016

If you've been thinking about buying or selling a home early this month, you could be all fired up to seal the deal – only to encounter delays. It may be better to hold on for the time being. A distant relative shows up for an extended visit on or around the 10th, thinking it's all-good if he or she hunkers down in your space. Thanks to this moocher, you may have difficulty finding time for regular routine of gym work-outs, sit-down dinners with the family or Epsom salt soaks. A word of advice - be pleasant to them, even if you don't feel like it. This person is well connected and may turn out to be quite useful to you a few months or years down the line. Between the 10th and the 13th, there are signs of trouble on the horizon with a female relative, parent or child. This might necessitate a "time out" while you both regain perspective.

Valentine's Day surprisingly turns out to be a dream. You get more flowers than your neighborhood flower shop – even from secret admirers who you vaguely remember seeing somewhere around town. This gives a big boost to your self-image and confidence. But just because you can reel 'em in, doesn't mean you'll want to keep 'em. That romance bubbling up within you is for real, Virgo mine. You may find yourself in love with a few at once. Save that special rose for someone who can enchant your mind, body and soul. And don't be shy. Sometimes you are known to use work as a crutch (you know, the old 'oh, I'd love to go on a date with you, but I am way too busy with work!'). Try and avoid such evasive behavior in the coming weeks.

Fitness and well-being become a predominant theme during the last two weeks of this month. Track your nutrition and exercise in an app or (why not?) a Fitbit. You could even make notes in a food diary to get a sense of your current eating habits. An upgrade to those exercise programs and equipment could be in order as well. Are you intrigued by intricate yoga poses? Check out the nearest yoga center and enroll for a few classes. The 24th is an excellent date to launch a new health plan. Work on your body. You'll see exponential results within a few short weeks.

VIRGO - March 2016

Romance turns a tad more serious this month. Planets are activating the sector of your horoscope ruling committed partnerships from the 3rd to the 10th. Instead of just locking lips with some attractive stranger you met at a bar, you're likely to view potential partners through the lens of "happily ever after". Coupled Virgos will now find the harmony that they've been seeking. Enjoy togetherness time, perhaps even talking about shared visions as you tread sandy shores or score some relaxing hammock time. If you've had issues with your sweetie, this is a great time to find an amicable solution. Under this planetary influence, you don't care much about being "right" as much as about being happy.

By the time you reach the middle of this month, planets are pointing toward knowledge, travel, expansion and wider horizons. Talk about letting in some fresh air! In case you feel lost in life or have been tripped up by tunnel vision, you are able to lighten up and regain perspective now. Or, if you've been (terminally) single, you remember that there's not just a handful, but a land full of options. Drop the worry baggage and have some full-throttle fun. Get out of your head, Virgo. Book air tickets and fly away on an adventure cum learning trip. Since this adventurous cycle is all about expansion, you could find rollicking romance somewhere along the road or while flying the friendly skies or even as you're broadening your intellectual horizons by joining a class or signing up for a course in French or Mandarin.

Between the 22nd and the 28th, you could find yourself overwhelmed by a packed inbox of emails. Or maybe a piled-up desk keeps staring daggers at you at the workplace. There could also be a little tension with an administrative assistant or someone who works for you in a supportive capacity. You will find you can keep a cool head, as long as you lock your inner eye on the efficiency prize. And if you're simply not getting the quality of help that you need, maybe it's time to hire someone else.

VIRGO - April 2016

Early April brings you an "aha" moment of clarity about what you truly desire. This could also bring about a huge change in for you that results in a reshuffling in your relationship. If you're single, the revelation could be simply remembering just how well you manage on your own. Or perhaps you realize that you do, in fact, want kids, even though you thought you didn't, for many years. Or you finally decide to pen that novel or memoir that for too long has been a mere thought bubble. Maybe sitting behind a desk or attending to customers was never meant for you. Your real beckoning could be something so zany as Holly-wood. Now is the time to claim your power in pursuing the artistic or romantic dream that means everything to you. Put it out there, Virgo. This time is all about self-expression. There is no moment like the present to make your desires known to the universe.

Planets indicate a strong possibility of a few structural repairs to your home between the 11th and the 20th of this month. Around the same time, you may also have to make a decision about a forthcoming move or some other aspect of your living situation. Any property deals, leases or mortgages that did not go through in February finally materialize now. Be certain, if you're a buyer, that the agreement is ironclad and that you've fully inspected every nook and cranny of the property. Also, if you're working with contractors on a home improvement, make sure everything is spelled out clearly. You really don't want to learn on the first day that their non-negotiable start time is 6:00 a.m.

This is also a good time to invest in homeowner's insurance, or potentially upgrade to a better health insurance plan to make sure your home and family have the best possible coverage.

Theatrical emotions alert! From the 22nd to the 27th, emotions may tend toward the dramatic. You experience stressful moments due to a lack of boundaries or unclear terms with a particular family member. This is likely to be your well-meaning cousin Jim or aunt Wendy who always takes his or her inquiries into your love life just one step too far. This person has an annoying habit of offering unsolicited advice. This time it could be about someone who you broke up with months ago. In their opinion, you should rethink your decision. Let them know (albeit politely) that you are capable of making your own decisions. Then back off. Do not allow yourself to get sucked into verbal arguments. Mercury is going retrograde on the 28th. Be prepared to see things get muddled.

VIRGO - May 2016

The communicator Mercury remains retrograde from the 1st to the 22nd of this month. Back up your devices and data. During this three-week period, you might notice certain communications going awry, especially those that occur online. Be wary of going tit-for-tat in the comments of a public blog. Also, avoid scolding someone on email. Your words could boomerang back to haunt you. When sending emails, check and double check to make sure you've included the correct recipient. If you're launching anything, especially digitally, wait until Mercury goes direct. Otherwise, a careless mistake could easily fell your best-laid plans. Give your posting trigger finger a rest on social media now, too.

Jupiter, the ruler of global connections and higher education is in a benign mood after the 13th. What this means is you have the trappings of prosperity at your fingertips—especially if you stretch your limits or take a well-calculated risk. Expand your horizons and your pay scale could follow suit. Read through the latest research in your chosen field or industry. Give yourself a competitive edge. Sign up for that online course or webinar on Wordpress that can put you ahead of the pack. Or speaking of a more global reach, you might do well to learn a foreign language to engage with your counterparts overseas. Getting admission into an Executive MBA course is also not a bad idea.

After Mercury retrograde ends on the 21st, several opportunities to be a part of charitable collaborations and other group projects come your way. You might choose to join a marathon or fundraising event. Or perhaps you find a bunch of kindred spirits who want to revitalize a community garden. It is also possible to join forces with some driven, idealistic folks determined to rebuild areas stricken by natural disasters. If you're a business owner, it would be ideal to add a charitable component to your company and mandate "giving back". The wealth you distribute will come back to you manifold.

VIRGO - June 2016

If last month inspired you to get involved with charitable activities, the heavens foretell a passionate interest in religion and philosophy early this month. A chance visit with a friend or relative can spur you to join a seminar on spirituality between the 4th and the 12th. Or you may browse through a few books on these subjects. Once you read more, you are likely to get hooked on metaphysical topics and remain on a quest to acquire true knowledge and wisdom for several weeks. If you go deeper, the concepts that you learn may turn out to be radically different and even challenge your existing beliefs. Initially this quest and its outcome may seem overwhelming. It would make sense to join an Internet discussion group (there are plenty of those around) and ask some key questions.

From the 18th onwards, the planets are conveying an electrifying and stimulating influence to your career, ambitions. Look out for professional honors nudging you into a more senior professional position. Some of you will get promoted and rewarded. If you've been shy about exerting your expertise, now you will have more than your share of opportunities to shine. But beware! With your career zooming ahead on all six cylinders, you might find stress accompanying this otherwise wonderful phase. With new gigs, demanding clients and extra responsibilities, you could find yourself guzzling those Red Bull cans or gulping an extra espresso just to keep up. Work hard. But do try to clock seven or eight hours of sleep at night.

You may have been taking your health and fitness seriously for the last few months. From the 22nd to the 27th, you will find yourself examining your deeper psychological motives for having indulged in negative habits. I will admit that it's not as easy as it looks to probe one's own depths. But if you want to kick a bad habit -whether it's smoking, drinking, overeating or nail biting—you will need to take out your inner magnifying glass and examine that part of your psyche that you usually gloss over. The good news is that if you make a sincere attempt now, you will be able to get over harmful addictions in due time. Visit a naturopathy clinic and detox. Goodbye cancer sticks, hello celery sticks!

VIRGO - July 2016

The first and second weeks of July show you struggling with stagnant energy at the workplace. You could find that you have a hard time letting go of that ingenious business plan - even though it may not be working. Or you could find it difficult to let go of a particular person. For instance, if you're a business owner, you might be keeping ineffectual staff around out of guilt. You've already outgrown somebody's skill set. But every time you feel like handing over the pink slip, you remember the story about their sick mother and sigh! Oh...maybe next month! If you are an employee, someone around you who was once helpful has now become an energy drain. Does this colleague always turn casual conversations around the water cooler into complaints about why the company sucks or other places that do it oh so much better? Well, these seemingly minor moments add up, deteriorating the fabric of a healthy work environment. To deal with this liability, you may need to cut ties or move away, realigning yourself with someone more positive who will add to your life rather than subtracting from it.

What goes around comes around. Between the 12th and the 16th, you will perform a random act of kindness for a perfect stranger. Maybe you will help an elderly citizen in distress. You may give them a lift to the hospital, and wait for them while they're with the doctor. Or you may prevent them from getting scammed by a hustler. The warm feeling you get is the real reward for this selfless karma. But, you will be surprised, a couple days later, someone will do you a good turn. You'll either forget your cell phone somewhere or will be struggling to get something crucial done. A benevolent stranger will find and return your stuff or assist you in completing your important chore.

If you are in a business and things have been slow on the financial front (perhaps due to stingy clients) you will see improvement after the 26th. Until then, review your priorities. Settle any issues with your customers. Get your budget in (real) working order. Pay off debts and trim down expenses. While you may not be able to charge ahead with new endeavors right now, reconnecting with a former client or colleague on or around the 25th could bring a hefty new source of cash.

VIRGO - August 2016

The first week of August puts the focus on your partner. He or she may be working hard and keeping late hours. Or he may be racking up business travel miles. He might also be occupied with a family obligation, such as an ailing parent. Whatever it is will leave little quality time to spend together. This could leave you to shoulder the weight of being your honey's rock as he or she traverses some tough waters. Be supportive and understanding. Assume whatever burdens you can yourself. Now is the time to show your sweetheart that when you say you care, you really mean it. Reality doesn't have to derail romance. Focus on the quality, rather than the duration and frequency of your interactions. Make an effort to schedule fun dates that fit their busy schedule.

Lady luck shines on you from the 12th to the 19th. If there are competitions and prizes to be won, put your name in the hat whenever possible on those days. Make a bet on a horse race. If you've never done it before, get a knowledgeable friend to help you. Follow your instincts on which horses to pick. If you are slightly risk averse, you could also choose spread betting, depending on where you live (i.e. where online betting is legal). Alternatively, you could organize a poker or bridge night for one or more of those dates. Investing in stocks now may also reap excellent short-term returns over the next few weeks.

Planets indicate laziness patterns creeping in slowly this month. Ask yourself if you have been doing anything to avoid getting fit lately? Do you keep ducking out of the gym right before your dance class starts? Or 'accidentally' spend so long drinking coffee that you 'miss' your yoga class? It's time to tighten your belt, get out there and get fit. There is no time like the present! As the month draws to a close and Mercury retrograde approaches on the 30th, some relationships may begin to show signs of strain. Irritable tempers and foul moods waft in and out. Strive to evade these by being on your best behavior. Your calm in the face of their exasperation will have the desired effect.

VIRGO - September 2016

Mercury remains in a retrograde right up till the 21st. These phases are a great time for reunions. So make use of your energy constructively. Open up your contacts and scour names for people you'd like to reconnect with, especially a mentor or favorite colleague. If you're self-employed, a routine check-in with former clients could yield an interesting opportunity for you. There is, however, a flipside to this discombobulating retrograde. It may cause a petty squabble with a sibling or a relative on the 13th. Let this be your cue to detach. As hard as it is to watch near and dear ones become upset with you, rushing in to clarify your stand won't help now. It could even complicate matters further. Just text them the famous Arnold Schwarzenegger dialogue from the movie Terminator – "I'll be back". And disappear from the radar until the 21st. Absence makes the heart grow fonder. Once Mercury goes direct, you can meet for coffee and work through the knots.

Between the 13th and the 19th is a fine time to try collecting on I.O.U.s. But don't be irritated if payments come in a tad slowly. If someone can only pay part of what they owe, show them compassion. Hark back to the times you felt ashamed yourself for not covering debts in a timely manner. Health-wise, mid-September is a slightly tricky time. Seasonal changes affect your mood and awaken your allergies. Eliminate caffeine and sugar. Try not to let any strong drink pass your lips more than twice in the month. If you feel the least woozy, switch to mineral water.

By end of this month, you are bursting with red-hot energy. The creative juices are flowing. Feel like reconfiguring large swaths of your life in bold strokes and brighter colors? Begin with your immediate surroundings – your home. Let your imagination be your guide. I wouldn't be surprised if you find yourself tie-dyeing the drapes, painting the walls lime green or ripping out that drudgery-inducing lawn and replacing it with ivy or pachysandra. A few elegant decorations will give guests much to compliment you about.

VIRGO - October 2016

In early October, you find yourself in a reflective mood. Lot of confusing thoughts and doubts pop up in your mind. You may begin questioning all that you've believed in and followed up until now. Perhaps you have been a die-hard follower of some spiritual discipline, only to discover that it's not giving you clarity in several areas. Or you find yourself doubting a teacher or a mentor. This person has been a guide to you in times of distress and you swear by him or her. You've put this person on a pedestal for a long time. But now you are either angered or disappointed when you notice something untoward in his or her recent behavior. Try and accept their "human" side. Nobody (we already know this) is perfect. If you cannot forgive them a trespass or two, then steer clear of them for a while. When you have had time to ponder this muddle, you can ring up, meet somewhere pleasant and tactfully discuss your feelings with them.

An upcoming business partnership or contract comes into focus around the middle of this month. This person is a close friend. Exercise caution before you sign on the dotted line. Going into business with someone is no small matter. So, just as you'd scope out a potential long-term romantic partner, perform the due diligence here too. You want someone who is sound, reliable and whose skill-set compliments your own. If you've already rushed into a joint venture, you may find yourself needing to backtrack and put some clearer agreements in place. If a partnership has already soured, you could be headed for Splitsville way too soon.

Your reproductive systems will be primed for baby-making from the 24th to the 29th. Perhaps you'd love it if the stork left a little moppet on your doorstep in nine months time. If that's the case, cancel all appointments, throw away those condoms, buy a lock for your bedroom door, grab your love partner and get to reproducing. If you're having trouble conceiving, this is a good time to meet with a specialist who can hone in on the underlying issue. If a child is not in your immediate plans however, you'd best be very careful when making love on these days. Make sure to use protection, especially if your quickie partner is a stranger. If you don't, rather than just sharing a night of passion with an attractive stranger, you could end up sharing the lifetime commitment of parenthood with them. Remember, it only takes one time to get pregnant. Once!

VIRGO - November 2016

November is probably the best time for you to get yourself a swanky new set of wheels. Do your groundwork. Go online and surf a few automobile websites. Decide on the two or three models that interest you the most. Then scour the newspaper classifieds and online ads for bargains. You should be able to find a super deal on the 4th or 5th without much effort. Go for any one of your lucky colors – green, yellow or silver white. Avoid dark red or black shades (even for the Upholstery). Obtaining a vehicle loan is also going to be a breeze. This is, moreover, also a good time to acquire expensive gadgets for your kitchen.

Things are getting better at the workplace after the 10th. Co-workers are happy with your performance and are voicing positive feedback. Your efforts over the past few weeks are finally being recognized by your superiors. But that recognition needs to eventually result in larger sums of money pouring into your bank account every month. It is indeed lovely to receive praise; but most of us prefer to be shown the money as well. Do not be afraid to give your boss a bit of a nudge if he or she does not appear to recall how much of a contribution you are making to the firm. Could it be time to talk about a raise?

Differences of opinion about your partner's work and/or finances (or both) may throw a monkey wrench into the workings of your primary relationship after the 21st. Whether you have a long-term partner or are just starting to see someone, this snag could prove harmful to your future prospects as a couple. How deep can you really go with someone who depends too heavily on you for material and emotional survival? Sure, your honey may be passionate, but if you're always paying for expensive outings and dinners from time to time and your love conveniently keeps forgetting how much money they owe you, your chemistry may fizzle out soon. The most promising solution is to discuss and gauge your reciprocal monetary situations and mutual goals at length and openly. He or she has to agree to share the burdens of running an efficient household. Relationships work best when they are between individuals at similar levels and are mutually beneficial. If your partner is still not getting the point, heading off to a couple's therapy to work out the finer points of sharing your lives is strongly recommended.

VIRGO - December 2016

A grizzled, clever person will enter your life sometime early this month. This character is going to act as your moral (or spiritual) compass for a long time to come. Initially, he or she will just be a casual new friend. They won't preach to you or try to sell you any belief system. But after some long, profound conversations you will begin to realize that he or she has a fund of information to share with you about the spiritual side of your own nature. Their wisdom comes from having suffered a great deal of tragedy in life. Learn from his or her lessons. Meeting this person is a special gift from the universe. While this new relationship is still developing, a old "frenemy" who once abandoned you will sheepishly re-enter your life around the 9th or 10th. You and this person were once in a very problematic (dicey) situation together. You stood fast. They fled. Now they're back and want forgiveness. For the sake of old times, you might want to forgive them in your heart. But keep your head. Don't entrust them with anything you care about - especially your life.

Mercury goes retrograde from 19th December onwards. During this particular retrograde, guard against identity theft, credit card fraud or erroneous bank charges. Make sure to read your credit card statements. Check your bills before paying them. There can be inadvertent errors. This is prime time for money mischief, so keep your eyes open. Also remember, if you're in a pinch, borrowing money could lead to some tricky dynamics. So be extra-cautious about whom you ask to spot you. The same applies if you're the one shelling out extra cash. Do you really trust this person to repay you? Are you prepared to wait patiently until he or she gives the money back? If not, you might as well *give* the money away instead of building up hopes of reimbursement only to be disappointed when the funds never return.

Christmas is going to be joyful this year. But keep a watchful eye on the foods you eat around the 25th of December. You are going to be particularly susceptible to stomach bugs. Worst-case scenario is serious food poisoning and a hospital visit. Avoid packaged foods. They are loaded with chemical allergens. Sushi? Don't even think about it. If you are doubtful about any food item you are served, simply reject it by discreetly hiding it under that lettuce leaf garnish at the side of your plate.

VIRGO - January 2017

Forewarned is forearmed. Mercury continues in retrograde till the 8th of January, I hope you have already backed up your smart phone, laptop or other electronic devices. If you haven't done so, do it as soon as possible. Ignore this warning and you could end of up tearing your hair after losing years of valuable data. One of your New Year's resolutions is certainly about steps to improve health and fitness. First things first. Begin with checkups. Get a full body scan, teeth cleaning, blood tests, mammograms, colonoscopy or whatever else you've been putting off. Love your body and it will love you back.

Speaking of resolutions, try and implement some structure in your life this month. Exercise routines are necessary. But they are not something you are always comfortable with. However whether you're eager to commit to a sweaty, boot camp style workout or get back on the meditation wagon, regularity is of key importance. If you need help sticking to a regular schedule, say, of rising at 5:00 a.m. to stretch or get into tip-top shape, don't hesitate to tap an expert to help you achieve your goals. Make exercise a first priority. Stay away from expensive rich foods and drink. Spend the money on a trainer or coach. That's where it will do some real good.

Planets may inspire you to kick-start a blizzard of meticulous cleaning on the 22nd or the 23rd. You might tackle some area of your home or work life which has become disorganized. Maybe you finally realized you will never again fit into those clothes from high school that have occupied the bulging closet in your spare room for more than a decade. It's no use punishing yourself for not being the same size as you were at 18, Virgo. Give those clothes either to a charity shop or to a young friend or relative who may actually see them as vintage gear. In the same cleansing mode, you may finally decide to go through yellowed files that have been collecting dust in the attic. Throw out old paperwork. Organize those piles of photos that are all stuck together in years-old cartons. And finally, make sure to protect yourself from possible identity theft by either burning or shredding any documents, which might reveal private information (passwords, pin numbers, love letters from old flames etc).

YOUR MONTHLY FORECASTS FOR THE FIRE MONKEY YEAR

2016

LIBRA

Author's Note... Mercury Retrograde

Sometimes planets appear to be zooming backward through the zodiac. Of course this backward motion is only an illusion. The planet has not turned tail. But it appears to have. Astrologers call this apparent reversing: **"retrograde"**.

Any planet can be retrograde. But only Mercury's retrogrades cause communications to break down. Mercury has its retrograde period for a few weeks 3 or 4 times each year. Whilst Mercury is retrograde, we humans are encouraged to take stock, make plans and discuss different approaches to a variety of subjects. But because information is often muddled, promises broken and electronic devices on the blink during Mercury retrograde, we must remain flexible and open-minded. Advice? Always allow extra time for travel. Schedule changes are common. Do not sign any contracts or cement agreements during Mercury retrograde. Make no irreversible promises. Watch out for con artists. Make no final decisions, binding engagements or major purchases during a Mercury retrograde. You are allowed to have tantrums or rail against your fate. But Mercury will continue to be retrograde till it decides to go direct again.

Mercury Retrogrades
2016

January 5 thru January 25
April 28 thru May 22
August 30 thru September 22
December 19 thru January 8 2017

OVERVIEW OF 2016 THE YEAR OF THE MONKEY FOR LIBRA

Diplomatic Libra,

This year you will have to do some fancy dancing to avoid financial pitfalls. The Monkey doesn't mind peaks and valleys, but you are always seeking a level playing field. You prefer the company of collected, calm people who don't make a point of dramatizing what you see as resolvable issues. And you prefer maintaining a positive bank balance as well. Your strength, of course, is that you see both sides of all situations. The Monkey is a terrific problem solver too. But his or her methods are not yours. Monkeys zoom to the heart of the dilemma, tear it to shreds and then decide what to do about it. You study and weigh and think about the problem before you even go near it. The difference in approach and style between you and the Monkey can make life a bit bumpy for you in 2016.

The warmer months promise to bring you either new romance or a renewed passion in the romance you already enjoy. Take full advantage of this smooth sailing period as in the late Fall, family issues will come up that can cause rifts in your love life. A meddling mother-in-law? A snarky teenager? A jealous ex spouse or lover? Something along those lines will interfere with your balanced home life. Best bet? Engage the complicity of your significant other and embark as a team on a defense plan. Little matter whose child or mother or ex is manifesting. If you work in tandem, nobody will be able to throw a monkey wrench into the harmony you two have worked so hard to establish.

Toward the end of the year, take stock of your shape and assess your fitness level. After all, your work, private and social lives depend on how you look and feel about yourself. Too heavy? You lose con-fidence. Out of shape? You hate getting dressed up. Go to the gym or begin doing yoga or Pilates seriously. If you prefer group activities, take up hiking or attend Zumba or cycling classes. sw

LIBRA - January 2016

First few days of January may find you shrouded in a "don't talk to me" aura. Morbid thoughts occupy your mind. News of a loved one struggling with a chronic disease. Or an elderly relative may pass away around this time. Mercury is retrograde most of this month starting from the 5th. Be meticulous about details of travel plans and hotel bookings. Check your email communications thoroughly. Sort through your Spam folder and eliminate anything and anybody you do not directly know. Never click on links unless you are expecting on from a friend. Chances of misunderstandings and glitches with electronic devices are high now.

Guard against a sudden temper flare up with your partner around the 13th. The argument may be related to an innocent goof up. (Blame it on Mercury.) If your lover is at the boiling point, do not add further fuel by making statements like "I knew this would happen" "I told you so" "He/she (your ex) would have handled the situation far better." Validate their anger. Give some credence to their reasoning. Do not underplay anger outbursts. True to your sign of course, you manage to spring back to balance fast after the 15th. Positivist and focus return now. Relationships get back to normal - whatever that is!

You may suffer from mouth related problems this month. It may also be an irritating clicking sound in your jaw (TM). You may find that an on and off painful tooth or gum needs surgical intervention now. Taking care of dental matters and curing mouth irritations is crucial to your well-being. An infection in your mouth can spread to your whole body. Postpone any surgeries till after 25th when Mercury goes direct.

LIBRA - February 2016

Early this month, your normally balanced feelings and reactions could be boomeranging out of control. Are you lusting after a married neighbor? Feeling a deep emotional connection to the mailman? Better take a few mental cold showers... In addition, a newfound tendency to snap at others will not make you any friends. At this time, you vacillate between insensitivity and aggression. Be extra cautious. Turn your tongue over seven times before lashing out at an unsuspecting soul. As Valentine's Day looms, the plot thickens. You might find yourself attracted to an ambitious older character. Have you grown attached to a workplace mentor? Does a sharply dressed superior have you daydreaming in your cubicle? This attractive person is extremely intelligent, has a solid work ethic and operates under clearly defined principles. Their very presence is electrifying. If you are free, why not drop a hint? They are likely to take it.

Around the middle of February, watch your personal finances. Impulse purchases and shopping sprees tempt you. Before rushing out to buy that talking refrigerator you so covet, sleep on the decision. Mind you, if someone else offers to pay for that dream television or leather jacket, accept the gift with humility and grace. The time is propitious now to have your way without breaking the bank. When it comes to your entertainment budget, exercise patience and prudence. Remember that "rainy day" you've always been told to save up for? Well, there could be a spell of them in the coming months. If you are mindful of your resources now, you will not have to scrape by on peanut butter sand-wiches or refried beans when the downturns occur.

The 23rd and 25th are perfect days to map out your master plan. Have you been yearning for a little guidance? A career guardian angel of sorts? That person should appear now. Perhaps a friend will introduce you to a distinguished member who is an expert in your field. Or a blind date will turn out to be more useful as a work connection than as a lover. Even Librans who are fresh out of university may get chances to intern or work at excellent companies. This relationship will help you generate self-confidence. Your own sense of self should grow exponentially in the coming months.

LIBRA - March 2016

Early in March, do lonely morning jogs bore you to extinction? Are you sick of pumping the same sweaty weights? Investigate some less miserable options for getting your heart rate up. What's the use of being a Venus-ruled sign if you can't bob and weave your way to grea-ter health? Look into ways to maintain your fitness with Zumba or an aerobics class. Ever hear of Bikram yoga? If that idea turns you off, sign up for some ballroom dance classes? Contact a nearby center and find out more about what intrigues you. If you incorporate some fun, joy and art into your exercise regime, your motivation will skyrocket. And you will meet more like-minded people.

Feeling lucky during the second week of March? Perhaps you are ready to roll the dice on a solo project. Dreaming that your travel blog will blossom into a lucrative book offer? Trying to get a hotel rental cell phone app startup off the ground? Chances are, the ideas you generate during this period do have moneymaking potential. But you may not have the capital to implement them just yet. That get-rich plan? Put it on hold until the seasons change. Also, if you're considering signing on to a joint venture or investment between the 10th and the 16th, you might want to pause and reassess. Especially if real estate is involved. Do you and your partners really *need* to buy that multi-million dollar ocean-view estate? The oceans are rising. Maybe a quiet suburban location would better serve your interests. This is an ideal time to review your finances. Consolidate student or home loans and do likewise with credit card payments. If you get money matters under control now, you will have a solid foundation from which to spread your wings and fly higher with that new venture a few months down the road.

Toward the end of the month, you are filled with a crackling energy to do something new or adventurous. Want to scale a lofty mountain? Or learn some complex new language? How about apprenticing to a chef to become a gourmet cook? Go for it! Break out of your routine. Release your inner child. Move "have more fun" to the top of your to-do list. In addition, if you've been depressed of late, a change of scenery could be just what you need to rev up that mojo again.

LIBRA - April 2016

Normally, spirituality is not your bag. However, as April begins, a chance encounter with a religious person is likely to (temporarily) spur your interest in matters divine. Perhaps a street preacher's *love everybody* message will catch your ear during your daily commute. Or just when you cannot find the remote, a charismatic televangelist will surge onto your TV screen. Or... the passing of an aged relative or childhood friend or close neighbor may be the impetus for starting to ponder life's mysteries. Read some literature on life after death and reincarnation by Dr. Raymond Moody Jr. or Brian Weiss. Their philosophical enquiries will help you make sense of these new feelings.

Around the 15th, you may be preparing for a grand event. Is a local theatrical event debuting? Are you gearing up to help manage an athletic tournament? Whatever the stage, it seems you are working behind the scenes and will not be in the spotlight. You could be the director or the coach - the referee or the prompter. In any case, when the big day comes, do not lose your cool. People are expecting you to set an example. On top of whatever pressures your backstage performance is exerting, a sick child has you worried sick as well. The little poppet will probably be laid up with something banal like measles or chickenpox. All will be well. Just make sure he or she is eating healthy foods and staying the prescribed time in bed. If you round up some electronic entertainment to occupy your cherub, you won't hear too many whines or peeps out of them till they realize it's time to go back to school.

During the final week of the month, the phone is ringing off the hook. Not to mention the barrage of texts and emails. You are much in demand. Around the 24th, a job offer could even be wafting your way. Are you tempted to accept? Don't give an answer right away. There may be something the interviewer isn't telling you. Research the history of the company. Make a list of pros and cons. You have some time to think it over as Mercury goes into the first retrograde of the year on the 28th and signing on the dotted line should be avoided for the next three weeks. If you must, you can agree verbally to a contract during this phase. But do scan the fine print with care and ask for a postponement till after the 28th. Do not hesitate to inquire in detail about any ambiguities you intuit.

LIBRA - May 2016

Until the 22nd of May, Mercury remains in retrograde. We will all be dealing with travel mishaps, technology breakdowns and all manner of miscommunications. Retrogrades are notorious for scrambling inter-personal communication. Some of your closest relationships could become dicey now. Simple Facebook posts or innocent text messages could be misinterpreted as antagonistic. Choose your words carefully or expect a headache when sorting things out later on. In addition, a lost figure from your past could resurface. Might be a steamy ex or a long-forgotten mentor. Guard your heart carefully. They disappeared once. It could happen again. Restrict leisure or business voyages as much as possible now. Flights get delayed. Baggage could be mishandled or lost. And travel mishaps are just the tip of the iceberg of on-the-road dramas that the littlest planet's reversal can cause. If you must travel, double-check hotel reservations and airline takeoff times. Then triple-check them. While you're at it, back up your computer and electronic data. If you shop online, make sure you do so only on ultra-secure sites. If you take such precautions, you just might escape this wonky period unscathed.

Are your stock market or other investments not paying off? Is a piece of real estate you own dropping in value? Toward the middle of the month, consider selling your assets and cutting losses. A potential client or investor may show interest in one of your projects around now. Feel free to talk business. But in either case, wait until Mercury reverts to his normal orbit on May 22nd to make a final decision.

The last week of May you may feel weighed down by the excess loose change in your pockets or purses. Your finances are healthy now. Perhaps it's time you decided to sacrifice a bit of that 9-to-5 security in the name of chasing your true passion. Or you might just string together a few freelance jobs to stay afloat whilst you pursue your lucky star.

You could also earn some extra holiday cash by unloading key items on EBay. If someone owes you money, this is a prime moment to collect outstanding debt. Give any and all borrowers a ring. Chances are they will be able to afford to repay you now.

LIBRA - June 2016

Is your live-in partner reckless with your joint credit card? The first week of June could spark some arguments about money. Your sweetie's spending habits are keeping you awake at night. If you are planning to co-sign a mortgage or raise children with this character someday, better to agree on rules of spending as of now. You may have been racking up expenses yourself: expensive gadgets, gasoline bills, swanky dinners—the trappings of modern life do not come cheap. Time for some home-cooked meals. Some long-dormant self-confidence issues may also resurface around now. Do not keep any insecurities about your appearance or intelligence to yourself. If you confide in your significant other, those self-esteem concerns will cease to weigh on you so heavily. Sharing one's burden tends to lighten them.

Sick of the noisy neighbors? Disgruntled with the outmoded style or inconvenient location of your humble abode? After the 12th of June, dip your toes into the real estate market. Even if friends and relatives are carping about how "impossible" it is to find reasonable rents or mort-gage rates, investigate these areas for yourself. Who knows? That dream home may be within your grasp. An odd surprise could come in the form of a message from an overseas family member who is headed your way. Or an email from a long-lost cousin might appear in your inbox. Or you may get a phone call from a sibling who is supposed to be studying abroad. This character wants to know if they can crash at your pad. Considering your blood ties, this is more of an entitlement demand than a request. Relax. They mean well. But hide the expensive food and imported booze. This person, it turns out, is a bit of a mooch.

Balance is the key to a successful Libra life. During the final week of the month, shine the spotlight on your health. Have you been binging on greasy cheeseburgers? Wearing your cartilage to the bone by running on the treadmill eight hours a day? Enlist some help. Get a workout partner. Someone who can push you when you're feeling lazy, but who will also tell you when it's time to quit. Visit a nutritionist to help develop a proportional diet suited to your needs. Having such a supportive person to both inspire and ground you is the blueprint to maintaining wellness.

LIBRA - July 2016

Fried nerve alert! During the first week of July, you find yourself reeling under incredible emotional stress. Why? The opinions of others have started to affect you negatively. Perhaps someone's insult or blunt comment is replaying in your mind like an endless tape. I'm going to be quite frank here. You need to snap out of this gloom. Don't let coworkers or acquaintances talk down to you. Tell that overbearing parent that they should respect your opinions when the conversation turns to politics. Ask your boss to stop referring to you by that demeaning nickname. If you don't like certain things, you need to take a risk and say so. In the meantime, take a warm bubble bath to soothe yourself. Bring along an engrossing book. Lock the door. Light some candles. Once you are feeling better, go see a live performance. A play or concert should fill the bill. Afterwards, relish the feeling of sinking into your bed stress-free.

Between the 11th and the 15th, exercise patience with business and domestic partners. A disagreement about strategy approaches. Does an associate want to change the company's title to that of a celebrity's last name? Is someone advocating slashing the advertising budget in half? Does your significant other want to move to Texas? You do not need to raise your voice or flip the table to express your dissent. Has there ever been a successful enterprise or relationship that did not hit some bumps in the road? Sip a cup of chamomile tea. Calm yourself. If you can relax and take your mind off the dicey topic at hand, you may be able to reach a compromise upon returning to the office or bedroom.

An entrepreneurial effort that has been on standby could get a big push on the 24th. You might also have a chance to travel internationally for a few weeks. Perhaps as a volunteering effort to build houses in Liberia or install running water in the Amazon. Dust off that passport. If you will be working with your hands, bring the proper clothing. A pair of reliable gloves is a must. If this trip is for pleasure, relax and enjoy the visit to a foreign land.

LIBRA - August 2016

Bells of change are ringing! Early in August, a big move could be in the offing. Feeling burned out on your current line of work? Always wondered what it would be like to make a living with your hands? Been dreaming of getting your shot as a business analyst? Now is the time to investigate making a career switch. If you choose to remain in the same field, take the opportunity to reflect on what motivates you. What do you look for in a job? What did you detest about past positions? If you can articulate what you truly desire in a gig, the process of finding the ideal one will become infinitely easier.

Around the middle of the month, two members of your circle (maybe relatives) appear to be having a huge disagreement - a tiff over a thorny love triangle or a cousin's alleged drinking problem? Although you had nothing to do with the genesis of this mess, both parties will expect you to take their side. Even if it is obvious who is in the wrong, remain neutral. You're a Libra, remember? Put those diplomatic skills to the test. Lend a sympathetic ear. But keep your own opinions to yourself. If you reveal your true thoughts, you risk terminating a valuable relationship. Do not fret. Time heals all wounds. Those two will (or not) sort themselves out eventually.

During the last week and a half of the month, you may find yourself warming up to a casual acquaintance. Is the sight of that tennis partner stretching making you see him or her in a new light? Is that yoga newbie distracting you from your poses? Don't be bashful. Invent an excuse to chat. Fortune rewards the bold. After the 27th, an older family member may require your rescue. During brunch or over tea, they claim to be dealing with a series of health issues. What they really need is attention. In this day and age, it's easy to get wrapped up in our own problems. Do not forget those who lack Facebook accounts or email addresses. Make it a point to phone or visit your elderly relatives. And not just when you want something! By the way, Mercury turns back into retrograde orbit on the 30th. Prepare for the usual chaos.

LIBRA - September 2016

Embarking on a short-distance trip toward the beginning of September? Planning some family fun in the sun? That might not be the best idea. Mercury, ruler of travel, technology and communication, is in retrograde until the 22nd. Expect the radiator to overheat as you drive to your destination. Or a sibling squabble might ignite and ruin the picnic or outing for everyone. Luckily, there are some things you can prevent. Back up any vital electronic files. Make sure your passport is up-to-date. And check the trunk for a spare tire and emergency flares in case of mechanical problems. Better yet, use this retrograde cycle to polish off long-overdue repairs or tasks around the house. Returning to previously begun but as yet unfinished tasks is the best way to avoid the littlest planet's trickery.

Around the 15th, a youngster close to you may win an important award. Maybe a football MVP trophy. Or a scholastic achievement certificate. Buy him or her a present to show how proud you are. Perhaps a necklace, ring or top of-the-line watch. Something that will last for many years. Tuck an encouraging note into the wrapping paper or gift bag. If the child considers you a role model, start making a concerted effort to showcase your best side in front of him or her. Turn down that fifth beer at the family reunion. Mention that you volunteer at a soup kitchen. No one can be saintly all of the time. But when you're the presence of this impressionable youth, set a shining example. He or she will want to follow your lead.

Between the 22nd and the 29th, Jupiter and Venus are influencing your verbal and mental acuity. During this period, stretch your mind. Launch an original website. Take an eye-opening class. Write a science fiction novel. You have the chance to develop fresh skills in the realms of marketing, public speaking, writing, and social media. If you are some-what timid when it comes to networking, you could blossom into a confident communications maven around now. In addition, a relocation is likely in your future. Perhaps you will be moving to a more tranquil neighborhood. Or your company is breaking ground on a new building in another part of town. Either way, the change of scenery will do you good.

LIBRA - October 2016

In early October, prepare for the return of a mysterious ex. Perhaps you will bump into this person at a party. Or you might mistakenly dial a former flame and strike up a dialogue that way. This character has always been intoxicating. But he or she is not necessarily the healthiest partner for you. Tune out their honeyed promises about how much they've changed. Do not try to convince yourself that one more roll in the hay would be harmless. Instead, identify what pull this person has over you. Are you attracted to hard-to-get, emotionally distant types? Do you unconsciously relish the challenge? If possible, work through this complex issue with a therapist or skilled healer. With a little outside assistance, you should be able to resist this hazardous temptation.

Toward the middle of the month, personal finances occupy your attention. Do you have a hefty tax bill to look forward to? Contemplating dipping into your savings to pay it off? Do not try to estimate the numbers alone. Obtain the services of an experienced accountant. This is also a prime opportunity to consolidate student loans or credit card debt. Are you planning a business expansion or property acquisition? In either case, seek counsel only from top-class lawyers or financial planners. Check reviews in Consumer Reports or online forums to make sure you're working with a reputable company or firm. If you cut corners now, you will pay for it down the road.

Around the 21st, an elderly relative's health may take a turn for the worse. Perhaps a recovering parent will relapse. Or a grandparent will take a nasty spill while rushing down the stairs. Obviously, this is an upsetting issue. No one in the family can think clearly enough to choose the best course of action. That leaves you and that balanced Libra disposition to save the day. Is a sibling refusing to admit that Dad has signs of dementia? Are the cousins fretting about the cost of a full-time care facility? Trust your judgment. If this person would receive better care in a nursing home or living with you, do not second-guess yourself. Your sensible nature makes you the best equipped to make these tough decisions.

LIBRA - November 2016

Have you been feeling stagnant in your current job? Do you have an idea to propel the company into the stratosphere that you've been too nervous to suggest? As November begins, take a gamble on yourself. Stop hiding in your cubicle to avoid confrontation. Voice that bold opinion during a mandatory meeting. Get to know your coworkers. Network. Socialize. Bond. Discuss mutual goals and anecdotes. On the 3rd or 4th, you are likely to cross paths with a valuable contact. Keep in touch with this person. Their emotional and logistical support will help you greatly in the next three to six months. After the 10th, special accolades are in the works. You could receive a promotion, a raise or an invitation to join an exciting project. Let those champagne corks fly! This occasion calls for a celebration.

The middle of the month sees you bonding closely with your family. Is an elderly aunt laid up in bed? Is a sibling having a tough time recovering from a divorce or breakup? Make some small sacrifices. Drop by their pad with a homemade cake and a box of tissues. Use a personal day to run their errands and stock their fridge. Soothing this relative's wounds will, on some level, soothe your own. In addition, carve out some time to beautify your own home and surroundings. Remove that mountain of old files from your living room. Sort through your long-departed Grandpa's old belongings. The more comfortable you feel in your dwelling, the better your overall health and vitality will be.

Between the 25th and the 30th, enjoy some quality time with your family. Cook a complicated meal together. Plan the next beach getaway. Spend a day frolicking in the park. Do some of the relatives live too far away to join you? Schedule a giant reunion. Seeing all those familiar faces will bring a smile to your face. As the month peters out, somebody may surprise you with jewelry or an expensive outfit. Your benefactor could be a love interest. Or just someone who cares a lot about you. Regardless, you are aware that this present did not come cheap. Show your gratitude by wearing the gift whenever you are in their company.

LIBRA - December 2016

Toward the beginning of December, be on guard for the green-eyed monster. Especially if you are in a relationship. Is a partner "ditching" you for a weekend? Claiming to be hitting the links all Saturday long? You worry. *They must be cheating!* You may be tempted to scroll through their old text messages. Or to hack into their Facebook or email accounts. A word of advice? Put down the cell phone or laptop. You will not succeed in confirming your outlandish suspicions about a secret lover. And there is a real risk of getting caught snooping. Before you explode in a fireball of jealousy, get the facts straight. They are probably planning an innocent friends-only outing. That game of golf? It is actually...just a game of golf. Stop looking for sinister motives where there are none.

Have a bad habit you want to kick? The period between the 13th and the 17th presents your best opportunity to do so. Whether you are trying to stop overeating, chain-smoking or binge drinking, you may finally discover the willpower to say no. Contrary to what you've been telling yourself, that chocolate bar is not calling your name. Neither is the bottle of whisky. Nor is that packet of cigarettes. Quit your current vice, and don't look back.

Surprisingly, when they're finally gone, you will not even miss the cigarettes, booze or extra jelly donuts. From the 19th until month's end, Mercury is in retrograde. You know the drill. During this stretch, communication will be a nightmare. Delay any business acquisitions or marriage proposals until January. If you must close a deal, ask plenty of extra questions about the arrangement. Terms of payment or nuptial agreement details may seem obvious to you. But the other party may have a completely different interpretation in mind. Discuss and write down all important points. The holidays will be (for the most part) joyful. You may have to play peacekeeper during a small family spat. Is a nephew jealous of his sister's present? Did a sibling drink too much and spill an old secret? Tempers may be running hot. Some are playing the "blame game". Smooth it all over with your native Libran savoir-faire and surprisingly, what seemed like the mother of all fights will vanish suddenly with hugs all around. Enjoy this unexpected reconciliation. You may not be so lucky next time.

LIBRA - January 2017

Some people are always trying to claw their way to the next rung of the corporate (or other) ladder. If their quest for success at any cost destroys their peers in the process, so be it. As January begins, prepare to deal with power struggles in the workplace. After that promotion last year, you may find yourself caught in a test of wills with an indomitable adversary. Is a colleague gunning for your job? Is an insecure boss angling to have you laid off? Do not attempt to talk your way out of any confrontations. Mercury remains in retrograde until January 8th. Trying to persuade others to come round to your point of view will be a waste of time. Instead, do some soul-searching. Is your own lack of self-confidence the problem here? Maybe you're imagining things. Maybe no one is actually aiming to knock you off your pedestal at all. To remedy the feeling of being a target, be proactive. Have you ever heard the expression "Fake it till you make it"? Instead of fretting about tension at work, start the morning with swagger and charm. Bounce through those office or shop doors. If rivals (real or imagined) see that self-assured pep in your step and that super new *coiffure* you are sporting, they will be suitably impressed and less tempted to meddle with your Libran good nature.

As we reach the middle of the month, turn that introspective focus toward your relationships. Is a romance faltering? Are your mood swings or jealousy part of the reason? If you do have a significant other, try to get onto the same wavelength as them. To do this, you may have to make some sacrifices. Grant your better half a jolly night on the town with friends. Rustle up a tasty dinner after putting in a ten-hour workday. Do not let simmering anxieties or deep-seated trust issues prevent you from achieving true intimacy. The line you envision separating yourself from your honey could very well be a figment of your current dark imagination. Use self-affirmation and visualization techniques to soothe yourself. If you can harness the power of positive thinking, your love life will once again thrive.

Around the 28th, you or your partner may be the victim of some nasty graffiti. The target could be the side of your house. Or your car. With any luck, your insurance covers vandalism. On a brighter note, use the end of January to reflect on the past year. What goals did you achieve? What failures did you persevere in spite of? What made these events possible? Scribble down your thoughts. When the going gets tough next year, flip back to this list for inspiration.

YOUR MONTHLY FORECASTS FOR THE FIRE MONKEY YEAR

2016

SCORPIO

Author's Note... Mercury Retrograde

Sometimes planets appear to be zooming backward through the zodiac. Of course this backward motion is only an illusion. The planet has not turned tail. But it appears to have. Astrologers call this apparent reversing: **"retrograde"**.

Any planet can be retrograde. But only Mercury's retrogrades cause communications to break down. Mercury has its retrograde period for a few weeks 3 or 4 times each year. Whilst Mercury is retrograde, we humans are encouraged to take stock, make plans and discuss different approaches to a variety of subjects. But because information is often muddled, promises broken and electronic devices on the blink during Mercury retrograde, we must remain flexible and open-minded. Advice? Always allow extra time for travel. Schedule changes are common. Do not sign any contracts or cement agreements during Mercury retrograde. Make no irreversible promises. Watch out for con artists. Make no final decisions, binding engagements or major purchases during a Mercury retrograde. You are allowed to have tantrums or rail against your fate. But Mercury will continue to be retrograde till it decides to go direct again.

Mercury Retrogrades
2016

January 5 thru January 25
April 28 thru May 22
August 30 thru September 22
December 19 thru January 8 2017

OVERVIEW OF 2016 THE YEAR OF THE MONKEY FOR SCORPIO

Sexy Scorpio,

As much as I would love to report that the Fire Monkey Year will offer Scorpios ample opportunity to indulge in the pleasures of the flesh, I can't. Instead of wallowing in sensuality this year, you can plan on being sumptuously busy. Not that being occupied full time is a bummer. It's not. But for you, who sometimes require down time to rekindle your furnaces, this year will prove testy. The Monkey is a meddler. You might be simply chopping onions or sawing wood and the Monkey will come along and point out the flaws in your method. What I mean by this is that the Fire Monkey Year might tend to make you unsure of your current path. In order not to let this happen, be vigilant. Steer clear of meddlers. Don't deviate from your well-trodden trail unless you yourself make that decision.

You will undoubtedly take up a creative project this year. It might be anything from learning to strum the ukulele to starting to make sculptures out of papier maché. But it definitely will come to pass. Whatever you embark on will be part and parcel of what promises to keep you so damn busy in 2016. Your work life already eats up at least 8 hours a day. Then there is your domestic situation to see to and after that (or before that) you need to take care of loving and being loved back by your partner or spouse. (And kids). Don't think that the painting or dancing or ukulele project can wait. Don't procrastinate. Steal the time necessary to build the creative part of yourself and your stress level will plummet.

Scorpio finances don't appear to pose a problem in 2016. You make money enough and can pay your bills. Do beware of overspending on gifts and trinkets to assuage the guilt you will feel about being too busy with your project to spend time with your lover. Small gestures of affection will suffice. Tender words and sweet nothings go a long way to keeping the fires of passion alive. sw

SCORPIO - January 2016

Last year was financially beneficial. As a result, early January 2015 is the time when you make the decision about getting some expensive repairs or renovations done to the interior of your home. You will have to dip into savings. However, you can't afford to put these urgent matters off for long. Safety would become an issue. It would be prudent to get multiple estimates and references from friends as to both the honesty and quality of service offered by their favorite carpenter, mason, plumber or mechanic. However Mercury turns retrograde between the 5th to the 25th. So it's not a proper time to start anything new. It may be better to start the repair work after the 25th. Retrograde Mercury can cause unnecessary troubles and glitches. You may have to realize that certain repairs at home present puzzling hurdles that will cause annoying delays. The preparation phase may be a challenge. But the final product will thrill you.

Small differences of opinion with your partner are hinting at an inevitable emotional firestorm around the 11th. Some discomfort in the family due to an outsider's influence is possible too. If the interloper is a sibling, be tactful and diplomatic while solving the issue. Your partner could need medical attention from the 14th to the 17th. He or she could suffer from eye or throat related issues. It may be time for a medical checkup. In case you have any loans to repay, now is the time to clear them up.

The three F's: Fun, Family and Friends will consume your time during the last two weeks of this month. You are going to have great fun catching up with a few people you haven't seen in ages. Some Scorpios may decide to work from home henceforth. There is something hermit-like about you. A home office could suit your operations. It would definitely allow you more family time. If you are over 65, you may decide not to retire, but rather to turn the guest room into your den and start working from home right there.

SCORPIO - February 2016

Your relationship status could change significantly this month. Planets are signaling a favorable time to move forward. There appears to be someone special at work who turns you on. You share a lot of intellectual and platonic harmony with them. You can feel the sparks with this as-yet secret crush, but are afraid to take this to the next level. Have you tried to convey your feelings earlier, but somehow get tongue-tied every time? Not acceptable! Stop pretending you're "just friends" when your heart wants so much more. Better to speak up than to keep quiet and risk missing your window of opportunity! Remaining in a one-sided romance is not Scorpio's style. Share your insightful thinking and brilliant concepts with them on February 6. Set the ball rolling. Valentine's day is nigh. Why not use it to advance your budding relationship? Invite him or her to your place for a quiet meal. Put on some soft music and initiate a deep, meaningful conversation. Their facial reactions to your comments will tell you a lot about what they are really thinking.

Woo Hoo! More good news! You are going to rake some cash from the February 15th to the 20th. Money flows in through various sources. Oddly though, you find your expenses increasing as well. An opportunity to put some money in a get-rich-quick scheme presents it to you between the 18th and the 21st. It looks attractive doesn't it? It seems like nothing could go wrong there. Stay your hand. Instead of making a chancy investment, put some money into a high earning, long-term account. Once we call it "savings" our cash has a way of making us less likely to want to touch it.

Teamwork and technology are coming into focus after the 23rd. Rather than cursing the "incompetent hacks" or remaining largely incognito in the virtual world, use this week to make some necessary changes. Maybe it's time to put your name in the hat for a leadership position within your organization. Why not draft a letter to the board with some constructive critiques? Be sure to offer up solutions too, or you could come across as a rebel without a cause. How your keen insights are received will tell you everything about whether you should stay or go from this posse.

SCORPIO - March 2016

On the health front, have you been more of a hedonist than a health nut lately? It's likely. A sedentary life is far too unsexy for you Scorpios. But luckily, the planets are likely to inspire you and your partner to hit the gym together between the 4th and the 8th. Burn off that excess energy and slough off the calories too. I am not asking you to stop eating cake. But first, polish off some lean protein and roasted Brussels sprouts. Feeling more inspired? Join a boot camp. When the drill sergeant blows the whistle, don't resist. Lace up those cross trainers, slap on the fitness tracker and bring your attention to your well-being once again.

You might be busy putting the finishing touches on a work assignment that's near and dear to your heart near March 13th. Whatever this is, it'll have sparked your creative side, and it will be something you're quite proud to reveal. It may have to do with the arts and entertainment and it just might put you in the spotlight among your colleagues. You'll know with absolute certainty that you're not meant to merely fit in. You're meant to stand out! If you've been waiting to submit an important proposal, email your resume, or contact a promising connection, there's no better moment. If you've been seeking broader support for a long-term project, you'll find it now. Consider the phase between the 12th and the 18th a time of career stardom for you.

It looks like you have been putting all your eggs in one basket for some time now. Either through some passive income or joint investments, you've probably become financially fit. But the landscape is changing. For the next four months, you'll need to be more discerning about your money. Try adopting a more strategic approach. Meet with a financial advisor. Diversify your risk. Spread your investments around in blue chip stocks, bonds and perhaps even in Gold or Silver. If you've been moving forward at a rapid rate, you may also be amassing some debt. You'll want to slow things down or even pull the plug on your urge to splurge. Consider the implications of your new money mindset. Give everything with a price tag a rigorous risk-reward analysis. You may be surprised in which column some things fall. And you may not always be on the same page as your partner. Be careful. If not handled delicately, dissonance of this sort can cause some rifts.

SCORPIO - April 2016

Try keeping the lines of communication open in early April. You could unintentionally send conflicting messages to your partner. Perhaps they are about nothing major, but when noticing his or her reaction to what you say, you can tell you are irritating them. If you have kids, try to get some couple time away from them. Even just 30 minutes a day helps. But of course, if you have the time and the means, escape together to an exotic holiday resort for two nights. There is nothing quite like meandering through the woods, over mountains and across the streams, hand in hand with your honey. If escape is not possible now, try tackling an organizing project. Dealing with life on the nitty-gritty level together actually helps to cement your bond. Perhaps a garage clean up, budget overhaul or office de-cluttering makes you feel more capable as a couple—and closer, too. Having a shared mission can really rev the romantic engines, too.

Between the 11th and the 20th comes a planetary phase supporting group activity, friendship, networking and reviving the spirit of fun. Your social calendar is abuzz, with fruitful happy hours and other promising invitations to connect with like-minded souls. All this moving-and-shaking has a clear agenda: to meet-and-greet with people whose own objectives may dovetail perfectly with your own. You now have the chance to assemble a star team in whatever your area of interest is. Or you may just want to mingle with a crowd that suits your current trajectory/state-of-being. It is time to lighten up where the burden of duty is concerned. Jetting off for a day trip with friends or your main love interest could be the perfect thing to do on the 16th or 17th. You might even add an athletic component like a snowy hike or some slope-time followed by dinner before the roaring fireplace of a ski lodge.

Thanks to ever-expansive Jupiter, your communication skills get a big boost after the 22nd of this month. Any simmering ideas and intellectual insights you've had for the past few months can be translated into real-time action. Utilize this phase to your advantage and gather attention and accolades. Take up any writing, speaking or teaching opportunities that come your way between the 25th to the 30th. It is also beneficial for you to take up short-term courses to improve your knowledge in an area of special interest now. Be prepared to face the retrograde Mercury phase beginning on the 28th of this month and not ending till May 22nd.

SCORPIO - May 2016

Nobody likes ripping documents apart with their bare teeth out of total frustration. So be careful with any botch-ups regarding official papers during the cycle of this Mercury Retrograde - between the 1st and 22nd May. This phase will deliver delays, changes and perhaps complete u-turns in several areas. Your Plan B may need to involve a Plan C. The issues you face may be related to your house, business or some other precious possessions. Refrain from making any grand announcements of your plans. They can often turn out to be hollow later on - or simply be reversed. So avoid finalizing any hot deals on the spur of the moment. Delay that business trip, relocation, web project, book, learning course or workshop until the 22nd. There may also be problems with post, transportation, electronic equipment or Internet connections – obstructing the normal verbal or written communication between you and others.

The 12th or the 14th shows you feeling swept away by waves of unbridled passion. In the heat of the soul-merging moment, you could feel like spilling every dirty secret, thinking that it can only bring you closer to your honey. But think twice: confessing that you had a secret momentary make-out session in the supply closet with the bartender or the barmaid at your local hangout ten years ago might not be the best course of action. Even if you weren't officially dating your sweetheart yet, this kind of confession usually leads to suspicion. Don't be too eager to get everything off your chest. Any breathless admissions are likely to undermine your honest intention to create closeness. What it definitely WILL do is – cause your partner to suffer jealousy and become more possessive.

Humanitarian causes and philanthropic activities are your calling early in June. You are likely to bump into or be introduced to some social activists between the 23rd and the 27th. This meeting will be an eye opener. You have lived for yourself and family along. Why not turn a fresh page and consider how you can use your spare time to better serve humankind? Perhaps you'll consider volunteering shuttling homeless families from shelters to permanent housing. Or maybe you'll visit a natural disaster site and just roll up your sleeves, helping folks clean up post-storm debris. Or you could simply organize a fundraiser to help raise awareness to save Tigers or the spare Blue Whale.

SCORPIO - June 2016

Leaving familiar places is definitely good for your love life during the 1st and 2nd weeks of June. This is the perfect time to take off on that foreign holiday. Venus rules global travel now and any cross-cultural connections will enhance your life. You're likely to find romance, or pump up the passion with your sweetie or, if you are already spoken for, you two will explore new terrain. Sparks could fly with a fellow passenger as you fly back home. Or, you may strike up a long-distance romance that's worth exploring. If you can't hop a plane and go diving in the Seychelles, perhaps you can infuse some of that travel urge into your daily activities. Why not pick up a mind-expanding book on the best and the most exotic locations to visit in the world? Start planning and saving. Contact your local travel agent and find out about up-coming tours and payment options.

Health issues, minor irritations and a need to streamline and organize take up your time and attention after the 14th. Have you been facing intermittent pain in your legs for last few months? No amount of medication seems to help. Worry not! You might get to the root of it now very soon now. Consult an Acupressure practitioner in your area. You will reap amazing relief.

Someone is likely to get on your nerves on the 18th. Perhaps you go to the gym in the morning. You meet your irritating and nosy neighbor there who decides that your time on the treadmill is a perfect moment to chat your ear off about your other neighbor's loud cats. Don't respond to their ramblings. Answer in mumbling monosyllables. Nothing is more effective to deter chatterboxes. Between the 25th and the 27th, you may need to face certain stressors, or deal head-on with problems you've been repressing and avoiding. If your sleep is interrupted from a surfeit of subconscious activity, get yourself some earplugs, a facial mask and lavender oil. Oh, and don't forget that warm mug of bedtime herb tea to accompany a nice pre-slumber soak in the tub. For the remainder of the month, shift gears, ditching the social butterfly schedule for unstructured free time at home lounging, listening to music, letting your imagination unfurl.

SCORPIO - July 2016

I see you battling with trust issues during the 1st and the 2nd weeks of July. Your Scorpio suspicion meter may go through the roof on the 5th. If you're overly mistrustful, do a serious gut check before accusing your love of giving bedroom eyes to the local barista. Is your vivid imagination working overtime? Or is there a legitimate cause for distrust in this relationship. You could be projecting a fear from past indiscretions or from one of your own subconscious desires. Maybe you're the one who wishes you could spend lunch break flirting with a cute colleague - crime that you're accusing your innocent partner of. Perhaps you've been Facebook-stalking that ex, only to turn your own sex-capading reverie around on your partner. It's easier than you think to convince yourself that he or she has been unfaithful when the indiscretion is really embedded in your own subconscious.

Multiple sources of income from various business ventures engage your attention from the 12th to the 20th. The planets indicate that you probably have more than one project in the works. And your respective ventures are vastly different. It's time you ordered visiting cards for each of your different identities. And by the way, the 15th is a banner day for launching a new online venture. Or, you may want to join a professional group to boost your credentials and spend time with kindred spirits in your field. You could also choose to make an important strategic collaboration or partnership official. Sealing the deal on this date or during the week hereafter heralds a whole new chapter in your work life, as you link up with a group of people who can put your career on a stratospheric trajectory.

There is so much happening around you that you are literally gasping for breath by the 25th. You may wonder if showing up at the artsy cocktail party for a 30-minute drive-by is truly meeting the needs of your soul. It might be. But it could just as easily cause you unnecessary stress. Personal energy levels may feel a little diffuse now. If your drive is dimmed, maybe you're ready for a rejuvenating break. Instead of staring blankly at an Excel spreadsheet, get your creative right brain into play. This is a great time to explore an artistic medium – painting or music for relaxation. Try and go hear a concert or visit an art gallery in your city.

SCORPIO - August 2016

This month, keeping the peace with loved ones is more imperative than ever. The planets render your personal life somewhat hectic and stressful, with lots of action on the home front from the 5th to the 15th. Picture it: plumbers or electricians coming, kids going, your partner chatting away with his or her friends on the phone, the cable repair person troubleshooting your remote, all while your phone pings and bleeps with Tweets, texts and voicemails. It will be difficult to react calmly to any of this. You might want to stock up on those extra snacks at home as well. In the spirit of the moment, if you have children, your home could become the designated crash pad or play space. Worse, your Aunt Lucy might just decide to stop by unannounced. Or some other relative or friend decides your home is just the place for him to chill out for a weekend. If this frenetic family energy starts to invade your personal space, lay down some clear limits. To add some joy to the confusion you could receive news of a pregnancy in your own family – of one in your immediate circle on or around the 13th.

The 15th to the 21st is a red carpet moment. You've been toying with the idea of a move, possibly even to depart from your current line of work. Or you have been planning to reconfigure the way you approach your career from now on. There is no major hassle at your workplace but your current profile doesn't quite do justice to your talent. And after all, just because you are handling a job well doesn't mean it's your destiny and set in stone. You may be motivated to relocate, for an exciting (and possibly long-term) offer. This move will be something totally new and a better fit for you.

The 24th to the 29th is a time to exercise your trademark Scorpio sensuality. Single Scorpios might very well find love close by. Try and look your best, even when you're just racing to your morning yoga class or to pick up a cappuccino at your favorite café. Cupid has you on his radar and you don't want to get caught wearing tattered gym pants. Actually, on second thought, it doesn't really matter. Your sex appeal is going to be unstoppable even if you are wearing pajamas with holes in them. This would be a key moment to ask friends to set you up.

Perhaps a cousin or sibling knows someone you need to meet. Try blind dates, and flirt with wild abandon. Your chances of meeting someone when you're reveling in your own sensuality are sky high. Be prepared to endure Mercury retrograde from the 30th of August till the 21st of September.

SCORPIO - September 2016

Mercury is retrograde between the 1st and the 21st September. This phase may cause technology, communication and travel breakdowns, so take preventive measures. Back up your important data well in advance and if you're traveling, plan around some likely delays. Make sure your passport is up to date and that your plane tickets are actually booked for the day you think you're leaving town. During this period, beware of gossip and getting ensnared into someone else's drama. If you have the feeling that something is not quite right, don't dismiss it. Pay attention to your dreams and subconscious hunches. They will point you in the right direction. This is also not a good time to divulge your most personal stories and secrets to people you don't know very well. Beware the houseguest from hell who might snoop. Keep your passwords in a protected document or safely stashed somewhere and lock your medicine chest.

A family feud might suddenly erupt on the 11th or 12th, taking you completely by surprise. You may be present when this happens. Your high-strung sister or brother may take offence to an innocent remark made by you. Don't blame yourself for it. It's not your job to make sure everyone find your remarks agreeable. Just because you can see exactly what the nature of the problem is, doesn't mean it's your responsibility to mend it. Make your stand clear and then go quiet. Don't give too many justifications or arguments. In time, this, too, shall pass away.

"Anger is a brief madness" – says an ancient Roman saying. The week starting the 25th is going to make you feel slightly hotheaded and impetuous. If a colleague asks something, answer politely. Don't bark. Be careful not to push your own agenda too forcefully. You could find that your ruthless pursuit of personal work goals needs to be tempered. You do possess intense, demanding needs. But maybe the other person does not. They prefer the status quo. Accusing a colleague like that of any ill intent is about as conciliatory as putting out fire with gasoline.

SCORPIO - October 2016

Early October brings a toxic relationship from your past back into your life. An old friend or lover friend wants you to patch things up and rings you about it. This disgruntled "frenemy" was very close to you once. He or she wants to talk and clear the air - find closure. But you're a Scorpio. Deep in your heart you still harbor resentment. All this discord between you two may have begun with a small argument a long time ago and then escalated. The rift may not have been your fault at all. But Scorpio, *c'est la vie!* If this person is trying to get back into your good graces, it may simply mean that you have some healing and forgiving to do. Of course those – even if it's not in your nature. The planets are giving you a chance to learn a valuable lesson in this episode. Go and meet with them with an open mind. It is easier to destroy relationships and far more difficult to re-create one. If you've been waiting to meet a powerful new contact for coffee, the 5th or 6th might be the right days for you to have that life-changing espresso meet up.

If possible, stick to public transport during the 2nd and the 3rd week of this month. Not only will you be doing Mother Earth a good turn, but you'll save yourself a lot of hassle. Driving across town in your own car this month has the potential to result in fender benders, arguments, wrong turns and general stress between the 13th and the 17th. To avoid new worry lines on your brow, take the bus or the train. There is also a chance of your car developing a flaw around the same time. Have you been thinking of going in for a new set of wheels? If so, start looking around now. With the extra cash you have made during the last few months, you should now be able to afford a deposit on a newer auto-mobile. Focus on a model and color that reflects your personality. Search online and do comparison-shopping. Make the purchase either later in this month of October or early in December.

A few uninvited guests - parasites or pests could invade your abode from the 25th onwards. Ants, termites, fleas, fungus, mold – some insidious wee menace will attack in waves. You may feel you are too busy to deal with it right away. Find the time. If you do not take steps to cleanse it from your house, this minor annoyance could develop into a real health hazard within a matter of weeks Get in touch with a few pest control companies. Compare estimates for definitive extermination.

SCORPIO - November 2016

Regular exercise is always positive. But *overdoing* it is not. Scorpios, do keep your innate aggression and competitive streak in check while working out now. Listen to your body! If you're feeling depleted, don't push yourself. Do something restful and restorative instead. You don't have to outshine both your aerobics and Zumba teachers. Always make sure to warm up sufficiently and then just do your best. Right about now you could be subject to a pulled ligament or strained muscle. Better to be fit than burnt out. Between the 5th and the 11th is a perfect time for a single Scorpio to cozy up to someone sexy at the local club. Love connections can happen countless ways, so be clear on what you want and at the same time, be flexible and imaginative about how it happens. Coupled Scorpios may enjoy double dates or short trips with mutual friends. You and your partner feel even closer when spending a raucous evening with your tribe. Let your hair down for some silly fun.

Keep an eagle eye on your finances from the 15th to the 21st. An austerity plan is not easy for someone with high-end tastes such as yours. But it's a little too easy to overestimate your cash flow now. Budget wisely so the year can end on a happy note. Start flipping through your old contact database. The name of a long lost colleague or client could set off some inner light bulbs. Reach out to them with a friendly call or jolly email. Some exciting synergy could happen between you. Synergy which may spell some moolah in the bank for the both of you later this month.

A sudden phone call or SMS from an ex on the 23rd sends you down memory lane. You are suddenly plunged back into the bitter moments that led to the final separation. Dissension is in the air. A conflict in your current relationship might also arise on this date. As a result, you may be asked to make a compromise in a matter of the heart. Will you bend or break? Don't be too contrary. A healthy heart is an adaptable one. Certain planetary aspects around Mars between the 23rd and the 29th may make you feel more argumentative, headstrong and scattered. Be more indulgent. The person you're closest too now could serve as a mirror of some of your less savory qualities, magnifying the areas you need to improve. Having a hard time getting your point across to your sweetheart without causing friction? In between nights at the ballet, wine tastings, and road trips, why not sneak in some couples therapy? Or take a workshop designed to foster harmony between you two. There's always more to learn and discover about the one you adore.

SCORPIO - December 2016

A negative planetary aspect between the 2nd and the 8th could translate into lower energy levels for some Scorpios. For others, it could mean weathering sleepless nights as a result of an overloaded schedule. In a nutshell, too much on your mind—and your plate—is your dragon to slay in this month. And this is a tough one for you, Scorpio. You tend to keep too tight a grip on the wheel. If you are not madly striving for perfection, you fear being seen as weak. Slow down! Pull an intervention on your inner workaholic or control freak. Wake yourself up. This is a good time to do some nature therapy, holistic healing, Reiki and/or meditation.

The 15th or 16th could bring health food or diet-related news. Perhaps you had been struggling with high cholesterol. Now you learn that four weeks of the Mediterranean diet has paid off in a surprisingly lasting way. If the news is disconcerting, you should decide to completely overhaul your approach to your diet, exercise and wellness habits. Any healthful change you effect now will become part of your larger life philosophy.

Mercury remains retrograde from the 19th to the end of this month. Have you been working on a solo project? This is an optimal time for tightening up the ship before you launch it from the port. Beta test new initiatives with your close friends or trusted colleagues. Take helpful feedback from them on how to improve your product. Polishing up your professional presentations for January would be a wise idea, too. Challenge yourself to raise the bar a bit higher. Planning on roasting chestnuts on an open fire on Christmas Eve? Christmas Day won't be so relaxing this year. You could be pulled between conflicting desires for low-key private time and the excitement of glittering crowds and big parties. You crave both intimacy and a rollicking good time with other. Yet your inner self requires some enriching down time. Warn everyone around you about how too many people surrounding you makes you feel jittery. Don't hesitate to request a timeout.

SCORPIO - January 2017

Why are you encountering roadblocks and potholes during the 1st week of the New Year? Just when you think you were snugly on your way to get crowd funding for your innovative new project from Kick-starter.com, you run into an unexpected setback. Chalk the glitches up to Mercury retrograde which lasts till the 8th. But whatever you do, don't give up now. If this endeavor is really the right thing for you, you'll persevere. Tweak a few aspects of the plan and you will be right back on track. It may, however, take until the 15th before the momentum really gain traction. Know that this venture has everything it takes to succeed. You have put much careful thought and planning into it. All of those hours behind the scenes will begin to pay off.

At work, you could be called on to make a critique or give someone a performance review on the 9th or 10th. Be gentle, but honest. If that intern just isn't cut out for the art auction life, let them know that's what you think. But be sure to point out what they are good at, and give them some positive input about what you think might work better for them.

Be on the alert! Your extended family and relatives will be begging for your attention (and a share of your savings) around the middle of this month. Siblings or cousins in dire financial straits could come knocking on your door. Sympathize with their circumstances. Offer them your suggestions, optimism and a few meals if you can. If need be, try and find them some paid work. You might even let them stay at your place for a specific amount of time. DO NOT lend them money.

Since work will be busier than you expect after the 20th, it will be prudent to make time for an efficiency mission. Rather than scattering your energy in multiple directions, revamp your timetable so as to group similar tasks. For example, block out times for returning calls and emails, then shut off your ringer when handling more focused missions like writing or research. You can "get by with a little help from your friends", but beware of using them as distractions from what you ought to be doing. It may be wise to pay for a part-time assistant, babysitter, or other service worker who will lift some of the excess work weight off of your weary shoulders.

YOUR MONTHLY FORECASTS FOR THE FIRE MONKEY YEAR

2016

SAGITTARIUS

Author's Note... Mercury Retrograde

Sometimes planets appear to be zooming backward through the zodiac. Of course this backward motion is only an illusion. The planet has not turned tail. But it appears to have. Astrologers call this apparent reversing: **"retrograde"**.

Any planet can be retrograde. But only Mercury's retrogrades cause communications to break down. Mercury has its retrograde period for a few weeks 3 or 4 times each year. Whilst Mercury is retrograde, we humans are encouraged to take stock, make plans and discuss different approaches to a variety of subjects. But because information is often muddled, promises broken and electronic devices on the blink during Mercury retrograde, we must remain flexible and open-minded. Advice? Always allow extra time for travel. Schedule changes are common. Do not sign any contracts or cement agreements during Mercury retrograde. Make no irreversible promises. Watch out for con artists. Make no final decisions, binding engagements or major purchases during a Mercury retrograde. You are allowed to have tantrums or rail against your fate. But Mercury will continue to be retrograde till it decides to go direct again.

Mercury Retrogrades
2016

January 5 thru January 25
April 28 thru May 22
August 30 thru September 22
December 19 thru January 8 2017

OVERVIEW OF 2016 THE YEAR OF THE MONKEY FOR SAGITTARIUS

Spirited Sagittarius,

In the Fire Monkey year 2016, it will be your turn to speak up, say what's on your mind and hide "nothing from nobody". Very often you clam up, twist the truth and even hide your feelings because you don't want to hurt anyone. This practice, of course, turns your emotional baggage to lead weight. Yes, it's kinder not to speak your mind in dicey situations. But concealing your real thoughts takes a toll on your good nature. These subterfuges (and you are not built for subterfuge) and glossings over of the blatant truths that you so readily perceive can be your undoing. So way in the beginning of the Fire Monkey year (starts Feb 8) take yourself aside. Sit quietly somewhere and ruminate. Imagine how much better you would feel if you told your sister-in-law that her hot pink lipstick looks cheap or if you spilled the beans to your crony at work about his repellent body odor. Once you have decided to make your real feelings known, concoct ways to deliver your words so they don't sound harsh and nasty. Speak softly. But speak honestly.

Money? Read your horoscopes for 2016. Details are in there. Your health picture looks excellent in the first part of 2016. Perhaps some minor aches and pains will niggle, but after September you could be looking at the onset of something that's "going around". If your immune system is, in any way compromised, a simple flu or stomach complaint could develop into something more serious. Make certain you eat fresh organic foods all summer and fall. Avoid ingesting anything packaged, Build your immunity before winter sets in. The Love scene this year is not exactly tepid. But it doesn't have the sizzling character it did last year. You may have one or two romantic setbacks. Remember. There are lots of fish in the sea. sw

SAGITTARIUS - January 2016

Mercury is retrograde most of this month starting from January 5th. Be careful because communications may go awry and some skeletons may pop out of the closet leading to embarrassments around the 8th to the 13th. Someone you respect a lot and have treated as your guardian angel and well wisher for years may cause you disappointment around the 6th of January. You may turn to this person for counsel for some important family matters but receive some misguided advice, which leads you into a mess. The advice given is likely to be biased or prejudiced. It may pain you to think that your mentor is not infallible and perfect. This person could be an elderly uncle or aunt or even older sibling. Do get another opinion before you decide on your course of action. This is not a good time to sign any papers for property investments, settlements, negotiations and agreements. Avoid business travel on 13th and 14th January.

Socializing and networking is favored in the New Year, but don't neglect loved ones in the process. The 17th or 18th finds you locked in a heated argument with your partner. He or she complains about getting cold vibes from you. You are accused of being selfish and unreasonable. Another reason for their anger may be that you are too lost in your work. You don't express love anymore. Listen to some of the gripes silently because they are likely to make sense to you. Don't overreact or your will end up in a stalemate. Swallow your ego and put yourself in their shoes. Acknowledging your mistakes will not make you appear small. It will only end the argument from blowing up into something much worse. Be respectful of your partner's feelings. Avoid saying anything condescending. When it's your turn to talk, you can share your own concerns without accusation. Make reconciliation and compromise your goals in this discussion. Hug your partner tightly and apologize. Make love and put an end to the story.

Do not lend, borrow or donate money between the 20th to the 25th. In fact, back away from anyone who is trying to get something from you. If you let your heart rule your head, you are likely to lost both emotionally and financially during this phase. Focus on self-improvement and picking up additional skills at the workplace. All projects concerning personal growth will turn out well now. Some diplomacy may be required to take advantage of a business and career opportunity at this month's end.

SAGITTARIUS -February 2016

Your ruling planet Jupiter is conferring the teacher's mantle upon you early this month. Well, at least in a small way. The 3rd or the 4th of this month might set you up to guide or teach someone a valuable lesson. This person is likely to be one of your cronies who is constantly wallowing in self-pity and is unduly sensitive by nature. They need to be told. However you have always held back for fear of hurting their tender feelings. But this time, he or she may actually turn to you asking for honest advice in order to genuinely improve. Give them a couple of hours of your time. This is the perfect opportunity. Don't be shy about sharing what you know or what you've seen go awry in their nature. You may need to be slightly ruthless to drive your point home. But don't worry. The results will surprise you. You and your friend will see a change for the better after this conversation. No one other than you can handle this matter with more aplomb and discretion.

Many a time, your enthusiasm and firepower have been known to make you leap before you look. Do restrain yourself between the 11th and the 20th. Otherwise you could end up making some costly mistakes. The words, "Let me get back to you on that," could be lifesavers during these days. Why not try a little centering exercise before you start a task or pick up the phone to make a call? Close your eyes and take three deep breaths. You might even light a gorgeously perfumed candle before you inhale. The point is to quiet your mind before you act. Visualize yourself moving through each situation with grace and ease. Hold a picture of the outcome you'd like to create in your head. How do you want to feel have once everything is complete? These forethoughts accomplished, go ahead with your activities.

The 22nd and thereafter are days that encourage your recreational desires. This is an optimal time for a couple's getaway. Book tickets in advance and fly off to the tropics. Let those escapist urges lead you to a mountain spa or some hidden jewel. Unwind and relax. Sip fresh coconut drinks and cuddle with your partner in a hammock. Most importantly - enjoy!

SAGITTARIUS - March 2016

You will have more energy at your disposal for domestic projects this month. Between the 3rd and the 9th is the perfect time to make a few changes in your home décor. Add a mystical touch to your ambiance? As you are ruled by Jupiter, why not employ the auspicious shade of turmeric yellow? Use this color liberally in your candles, curtains, carpets, tablecloths or other accessories. The vibes you will receive from this warm, bright color will give you a more balanced perspective toward whatever unfolds around you. A spattering of orange might seem like a bit too much. But trust me, it will further enliven the spirit and mood of your living space. These lustrous colors improve relations in the household as well.

The 11th to the 14th will make you want to get outside and have fun! Hiking? Biking? Tennis? Golf? Or just to go walking in the woods with your sweet pea? Whatever it is, drop all your chores and get outdoors. On the 18th, you could be feeling slightly pent up. Luckily, it's nothing a little honest sweat can't improve. So get to the gym or run around the block a few times. At this juncture, a certain should-you-shouldn't-you question could trouble you a bit. It looks like you have spotted someone interesting. And you are dying to talk to them. Should you? Shouldn't you? Don't wait for him or her to make the first move. Approach them directly. They will no doubt respond favorably. Such a spontaneous relationship could turn out to be sweet. At the very least, you might make a valuable and lasting friendship here. At best, this new kindred spirit may turn into a lover.

Your home is going to be buzzing with activity from the 26th to the 29th. A parade of uninvited people comes marching through your place — a plumber shows up out of the blue. Or maybe a neighbor brings over a homemade pie. You will receive a none-too-welcome visit from a relative. Or few kids turn up for a pajama party. What with all the noise and activity swirling around, you notice your partner is feeling cranky or even unwell. He or she is stressed and needs a little peace and TLC. Make it your business to find ways to please them. Help out with chores. Buy them a small thoughtful gift. Or... just for the hell of it, whisper some sweet nothings.

SAGITTARIUS - April 2016

Early this month, someone may ask you to offer aid in an area outside your usual comfort zone. Maybe an ailing friend asks you to baby-sit her toddler. Or your partner asks if you can build shelves in the bedroom closet. Or someone who is a poor driver wants to borrow your car. Explain as well as you can that you cannot fulfill the person's request. But say that you will, instead, recruit someone for them. Find a knowledgeable friend or call a service which can intervene in your place. During this phase, it is especially important for you to develop your ability to help others in practical ways.

If you are feeling cooped up in a cubicle or at your home office between the 11th and 15th, you might not be doing your best work. You need some fresh air. Is there any way you can get outside? A walk through bustling downtown (Or through the nature reserve behind your office complex) would really jump start your brain, body and soul. Physical activity is really the best way to get out of this spinning-your-wheels rut. Ask, demand, wheedle — or just slip out. Everybody will benefit! And make escaping to the outdoors a regular habit. Your optimism about a work project looks to be very, very justified on the 15th. Expect and then graciously accept those compliments coming your way! You did do a terrific job.

Your partner undertakes a new health regime during the last week of this month. The two of you may decide to go on a juice fast and give up gluten completely. Or you start getting up early to go to boot camp fitness classes. You will actually enjoy the challenge of this new routine. You feel invigorated. Your partner on the other hand, is a bit grumpy about it. Don't let him or her slack off though. With exercise, nothing is more motivating than a pal or a trainer or a lover who is keeping you honest about how much and how often you work out. Watch out! Mercury goes retrograde again on the 28th of this month and doesn't go direct till April 22, we are all well advised to think and act with caution. No binding agreements. No major commitments or purchases.

SAGITTARIUS - May 2016

As Mercury stays retrograde till the 22nd of this month, you may find that your best-laid plans start facing delays. It is, however, still worth planting the seeds of an idea by researching your options and taking baby steps. Extra care should be exercised when it comes to composing letters, emails, making phone calls, and with communications in general. There may be the need to revisit old, nagging issues with siblings or neighbors. Errands could go wrong. You might have trouble getting transportation from point A to point B. Emails or letters get lost, and so forth. Also, idle chitchatting during this period may have some nasty repercussions! People might misunderstand what you say. You may be forgetful during this cycle. It would make sense to allow yourself extra time to get to appointments, if they are not cancelled in the first place! It would also be wise to double-check your work and review all communications before sending them off. You might have less tolerance in conflictual business meetings at this time as well. Why not send a more charming and patient member of your staff or family to handle any difficult adversaries.

A planetary nexus between the 11th and the 18th could usher your talents onto the world stage. This happens because a project that slipped under the radar earlier gets a second life. Make sure you leave the house "camera ready" because the media could pop by to interview you. Heck, you might get stopped by a style blogger for your fifteen minutes o' trendsetter *du jour*! With Mercury retrograde until the 22nd however, resist the urge to chop off miles of hair, ink or pierce anything. A simple blowout and some edgy makeup or wardrobe selections will satisfy the dame kinky desire — and spare you any regret.

If you've been studying for a certification, license or advanced degree, you might complete your requirements after the third week of this month. You'll feel a brilliant sense of pride and achievement, as you should. You've earned it! Another possibility is that you'll tie up a legal matter, and be able to put a thorny situation behind you once and for all. Whatever the details, the outcome doesn't appear to be anything that will sour your mood.

SAGITTARIUS - June 2016

June is full of naughty, romantic overtones. There's a roguish charm in the air. Ambitious and hardworking though you may be, you also need to let your hair down at times. If you've been chained to your desk, you'll certainly enjoy the lighter vibe that this month brings. The days between the 6th and the 10th find you and a certain you-know-who at your workplace trading adorable emails. It becomes something of a game and you occupy a lot of precious time thinking up funny ways to reply. Feeling foolish and silly? Don't! Let your love life be flirty and playful. And even a little mischievous! Then focus on details and flourishes as the week progresses. Give this you-know-who a simple, unexpected present. And plan something for the weekend. Saturday is a perfect time for an off-the-wall date, something to get your heart racing. A picnic on a merry-go-round maybe?

Be slightly cautious with your trademark "Jupiterian" generosity on the 13th or 14th. On either date, you may bite off more than you can chew. A friend or colleague could sell you a sob story and send you on a guilt trip. You feel compelled to rush in for the save. Perhaps you may volunteer to handle an uneven share of the workload only to sit down and regret it later. Curb the feeling of brotherhood and codependence. It's not that you shouldn't pitch in or lend support, but make sure you're not going on a rescue mission that will leave YOU drained. The best defense to espouse when dealing with such situations is to take your time and make commitments only after due thought and consideration.

Speculation, investment and allocation of funds could preoccupy you on the days between 19th and 27th. Keep your wits about you while handling money. Buy stocks by all means, but subscribe to some reliable fundamental and technical analysis reports before you do that. Try and invest only for the long term. Greed and fear are responsible for many ruined fortunes. Always remember to keep your losses small by investing wisely in stocks or bonds that have already made money for your friends or family members.

SAGITTARIUS - July 2016

Is that a wish-granting fairy godmother sitting on your shoulder? Or is it a guardian angel, hovering over your head? In early July some divine presence will look after you. And you will be able to feel it intuitively. You could find some hidden desires being fulfilled right now. As if someone is reading your thoughts. For instance, you passed by a show-room window, ogling at that expensive watch. And a friend sends the very same item to you gift-wrapped. In a nutshell, you are being of-fered support, succor and sustenance, some of which may take a deci-dedly unambiguous physical form. I'm not promising cloud bursting miracles. But you certainly have the uncanny feeling of being sur-rounded by some otherworldly blessing. Make the most of this phase. If you don't have a habit of making wishes or praying, then develop one now. Some of the wishes you ask for are likely to be granted in the days to come. The 5th to 8th could bring some amazing news, perhaps about a raise, a coveted leadership position or a prestigious client. The offer could come out of the blue, giving you a massive opportunity for growth and advancement. You may even branch out into a new path or field.

You have been pursuing your current sweetheart for the past couple of weeks. But he or she doesn't seem to be giving in. Read the tea leaves, my dear. If you are exhausting yourself with this pursuit, you may be barking up the person. It could also be that you gave too much too soon and now the other party feels pressured. See what happens if you draw back and become a bit more elusive. Don't back off completely though. Dangle the carrot a bit. But don't make it too easy to nab a bite. If you play just a bit hard-to-get, they will indeed catch the bait. Maintain the mystery. Reel them in slowly.

With your planets indicating fun, passion and play active between the 18th to the 29th, you bring the sunshine everywhere. It might be cold and windy outside, yet you have warmth about you that can make any party or room feel downright tropical. Your *joie de vivre* returns, in full force! Take advantage of this sexy, glamorous period by dressing the part. Whether you go for punk rock or jazz, you definitely should push

155

the appearance envelope. I predict that you are definitely going to make many heads turn.

SAGITTARIUS - August 2016

If it was the fun and frolic factor that closed the last month, then its health food and wellness that opens this one. I hope you enjoyed your passionate indulgences; because now it's time to repent. Out with the gins and the vodkas! In with the ginger and turmeric! Clean up your act and get healthy for the entire month of August. I can see your needle and spotlight hovering on holistic health. Book an appointment with a naturopath. Check your adrenals. Give your body a boost using the latest "green" trends or natural remedies. When it comes to your well-being, you're ready to get a grip!

Mid-August is the time when your personal finances and possessions receive maximum attention. You are brimming with new ideas. Think passive income sources. Pour your energy and creativity into your ideas, and you might just be able to take them to the bank. Extravagance with your pocketbook is something you may want to look out for however. Lately, your personal expenses are splashing overboard. If you find yourself itching to make "unnecessary" purchases, know that at the root of this urge is the desire to pamper and comfort yourself. Nothing wrong with that; but there are inexpensive (and even free) ways to make yourself feel better.

The planets lead you on to a rocky stretch on the 21st. You find yourself interacting with some people who are right difficult to deal with - awkward, argumentative, belligerent or just plain old non co-operative. While you will mostly be able to deal with everyone else, you are at loggerheads with this particular person in your group. You really wish you could be treated with more respect by him or her. Avoid direct confrontation or verbal battles especially after the 29th when Mercury turns retrograde - again! Simply blind this person with affection. Be sweeter than they and watch how they melt.

SAGITTARIUS - September 2016

With Mercury retrograde between the 1st and the 21st, be cautious when purchasing big-ticket items or buying online. Though you may think you're getting a bargain, there's a good chance you may not be. It helps to keep receipts and paperwork, as you'll be needing them later. During this tricky transit, even your most strategically plotted efforts could still hit a snag or two. This is a better time to tweak your grand plans than to actually launch them. So, take a step back and run another round of quality control on your ideas. Take a moment to check: are you on track with your goals and plans? Is there paperwork left to fill out, bills that you've been ignoring, calls left to make? As much as you hate to rustle through those piles and stacks, continuing to ignore them is only going to leave you with a low-grade stress hangover.

Are there any bright sides to this Mercury retrograde? Yes, there are. It's a great time for reunions. So gather with the good friends in your life between the 14th and the 21st to make sure those relationships are on track. Especially call and meet up with those who have been out of touch for some time. Clear the air around any misunderstanding, and take special efforts not to push each other's buttons. Steer clear of controversial topics unless you can address them from an open-minded, solution-oriented perspective.

A taste and desire for everything different, exotic and foreign takes hold of you from the 21st. This shows up suddenly in many areas of life – people to whom you are attracted, what you buy, the kind of art or entertainment you enjoy, and so forth. Visiting a foreign film festival or an art gallery will be an enriching experience. Speaking of attractions, you are irresistibly drawn to someone who you previously wouldn't consider the least bit tempting. Or you may feel some new excitement about someone whose cultural background is very different from yours. If you are straight, you may come across a charming gay or lesbian personality who forms a lasting friendship with you. If you belong to the gay community, the reverse is applicable.

SAGITTARIUS - October 2016

A brush with an illness will have you reeling on or around the 4th. Looks like you, or someone very close to you has been harboring a non-fatal but chronic disease for some time. Diabetes or heart disease are a couple of possibilities. Ensure that you and your loved ones have been tested for similar surreptitious illnesses. Whether the patient is you or someone else in your family, there is a need to alter the lifestyle and get back to fitness routine. Load up on preventive medicine, ensure sufficient intake of vitamin C and D and eat only fresh produce. Getting sufficient and timely sleep is a must. Get yourself a trusty monitoring device to track your vitality and keep you accountable on your self-care mission.

On a happier note, your hard work last month has resulted in you being up for promotion on the 12th. In the days leading up to the decision, make your presence felt around the office. Put yourself in the spotlight by speaking up at meetings, talking with your superiors on a regular basis, and even dressing particularly well. Remain modest. But be visible. When they sit down to decide on who will be chosen for the position, make sure you're in the forefront of the important peoples' minds. In truth, there are several candidates who are more qualified than you at this stage. So don't be too disappointed if you're not selected this time around.

You could well fall for a sultry charlatan between the 23rd and the 28th. So be extra careful whose blather you believe. This potential lover will promise more than they can deliver. If you want to, consider this a fling and nothing more. But don't be surprised or devastated if your dream of passionate nights of bliss remain but a one-night stand. Also insist on using condoms. I know it's not as much fun. But I would advise you not to play Russian roulette with your life. There is a chance of catching a sexually transmitted disease during this phase.

SAGITTARIUS - November 2016

You have an increased desire to rule the roost early in November. We all need to maintain our egos in order to progress, don't we? While it is only fair that you have this feeling, it will unfortunately stimulate a few conflicts or disputes around you. Some of these are likely to be family-related. You may have arguments with them, about them, or on their behalf between the 5th and the 9th. You may also encounter opposition, resistance and outbursts from a few of your not-so-friendly colleagues. Mind you, much of this rough treatment will be undeserved. Don't wilt like a milquetoast or be cowed by workplace bullies. Do whatever you damn well please. Be bold, be brash and be really annoying right back. In the end you will get your way. You just will. It is in your jaunty nature to joke around sometimes which may have led some people to think you are a clown. When they see what you are really made of, people will start taking you more seriously.

You are likely to pick up negative vibes and get affected by others' suffering on the 12th or 13th. Be particularly careful if you have some ongoing addiction issues. It's entirely possible that you're having a fabulous, sunny day, only to cross paths with a draining person whose bad mood becomes yours, as if by magic. And it lasts for several days! Odd phobias could pop up, too, possibly making you feel like you're under some psychic, demonic, black magic attack. Relax. You're not under any cosmic fire. It's just a mood. And moods are contagious. Believe me, they are! Instead of reaching for a vice to help you cope, make sure you have healthy go-to outlets. Try running a few laps. Watch your favorite comedy show on TV. Sit silently and mentally relive happy incidents in the past. You will snap out of this slump in no time.

Domestic harmony is easy to achieve during the last week of this month with relatives as well as your partner. If you are truly in love, you might feel extra comfortable integrating your lover into your family now. If you haven't yet introduced him or her to your clan, this is a great time to do so. Perhaps you and your lover are considering moving in together. Or decide to purchase and own a piece of real estate jointly. All relationship scenarios are favored now. Regrets are unlikely.

SAGITTARIUS - December 2016

Early December is a time for completions and endings. Planets are going to shove you toward some exit strategies between the 4th and the 9th. Don't lie to yourself: have you known for a while that a chapter of your life was over? Are you feeling claustrophobic in a relationship, friendship or work situation? (Help…gasp….air!) In some cases, you might opt out and go your separate ways. At the very least, create a little (or a lot) more breathing room for yourselves. While you may have hung on to things longer than the average bear, it's time to strap on flying machine and fly, fly away. No more procrastinating. Wrap up a project that's been dragging on and declare it done and dusted. You have bigger fish to fry, new vistas to explore! Brace yourself for a wave of liberated energy coming your way.

If you've broken up recently, you should refresh your online romance profiles. You will enjoy a high click-through rate from the 10th to the 18th. If you're more of a "Facebook, Twitter and online-dating hate club" type, simply get out and mingle. You could meet a mate through the introduction of mutual friends or a group activity like a ski trip, book club, or self-development workshop. Already attached to someone? Make a point of socializing more as a couple. You and your partner could become the reigning royals of a new scene, calling your respective friends out from their hibernation for some rollicking good times. Host a dinner party. Organize a weekly night at the movies. Or gather everyone for a winter sports lodge rental where you might even trek through the snow to an outdoor hot spring.

Mercury, the speedy messenger retrograde from the 19th December till January 8th. Luckily, it's during the holiday season. So you will be partly spared confusions and troubles at the workplace. Although Mercury retrograde is never the best time to launch anything, it's perfect for reviewing what you've already done. Go through your social media pages with hawk-like attention. Delete the lame timeline posts and tipsy tweets and put up some new selfies and photos that tell the story of who you are today. This Mercury retrograde is also particularly good for reviving any collaborative projects that got stalled earlier. Don't try to complete anything or sign an agreement now. But this is an ideal time to plan ahead.

SAGITTARIUS - January 2017

Mercury continues on its back-pedal movement between the 1st and the 8th of January. What does that mean for you? - A medley of confusion and zigzag events at work and in your personal life. And yes, there will be drama. With every emotion heightened to a fever pitch, you'll have to keep the soap opera tendencies down to a respectable level. Feelings could easily be confused with facts during this phase, and no one will be in the mood to back down from his or her righteous stance. An influential friend you bump into on the 6th or the 7th may try to rope you in for something. However this person will not live up to their hype or promise. He or she could even have some shady activity going on behind the scenes. Keep your guard up. It would be best to just enjoy the view instead of actually getting involved now. Take extra care to guard against identity theft and security breaches on the 13th. The planetary influences can lead even the most "confidential" Info to slip through the cracks. Don't want your rant to get back to your boss or prized client? Then avoid the water cooler in your office and hit "delete" before you send or save any gossipy emails. Keep everything above-board.

The days between the 9th and the 16th could bring major downloads of creative and business inspirations. Don't be surprised if you wake up in the middle of the night to scrawl and sketch pages and pages of ideas. With entrepreneurial Jupiter's touch, these could be the seeds of a business plan or even, if you are a writer - a full-length book. Some of you are going to be laughing all the way to the bank in this coming year as a result. The bubbling inspiration might even come from your own emotional pain and experiences. Whatever you apply these ideas to will later blossom into something that inspires many others.

Acting a bit heavy-handed in your deal-making tactics? You could be making other people feel hustled and rebellious. Especially exercise caution between the 19th and the 24th. If you rushed through a project earlier, this planetary pairing will expose the weak spots. Don't wait for a breakdown to occur — one that could potentially damage your good standing. Go back and batten down the hatches, even if you have to own up to making a mistake. Someone who you worked with in the past could show up with an interesting proposal or project worth considering on the 27th. Could be anything from a group vacation plan to a revolutionary invention her or she has up their sleeve/ Review it. But before you make a final decision about how to proceed, get a few outside opinions.

YOUR MONTHLY FORECASTS FOR THE FIRE MONKEY YEAR

2016

CAPRICORN

Author's Note... Mercury Retrograde

Sometimes planets appear to be zooming backward through the zodiac. Of course this backward motion is only an illusion. The planet has not turned tail. But it appears to have. Astrologers call this apparent reversing: **"retrograde"**.

Any planet can be retrograde. But only Mercury's retrogrades cause communications to break down. Mercury has its retrograde period for a few weeks 3 or 4 times each year. Whilst Mercury is retrograde, we humans are encouraged to take stock, make plans and discuss different approaches to a variety of subjects. But because information is often muddled, promises broken and electronic devices on the blink during Mercury retrograde, we must remain flexible and open-minded. Advice? Always allow extra time for travel. Schedule changes are common. Do not sign any contracts or cement agreements during Mercury retrograde. Make no irreversible promises. Watch out for con artists. Make no final decisions, binding engagements or major purchases during a Mercury retrograde. You are allowed to have tantrums or rail against your fate. But Mercury will continue to be retrograde till it decides to go direct again.

Mercury Retrogrades
2016

January 5 thru January 25
April 28 thru May 22
August 30 thru September 22
December 19 thru January 8 2017

OVERVIEW OF 2016 THE YEAR OF THE MONKEY
FOR CAPRICORN

Tenacious Capricorn,

Last year prepared you for this one. The Sheep year was more than a tad confusing for Capricorns. You prefer to see things done "the right way". You are wedded to convention and are cautious about allowing for too much frivolity. The Sheep could care less about convention and frequently throws caution to the winds. So the sheeply confusion of last year irked your sense of propriety and sometimes even caused you to doubt yourself.

With the advent of the Fire Monkey year, you can begin to smile and even feel a rush of playfulness coming on. You can shed the weight of the madness inflicted by the Sheep year and begin to get your checkerboard patchworky life under control again. The Sheep year ruined your schedule, stole your sleep and imposed great swaths of new responsibilities on you. All hail the merry Monkey who comes along on February 8 to make order out of chaos for Capricorn. Your love life becomes passionate again. Your body begins to look like its old self and your finances move off the charts. Take a deep breath and read a gripping novel. You earned it.

Family matters may cloud the Fire Monkey year for you Capricorns. One or more of your relatives will require major treatment and not be able to pay for it. Or perhaps an ageing parent will begin to lose his or her memory and cause you untold sadness. God forbid a child should fall ill, but in the Monkey year, it's possible. Sorry to say there is nothing you can do (and Capricorns like to DO things) to prevent these occurrences. Just gird your loins and enlist aid where necessary. Keep smiling. sw

CAPRICORN - January 2016

Mercury is retrograde most of this month starting from Jan 5th and ending on Jan 25th. This month is going to present an opportunity to make a major decision regarding your career. You may be contacted by a headhunter with an offer of a dream role with a multinational organization between the 8th and the $14^{th\ of}$ January. However it comes at a price. This role may necessitate relocation to a distant city by February or March. Due to the mercury retrograde there may be several rounds of personal and telephonic interviews and negotiations. So don't expect a quick selection. In fact, you should insist on a written offer. And negotiate aggressively. Ask for joining bonus and stock options. Things are likely to go awry with any verbal promises made to you during interview. It is easy to backtrack with things that are not in black and white.

Expect a positive change in your social status and reputation in the middle of January. You may be conferred some kind of an award or recognition at workplace. You are likely to take advantage of this phase and some image building exercise is indicated. Watch out for a minor injury to the legs around 17th or 18th. Ego hassles are likely to crop up between business partners due to some miscommunication or inaccuracy in official documents. This will get sorted out once the Mercury goes direct after 25th January.

The phase after 20th January shows you working on restructuring personal finances. This is a good time to recover any debts owed to you and address your own debts. Take steps to clear any lingering financial burdens from the past. Do yourself a favor and keep friends and finances apart from now on. As a matter of fact, be aloof and detached from affairs of friends for a couple of weeks. You may develop serious misunderstandings with them now. Play neutral if called to intervene in a tricky issue between two friends between 25th and 30th January.

CAPRICORN -February 2016

Early February brings you more down time greater opportunities to indulge in hobbies and pastimes which interest and benefit you. Most of you may feel like taking up one of the creative "P's" - painting, poetry or photography now. This doesn't mean that you can't or won't take up gardening or some other creative pursuit. You may have the inspiration to start writing poetry on nature while trimming your garden roses. So if you have been dilly-dallying over embarking on an artistic journey, don't wait any longer. This is the perfect time to nurture your enthusiasm for a new pastime. You may begin checking books about your hobby out of the library. Try attending monthly poetry readings or photography exhibits in your city. Visit some art museums. If you really want to nurture your interest, interact with like-minded people. Make yourself a few friends who are involved in the same activity as you. This new sideline will soon become a passion. Stick at it. Practice makes perfect.

You are in for a slightly awkward encounter between the 8th and the 10th. It looks like you might run into an ex-flame. Your relationship with this individual was quite rocky. You had fallen head over heels in love. But eventually she or he took a vivid interest in someone else. The separation was quite painful for you. This person may gaze lovingly into your eyes and try to initiate a conversation. This could make you uncomfortable. Do not fall for their advances. There is no chance of renewing this relationship. Your old flame is fickle-minded by nature. You will be better off concentrating on someone new. Time to move on.

Stable unions are favored at this time. A very long-lasting business relationship is likely to evolve during the last week of this month. Depending on your individual horoscope, this may also be the perfect time to get married. Capricorns who are already married and those in live-in relationships will draw closer to their partners now.

CAPRICORN - March 2016

Early March is the right time to do some renovations in you living space. You have a traditional way of looking at things and do not like frequent changes. So this remodel could be happening after a long wait. If you are looking forward to shedding worn out negative energy, begin with practical modifications. Clean out the attic and the basement. Clear out your closets. Throw away moldering papers and books. Create a little corner for a studio space. As you are responsible and disciplined by nature, you don't like to leave any office business unfinished and often bring files home. Creating this dedicated space will help you work on your projects more efficiently and in an orderly manner. You favor a down-to-earth style. So you may go in for solid wood furniture and fine leather armchairs in your living room. You could also add a few accents that evoke comfort, like piles of brightly colored cushions and oriental carpets. Since you would rather jump off a bridge than have your interior constantly changing, you should pick decoration pieces carefully. Choose discreet items that don't scream "décorateur".

Some small financial gains are likely to brighten your days between the 8th and the 12th. Be careful about over-committing yourself to trivial tasks and other not-so-necessary social obligations. You have a backlog of chores to catch up on. An old friend is coming to town. It will even be difficult to find time to meet with them. Your work and family life is likely to be out of balance till the 18th. Things may fall into place as long as you don't keep jumping from one activity to another without finishing anything. Inconsistency will hinder your progress.

The days between the 23rd and the 27th will be dreamy and emotional. You're mentally preoccupied with some crucial event that happened in the remote past. You don't feel mentally sharp at this time. Logic and reason seem to have taken a backseat. Postpone any important business and personal meetings till the 28th or thereafter in order to avoid making faulty decisions. Long distance travel during the last week of March could involve delays.

CAPRICORN - April 2016

You may be seeking some advice from a distinguished personality early in April. This is not a medical or health matter. However, you may be facing some distressing emotional turbulence. This lofty personage may meet you between the 3rd and the 9th. There will be immediate attraction, but not of the romantic kind. You will find him or her quite knowledgeable, sympathetic and intuitive. He or she exudes power and charisma. They also come with a strong academic or spiritual background. You could be meeting with a psychic or an astrologer you meet for a consultation. One way or the other, this encounter will affect your point of view. Your interaction is going to lead to a long lasting friendship. Consider their advice seriously. This character has answers to your most urgent questions.

An acquaintance you thought was your well wisher suddenly makes some nasty comments about you to a few close friends on the 14th. Their complaint is about your snobbish behavior and may stem from the fact that you forgot to invite him or her to a small party you threw for close friends. While you may be taken aback and feel like confronting them about this issue, don't do it. Handle it differently. Everything will be forgotten and forgiven if you invite them to have a drink or share a meal with you. Give them a chance to feel they belong in your life. Chances are, the rumors will stop.

A reshuffle in the senior management roles in your workplace will result in significant adjustments after the 21st. Though you will neither be moving up nor down in office hierarchy, some kind of lateral repositioning will be required. You may not find the new boss so congenial. And the new working conditions are sure to take some getting used to.

Don't fret too much. It may take some time for the boss to get used to you - and vice versa. Mercury retrograde begins on April 28. Prepare to be patient.

CAPRICORN - May 2016

Then Mercury retrograde that began on the 28th of the last month will continue till the 22nd of this month. Until then you ought to take things a bit slowly. Be cautious. Do not act on impulse or emotion - especially where emails and verbal communications are concerned. During this phase, it is easy to blurt a secret in a moment of weakness. Avoid listening to malicious gossip. Ignore this advice and you risk making a bad name for yourself. Oddly enough, you may notice your mobile phone or computer malfunctioning due to a virus or other glitch. This is quite common during Mercury retrograde. Avoid purchasing any new electronic equipment during this retrograde. Any misunderstandings which crop up between you and your partner now will sort themselves out after the 22nd.

You may be sniffing around for an investment. Some surplus funds are at your disposal after the 16th. Though you may be inclined not to think so, investing in the stock market is not lucrative at this time. You may be approached by someone promising you trading tips that give hefty, quick profits. Research their claims. They may have an ulterior motive. This is however a good time for you to invest in residential property. Contact a few property brokers and get their input on real estate trends. Do your digging for information. Look for distressed property sales in up-market residential areas. You are likely to achieve excellent returns on your investment within the next 2 years.

Your creativity shines in its entire splendor on the 21st and a week thereafter. Those Capricorns who want to get seriously into public speaking, singing, theatre or politics will find excellent opportunities now. You will be assisted by worthy boosters. And you will effortlessly absorb the limelight. Do not resist. An appreciation you receive from someone of eminence and status during a public event could open up many new connections to powerful people from all walks of life.

CAPRICORN - June 2016

The planets are indicating a major impulse for Capricorns to rid themselves of a laziness streak and begin to focus on health and well-being. You will have extra energy and motivation to kick start a new diet or exercise program between the 4th and the 10th. If you are already actively exercising, you will benefit from assessing what needs improvement. Perhaps you want to add more stretching to your gym

167

routine. Signing up for Yoga and/or Pilates classes would be ideal. You may also want to modify your diet. Add more organic fresh fruits and vegetables. Make salads and soups instead of meat dishes. Visit a farmer's market for the delicious variety of produce. Cook more vegetables more often. Cut back on meats and dairy products. With more greens and fruits on the table, your energy levels will receive a hearty boost.

There may have been a legal struggle related to the apportioning of a legacy in your extended family last year. It is likely to get resolved after April 22nd. The outcome will be favorable for you. This is not expected to be a windfall, but it may nevertheless land a tidy sum in your kitty. You may also be entrusted with some papers concerning the will of an elderly relative. Put them away for safekeeping. If you see that you are one of the beneficiaries, keep it a secret. Discuss it with no one. The slightest leak to one of your greedier siblings may lead to jealousy and arguments. Why stir up a hornet's nest?

One of the youngsters in the family may be a cause of concern to you between the 22nd and the 28th. You could be contacted by school authorities about his or her pranks. Or a neighbor complains to you about this child bullying other kids. He or she may also be lagging behind in the classroom. You will need to figure out whether the kid needs some private tutoring or perhaps some psychotherapy. Do some detective work to find out if they are keeping bad company. If so, do discipline the child with love and care. Shouting won't help and could cause them to rebel.

CAPRICORN - July 2016

Early July appears to be a time of celebration about a happy reunion of some sort. Potentially big news on the home and family front is coming to you. It could be a visit from the stork. Or it may be about a family member who was away from home for quite some time for work or studies. That person may be returning at this time. Who or whatever comes along now, be sure to offer them a hearty welcome. Visits from other family members and friends are going to keep your house buzzing with activity at least till the 13th. Ensure to stock your kitchen with snacks and drinks and food aplenty. Food is never a problem for you hungry Capricorns. But do be certain you have enough to go around.

Be wary of a cunning foxy personality among your acquaintances on or around the 15th. This person has moved to your area recently. You and your group of friends don't know him or her too well. But everyone in your group has been raving about how witty and intelligent they are. Be

168

cautious. This character might be amusing, but he or she is definitely not a subject for a long-term friendship. They may even ask you to do them a small favor such as lending them some money. Say no.

Be careful with your household spending around the 25th or thereafter. There may be an unexpected expense this week. Either your vehicle or a huge kitchen appliance may need urgent repairs. The upshot could put a big dent in your bank account. It's a good idea to be prepared with a backup budget. Chop the frills from your shopping list. Look for deals everywhere. Swap the snootier brands for the more sensible low cost items. Take your lunch to work rather than eating out. Simple steps to save you worry when the oven explodes or your car blows a gasket.

CAPRICORN - August 2016

If you have been job hunting, you may find exactly what you are dreaming of during the first week of August. And if you are already happily employed, you will be feeling your oats. Nothing will seem impossible at your workplace. The boss is singing your praises. Colleagues give you credit for your efforts and hard work. What more do you want? To improve your luck further, keep a small two-layered Feng Shui Bamboo plant next to your workstation. Studies have also shown that plants in the office significantly improve performance satisfaction, employee concentration and air quality. A long distance journey related to work seems to be in the cards on or around 10th. However, a fuzzy restlessness and mild apprehension may muddle your mind about this trip. There may be no specific cause. Even as the plane takes off, you are sure something is going to go wrong. This time, you can safely ignore your "intuition". The trip will be hassle free. Practice deep breathing to release some of that accumulated stress. Breathe in through your nose, expanding the abdomen with that air. Hold your breath for 12 counts. Then let the air out very slowly to the count of 12. Do this exercise ten times. You will be amazed at how calm it makes you. Your previously negative thoughts will have faded away.

Looks like you are going to be playing with fire on the 16th. I mean both literally as well as metaphorically. You could end up burning your fingers while cooking. It's a bad idea to put ice immediately after the burn. Ice may soothe. But it doesn't heal. Also, never throw water on burning oil. Drench a towel with water and smother the pan with the soaked cloth. Metaphorically, you'll be putting out a few fires at work as well. A colleague or a subordinate of yours will mess up big time. You will cover for them and then face the heat from the higher ups.

You may have to attend a party around the 25th. Though this will be a routine affair, something will make this event turn out to be significant for you. Even if it's not apparent to you right away, you'll be introduced to someone who will mentor you in the coming years. This person could also have a strong influence on you spiritually. Mercury is turning retrograde on the 30th of this month and will be moving backwards till September 21st. Prepare to face a few communication-related glitches.

CAPRICORN - September 2016

The effects of Mercury Retrograde from the 1st of September through the 21st could mess up your day once or twice. Double-check the functionality of all electrical appliances and complex electronics. Replace the batteries in your smoke alarm. Are your computer databases, contact lists and hard drive backed up? In the event of storms, be sure to unplug all electrical devices. Mercury retrograde can play havoc. Are you freelancing? Even if you are not, it looks like you are taking up a major, long-term project between the 5th and the 10th. This endeavor could concern anything from software development, to writing a gripping novel or opening a restaurant. Whatever it is, it's big and prestigious. And it's going to gobble all your time and energy this month. But do remember, you're laying the foundations for something grand here. So brush aside any distractions and prioritize wisely.

Speaking of distractions, don't get sidetracked when an intruder appears on the scene. This person not a burglar or anyone truly dangerous. But their presence and their problems are intrusive. They will no doubt attempt to tear you away from your goal. This character has some clout with you (relative or ex or child who has flown the nest for example) could prove to be a rather large pebble in your shoe. Right now you don't have any time to waste. There is too much at stake on the work front. Resist all temptation to meet with them. It's difficult. But sometimes we have to make our positions clear with others or they will eat us alive.

You could find yourself suffering from a niggling ailment after the 23rd of this month. Could be and itchy, irritating rash, frequent headaches or lower back pain. Olive oil, Aloe Vera and Apple Cider vinegar work like magic for skin rashes. Back pain can be managed with a few alternate leg yoga stretches whilst lying on your back. You won't need to see a doctor for the headaches either. You probably need to change your sleeping position.

CAPRICORN - October 2016

Early October sees you grappling with the blues. You are likely to be in an inexplicable sad frame of mind. You seek to overcome this mood and you may even succeed. But shortly after you think that you have gotten over it, the damn thing returns. It's more than likely stress-related. Capricorns under duress tend to seize up and go crisp. Why not avoid challenging activities. Take some time off from work. Watch movies, attend a concert or visit an exhibition. Light entertaining pastimes with your family are just what the doctor ordered. You are deeply sentimental, so browsing through old photographs will be relaxing too. While your mood stabilizes completely after the 5th, a sudden snafu with finances can leave you flummoxed on the 11th. Don't try to sort it out all by yourself. Talk about it to savvy friends or acquaintances. Look like an older person in your circle will help you resolve the issue. Make sure you return the favor at an appropriate time later on.

On a happier note, your diligence last month will result in you being one of the strong contenders for a promotion or an award between the 12th and the 19th. In the days leading up to the decision, make your presence felt around the office. Place yourself in the spotlight by speaking up at meetings and interacting with your superiors on a regular basis. Do some networking. Pay special attention to your attire. Remain modest. But be visible. When they sit down to decide on who will be chosen for the higher position, you will be in the forefront of the decision makers' minds.

Between the 21st and the 30th is a good time to get good deals on new electronic gadgets. At this time you are particularly receptive to learning new technology and using it to your advantage. The more cutting edge and fresh this technology is, the better. Visit your local electronics retailer and pick out the items that dazzle and surprise you most. You will make short work of becoming familiar with their function. That assimilated knowledge will simplify your life.

CAPRICORN - November 2016

Early this month you will feel intellectually stimulated by what is going on in the world at large. You feel more and more like watching and actively debating all political news. On or around November 6th, you may also be moved to become involved in local government or social service. If a particular faction or politician inspires you to take action, why not head into party HQ and offer your assistance? Whether your talent is speech writing, handing out buttons, or baking cookies, there's something you can do to assist in the campaign of your favorite candidate. It is much better to take action, even if it's in a seemingly minor way, than to sit at home on the couch complaining about how things never change. Participation in charity or fund raising activities is also indicated now. Mercury and Venus are providing you a lot of extra energy to develop a reliable social network. You are proud of your ideas and are good at expressing them to others. Take advantage of this increased spontaneity and use it to advance your opinions and strengthen your value among your peers.

One day mid October, you suddenly wake up and notice the crow's feet and fine lines on your face - telltale signs you are aging. Bad news? Yes. But here is the good news: wrinkles can be delayed and you can prevent them from appearing too young. Start drinking 3-4 liters of water daily. This will keep your skin hydrated and flush out the toxins from your body. Swap your coffee with herbal tea because caffeine causes dehydration and makes your skin dry and rough. Indulge in aerobic activities that increase blood circulation. Eat fresh, non-processed foods which encourage your skin to renew itself. And finally – reduce stress. Meditation, yoga, gardening, walking and playing with kids and pets can help you on the path to becoming wrinkle free.

Sexual tension fills the air after the 25th. There is somebody you work with whom you are lusting after. And you have the feeling it's reciprocal. You know in your gut that you shouldn't act on your desire. The person you long to know more intimately is already in a relationship with someone you know. Perhaps you should take a trip for a few days to clear your head. Think about how the consequences of your actions vis a vis this colleague would play out. Quash your incipient sexual appetites now by being reasonable, thus saving yourself from yourself.

CAPRICORN - December 2016

Time flies. Early December will catch many Capricorns in a pensive mood. You will be mentally analyzing your past experiences, thinking about the people who really made a difference in your life this year - encouraged you, believed in you, gave you breaks and helped you. Once you have your list – call those folks and acknowledge their contributions. Let them know how grateful you are. Research has shown that expressing gratitude somehow makes us happier and healthier. Unpleasant though it may be, you might also want to think over the times you fell flat on your face in 2016. Make a mental note of the mistakes you made. You can draw valuable lessons from each one. Our trials can be our greatest teachers. Think back, take heed, but don't obsess over past failures.

Mercury is retrograde from the 19th December through the 8th of

January 2017. Communication errors will abound. Look out for missed messages, computer glitches and identity thefts. You need to be especially careful while shopping online this holiday season. Do not click and open suspicious emails asking you to track packages that you did not order. It's called "phishing" and its purpose is stealing your login credentials. Don't trust emails that ask you to call a number or click a link to your banking site. Whenever possible, choose a cash-on-delivery option. This is a time for money mischief. So keep your eyes and ears wide open.

Between the 16th and the 19th, a surprise is coming your way at work. It looks like a monetary bonus, but it might be in the form of a snazzy gift or a brand new perk. Whatever it is, it's nothing less than you deserve. You have really put your shoulder to the wheel this past year. If the gift is money, don't be tempted to squander it on Christmas presents or holiday entertaining. Put it aside until after the festivities and then... why not spend it on yourself?

CAPRICORN - January 2017

The New Year begins in Mercury retrograde till the 8th. Traveling may be subject to annoying delays and hindrances. You feel a tad irritable on the 5th and the 6th. Your vexation hints that someone at work is withholding crucial information that you need to move ahead. This person could be a colleague, a senior officer or your boss. There appears to be a slight malicious intent. Arrange informal meetings with key people after the 8th. Or simply shoot a few emails around to see if any0one else knows what's going on. Ask questions and don't stop until you are satisfied with the answers. If you find ambiguity or hostility in any of the responses, make certain you have allies before staging any open confrontations. Settling personal scores with your detractors may be counterproductive. Family members are supportive and patient with you. But displaying your ill temper around the house may upset them. Try to avoid bringing work related worries home. Leave office politics behind on your doorstep. Any misunderstandings with your sweetheart are best cleared up with an open discussion after the 10th.

You feel quite upbeat and sexually charged after the 12th. And your physical energy is also gradually beginning to peak. Why not use this upbeat mood to your benefit? It's a good idea to look for exercises to boost your sex life. Certain yoga poses like 180 degrees split, butterfly and the mountain climber pose enhance flexibility in the pelvic and groin region and tone the sexual energy channels and organs.

A verbal faux pas on your part could make things difficult for your partner between the 25th and the 29th of this month. If you speak out carelessly, he or she may have to face consequences in some way or the other. Try to stick to just one glass of wine at social events that you both attend. Alcohol may loosen your tongue just a bit more than is wise right now.

YOUR MONTHLY FORECASTS FOR THE FIRE MONKEY YEAR

2016

AQUARIUS

Author's Note... Mercury Retrograde

Sometimes planets appear to be zooming backward through the zodiac. Of course this backward motion is only an illusion. The planet has not turned tail. But it appears to have. Astrologers call this apparent reversing: **"retrograde"**.

Any planet can be retrograde. But only Mercury's retrogrades cause communications to break down. Mercury has its retrograde period for a few weeks 3 or 4 times each year. Whilst Mercury is retrograde, we humans are encouraged to take stock, make plans and discuss different approaches to a variety of subjects. But because information is often muddled, promises broken and electronic devices on the blink during Mercury retrograde, we must remain flexible and open-minded. Advice? Always allow extra time for travel. Schedule changes are common. Do not sign any contracts or cement agreements during Mercury retrograde. Make no irreversible promises. Watch out for con artists. Make no final decisions, binding engagements or major purchases during a Mercury retrograde. You are allowed to have tantrums or rail against your fate. But Mercury will continue to be retrograde till it decides to go direct again.

Mercury Retrogrades
2016

January 5 thru January 25
April 28 thru May 22
August 30 thru September 22
December 19 thru January 8 2017

OVERVIEW OF 2016 THE YEAR OF THE MONKEY FOR AQUARIUS

Visionary Aquarius,

This Fire Monkey year begins in emotional turmoil for you. Someone you love has either betrayed you or moved far away never contacts you anymore and doesn't answer calls, texts or emails. You get the obvious message that they prefer not to be in touch. This rejection wounds you deeply and is worsened by the fact you don't know why this character has forsaken you. Try asking people who are close to him or her. If they don't know the answer, it's probably best to close that chapter. Recovering from desertion takes time and can seriously diminish your self-esteem. Don't hesitate to talk about your loss to friends and family. Keeping the hurt inside will only make it worse.

From a career standpoint, this year looks bright for Aquarians. Your oddball approach to your work life will garner approval among your colleagues and superiors. You are able to view complex puzzles in a unique way that they could never begin to fathom. It's not that you sort out the problems so much as you see how it can be done and know how to delegate. Money won't be too tight in 2016 for members of the Aquarian persuasion. You should have ample funds to afford a super swanky holiday this year.

Your own health picture looks fine for 2016. There is however some concern about a relative who has been suffering from a chronic illness for some time and is losing hope of a full recovery. Visit this person often. Boost their morale. As for your love life in 2016, it will be spotty at best. You can't seem to make up your mind whether to hang onto the person you have been with for some time or leave them. If it's hot nights of steamy passion you're after, make the break. But if you prefer the status quo, hang in there and work on keeping the relationship fresh and alive. sw

AQUARIUS - January 2016

Another Mercury retrograde falls between Jan 5th and Jan 25th of this month. The month shows intermittent communication issues & stress related to your sweetheart or your offspring. Your partner may misplace some important papers related to a will or inheritance around 8th Jan. You see red & stage a heated argument with them. One of your older kids could scratch a fender while parking or even put a dent in your vehicle. Your phone malfunctions & starts dialing people on its own. Be careful before you blame others around 14th. Do not engage in stressful conversations or lock horns with anyone. A caustic remark you make casually about a sibling or a relative will backfire. They will retort and give you a very large and upsetting piece of their mind. You quail and feel terrible. Apologies cost nothing. And they work.

Your partner really could do with your company & support this month. He/she is likely to experience a bereavement or lose an important friend around 20th Jan. This friend may perish from some chronic malady or they may be moving far away to another country. Offer as much solace as you can to your partner during this time of emotional distress. Hold him/her close to you and reminisce about some positive events concerning the person they have lost. Distractions sometimes help. Go to the movies or theatre together. Choose life-enhancing films or plays to see. Boost morale.

A newly launched project at the workplace is likely to go from strength to strength now. The remainder of the month after 10th Jan is focused on your involvement in it. Relationships within your team should be harmonious & friendly. You do, however, have to factor in other people's feelings and goals before making any decisions now. Be open and direct about your own objectives. Honor their opinions.

AQUARIUS - February 2016

Early in this month, you are about to embark on a phase in which you can resist everything except temptation. This is especially so if it comes in your favorite flavors. Try to limit the damage and be especially careful about comfort eating. You'll be feeling much more romantic and lovey-dovey than usual. And that is good news if you're part of a couple. However, this time, you are also attracted to someone who is intimately involved with someone else. This person is likely to have a similar bent of mind. You hit it off like two houses on fire. This could lead to plenty of secret trysts till the 12th or so. After this, your love balloon gradually floats to the ground. Enjoy it while you can.

The planets are planning a whirlwind of changing and transformative activities for you from the 14th to the 19th. There are changes at your workplace, within the family and among friends. These shifts are a godsend because you have a swarm of personal issues concurrently running that aren't exactly wonderful. You've known for a long time that changes are overdue and needed in several areas. This time there is no escaping. However be gentle with yourself. Let things happen in their own time. Don't go snooping for excitement. For instance, in the professional sphere, you are tempted to show excessive zeal and act impulsively now. You may want to completely alter the way you look. Fact is, your appearance is fine. Except that you feel it could use a slight tweak. So tweak it and you will suddenly be able to make quite a statement with very little effort and expense. A lot is riding on your ability to husband your energy wisely these days. Keep in mind that random interferences will always try to trip you up. Aquarians are able to keep a cool head and work around them.

Legal issues and disputes may irritate you between the 22nd and the 28th. It is time to retrace your steps and pause for thought before launching fresh attacks on your opponents. If it's office politics you are embroiled in, take a breather now. While you are engrossed in all this and accomplishing your goals, your family and loved ones may be feeling neglected. You need to work toward achieving a harmonious balance between work and home. Think in it. Then act accordingly.

AQUARIUS - March 2016

Early March keeps you busy with work-related issues. You may become obsessed with an idea or problem until you have figured it out. The irony is - it's not your problem. The dilemma belongs to someone else, who probably doesn't care about it as much as you do. Don't try to control your colleagues' issues. From the 5th to the 9th are good days to lead the way on a new project. Your energies are at an all time high. However do concentrate. Work quietly and steadily. Rely only on your inner resources. Your patience and hard work will pay off. You will benefit most if you keep a low profile for now. Be careful where you leave your possessions on the 12th or the 13th - house keys, wallet, mobile or your expensive watch. Thieves abound around this time.

While work is going well, don't forget your sweetheart. Try to be more responsive and forthcoming in matters of love and affection. At this time, your partner wants to shower attention on you. Of course they expect the same in return. Cupid strikes the hearts of many Aquarians after the 15th. If you are single, you are about to embark on a sup-portive relationship. Be prepared for a flash of passion on the 17th. It may take you by surprise and unfortunately could die down just as fast as it began. You will be deeply moved by someone or some event on or around the 20th - the death of someone's beloved pet or the loss of one of their aged relatives. At the same time, there is a possibility you might discover a secret or uncover the hidden aspect of some dicey situation. This discovery and the resulting realizations will gradually trigger lot of improvements in your own personal sphere.

Social and cultural activities keep you busy from the 23rd to the 27th. A failed romantic encounter with a charming acquaintance may leave you feeling flat. But an evening of music and dance will lift your flagging spirits. You will gain several new admirers at this time. Your self-esteem continues to rise. The 29th is slightly tricky. Those in writing and publishing professions and students waiting for the results of an examination or thesis evaluation may experience setbacks on this date.

AQUARIUS - April 2016

A legal or business matter that has been weighing on you could clear up in early April - and to your great satisfaction. Steer clear of any underhanded dealings or offers made to you between the 4th and the 8th. They look quite tempting but do not have much of a chance of working out positively. I fear however that that greed will get the better of you. You will ignore my advice and go ahead anyway. The regret will blow over by May. Your romantic life is going to lead you to a proverbial fork in the road after the 9th. You will either need to double down on your commitment or ready yourself to venture down the path of the unknown. Make this decision with care. Turning back will not be as simple as making a U-turn.

By and large, the positive financial trends of the previous months will continue from the 14th to the 20th. Many events will transpire so fast that you won't know what is happening. Plans that had been lying dormant start showing sudden promise now. Business Loans that were stuck for no apparent reason start showing positive indications. Your proposals will move faster and smoother. This is a good time to colla-borate with friends for professional, creative or business ideas. Partner-ships are favored. A senior male family member or even a distant relative will offer you precious advice on the 17th or the 18th. Follow their words of wisdom. They are likely to work to your advantage.

Planets indicate leisure and entertainment between the 23rd and the 29th. Your partner may be in the mood to splurge. And you won't have the heart to say no. Going out for a family picnic or pizza is not a bad idea. A younger family member has been begging you for a pet for quite some time. Have you been discouraging him or her? It might be time to give in to the child's request for a little four-legged buddy. Contrary to beliefs, engaging with pets is emotionally productive. Cuddling during breaks help one to de-stress and remain calm.

AQUARIUS - May 2016

Mercury is going retrograde from the 1st to the 22nd of this month. Check essential paperwork and any files that you handle now for possible errors or miscalculations. Take care when communicating with those you see on a regular basis. It's like everyone you know has suddenly gone mad! You might find yourself getting into bizarre arguments about minor things. You may at times be unable to finish sentences properly. Or you may barely even be able to form a coherent thought. Your computer and other electronic equipment are more likely to go on the fritz. You could experience travel delays, too. Double-check your flights and take a book to keep you occupied while you wait for the train! Read contracts thoroughly and avoid signing anything to be fully aware of all the contents. We don't tend to get all the information we need during this retrograde period. Proceed with caution.

There is a sudden surge of workload from the 12th to the 17th, and your priorities may go haywire. You may be in a hurry to do too many little things simultaneously. Such fragmenting of energy impedes substantial progress. Don't be surprised if you start feeling low as a result of this paddling aimlessly in too many directions. Avoid taking risks in order to make a fast buck. Fast bucks often backfire. Sales and marketing personnel may also find it hard to meet targets now. On the health front, minor ailments lead to frustration, especially if you delay treatment. A too long-delayed visit to the dentist or skin specialist will prove advantageous during this phase.

The 23rd and thereafter is quality time well spent in the company of a close friend. This person has always been there for you, come rain, thunder or sunshine. Now is a perfect time to tell him or her how much you value their friendship. And although this gentle soul does not expect favors in return, you would do well to plan a fun outing for this person or purchase a thoughtful gift for them. During this period, any generous or kind action on your part resonates more strongly. If you want to undo any misconceptions others have about you, this is the time to show your real worth through acts of kindness.

AQUARIUS - June 2016

Early June is a time to hit the road or head to higher ground. You've lost your taste for whatever's going on around you. It's not that there's anything so wrong in your life. This slump is more about needing to redefine everything. A trip, or even a day or two away, will allow you to step out of your routine far enough to see yourself and your life more objectively. Pack your travel bags and set out with or without your partner. Stay in a place with tranquil surroundings. Ponder, deliberate and go for long walks. Make a list of achievements and future goals. Don't hesitate to dream big. Imagine the most idyllic setting possible for your life. The planets are in a very benign alignment now. Your thoughts will have more impact than you realize. And if you visualize them, your wishes and aspirations are likely to come true in the very near future.

The 15th and the 16th are good days to heal old wounds. While you had been reflecting and looking back in order to move forward, you realize that your peace of mind is troubled due to one or more past relationships. This feeling is holding you back. The subconscious memory has to do with a troubled relationship with an older person – mentor, teacher or relative. If you are able to reach them, why not confront them and talk it out? If they are no longer in touch, use some other way to find closure. Write them a letter or make a phone call - at first just to say hello. Then get to the point in a future conversation. You can also try healing therapies such as self-hypnosis or NLP. Perhaps talking to a therapist or someone older whom you trust and respect will help. The bitterness, resentment and anger are harming you. These negative feelings need to be released.

Look before you leap – especially between the 21st and the 25th. An impressive talk with an associate about a new non-profit may inspire you to think toward a diverting venture. However, don't rush in too quickly. Do your homework. Discuss the idea thoroughly with your partner and family. Take your time to examine all the details before you take the plunge. This idea is likely to offer emotional profits in the long run. But it may be a wee bit slow in the initial stages. There are no big risks visible. But in all prudence, you should invest only time that you can afford to lose without affecting your finances negatively. And don't be in a hurry to quit your day job before this fresh new project becomes fully developed.

AQUARIUS - July 2016

You are in one of your sparkling, witty moods that will win you several admirers early in July. Your ego and self-esteem are likely to get a big boost as well. Participation in a fun outing with a group of buddies on the 7th or the 8th is enlivening and stimulating. A group family event around the same time makes you wish for more kindred spirits. You don't really share friendly vibes with all of them. But you have future plans, which need a nod from everyone. So there's no way you can avoid having to sit down and talk things over with people along with whom you don't get. If you time it right, you can come out the winner. There is nothing wrong with using a go-between either. Get some family member you trust to break the ice. Then come in with your plan. You may be surprised to find out that the whole lot turn out to be more agreeable than you feared.

A senior colleague pushes you to take the lead in a prestigious project on the 13th or the 15th. You will be able to envision your future career path now. What you're doing, what you could be doing, and what you should be doing, will all become clearer during the next two weeks. Work to gather and exchange information with colleagues. It will help you to stay aware and alert to important professional matters concerning you. You could bag a big real estate deal during a presentation with prestigious clients between the 18th and the 21st.

As far as love and romantic relationships are concerned, there isn't too much to be concerned about right now. Your partner is more or less in a happy, non-complaining frame of mind. However if you do notice minor chinks in your relationship from the 23rd to the 25th, I would advise you to refrain from trying to point them out, heal or fix them. Your efforts may go horribly wrong at this time. Those who are single may stumble on a sudden opportunity to hook up with a person much younger. There is chemistry between you. Turns out, this character is actually much more mature than his or her age. The 27th to the 30th are good dates to purchase a new vehicle or invest in an expensive gadget.

AQUARIUS - August 2016

The planetary movement in early August is bringing you some rewards that come from past deeds where you expected nothing in return. The good deed could have something to do with your background and upbringing. A stranger whom you helped in a time of severe distress comes by and drops an expensive gift in your lap. The 5th to the 7th are days that are heavily packed with traveling for work or business. Your needle of attention is hovering over your financial position after the 12th. Are your bank balances in the red? Cash levels could be dipping due to some impulsive overspending. It's time for you to do some financial planning. Try to reduce the credit card spending. Figure out a sensible repayment schedules and stick to them. Be thrifty while shopping for groceries. Leave the smoked salmon and choicest cuts of meat for later on when you are once again flush.

You wish for some form of freedom in social and love relationships from the 18th to the 20th of this month. However you could feel a bit caged and restless. You could be exchanging late night messages with a certain good-looking colleague. Even if these messages are official in nature, your partner may be madly jealous. Howsoever hard you try you may be unable to explain your point of view convincingly to your partner. Do not retaliate with a dismissive remark. You know by now that love relationships are always a bit of a seesaw. The situation can be better handled with compassion and understanding. Many of you suddenly find yourself in consultant or advisory positions between the 20th and the 24th. Good publicity will come your way. Those in public relations or the travel business can expect success and popularity.

Mercury turns retrograde on the 30th of this month. As if announcing its backward journey, some minor money glitches may create a hassle for you between the 29th and the 31st. Perhaps a payment you that made on your credit card or to a utility company does not get recorded. Or your bank may inadvertently make a glaring accounting error which results in an overdraft. Make sure your financial records are in order. Have emergency cash on hand. You may temporarily lose access to some funds. This mess could take a week or two to sort out.

AQUARIUS - September 2016

As the month begins with Mercury transitioning into reverse gear, be prepared to lose a trickle or two of time going over old ground. These retrograde periods of the smallest and fastest moving planet of our solar system can tie communication and travel matters in knots. This particular retrograde period lasts until the 21st. Do not sign or promise anything you can't get out of. A couple of vexed business issues may have been hounding you for the past few weeks. Consider putting your ideas on paper. It is likely to help you to come up with a perfect solution. An unexpected event on the 5th or the 6th puts you up against the wall in the professional sphere. You could be asked to justify some disappointing income figures. As accounting is not your specialty, this display of failure could undermine your confidence.

Family assets, property and other related matters concern you a great deal now and come up for discussion from the 8th to the 15th. You will need to prioritize and focus on the larger picture while making decisions. Another family member who has been less fortunate with career and life in general may have more needs than you or others staking their inheritance claims. The poor soul may stay quiet in the corner and not raise a hair. Do be considerate of him or her. Compassion counts. The difficulty will be convincing less generous relatives of the quiet person's dire needs. The Mercury retrograde phase ends on the 21st.

Those who are involved in garment exports, foreign trade and speculative activities will fare very well after the 23rd. An almost global reaching-out will be experienced. Collaboration, links and some travel are all included. You are a dynamo at your workplace. There is a sense of mission in everything you perform. Love relationships are zany and capricious. You show willingness to take risks. If the gesture gets you what you want, you are ready to lay down your heart for your sweetheart to trample over. Take care. A lot of irreparable damage comes from such situations. Don't overplay your role. At this time, do not allow anyone new into your life who hasn't already figured out who they are. Spare yourself the heartbreak or dealing with folks who are lost.

AQUARIUS - October 2016

Loans and repayments are the highlights in October. You will be able to reimburse an existing loan early in this month. This is also an excellent time for those of you who are eager to acquire long-term loans. Several major outstanding personal rewards will be forthcoming around this time. A close female relative may have an axe to grind with your partner. As this relative has been very kind to you on several occasions, you are caught in an extremely delicate situation. Beware of a confrontation between the two from the 6th to the 9th. You have been discreetly trying to strike a compromise for them, but your efforts haven't yielded fruit yet. The clash will not last forever. Especially if you add a touch of Aquarian diplomacy to your methods.

Rather than pay attention to society's or nature's dictates, you are restless with routine and tend now to dance to your own beat. Progressive, part-time or unconventional ideas appeal to you these days. From the 15th to the 22nd irregular work schedules are demanding. This causes disruption at your workplace. Your working hours may become nontraditional. Either this will suit you or you might move toward a more unconventional job. Tensions are possible as you adjust to this disruptive influence. It would be wise to find work that offers you not only variety and stimulation, but also the chance to invent and create.

In the last week of this month you are taking an interest in dieting, fitness, nutrition and alternative healing methods. It is also possible to benefit greatly from yoga or other mind-body therapies now. If you are a video game freak, then your fitness routine can become fun and interesting during the winters. All you need is a game that works on motion sensor. Having your partner join in will make the activity more exciting. Include fruits rich in Vitamin C in your diet. It will not only keep the skin fresh and moisturized but will also help the body fight colds and flu. You may very well receive some money from an unexpected source on the 28th.

AQUARIUS - November 2016

November starts with you going about with your usual tasks with an almost comical alacrity. It is as if you are in a hurry to get somewhere. Slow down and breathe. Heaven is not going to land in your backyard if you delay watering the petunias on your porch by 15 minutes. While you are in this whirlwind mode, a child may come to you for assistance around the 6th. Do not brush the kid off with cliché advice and walk away. Listen carefully to all the details of the problem and consider your answer thoughtfully. Children's problems may seem frivolous, or even amusing. But from the child's perspective, those same issues appear immense. It's vital you demonstrate a vivid interest and a willingness to help. Even if you can't affect the situation tangibly, your attention and acknowledgement will serve as comfort. If it is your own child is going through disturbing phase, try using Bach flower remedies to calm the choppy waters. They are safe and have no side effects.

There are changes in your partner's work situation around the middle of this month. This can create undue pressure on them. He or she must work longer hours than previously. Both of you have such busy schedules that you have been a weekend couple. Weekday communications about practical matters are mainly through texts, e-mails or notes jotted on a scratch pad on the dining room table. Be sure also to intersperse the reminders to buy groceries with a few romantic messages. Or leave a small, thoughtful gift in your partner's briefcase or lunch-sack. Don't let the romance wither under the pressure.

The bold and beautiful side of you will take over after the 22nd. The planet Venus is in benign aspects by other friendly planets. Invitations to clubs, organizations, parties and social events will start pouring in. Say yes, because it will be beneficial to socialize now. You will also be fascinated by people from foreign cultures. This mostly has to do with their language, food, art, music and culture. Try to visit an international food or a film festival in your area. You are likely to bump into someone friendly and highly motivating for you.

AQUARIUS - December 2016

December means planning for the holidays. There's a chance your family members may be at loggerheads with each other due to a disagreement starting on the 6th or the 7th. It may be about where to holiday this year. Or it may be about modes of transport and/or the travel dates. No one will be willing to give in. There will be no easy way out of the dilemma. Just weigh up both sides of the argument with an open mind. Offer the best solution possible and then try to get them all to agree to it. Don't give them too many choices. It will only confuse them. Be the peacemaker. Do not be partial to anyone. Be fair. Otherwise you will see a few sulky faces giving you dirty looks every day for the rest of the month.

A minor but chronic body ache comes up suddenly on the 10th. You may be wondering if you ought to take the complaint to the doctor or just self medicate. Those headaches or joint pains may simply be diet or lifestyle related. If you tend to sleep late, you are likely to develop backaches in the lumber region and kidney related issues. Restful and timely sleep, regular eating habits and exercise are the key to good health. But there may also be deeper medical causes and are best nipped in the bud. Why not try out acupressure or acupuncture for a change? Holistic healing therapies provide more relief than conventional medicine in the long run.

A big bad wolf comes knocking on your door on December 19th. Its name is Mercury Retrograde. This one lasts till January 8th. Holiday travel plans are in danger of being jeopardized during this phase. Be ultra careful with your plane tickets. Check the dates thrice. Make sure that you have already booked the cabs for airport transfers. Keep your money safe in a money belt. Make sure each family member knows where to assemble and which numbers to call in emergencies. Create a plan B in advance for every situation.

AQUARIUS - January 2017

As mentioned above, Mercury remains retrograde until the 8th of January. While you will welcome the year with hope and enthusiasm, something seems to be bothering you. It's your waistline. Are you wondering why the diets you have been trying lately are not working particularly well? With all the variations you are attempting, you are actually making it more difficult for your body to maintain its natural rhythms. Forget fad diets.

Don't pay attention to what every quack doctor on TV or the Internet has to offer either. I will reveal the secret to you. And it is extremely simple - Have your breakfast like a king, lunch like a prince and supper like a pauper. Eat only soups, fruits and salads in the evening. Finish your dinner early. Eat light. Do all this for 15 days, and your weight will reduce and stabilize on its own. Expend less energy cooking up excuses not to get regular exercise. Slap on some trainers and jog or walk home from work instead of bussing it. Walk everywhere you possibly can. Indulge in vigorous bed exercises with your partner every time you can. Yes, sex does eliminate calories. It doesn't take much to improve your health and as a consequence, refine the shape of your body.

You could be interacting with some well-known public authority figures from the 12th to the 18th of this month. Unfortunately, you may experience a sense of insult or betrayal. The person concerned will turn out to be a hypocrite and is likely to go back on promised words. Perhaps you're partly at fault for putting so much faith in someone you didn't really know well. Henceforth, endeavor to be a tad more cynical and probing.

The 22nd or thereafter is a good time to reconcile with someone you previously had tension with. This person is likely to be an office colleague who likes to compete with you in everything you do. Both of you have been critical of the other. Both have been vying to catch the senior management's attention. But you finally realize that chopping off others' heads does not make you taller. Why not discuss the uncomfortable relationship directly with the person in question. You will be surprised at how the relationship can change into a cordial understanding.

YOUR MONTHLY FORECASTS FOR THE FIRE MONKEY YEAR

2016

PISCES

Author's Note... Mercury Retrograde

Sometimes planets appear to be zooming backward through the zodiac. Of course this backward motion is only an illusion. The planet has not turned tail. But it appears to have. Astrologers call this apparent reversing: **"retrograde"**.

Any planet can be retrograde. But only Mercury's retrogrades cause communications to break down. Mercury has its retrograde period for a few weeks 3 or 4 times each year. Whilst Mercury is retrograde, we humans are encouraged to take stock, make plans and discuss different approaches to a variety of subjects. But because information is often muddled, promises broken and electronic devices on the blink during Mercury retrograde, we must remain flexible and open-minded. Advice? Always allow extra time for travel. Schedule changes are common. Do not sign any contracts or cement agreements during Mercury retrograde. Make no irreversible promises. Watch out for con artists. Make no final decisions, binding engagements or major purchases during a Mercury retrograde. You are allowed to have tantrums or rail against your fate. But Mercury will continue to be retrograde till it decides to go direct again.

Mercury Retrogrades
2016

January 5 thru January 25
April 28 thru May 22
August 30 thru September 22
December 19 thru January 8 2017

OVERVIEW OF 2016 THE YEAR OF THE MONKEY
FOR PISCES

Pensive Pisces,

If last year was chockablock with change and upheaval, this one will be more so. Of course, by this time you are used to being buffeted about and asked to switch lanes every minute. Just when you think life has smoothed out, Bam! You have to move house, change offices, receive an unwanted guest or effect a major repair to your car or your computer. Monkey years are known for making unusual demands on Pisces' gentle nature. Buck up! Of all the signs of the zodiac you are the most flexible. No matter what life throws at you, you either catch it or you swim elegantly out of its path.

In the middle of the year you will meet someone terrific who wants to help you out - either financially or in some practical way. Accept the presence of this new character in your life graciously. This encounter doesn't look like a blazing love affair or even a fling. It's more likely to be someone older with more experience than you whose ideas will suddenly make sense. Listen to them. Heed their counsel. Then make a plan which correlates to what they have advised. This re-design of your lifestyle will be well worth whatever it costs in the way of shifting gears.

In early September, you may suffer from dizziness or headaches. Schedule a doctor's appointment for a full checkup. The symptoms you are experiencing are probably emotion-based. Passion will engulf you toward the end of the year. A surprise meeting with someone ultra attractive will bowl you over. If this is the start of new relation-ship, it should be safely in place by Christmas. You can kick back and enjoy sharing the holidays with your new love. sw

PISCES - January 2016

This month is a harbinger of wealth and prosperity for Fish people. There is, however, a catch – Mercury will be retrograde between Jan 5th and Jan 25th. Do keep your hard drive backed up. The highlights of the month include enhanced status and prestige at the workplace. The boss finally appreciates your work and hints at a reward coming your way. The domestic atmosphere is full of light and goodwill. Expect happy news from immediate family members too. A birth in the extended family is possible. Parents feel proud of your achievements and are lavish in their praise. You are in a better frame of mind now and can throw yourself into working and networking. You are scouting for mega projects and bigger money. Dreaming big – larger than life.

After Jan 12th, there may be discussions about selling some property that you or your partner inherited. Seek advice from friends. Prefer professionals who have already been doing this type of transaction for years. Why not consult an elderly relative who could give you solid, insider information on how the real estate market works? Caution however. Due to Mercury retrograde, it is advisable to postpone decisions about contracts till Jan 25th. You stand to make a solid profit now or even a couple of months from now – whatever you decide. No matter how much you need them, resist the urge to buy fancy electronic devices during Mercury retrograde. Electronics fail all too often during these phases.

22nd Jan and beyond indicates problems for you or for your spouse with an authority figure. The situation seems to be connected with a piece of property or a vehicle. Perhaps you receive a speeding ticket. Or your significant other gets a late fee notices from the property tax authorities. If you are obliged to meet with any official representatives, maintain your dignity and stay cool. Exercise both tact and prudence. Be at your diplomatic best. Respect and aplomb. The officer or functionary in questions may behave imperiously. Turn your tongue over 7 times before you utter a high-handed response. One snappy answer and you could find yourself entangled in an administrative basket of crabs.

PISCES -February 2016

The early part of February is dedicated to relationships. The harmonious ones, the unsettling ones, the silly ones, the work related ones have all got your number. You may be dragged in three or four different directions. And all this because of numerous commitments made to your colleagues, friends, your partner, your mom and so on.

Try to learn to say no. You will save yourself many headaches. Interpersonal dynamics are going to be on your agenda. The 5th to the 7th are better spent doing some indoor activity. The more intimate relationships at this time are the juiciest. Treat yourself and others with compassion. We are all here for each other to experience depth of feeling and soul connection.

Talking of soul connection - some of you will likely give way to temptation and enter into relationships around Valentine's Day. These sudden unions are mostly those that you later find difficult to get rid of. A tempestuous relationship that you recently entered could begin to look shaky around the 19th. If it suddenly snaps due to lack of interest from your lover, please don't say you weren't warned. In any case, it is unlikely that you will linger or look back. A minor financial issue between the 16th and the 20th may give you worry and heartburn. But it looks like you will be able to manage it after a little struggle juggling figures and even perhaps requesting a loan from someone near and dear.

A fun filled celebration with young ones in the family is indicated near this month's end. The reason for this is related to good news arriving between the 27th and the 29th. This party could either be about your own child or the child of someone fairly close to you. Perhaps they've been picked to represent their town or county in a sporting event. Or they've won a prize in some prestigious competition. Either way, festivities are planned. Even if you're on a diet, one night indulging won't set you back. Enjoy yourself.

PISCES - March 2016

Early March promises to be eventful. Choose carefully from the plethora of opportunities that come your way now. However, do not let yourself become so busy that you neglect your soulful side. If you do, you will grow frustrated and anxious. You require major periods of down time to chill and find your own direction. Any part-time job or volunteer project you began earlier this year begins to pick up momentum between the 7th and the 10th. Suddenly, your talents are being recognized. Your good work is receiving kudos and your opinions seem to be valued. Important people start seeking you out. It is also very likely that you are asked to join forces with them in another venture. Your creative projects can continue to supply you with a regular source of joy. This is a crucial time, which may well change the very course of your life and way of thinking. It is time to make fresh evaluations, assessments of goals and new orientations.

The week between 14th and 18th promises monetary gains. At the same time, you are developing stronger bonds of love with those that matter to you. A few meetings with loved ones will reinforce the feeling of companionship and togetherness. You could also find yourself wanting to delve deeper into spirituality and be moved to altruism. Try reading books on eastern mysticism and investigate past lives to satisfy your quest for more knowledge. If you have already been meditating, the dry spell you have been facing ends now. Now is the time to pursue your meditation with renewed zeal and intention. A close friend and acquaintance is intrigued by your learning and wants to explore and discuss these topics with you.

A dear friend of yours may be moving away in the last week of this month. For professional reasons, their move is necessary. You have had the pleasure of living and being emotionally close to this person for a number of years. He or she has given you lot of succor in times of distress. No doubt, there will be chances to visit each other in the future. But in the interim, you are likely to be affected deeply by this separation. And this one promises to be a teary farewell.

PISCES - April 2016

Romance rules early in April. If you are single, you will finally run into someone who steals your heart. What is more bizarre is that we are talking about someone you currently work with or have worked with earlier and had not yet noticed. It's only now that you realize that the person has been trying in subtle ways to gain your affection. He or she may play a much greater role in your life in future. This romance could be an opportunity for an unusual and unlikely combination of mind and spirit that could reach loftier dimensions. This unusual person will complement you and enhance your image or belief in self. Yes, there is a physical attraction. But at the same time, there is also something platonic and heartwarming about this friendly and loving relationship. Go out for coffee and on movie dates. Get to know each other as thoroughly as possible. This relationship will draw closer as you share dreams and discussions with each other.

Winds of change are blowing around the middle of this month. Someone at your workplace at the senior management level may be instrumental in providing you with an exciting new work opportunity between the 15th and the 20th. This could be a plum offer with a fantastic salary and benefits. With this proposal, you may also get the chance to travel and work out of a new and exotic destination for a couple of months. Taking up this project and work-related trip could mean missing a major family event. However you should not think twice. Say yes to the offer and express your sincerest regrets to family members.

A minor accident while driving is possible on the 24th. No injuries to you or anyone else are foreseen however. In light of this ambiance, drive more carefully and ensure that your vehicle insurance papers are up to date. Bones or teeth related issues could cause your partner lot of discomfort between the 27th and the 29th. Could be a tooth infection of which will result in a fair amount of pain and several trips to the dentist. Show compassion. Mercury is turning retrograde from the 28th of this month the 22nd of the next. Be prepared for communication and transportation glitches.

PISCES - May 2016

The current Mercury Retrograde has the potential to ruin many of your well-laid plans. Your partner may inadvertently play spoilsport and be a cause of cancellation of a pleasure trip. You could also be susceptible to fakes and fraudsters. Beware of smooth talkers. If someone comes to you with an investment proposal that sounds too good to be true, it probably is. Don't fall for it, no matter how much sugar coating they slap on. Likewise, if a gorgeous stranger seems too, too perfect, try to avoid falling for them. There are likely to be some severe chinks in their armor that you have not yet been able to discern. During these backward Mercury periods, things are often not as they appear. Most assuredly until after the 22nd, do not accept any binding romantic proposals - even if they come from a long-term partner. Events are likely to conspire against you and muddle everything. Even if you are sure about the decision you want to make, hold your horses. Delay it until after May 22nd.

Some of you have been contemplating a change of residence. The middle of this month and thereafter is the right time to start looking for properties. Check out the classifieds in the new area. East and North directions from your current residence are luckier at this time. Contact agents and question neighbors to make sure you are not moving to a less than savory neighborhood. Do not commit to anything till the Mercury goes direct again on May 22nd.

The last week of this month could bring some difficulties with your partner. One of you is feeling overloaded with work and future planning and is stressing the importance of cooking, cleaning, saving money and paying bills on time. The other of you just wants to have fun and worry about winter when it comes. There really is no middle ground. Long talks over quiet dinners at home may help balance the books between you. Music, art and dance also offer you serenity now. This is a terrific time to take guitar lessons, commune with nature by going for a long hike in the woods or taking in some live productions of plays or opera.

PISCES - June 2016

Celebrations are in the offing early in June. A close friend, colleague or relative gets married early this month. You are likely to be asked to lend a helping hand with arrangements and planning. You may also serve as best man or bridesmaid. An unexpected networking opportunity is likely to emerge on this occasion. And it will pay rich dividends for some time to come. You are sure to make some influential contacts. So keep your eyes and ears open while at the wedding. Stop, look and listen to each and every person to whom you are introduced. Talking of celebration, there is a significant birthday between the 7th and the 10th that you have probably forgotten. Rack your brain to recall whose birthday it is. Rather than firing off a text message or jotting a quick email, make an effort to talk with or see this person on or around their birthday. They have something crucial to reveal to you.

You have been carrying a few insolvent and emotionally dependent people on your back for much of this and last year. These may be co-workers, family members or friends. Between the 14th and the 19th you have confused feelings about retaining these dependencies. My advice? Start shrugging them off. They are slowing you down by taking advantage of your kindly nature. You like the feeling of being the rescuer. But you can't be responsible for everyone around you. If you want to maintain peace of mind and sanity, it's a good idea to teach yourself the difference between promising folks who need a leg up and hopeless cases. Make your peace with the idea that your charges will themselves benefit from being cut loose at this stage. Be gentle about letting them down. And try harder to stop picking up stragglers and trying to reform them.

The last week of this month sees you fending off advances from an ardent admirer. This person just won't quit or take no for answer. The best solution will be to make it perfectly clear verbally and in person that you are already deep into a felicitous, working relationship. If your partner is not known to this character, take steps to see that they meet. But if you are single, ask a friend to assume the role of your partner. No hurt feelings.

PISCES - July 2016

Pisces is a sign ruled by Jupiter – the planet of wisdom. It looks like you may be in a knowledge-sharing and teaching mode early in July. Some of you may be planning to provide some kind of tuition or classes in your favorite subject. Look around and see if there is an organization seeking adults to mentor or tutor young people. Also check to see if a community center or local library needs tutors for an after-school program. Maybe a professional organization in your field has a Big Brother or Sister program which can afford you the opportunity to share your expertise. This kind of volunteering is a marvelous way for you to offer others the benefit of your accumulated wisdom and not assume them as your full responsibility. You can inspire and offer practical advice to youngsters. The children or teenagers will benefit greatly from your help. Then they will go home to their parents. You can help. But you must not encourage dependency.

Mid July heralds an excellent phase to update and sharpen your own professional skills and continue some form of higher education for yourself. Many of you are likely to join weekend or evening courses in your areas of interest now. If tuition fees are an issue, look at free online learning tools from prestigious universities like Harvard, MIT, Yale, Purdue and the like. Their excellent courses can be taken at your own pace. There are innumerable subjects to choose from.

A lucrative investment opportunity falls in your lap between the 22nd and the 29th. However you may be faced with several choices. Only one out of these selections might be worth the effort. Do research. Don't jump into any investments suddenly. Talk to someone who knows the subject. Do your due diligence. Study up on the companies and individuals involved. Curb your enthusiasm till you know you are putting your money somewhere safe. Having said this, there is an excellent chance of your chosen placement paying off handsomely in the next two years.

PISCES - August 2016

The focus between the 3rd and the 9th August is on food, health and nutrition. Many of you may be worried about your weight around this time. You may come across an informative article or watch a TV program that inspires you to think in this direction. Taking some steps to reduce unhealthy fat and boost your metabolism is really not a bad idea. Eat fresh, seasonal fruits to aid your digestion and boost energy the natural way. Choose fresh juices over canned ones and avoid all carbonated drinks and sodas. If you happen to be over 40, adding a broad spectrum multivitamin to your daily diet will go a long way to keeping you fit. Focus especially on getting enough iron, Vitamin D and vitamin B12. Deficiency in any one of these can develop into fatigue, muscle loss and/or insomnia.

You may misplace an essential or valuable item on the 12th or the 13th. Could be your car or house keys, the TV remote or even your wallet. It may also be an item of jewelry. Do not spend more than a couple of hours sniffing about on a hunt. It is unlikely you are going to find it yourself. Recruit a helper. Or assemble a search party. Others will probably have more luck than you in this case. The days from the 15th to the 18th are likely to be spent concentrating on hobbies. Some dilemma or niggling issue that has been perturbing you for quite some time will all of a sudden untangle itself on the 19th. The simplicity of the solution will make you laugh.

Many of you are contemplating shifting to a new location now. A short reconnaissance trip between the 25th and the 27th will help you set markers for a future, more permanent place to abide. Be especially aware of the effect the new venue has on your mood. Your state of mind when you visit this new location will indicate whether a long-term move is a wise idea. Mercury is going retrograde on the 30th. There is nothing to be afraid of, but a little planning on how to tackle this phase will save you unnecessary headaches.

PISCES - September 2016

Mercury is retrograde from the 30th of August to the 21$^{st \, of}$ this month. All communication devices could backfire now. This might manifest simply as malfunction or theft of your mobile phone. Or it might be more involved - an email regarding your new work responsibilities disappearing into the recycle bin instead of reaching you. The key is to be patient and not force any issues. Somehow you don't seem to be clicking with your friends and your usual circle of cronies now. You may think they are avoiding you. But in truth, the feeling is not coming from them. It's just that you are in a social slumps and do not derive much pleasure right now from mingling. You would be wise to wait until you are in a better frame of mind before deciding to throw anyone out of your life and/or your heart.

There is a good chance that you will receive a gift, inheritance or legacy between the 12th and the 17th. If it happens, refrain from any grand plans to invest in a startup business. In other words, do not invest this precious gift in anything which cannot guarantee success. Solicit advice from a professional money manager. A visit to the doctor is in the cards now. Schedule an appointment. The headaches and blurred vision you have been dealing with lately could prove to herald something serious. Your once-a-year checkup is probably overdue. It's probably nothing. But do make sure the doctor orders all the appropriate tests.

Mercury retrograde ends on the 21st. Some important documents that may have required your attention earlier should come up for discussion after this. They, more than likely, relate to a business venture offer. Or a job contract. Read over them carefully. There will be some things you want altered before you sign them. Anything you leave in right now could cause future headaches. Look at all sides. Spend a more time with family now. Enjoy a romantic evening with your partner. Or take the family out for a picnic at a nearby scenic location. This is a perfect time to show them how much you care.

PISCES - October 2016

From the 4th to the 9th of October a peculiar hallucinating effect enters you mind. You may suddenly become jealous and possessive. Even though you don't have any concrete evidence, you imagine your partner could be two-timing you. Why should you trust them? Why not follow them and find out the truth? Or you might start worrying about others in the family. You may either begin spying on a sibling or on one of your older kids. You could be convinced that he or she is up to horrendous things on weekends. Perhaps they are into drugs or they are going to squander away your inheritance at the slot machines. Or could it be the health of an older relative that is preoccupying you? My advice here? Your imagination is working overtime. Stop obsessing.

While you may actually be able to stem the negative thoughts after the 9th, your mind turns in another direction after the 12th. Some secret desires and fantasies might start hounding you day and night. This is a time you will look back on someday, smiling and saying to yourself, "My God!! What was I thinking?" Consider everything you get up to very carefully now. Don't make hasty decisions. Do you really want to quit your steady job and pursue your dream to become a famous actor in Hollywood? Are you sure you want to buy that swanky car? I would advise you to wait a couple of weeks before leaping into any radical projects. If your current thoughts are correct, there will still be time to act on them next month. If, however, your visions are misguided, you will save yourself a lot of trouble by postponing things.

You may be approached by a close friend or associate for financial assistance between the 23rd to the 26th. This person has a penchant for

197

getting into trouble with finances. The ironic part is that they will present their request for money as an opportunity for you to do something useful. You know better. Say "Sorry but No." You must balance compassion with discipline. Don't give the impression that you are always willing to lend help and support without any hesitation. Otherwise, you could find yourself facing ever more harrowing "emergencies" from this source in the future. Be charitable. But don't be a fool.

PISCES - November 2016

November is heralding creativity, expression, fresh new sources of income and better finances. Those who are looking for employment will find it now. The 3rd to the 8th sees you making valuable new contacts and steady progress in whatever you undertake. A few necessary expenses you had been avoiding earlier will now be easily met by you. Bank accounts, tax or estate related matters are satisfactory. It may be a good idea to keep your own counsel about money now. Some form of speculation is likely to come your way this month. Investing your savings in long-term stocks can provide good returns over the next couple of years. Why not use some Feng-Shui tips for enhancing prosperity at your home? Hang some lilies or lotus pictures in your living room. They are said to increase luck, prosperity and positive energy in the environment. Now that you have tasted some success and improvement with your finances, you might start thinking of new ways to make money. A desire for upward mobility will motivate you at work between the 8th and the 14th.

"Fitness" is the mantra for mid November. You are going to suddenly find this word staring at you everywhere – from the TV, in the newspapers, in books as well as casual conversations with friends. This is the perfect time to start an exercise regime for those who are not into it yet. There will be plenty of encouragement from friends and your partner. Join a nearby gym and make sure you get a good trainer who can give you a few valuable tips. Beginning and ending your routine with a stretch will assist in toxin removal and increase oxygen levels in your cells. Exercising along with your partner can make it an even more fulfilling experience.

From the 23rd to the 24th, you may again be feeling concern for an elderly relative. This person was close to you years back. Now, some distance separates you. He or she could be feeling blue in late November. This gloom is probably related to the anniversary or the birthday of a lost loved one. Your older family member will be feeling especially vulnerable at this time. Call them more often. Pay them more visits and take along presents you know they will be grateful for.

PISCES - December 2016

You may receive an unexpected opportunity to draw on a hidden artistic talent of yours between the 4th to the 7th of this month. A friend may ask you to use your photography talents to make them look lovely for a dating site profile. Or someone sees the canvas you painted and gifted a dear friend and asks if you want to sell your creations at their store. Maybe your dance teacher asks you to substitute teach a class when she goes out of town. This opportunity could provide another source of income for you. So do say yes. You may be out of town on a short business trip between the 13th to the 15th. This trip will turn out well for your future.

Mercury backpedals again on the 19th of this month. Financial iregularities at home and office are likely to trouble you during this retrograde. Read the fine print on any documents related to business or property matters with excruciating precision. Delay signing anything of importance. These retrograde periods of the planet ruling communication and travel are the worst possible times for making long-term commitments. Do not accept committee assignments or board appointments. Avoid engaging in activities that don't inspire you. Intensify your meditation practice. Get more fresh air. If you can avoid being drawn into boring pursuits, you will fare better. Avoid drudgery. Use this time to concoct plans and research future projects.

You may be in a slightly pensive and reflective mood during the last week of this month. Planets show that you are interested in learning a new language. If you do try, you will succeed at your attempt rather easily. It may also be that you are introduced around this time to someone who has native level proficiency in the language that interests you. Research has shown that learning a new language strengthens your brain. Find some free language tutorials online and start practicing your new language at your own pace. If things go well and your interest sustains, you may want to attend a language school to secure a proper diploma.

PISCES - January 2017

Mercury continues to be retrograde till the 8th of January. Partnerships – both in business and love will be the area of focus. Be as non-judgmental as you can with a business partner. There may be a need to revisit old issues in a partnership. You can initiate a dialogue now, though it may take some time to resolve everything. If your current relationship is not running smoothly, make a joint list of all the areas you two need to work on. You two may be forced to come to terms with a painful reality. It's time to make a meaningful decision about this relationship. If after much discussion, it looks hopeless, it may be time to move on

The 14th to the 18th is a propitious time to ask for a promotion or a bonus. You are more than ready to shoulder additional responsibility. Your leadership skills will leap to the forefront this month. You will be pleased to note they serve as an inspiration to a growing group of followers. Your normally not-so-friendly boss is ready to recommend your name to the senior management. Your head is also going to be buzzing with business ideas this month. Keep a close eye on trade journals and classified ads. You may come across some fantastic investment opportunities.

Pisceans are known to have spiritual tendencies. You may suddenly find yourself drawn to some occult or metaphysical subjects after the 25th. Your intuition and understanding of spiritual concepts will expand to a new level. A friend or acquaintance could invite you to a spiritual retreat involving yoga and meditation. Try and go, as the experience will be both revelatory and comforting. Some participation in charitable activities is also possible now. This is a good time to donate old clothes, toys and books to charity.

YOUR MONTHLY FORECASTS
FOR THE 12 CHINESE SIGNS
FOR THE FIRE MONKEY YEAR 2016

YOUR MONTHLY FORECASTS FOR THE FIRE MONKEY YEAR

2016

RAT

Author's Note... Mercury Retrograde

Sometimes planets appear to be zooming backward through the zodiac. Of course this backward motion is only an illusion. The planet has not turned tail. But it appears to have. Astrologers call this apparent reversing: **"retrograde"**.

Any planet can be retrograde. But only Mercury's retrogrades cause communications to break down. Mercury has its retrograde period for a few weeks 3 or 4 times each year. Whilst Mercury is retrograde, we humans are encouraged to take stock, make plans and discuss different approaches to a variety of subjects. But because information is often muddled, promises broken and electronic devices on the blink during Mercury retrograde, we must remain flexible and open-minded. Advice? Always allow extra time for travel. Schedule changes are common. Do not sign any contracts or cement agreements during Mercury retrograde. Make no irreversible promises. Watch out for con artists. Make no final decisions, binding engagements or major purchases during a Mercury retrograde. You are allowed to have tantrums or rail against your fate. But Mercury will continue to be retrograde till it decides to go direct again.

Mercury Retrogrades
2016

January 5 thru January 25
April 28 thru May 22
August 30 thru September 22
December 19 thru January 8 2017

OVERVIEW OF 2016 THE YEAR OF THE MONKEY FOR THE RAT

Forceful Rat,

Here comes fun! You and the Monkey always hit it off. Monkeys are partial to surprises and excitement. They take kindly to movement and enjoy action for its own sake. Monkeys are social animals. But . . . unlike you Rats, Monkeys don't really care about power. They are willing back seat drivers who prefer to lurk in the wings solving problems and serving as the "brains" behind an operation.

So in Monkey years, you are free to take charge again. Go after that seat on the board. Run for office. Try to become the president of the world. Go after the power and you shall most likely receive your wish. One quick cautionary note: be prepared to be obliged to flatter a family member who is most decidedly not on your team. The person in question may only be a distant cousin or a nephew by marriage (could be Horse or Snake), but they are of a jealous nature and will do whatever they can to bend your spokes. As they are sensitive to adulation and praise, go ahead and slather it on. sw

RAT January 2016

January has Mercury moving backwards from the 5th until the 25th. There can be dicey communication problems. This is the perfect time to start a new non-verbal project. Or to finish an old one. Those bathroom floor tiles you always swore you would replace? No time like the present. That thousand-piece jigsaw puzzle you always wanted to make into a coffee table? Take another crack at it. It is also an excellent time to do some cleaning and clearing. But be careful what you throw away. You run the risk of overlooking something valuable. Did Granddad tuck his life savings into an old shoe before he passed? Is that dull little vase actually a priceless heirloom? Better check each item twice.

The middle of January is an ideal time to surround yourself with youthful fun. If you have children, take them to a park or a silly movie. If you do not have any kids of your own, borrow someone else's for the day. Or take a niece or nephew. Better yet, invite your neighbor, the single parent. Eat sticky foods with your fingers. Laugh till your sides hurt. It will wipe the wrinkles off your face and prepare your spirit for the coming year. After all, a Monkey year is in the pipeline. The Monkey is one of your favorite playmates.

The Sheep year ends with happy news. A wedding or an engagement is on the horizon. You will be invited. You may even be a major character in the event. But this is no ordinary celebration. It includes travel. Perhaps one of the partners is from a foreign country. Or they have simply chosen an exotic location for the ceremony - a safari or a tropical paradise event. Remember to take your sunscreen, Make a copy of your passport. If you lose the real thing, you have proof of ID. Be sure you have the all the necessary vaccinations.

RAT February 2016

The Monkey Year bounds into your life. Luckily for you, Rats and Monkeys get along. You should have a warm, fuzzy feeling about this partnership. A leadership opportunity has opened up in your life. In all likelihood, this vacancy will appear in your workplace. Perhaps one of your bosses is about to move on (whether they want to or not). As a qualified candidate with a burning desire to head the pack, do not be surprised if the powers-that-be turn to you as a solution. Make the most of this opportunity. After all, you are no reluctant general. This advancement has long been your dream!

Perhaps a painless transition will occur. If your company is expanding, management positions are soon to open up across the board. And the executives prefer to promote from within. Chances are, they have already noted any outstanding employees. Put yourself in the shoes of a hiring manager. Which would you rather do? Post a job opening, sift through hundreds of unqualified candidates, and risk hiring a sociopath anyway? Or promote a known reliable commodity from within? You can be that known commodity! You have already laid the foundation through your excellent performance. Now, you must sharpen your attention to detail. Learn the names and personalities of your boss' bosses. Volunteer for a difficult assignment. If your place of work has an annual day of service, sign up for a leadership position. Anything to stand out from the crowd. Management is always watching (if they are smart).

Your family situation seems stable. Relations with your significant other? Nothing but tranquil waters. Not surprising then that the siblings have not been bickering either. But all is not as it seems. Mounded by lush, fertile soil, the familial volcano lies dormant today. Sunny skies inspire a feeling of safety. But trouble lies ahead. Tomorrow (or three months from now) brings an unexpected eruption. Your climb to success will cause some ripples. Remember and heed this advice —Where there's a yin there's a yang - and it's just around the corner. One person's ascent breeds another person's resentment. So keep an eye on your back!

RAT March 2016

You are soon to discover one of the main themes of the Monkey Year. Let's call it Surprises. A familiar face reappears in front of you in early March. No. This apparition is no mirage. Perhaps you will bump into an ex. One whom you still have unresolved feelings for. Things ended poorly between the two of you. Actually, let's be honest. People could see the fireworks from ten towns over. But that unfortunate scene is in the past. Now, you both simply need closure. Seeking that catharsis does not necessarily translate to "start dating again." However, maybe you two can make a serviceable pair of friends. After all, who knows you more thoroughly than they do? And vice versa..

Someone in your family is putting pressure on you to clean up your house or apartment. Your entertaining rooms look passable. But away from the judgmental eyes of your guests, a heap of junk is stuffed away somewhere. This landfill could be squeezed into a closet, basement or attic. Who knows when you might need that set of multicolored pipe cleaners? Or when your grandfather's old set of scratched binoculars could come in handy? One of your Rat tendencies is to hold on to your old things. All of them. You are thrifty by nature, after all. Unfortunately, your current inclinations have left you a few years away from becoming the resident hoarder of your neighborhood. So heed your relative's words of wisdom. Recruit a friend. Take a Sunday afternoon to go through all your old garbage together. How to discern what is true crap and what should be kept? Trust me. Your companion will give you an unbiased (even brutally honest) opinion in that respect.

Inner tension has always been a health concern for you. Close friends and family know your nervous tics well. A leg constantly bopping up and down. Teeth constantly gnawing on gum or a pen cap. These telltale signs merely hint at the strength of the energy bubbling beneath the surface of your placid face. That energy has been and will continue to be a source of strength. But especially for my older Rats, the pressure wears on you. Take this opportunity to discover a new pastime. Golf, clichéd as it is, can be both calming and competitive. Even a new card game. Just take up something to alleviate that agitation.

RAT April 2016

Your reach for power at work is heating up. A new position is yours for the taking. If no one has offered you anything yet, take matters into your own hands. Traipse into your manager's office. Let him or her know that you are interested in the open position. If you feel so emboldened, relate a quick list of attributes that would make you a top performer in the job. This directness will do wonders for your career, at least this year. Ask, and you shall receive!

The financial cases of multimillionaire athletes are well-documented. Often, when someone overcomes the odds and breaks out of their economic strictures in a huge way, there can be negative consequences. Family members come out of the woodwork with their hands out. What? You don't remember that time cousin Will drove you to football practice? Or the pair of sneakers that Aunt Gracie bought you when your mother could not afford them? You may not (yet) be privy to such riches. Still, you have done well for yourself. Not everyone in your family has been so lucky. Be on the lookout for a greedy, entitled relative. As they gaze upon your success, they hunger for a piece of the pie. If you refuse it? Their jealousy will soon surface. Tread carefully. Let your words be as sweet as honey and as smooth as top-dollar whiskey. A tip? Go out of your way to praise this person's intelligence. Openly admire their "success." It may seem a cheap trick, but flattery may be the only way to avoid a sabotage attempt on your career.

On a positive note, your social calendar is filled to the brim this month. It is always cathartic to spend time with your friends. Especially for a social Rat such as yourself. Plus, you have been busting your butt during the week. Take care not to overdo it with the hard liquor though. You cannot ease your inner tension by getting roaring drunk. The distraction may work wonders at the time. But the next day will be more awful than the previous. Mentally and physically. Instead, take a healthy approach. Call on a friend you can trust to listen. Talk about your feelings and anxieties with them. Even if such candor makes you uncomfortable. Do it. Relieve the tension by talking things through.

RAT May 2016

On April 28, Mercury slips into that period of lunacy we call retrograde. He remains in that orbit until May 22. This is a critical juncture for you, Rat. As always, communication becomes murky. People's good intentions can be garbled as soon as they open their mouths. That means you should put off signing any important documents or making any life-changing decisions. So no lease or contract endorsing. Unless of course your career makes such activity unavoidable.

Still trying to get a toe in the managerial door? The higher-ups might choose the middle of this month to offer you that promotion. There is a caveat, however. The new position is in another town. Not so far that you would be forced to relocate. But far enough to require a massive daily commute from your current residence. This conundrum leaves you in a precarious position. Do you uproot your family? Or do you accept a galling daily travel? Keep in mind—Mercury is in retrograde. So ask the hiring manager by which date he or she needs an answer. If the deadline is after the 22nd, you are in luck. Delay your decision until then. Otherwise, you risk having the planet obfuscate your words. And you want to be on exactly the same page with your family when discussing your shared future.

How long has it been since your last vacation? Late May presents an ideal opportunity for a weekend getaway. Bring your significant other. Schedule some physical activities where you can avoid verbal communication. A horseback ride through the forest? Fits the bill. Attending a sports match? That could work. As long as this event is something your partner will also enjoy. Currently bereft of a romantic companion? Gather up some close friends and hit the town. Who knows, perhaps someone will catch your fancy. And who better to talk up your better qualities than your old compatriots?

RAT June 2016

As June dawns, you can anticipate a full month outside the scope of Mercury's bizarre influence. In spite of that freedom, you face some choppy seas in the office or workplace. Especially if you have been newly elevated to a position of power. You must learn the ropes anew. Your old peers do not understand your new responsibilities. They cannot help you get acclimated. Plus, in a higher post, you are duty-bound to treat people differently now. That change may rub some of your colleagues the wrong way. In addition, unbeknownst to you, a coworker you are close to also applied for your new job. He or she is bitter that you were chosen over them. So do not expect much help from your former office allies in your new duties. Instead, look to your new peers for advice and examples of how to conduct yourself. Better yet, ask someone at a similar level at another company how they handled their promotion. Their answer will help you succeed without revealing your confusions to your superiors.

Rats may reach a turning point in their romantic relationships in mid-June. A Rat needs a partner with high standards to match them in bed and live up to their deep sense of commitment. You have had some doubts about your partner. These worries have been floating around the back of your mind for some time now. An incident is soon to bring these questions to the forefront. Perhaps they will cancel plans on the eve of an anniversary dinner. Or... after spending six hours on the couch watching TV, they might claim they are too exhausted for lovemaking. Use this stimulus as a chance for some introspection. Is this person really the one for you? Love is a vital component of the answer, of course. But so is compatibility.

Remember that family member who was having trouble coming to terms with your success back in April? Well, the flattery with which you temporarily assuaged their feelings has worn off. This person is spreading vicious (but vaguely believable) rumors about you behind your back. Do not be surprised if another relative asks whether you are actually having an affair. Or whether you slept with your boss to get promoted. The time for delicacy with this jealous person has ended. Until you can confront him or her in person, offer them the cold shoulder. Do not speak, write or call them. Such silence may seem petty. But fear not. Your chance for redemption will come. Sooner rather than later.

RAT July 2016

As we are well aware, you rarely lack for friends or admirers. Your personal magnetism extends to people you barely know. Making and spending time with new friends is fine. But do not neglect your inner circle. Without them, you are merely a social butterfly with a secret loneliness. So set aside some time early in July to demonstrate your thanks and appreciation for your family's support. Have your children always clamored to go to a Disney theme park? Acquiesce (even if it breaks the bank). Besides, your kids will have a little less ammunition to throw at their therapist in twenty years.

Your finances are also performing well. Part of that is to be expected, what with your career advances. Still, be careful to put your money in smart places. IRAs, 401ks—they may not sound sexy now. But you never know when your income might dry up. Smart investments always pay dividends. They will provide you with a safety net, should life throw you a curveball. Want to become an English professor after twenty years as an accountant? Need to move to Jamaica to marry the man or woman of your dreams? If you have made good choices with your money, these challenges become less daunting.

As the weeks pass, the family silence lengthens. Now you have aunts and nephews ringing you up. *Can you* please *give Relative X a call? I cannot stand having a rift in this family! Whatever shall we do during the holidays?* Be polite, but firm with these meddlers. You were not the one slinging mud behind the other's back. Continue to bide your time. It is your relative's duty to extend the olive branch. Allow them a month to do so. There is hope yet. After all, you know that he or she is a reasonable person deep down. But still. If worse comes to worst, you still have that upcoming family reunion or gathering to talk things out face-to-face.

RAT August 2016

As August starts off, your neighborhood or local area is having some community problems. Perhaps a construction company is damaging the environment with their reckless drilling. Or maybe the issues are on a smaller scale. The mayor could be threatening to eliminate the annual town parade. Which happens to be the longest running such event around. Remember that you are in a Monkey year, Rat! Now is your chance to grab power. Consider running for local office. If local pollutants are your concern, host a town hall meeting. Become the focal point of the resistance. You have always had the ability and desire to lead. Now, with the stars aligned, you have the ability to make a difference!

On the home front, your extended family is gathering this month for an impromptu meeting. This reunion is due more to happenstance than a long-term plan. Several relatives happen to be staying in the same town at once. You know what that means...coming face-to-face with your feuding partner. Remain calm. You have the moral upper hand. We already know that this person is sensitive to adulation. If flattery assuaged them once, why can't it again? So assure this person that your success is entirely due to their influence. Stretch those vocal chords. Bend the truth. Citing facts is not important in this situation. If they feel responsible for your success, their jealousy will dissipate. They might even shock the whole room and apologize publicly for their rumor mongering. Just like that, months of familial iciness will come to a halt. The rest of your clan can breathe a deep sigh of relief.

The end of the month may usher in some minor health nuisances. Be careful trekking up and down stairs. You are in danger of a slip. And take it easy with your social schedule. Back-to-back-to-back parties will devastate your immune system. Plus, Mercury retrograde is approaching on August 30. So now would be an especially bad time to get stuck in the hospital. If you are relying on doctors and nurses to medicate and treat you, their communication needs to be checked and re-checked for clarity.

RAT September 2016

Unfortunately, my dear Rat, early September reveals your first slip-up in your new position. Until now, the transition into your new role has been remarkably smooth. But your boss is soon to assign you a project that you do not understand in the slightest. Resist the urge to ask him or her for help. That might indicate weakness. He or she could be looking for a reason to explode at you. Instead, accept the new task. Head back to your desk or table. Once there, go ahead and seek advice from your peers. Choose the ones you consult with care. Some folks could use this event against you one day.

As I mentioned in August, Mercury is in backwards orbit and will remain so until September 22. As usual, systems of communication will be difficult to decipher. This particularly affects family matters. You might come home to dinner on a seemingly innocent night in mid-September. To your surprise, there are no smiles around the table. Only glares coupled with a weighty silence. When prompted, your loved ones insist that nothing is wrong. You press further, but to no avail. Perhaps you can chalk this silence up to Mercury's negativity. But take note of it nonetheless. There are underlying problems in your inner circle which will, of course, surface at some point. Forewarned is fore-armed.

As you have little hope of accomplishing anything positive with words right now, why not retreat into the hobby you picked up in March? It can provide an opportunity for self-reflection and planning for the future. Go to a driving range and slam some golf balls into outer space. Take a long walk on your own to gather your thoughts. To include loved ones, you might host a family cards tournament. Poker, Cuarenta, even Go Fish. Keep the stakes light. Especially if children are involved. Such a tournament can be a great technique to bring the family together having to discuss thornier issues.

RAT October 2016

You have always been preternaturally fidgety and nervous in private. But lately, the pressures of your new career position have compounded your anxiety. The pressure is building inside you. By early October you need to find an outlet for it. Fast. And I do not mean using alcohol or drugs for temporary relief. That would be damaging to your family, your bank account and your personal health. You are a person who must talk through events - if only to figure out how you feel about them. Find someone discreet - a word-sponge who has broad shoulders you can cry on. Perhaps a valued relative or trusted friend. However, if you want to prevent people you know from worrying about you, talk to a professional. Shrinks are paid to provide a non-judgmental ear. And to give knowledgeable opinions. They possess professional solutions. Don't think you will shock a psychologist. They have heard it all before and have helped people to work things out to their advantage.

You will find your newfound calm cathartic. As you pull out of your own head, you subtly begin to notice the vibes around you. Things that you had completely missed before. In mid-October, you may finally realize that someone in your family is in trouble. Perhaps your son or daughter has been struggling with schoolwork. Embarrassed to tell the parents, he or she is despondent. Or maybe an aging parent has been hiding a medical issue. When you ring up Mom or Dad, you may observe that he is struggling to remember names and places. Is their memory starting to slip? Thanks to your observation, you can get him or her started immediately on a proactive course of medication. Now you know what you didn't before - these vital issues were causing all the unexplained familial tension in September. The rest of your family had recognized the problems. But you, imprisoned in your stress bubble, had missed the signs.

Set aside some time at the end of the month to relax. This is the calm before the storm. The next few months will be more difficult. Your job will be busier as the year draws to a close. So grab time now to read a good book. Catch up on your favorite television series. Binge-watch it, if you want to. Revel in your newfound mental peace. Luckily you have stockpiled a lot of goodwill and positive power. You may need to tap into your reserves to finish the year on a high note.

RAT November 2016

Pressure mounts at work as the end of the year nears. All of a sudden, deadlines loom larger in your vision. It had seemed like you had all the time in the world to finish your projects. Now, you curse yourself for your procrastination. But you already know the remedy. You will need to put in some late nights at the office. Your family might not adore that. But there is a positive angle to not being home as much. If you have teenage children, your absence will provide them a useful lesson on how to take care of themselves. Without mom or dad hovering over them 24/7, they will be obliged to cook their own meals, wash their own laundry, etc. Just be sure to tip a neighbor off to your plans. You do not want to arrive home from work to a raucous party in your living room!

The finances of someone in your family/social circle are about to plummet. Perhaps a relative has been fired. Or maybe the bank has foreclosed on someone's house. Tread carefully here, Rat. We know that you cannot stand to be in second place. At this point, you are a clear first. You are the most successful person in your immediate family. So act the part. Demonstrate some class. Do not grate on everyone's ears with anecdotal tales of your own triumphs. Such self-referencing comes across as condescending. Your task is simpler. Provide a sympathetic ear to vent to. A shoulder to cry on, even. If you can pull this off, your clan will appreciate it and return the favor one day when you need them to listen.

Rats are sometimes prone to fits of foolish spending. Out of character for one so thrifty? Perhaps. But all the same predictable. One such urge is set to hit you at the end of November. Perhaps you will feel a calling to purchase two large lion statues to line your driveway or to build a home cinema in your basement. Try to turn this foolish impulse into something positive and practical. Is there a gift for which your significant other has been begging for years? Or a kitchen or bath that desperately needs renovation? So happens that now is the perfect time to buy those diamond earrings or a fancy computer. Better still, invest in a new furnace or fix the roof. Spend on something that provides actual long-lasting value.

RAT December 2016

As December thunders in, your significant other has a favor to ask of you. He or she wants to get their business plan off the ground. Maybe your wife is trying to start a daycare facility. Or perhaps your husband is attempting to get a do-it-yourself publishing house started. How can you help? Specifically, they require your Rat charm. It could be that the neighborhood building committee is vetoing plans to break ground on a new structure. Or the publishing firm needs the backing of some wealthy investors. So it is time to put your schmooze hat on. As you float through your various social circles, see if you can convince a rich crony to invest. Or influence a businessperson to change his or her vote to pro-build. I am sure you can think of something. Any self-respecting Rat can wangle for gain.

When you have a chance, check up on your stock or bond investments. You are in for a pleasant surprise. Your gains may have exceeded predictions. That is the reward for smart investments in July. Do resist the urge to withdraw your money now. It is not necessarily wise to pull out while you are ahead. This is not a game of poker. Let your slow-growing investments increase at their own speed. There will be more years of plenty such as this. Unfortunately, there will also be periods of famine. Keep your long-term goals in mind. To use another cheesy analogy: the tortoise wins the race! Not the hare.

Just as you thought you could escape 2016 without additional unforeseen problems, Mercury retrograde rears its ugly head again. From December 19 to January 8, specifically. You know the drill. Methods of communication may dry up. Or at least become warped beyond belief. During this period, avoid fighting with family. Especially your partner. Your words can too easily be twisted. Yes, the mystifying effect will terminate in January. But the damage from the argument will not. So if you have a problem, use nonverbal cues to settle it for the time being. Hugs, cuddling, lovemaking. Wait until the next month to verbalize your feelings. Meanwhile, keep a weather eye out for electronic failures.

RAT January 2017

Holiday celebrations bring the best parts of your Rat nature to the forefront: multiple opportunities to socialize, schmooze, and meet new people. Just what the doctor ordered for an overworked Rat. So make the rounds. Live it up. But remember to bring your significant other along to some of the events. Sometimes he or she can feel left on the sidelines as your social command takes over a room. Including him or her (and making them a key cog in the festivities) will maintain goodwill between you. If you lack a partner... with your charm and charisma, you will not be lonely for long. With all the fiestas you are attending, you are likely to meet someone will who figure prominently in your life in 2017. Under the mistletoe? Or during an unexpected New Year's kiss.

In mid-January, set aside a day of solitude. Rid yourself of distractions. As the Monkey Year comes to a close, take stock of the advances you have made. The Monkey gave you an opportunity to seize some power in your life. And you did, rising to a new position. Or at least to some new responsibilities in your career. You survived a familial sabotage attempt. Pretty heady stuff. After you have reflected on the past, set some goals for the future. What would you like to accomplish during the Rooster Year? With your ambitious nature, I am certain you have multiple intentions. Then, brainstorm some concrete plans to reach those objectives. Write down your ideas. Your notes can help guide you if you lose your way during the feisty Rooster year.

One last note. That pesky relative? The one who gave you so many problems this past year? That volcano remains dormant, not extinct. When someone has that many blatant insecurities, they need constant reassurance of their self-worth. So be aware—if you continue to enjoy career success, you may need to repeatedly slather praise on that person's ego. It's not necessary to be less ambitious with your career or finances. But do keep on eye on that problem child. Something tells me he or she is not finished causing you grief.

YOUR MONTHLY FORECASTS FOR THE FIRE MONKEY YEAR

2016

OX

Author's Note... Mercury Retrograde

Sometimes planets appear to be zooming backward through the zodiac. Of course this backward motion is only an illusion. The planet has not turned tail. But it appears to have. Astrologers call this apparent reversing: **"retrograde"**.

Any planet can be retrograde. But only Mercury's retrogrades cause communications to break down. Mercury has its retrograde period for a few weeks 3 or 4 times each year. Whilst Mercury is retrograde, we humans are encouraged to take stock, make plans and discuss different approaches to a variety of subjects. But because information is often muddled, promises broken and electronic devices on the blink during Mercury retrograde, we must remain flexible and open-minded. Advice? Always allow extra time for travel. Schedule changes are common. Do not sign any contracts or cement agreements during Mercury retrograde. Make no irreversible promises. Watch out for con artists. Make no final decisions, binding engagements or major purchases during a Mercury retrograde. You are allowed to have tantrums or rail against your fate. But Mercury will continue to be retrograde till it decides to go direct again.

Mercury Retrogrades
2016

January 5 thru January 25
April 28 thru May 22
August 30 thru September 22
December 19 thru January 8 2017

OVERVIEW OF 2016 THE YEAR OF THE MONKEY FOR THE OX

Powerful Ox,

This Fire Monkey year bodes plenty of activity and a speeding up of pace for you Oxen. I know you hate to be told to move faster. But . . . Monkeys have no time to waste standing around tapping their feet whilst you Oxen ponder and plod through mountains of what Monkeys consider useless details, paperwork and administrative BS. Monkeys see a problem and get right to the core of it, solve it and get on to the next one. So you will have to drop the spreadsheets, abandon your precious red tape and learn to hurry. And (because you are hell bent on getting ahead no matter what) you will pick up speed. This, hectic cadence however may take its toll on your health. Be sure, during this Monkey year, to get regular checkups and tests for everything that can go wrong with Oxen (esp. digestion-related ills). Bottom line? You will thrive in a Monkey year because the Monkey is cleverer than all of us and knows when he has found a sane, safe ally. That cohort, my dear Ox friend, is none other than you. This year will be fruitful and you will not be sabotaged or refused much of anything. You will, however, have to pick up those clodhoppers of yours and get a move on. sw

OX January 2016

Wretched Mercury returns to retrograde orbit from the 5th to the 25th. What should you do to best mitigate the problems associated with this period? Stay in bed and avoid all encounters with other human beings. Or run away to a tropical island (preferably a deserted one). Obviously, most of us cannot accomplish either of these feats. The best you can do is to avoid long distance travel, be patient with communication glitches and postpone signing important documents until the month is over. As we move toward the new Monkey year, things will pick up pace. Brace yourself for sudden change, often at a second's notice. This starts with unexpected phone calls or letters. A painful family secret might be revealed around the 8th. It will hurt, but everyone is strangely relieved to have it out in the open. Finally, the healing can begin.

You have to work hard to assert your independence around the middle of the month. This applies to your work or business. You have been underestimating your ability to achieve success. It's time to toss those insecurities to the curb. Spread your wings. The take off will be bumpy at first, but you will be flying high soon enough. More sudden change arrives with news of a farewell. Someone you love and respect is moving far away. This is a charismatic person, confident and urbane. You look up to him or her with awe. This acquaintance has been there for you during many difficult periods in your life. Yes, you will miss them. But in the process of moving on, you will discover your own strength. Constant support can sometimes become a crutch.

Finances are somewhat volatile this month. Money comes and goes. Often at a speed which leaves you breathless. This is especially true if you have recently started a new business. Do not panic. The ship will right itself before the bank takes your home. In fact, the fast pace of events may leave you quite exhausted by the end of January. Set aside a day for total rest and solitude. Plug in your earphones. Lose yourself in some soothing music for a few hours. Run a hot bath and soak in relaxing scented oils. Avoid all phone calls. Sip some of your finest wines and plot your next coup.

OX February 2016

The FIRE Monkey Year is upon you! Oxen and Monkeys could not be more different. Oxen are methodical in their pursuits. Monkeys—well, they don't have time for any of that deliberation. The year will turn out best for you if you compromise your natural tendencies. You are already set in your ways at your current job. But a change of scenery would allow you to shake things up. Is there a lateral move available at your company? Perhaps you can simply rearrange your office furniture. If you lack an office, search for a new spot to get your work done. After this shift, you can accelerate your pace to match the Monkey's impatience. This new style will seem like a chore at first. But trying something different should reap benefits for you this year.

The middle of the month presents an opportune moment to meet someone new. Has your love life been a little on the lonely side lately? Change your approach. Take some social risks. Stick your neck out. Introduce yourself to perfect strangers. Stop to have a conversation with a passerby in the supermarket. This frivolity may run contrary to your nature. Oxen often prefer to remain aloof. Only after knowing someone for a long time do they allow them into their inner circle. Such high standards make you a great friend to have. But in order to get back on the romantic horse, you must leave your comfort zone. Even if you do not meet a potential significant other or find your future spouse this month, you will encounter some fascinating people along the way.

You may be in for a minor health scare at the end of February. All this leaving your comfort zone and trying new things has put your stomach in knots. Oxen carry a lot of natural tension and stress. The added pressure of changing your habits may lead to a stomach ailment. Compensate for this risk by monitoring your diet closely. Add more fruits and vegetables. These goodies will help you stay regular. Above all, avoid greasy fast food. Even on the weekends. The toxins in fast food lay another burden on your already-taxed digestive system. You don't want ulcers - do you?

OX March 2016

You are focused on the higher goals in life. Advancing in your career. Finding and keeping that special someone. The things that matter. So you become irritated when the beginning of March sees some family infighting. These squabbles seem petty to you. Who cares if your daughter's new boyfriend has a tattoo? The ink is to commemorate his grandmother! Never mind. The very idea of tattoos it so horrible to you that you forgot to wish your aunt a happy birthday. Or call your Dad about his retirement party. Yet, these seemingly insignificant problems insist on interrupting your peace of mind. My advice? Camp on your position of indifference. Save your energy for issues of actual importance. And pray for the wisdom to know the difference.

You are at risk for a fiscal scare toward the middle of the month. Perhaps your credit card number will be stolen. Or your investment portfolio will tank during a bad month in the stock market. The problem could be something smaller, too. You might misplace something as trivial as twenty crisp dollars in your pants pocket. Take solace in the fact that not all is as it seems. The bank will replace any stolen funds (as long as you can document the unauthorized purchases). The stock market will rebound. And the misplaced bills might even reappear in your jeans after the laundry. Faded and crinkled to be sure. But still legal tender.

Toward the end of March, set aside some time to travel. If you are in a relationship, book a long weekend at a bed-and-breakfast. If you are a single Ox, go exploring on your own. You may have a friend who recently moved to a new town or city. Doesn't this sound like a great excuse to visit an unfamiliar place? First, double-check that his or her schedule is open. Then brainstorm some activities to share with your crony. Hitting a trendy nightclub. Dining at a renowned restaurant. Even tourist-y activities, like going to a rodeo or taking a guided tour. Your evening itinerary is now in place. During the day, while your friend is at work, you can make progress with your own work projects. This wise use of your time will soothe any guilt you might have been entertaining about taking a wee vacation. Also doing recreational things each night will take your mind off your office duties. Your work and your humor should improve as a result.

OX April 2016

An early-April touch of depression may leave you unexpectedly morose. The reasons are unclear. There has not been any tragedy in your life recently. Your relationships are strong. If you don't watch out, you will drive yourself nuts trying to discover the cause of your blues. So don't even bother. Take a pro-active approach to pulling yourself out of the mire. Start getting some more exercise. Sign up for a gym membership. Swim some laps at your local pool. Walk around the neighborhood each day after dinner. The increased blood flow and change of scenery will work wonders for your state of mind.

In the workplace, your boss' frustration is mounting. The cause of his or her bad humor is not the quality of your work. That is excellent. The problem is your slow pace. I warned you that you would need to pick up the speed for the Monkey Year. So here is your chance to shine. Aim to finish a project ahead of schedule. If need be, bring your workload home and put in some overtime (without telling your superior). If you are a freelance worker, your client will be impressed if you submit some pieces before the deadline is up. This feels like a breakneck pace to you. You might worry about compromising the quality of the final product. The truth is, not everyone holds themselves to the same high standards as you do. So try not to fret over miniscule mistakes. Your boss or client will be happy with the current results.

As April ends, listen to your body. If nothing is complaining, you are in the clear. But if you are experiencing any pain in your midsection, take action. Make the trip to the doctor. With your predisposition for stomach ailments, you cannot allow this one to go unchecked. Especially if you were also feeling some discomfort in February. The doctor can run some tests. A negative result will give you peace of mind. In all likelihood, nothing serious is happening. But if there is something wrong, the laboratory will catch it. So it is important to be candid about talking to a professional.

OX May 2016

On April 28, we receive our first dose of 2016 Mercury retrograde. The effects will hamper communication processes until the planet reverts into its normal orbit on May 22. Computers have a tendency to go blank during this period. So make an extra effort to back up your digital files. Send emails to yourself with important documents attached (that way, you can access them from another machine). Or consider investing in an external hard drive. Such additional precautions may seem like overkill. But they will pay off if your brand-new Mac simply refuses to boot up one Mercury Retrograde morning.

If you have children, one is due for some hard-earned recognition toward the middle of May. This acknowledgment may come through the school system. Perhaps your child is set to receive an academic award. Of course, you realized they were putting in a lot of hours on homework. But you never thought it was enough to get the Math Award. Or maybe your child will collect an athletic trophy. MVP of the 8th grade field hockey team might not seem like much now. But if a few pieces fall into place, he or she could parlay those skills into a college scholarship. Who ever said sports had to come at the expense of class work? In any case, you are so proud of your kid's achievements that it might as well be a Nobel Prize!

You may have a parent (or grandparent) who is aging a bit too fast. Additional health concerns spring up by the week. As May nears its end, phone him or her more often. You must stay up-to-date with their progress. They may try to hide problems from you, not wanting to cause a scene. And there are few things worse than getting blindsided by bad news. As Mercury eases out of retrograde, they should give you a straighter answer to your queries. If they simply mumble, "I'm fine," take matters into your own hands. If they live close by, drive over and check on them in person. If they are a plane flight away, give one of their neighbors a ring. This nearby acquaintance may be able to give you the real scoop.

OX June 2016

In early June, you might make a silly error in your job. If you are an Ox accountant, such a silly error could cost someone a hefty chunk of change. A business-Ox? You run the same risk. In some way, this mistake is a consequence of speeding up your work. Normally, you plow methodically through your duties. Blunders are few and far between. So you are nervous as you face this new glitch. Luckily, you have built up a bank of good will with your boss. First, by being such a reliable worker. Secondly, as he or she asked you to in February, by changing your style of production to better suit the company's needs. This minor problem at the office is nothing to lose sleep over. Your job is safe.

Although picking up the pace caused some problems in the office, it has paid dividends in your social life. Perhaps a special someone has caught your eye. You would never have met this person if you had not stepped outside your comfort zone. You have probably been taking the relationship slow - as Oxen are wont to do. It takes a lot for an Ox to trust anyone. Let alone to fall in love. However, by mid-June, it is high time to take things to the next level. If you have been steadily going on dates together, ask your partner to come home with you at the end of the night. If that box has been checked, sit down and have a talk together. Be honest with your feelings. If you really like this person, they may not have realized it. Your thoughts can be inscrutable to those who haven't known you for a decade. So clear the air by once again exiting your comfort zone by speaking your feelings openly and without fear of rejections.

As late June approaches, you may find yourself bored. Not with your job. But with your leisure activities. Poker has lost its luster. Binge-watching TV shows depresses you. You decide that you are in the market for a new hobby. How about chess? The game forces you to use your brain. It eats a lot of time. And the satisfaction you get from winning satiates your competitive drive. Now, all you need to do is recruit a partner. Or join an online forum. Whatever you choose to do, besides work, has to be productive and offer you a sense of achievement.

OX July 2016

After your money scare in March, your finances have rebounded into good form as we head into July. Your account is stable enough to justify a splurge. Take the kids on a shopping spree (if you have a daughter, she may love you more at this moment than ever again). Outfit them in duds that will turn heads at school. Or perhaps aim a surprise gift at your significant other. Jewelry or a painting or a new computer perhaps. Picture the scene. What's the occasion, they ask, startled by your sudden largesse. "Oh, nothing. Just wanted to let you know I was thinking about you', you smile in response. For you single Oxen? Treat yourself! Buy that new videogame. Pick up a leather handbag. After all, it is just money. You can't take it with you. So you might as well put it to use.

Your immediate family is thriving in mid-July (your suddenly open checkbook may have helped, but still). They are putting pressure on you to take a vacation. The idea is tempting. Especially as you can see that colleagues are slipping out the door, and are not seen again for a week. The volume on your desk has been diminishing. But don't book the hotel in the Caribbean just yet. The lessening of work trend is about to reverse itself. Unexpected business is about to materialize. And you will be one of the few left in the office to handle it. This overload may see you putting in some late nights. But the higher-ups will also notice your rigorous work ethic. Your labors may not be for naught after all. Your name will now come up in discussions about promotions. Take a chance and stay home. The children and hubby or wife will be disappointed. Once again, you can explain.

Late July has an increased risk of injury for your loved ones. Counsel your children to take it easy in their athletic programs. A catastrophic break or tear could destroy any hope of a scholarship offer. Tell your spouse or sweetheart to be careful not to fall down while climbing stairs or settling into their car. The period is propitious for unexpected tumbles. People tend to break bones during this time. You might all want to take a yoga class. Or do some stretching together. Become more nimble of both body and mind.

OX August 2016

As August takes the reins from July, a family member is planning a big move. Your daughter might want to study abroad. Maybe a nephew has volunteered to provide aid to a foreign nation. In such a case, counsel them to question their motives. Are they running from something? Avoiding a certain someone? As you know, a move to a foreign land will not always solve the problems we leave behind. The stress of adapting to the ways of a new culture can lead the mind right back to the anxieties he or she left behind. . Maybe a younger relative is simply moving out of their parents' house. Still, it's a major lifestyle change. If the young person is becoming a tenant, check to see if you have an extra sofa or table lying around in the garage or attic. Those items would be mighty useful for a new renter.

Around the middle of August, you are in for a bit of an adventure in the workplace. One day, you glance to your left. A new coworker sits there. One who appears barely old enough to drive. This controversial hire will be the talk of the office or shop for a while. Are they the son or daughter of an executive? An intern or apprentice from a prestigious university? A small caution: take the entire rumor mill with a grain of salt. And definitely do not go spreading gossip of your own. Your fresh-faced colleague could turn out to be just that—a preternaturally young-looking person of 40 years of age.

Feeling lonely toward the end of August? Perhaps it was your son or daughter who moved out of the house. Leaving you with empty nest syndrome. Or you might have worked too many nights in a row without a diversion. For an amusing change, why not host a dinner party? Invite your closest friends. Ask for cooking ideas via email from the group. Someone may just the recipe you have been longing to try: An Indian dish, Peruvian gourmet fare, etc. And more importantly, they may offer to cook. The combination of friendly faces and delicious food will drive the empty nest from your mind. Of course you will have to use your hard-working Oxxy diligence to plow through that mountain of dirty dishes. A small price to pay!

OX September 2016

Unfortunately for your peace of mind, Mercury turns retrograde on August 30. Be on the lookout for faulty communications up until September 22. During this period, keep a close eye on your financial statements. If you read anything that says: "Click here to see our updated policy," by all means clicks! Do not banish it to the trash bin. Carefully scan the fine print for any notable changes. Your bank might be trying to attach new fees to your account without your noticing. If the jargon is indecipherable, set the notice aside. Come back to it after the 22nd to make sure you know exactly what is happening with your money.

Toward the middle of the month, your romantic life is perking up. You may be considering taking a crush out on a date. Here is a tip. Eschew that list of 101 Sweet, Romantic Date Ideas that you found on the Internet. None of those is your preferred style. If you use one of those suggestions, you are pretending that gooey and mushy is what you like.

That assumption will set certain expectations for the future. So instead, take your date out for an action-packed adventure. Windsurfing, jogging, something involving physical activity. If they cannot handle that, you probably will not enjoy being with them for long.

After some scares earlier in the year, your health seems to have stabilized. Take solace in the fact that Oxen have the most impressive longevity of all the signs. One cautionary note: if you live in a warmer clime, slather on some sunscreen before you go out. The sun's rays still have some power. If you do not protect yourself adequately, you may end up with a painful sunburn. On the other hand, if you do not live where it's warmth in September, make sure you are getting enough sunlight. Even if temperatures are unpleasantly low. Find reasons to go outdoors multiple times each day. The extra rays will boost your mood and help maintain your vitamin D levels.

OX October 2016

Early October brings a stroke of good luck. Perhaps you will find some money in the street. Or maybe you will discover the missing TV remote buried in the couch. Don't forget your umbrella when you leave the house. And when it downpours, make sure your electronics are protected. You do not want to be lugging a water-damaged smart phone back to the shop. Or worse, a drenched and ruined laptop. A leather case or plastic case should do the trick. Short of such supplies? Don't be too proud to use a resealable plastic bag. Sure, you might look like a nerd. But you will have the last laugh if you get caught in the rain.

If you have children, be prepared for some unforeseen expenses toward the third week of the month. Budgeting is much more difficult when kids are involved. So plan for the unexpected. Perhaps an unplanned doctor's visit will set you back. Apparently, those plantar warts had to be taken care of professionally. Or maybe your son or daughter will reveal a newfound love of sports. Which means investing in the proper gear. Now, your finances must compensate for these sudden costs. Luckily, you have the economic flexibility to manage.

Late in the month, your significant other has had enough. You did not even realize that tensions were rising. But apparently, he or she is tired of your monotony. Always plodding ahead in a straight line, you may indeed have neglected to inject variety into your relationship. This oversight was not really your fault. You probably tend to see things in black and white. You either love someone, or you don't. The rest of us are not wired the same way, however. So in this moment of crisis, you must do something to prove your spontaneity to your partner. You could offer to learn to dance. Perhaps the Tango. Or an easier genre, like salsa. Or suggest the two of you take French lessons together. Or learn about organic gardening *à deux*. Brighten up your sweetheart's horizons. Start doing things their way for a while. You will find the shift rewarding.

OX November 2016

The next month is going to be a tough slog in the workplace. Do not be surprised if you are inundated with assignments. It may seem like your boss is singling you out for extra work. Don't hold a grudge. It's not personal. The volume of business has grown. If you are a freelance worker, you should finish up any ongoing projects in a hurry. You will be asked to take on more work as November progresses. If you wipe the slate clean now, you will be less overwhelmed by new tasks. For my Oxen who are doing physical labor, aim for *at least* seven hours of sleep each night. For you, an increased workload translates to a higher risk of injury. Getting more sleep will help your body recover after each tough day.

All is tranquil on the family front in mid-November. That is one positive of spending a lot of time at work. This could be salutary and there is less time to clash with loved ones. Your romantic partner is happy to see your smiling face at the end of each long day. If child was injured in July, their bones or joints ought to have physically healed by now. The doctors have cleared them for some mild athletic activity. Despite the doctor's note, the kid continues to limp around the court or field. Perhaps another round of physical therapy is in order - especially if it's a ligament or tendon that is recovering. November does not look menacing in the entertainment department. You and your main squeeze will be invited to every kind of social event - from fancy dinners to evenings with friends at the theater. Go without grouching. You need to be stimulated. Otherwise you tend to stagnate.

By the end of the month, you might have got used to distractions. In this spirit, go out to see a movie. Go to a theater. Look for a drama. Avoid violent action-packed films. Get wrapped up in the story of someone else's life. Those screen lives contain a lot more heartbreak and upheaval than yours. Whatever your own problems, are right now, they will seem petty by comparison. After a heartfelt drama, you will exit the movie theater feeling refreshed and renewed and ready to take on another month.

OX December 2016

Early December reveals another mad stretch of business (busy-ness?) at your job. Everyone is trying to meet deadlines and finish projects before the holidays. But by all means, continue to mow steadily through your work. Do not allow everyone else's panic to raise your blood pressure. This rush is the last hurdle before the peace of the holidays. Peace is this instance is of course relative. You may be anticipating a family war when you all get together at holiday time. Let's face it, there are certain relatives who always bring a storm cloud to these gatherings. And there is invariably one secret (or obvious) alcoholic to add to the mix. But familial squabbles burn up a different energy than constant pressure at work does. This interval could send you on such an emotional roller coaster that by early January, you will be begging to return to the office or shop.

Whatever tradition(s) you celebrate, you are due to receive an unwanted present around the midpoint of the month. Perhaps it will take the form of a puppy or a kitten. The gift is somewhat exasperating as you think you do not have time to take care of such a needy creature! You will be surprised how quickly you become attached. Or... you might be offered a multicolored jacket that went out of style in the 90s. Do not trash this gift immediately. Allow it time to grow on you. Depending on your point of view, being different is just as fashionable as being fashionable.

Mercury again dips into retrograde in late December. As usual, systems of communication—and therefore, decision-making—are impaired. You may feel inspired to declare some outlandish New Year's resolutions. I will drink nothing but vegetable juice this year! I am going to start working nights so I can save up for a trip to Las Vegas! No matter where Mercury is headed, snap decisions have never been one of your strengths. Let's not swear any oaths before January 8, when the planet's confounding influence fades.

OX January 2017

When you return to work, the situation has got back to a leisurely pace. This pace feels much more your style. Take advantage of this period. While others lose motivation without the pressure of constant deadlines, you remain able to chug forward. This steadiness will allow you to finish several long-term projects. And also to clean up paperwork that your coworkers despise. Polishing off a stack of busy work is no chore for you. You can easily switch your mind off and charge through it all. Accomplishing routine tasks is more useful than sitting idly at your desk playing online poker and browsing Facebook - the way so many of your less industrious colleagues do.

A series of unfortunate events may take place within your immediate family during the middle of the month. Minor annoyances, for the most part. An important kitchen appliance -such as the dishwasher r the microwave - might break down. Does anyone relish the thought of washing dishes by hand for a month? Or reheating leftovers in a frying pan because the microwave has conked out? In addition, one of your loved ones is at risk for illness. If someone starts coughing or wakes up with a sore throat on consecutive mornings, get them to a doctor. Without medical attention, this nuisance could linger for weeks. And take care of your own body as well. Do not overdo it in the gym. A pulled muscle is the last thing you need right now.

Take the last week of January to reflect on the FIRE Monkey year. The Monkey's influence forced you to step outside your comfort zone. You had to increase your pace, particularly in the office, or risk getting left behind. There were some ups and downs. But overall, it was a success. How was your romantic life? Did your family survive the year unscathed? What did you check off your bucket list over the last year? Process and appreciate all the ways you grew in 2016. Soon it will be time to gear up or the FIRE Rooster year!

YOUR MONTHLY FORECASTS FOR THE FIRE MONKEY YEAR

2016

TIGER

Author's Note... Mercury Retrograde

Sometimes planets appear to be zooming backward through the zodiac. Of course this backward motion is only an illusion. The planet has not turned tail. But it appears to have. Astrologers call this apparent reversing: **"retrograde"**.

Any planet can be retrograde. But only Mercury's retrogrades cause communications to break down. Mercury has its retrograde period for a few weeks 3 or 4 times each year. Whilst Mercury is retrograde, we humans are encouraged to take stock, make plans and discuss different approaches to a variety of subjects. But because information is often muddled, promises broken and electronic devices on the blink during Mercury retrograde, we must remain flexible and open-minded. Advice? Always allow extra time for travel. Schedule changes are common. Do not sign any contracts or cement agreements during Mercury retrograde. Make no irreversible promises. Watch out for con artists. Make no final decisions, binding engagements or major purchases during a Mercury retrograde. You are allowed to have tantrums or rail against your fate. But Mercury will continue to be retrograde till it decides to go direct again.

Mercury Retrogrades
2016

January 5 thru January 25
April 28 thru May 22
August 30 thru September 22
December 19 thru January 8 2017

OVERVIEW OF 2016 THE YEAR OF THE MONKEY
FOR THE TIGER

Peripatetic Tiger,

The Fire Monkey year will both delight you and try your limited patience. This next 12 months will offer you a spree of activity just the way you like it. Multitasking and multi-meetings and multi proposals for work, cultural. And sports experiences. Take the Monkey up on all of these propositions. You, more than any other sign, can surely multi manage such a variety of goings-on. Where other people might feel they have been bushwhacked by such a plethora of fresh things to learn and do, you revel in the "New" ness of it all. A change in your work environment is in the offing this year. You are a person whose enthusiasms need changing about as often as you change your clothes. So get cracking on finding that unusual job straightaway this year. You will not be sorry you did. Love life? Medium rare. I say that because the love situation you have been in for so long is well done by this time. Overdone in fact. Hence, could be time to make changes. Either see a couples' therapist or end it and bounce a bit now from prey to prey. See how it feels to enjoy seduction again. Change is what the Monkey year is all about for Tigers. P.S. Your current partner will more than likely be overjoyed to see your tawny rump slink out the door. sw

TIGER January 2016

Mercury goes retrograde on the 5th and stays that way until the 25th, making the end of the Sheep year somewhat frustrating to navigate. As long as you remain conscious of this confounding influence, you will survive the month unscathed. Thankfully, work is going well. Also, the holidays have left you at an all time high in your social circles. So spend the month of January getting simple things done. Tidy up at home or work. Clean out your cupboards. Go for walks. Cook new types of meals. If they pass muster, prepare them again and invite the people you know will appreciate them.

Midway through January, you may need to visit a family member in hospital. The complaint is probably nothing serious. Still, make it a point to go. The patient will appreciate your presence. While you are there, be careful in the parking area. Someone may scratch your car. Or if you are on foot, nearly run you over. Look twice before you venture into the street, especially if the weather is bad. If there is a minor accident, be careful when exchanging insurance details. Mercury's influence still hangs over us till the 25th. All you need to do is remember the three Mercury Rx monkeys. "Say nothing," "Sign nothing" and "Read everything twice."

As the Sheep year limps across the finish line, the retrograde is attacking communications systems. Your phone starts sending texts in Mandarin. Your computer decides to spell-check in German. Your email is hijacked by a third world banking scam. When you phone for help, the voice recognition network thinks you are speaking Swahili. Your path through the mire is long, arduous and inescapable. Power down all of your technology. Pour yourself a strong drink and hibernate until the 25th. The Monkey year is about to begin! And that, Tiger, will bring you a barrelful of excitement.

TIGER February 2016

The FIRE Monkey Year will play to your strengths. It should progress just the way you Tigers like it—with a lot of turnover, new experiences, and excitement. And February will not wait to give you a taste of what's to come. A move may be in the offing. You might feel the urge to chase a job in another city. Maybe you want to try to work things out with a certain someone. Or you could simply be embarking on a long trip. Whatever your motives, plunge into the challenge. You will enjoy hunting for housing. Bargaining with real estate agents fires up your competitive spirit. Plus, once you find a place, there will be so much fresh territory to explore. You can spend as many nights as you want prowling about the local haunts.

The middle of the month brings sad tidings. If you have a family of your own, you may experience some trouble with a child. Perhaps a son will get in trouble for drug use or underage drinking. Maybe a daughter will get a little too involved with an unsuitable boyfriend. In any case, your living room is soon to turn into a war zone. This incident will place a huge strain on your relationship with your significant other. The next step? That depends. This incident could drive you apart. Or it could solidify your bond. If you want to keep the group together, it will be hard work. Many late nights and emotional episodes are sure to come. But you live to fight for what is right. If there is a way to salvage the situation, you will find it.

Use the end of the month to espouse a new hobby. If you are the sporting type, you are accustomed to trying different games. It does not usually take long for you to master one. If you have the resources, give polo a shot. Being on horseback adds another wrinkle to the game play. Women, too, play polo now. You cannot rely on sheer willpower to dominate. You must learn to coexist and triumph with another creature. If you prefer more leisurely pursuits, teach yourself a new card game. Just stay away from gambling. Games of chance will fire up your competitiveness in all the wrong ways. Stay away from those crap tables or you may find yourself staring into an empty wallet at the end of the night.

TIGER March 2016

Early March presents myriad challenges at your place of business. There may be a new set of faces in management. People who fail to understand the previous delineation of duties. If they lay off or fire some of your coworkers, you will be expected to pick up the slack. This craziness would swamp a lesser creature. But not you. You thrive on multitasking. You should be able to handle the extra duties. Just make sure that your superiors realize how much work you are putting in. That way, you are more likely to keep your name in the conversations for possible promotions. Keep an eye out for open positions at other companies, too. 2016 might be the year you fly the coop from your current job. One way or another, the pressure is building. Something has to give.

You are currently relishing a period of good health. Don't let this sickness-free time make you complacent about your personal maintenance. Exercise is vital to your health. Monotonous workouts at the gym are not the best outlet for you, however. Find something that allows you to release some aggression. Perhaps boxing lessons? Although do not be surprised if you are smacking the teacher around after a few months. Unfortunately, in mid-March, one of your close friends is not sharing your good fortune with regard to illness. You may need to hustle over to the hospital to comfort him or her. Just remember—if you commit to a time, stick to your word! Your ailing comrade has nothing better to do than stare at the clock.

Watch your finances at the end of the month. Your spending is not the problem (as long as you stayed away from the casino, as I cautioned in February). Do you have a joint back account with your partner? Do a bit of sleuthing. He or she may have been swiping the credit card a bit too freely. Or signing up for services that the two of you did not agree upon. If so, it is high time for a sit-down. Confront them about their squandering. The atmosphere may get fiery. But perhaps there is a bright side. If an end to the relationship is the upshot, 'better close that join bank account in a hurry.

TIGER April 2016

In the beginning of April, you observe an intriguing trend. Your mornings are incredibly productive. At your job, you chew through assignments like oatmeal. Before noon, at least. On the weekends, sunrise sees you out in the yard. Mowing, trimming, weeding—no task fazes you. But when the afternoon creeps in, your energy vanishes. Lethargy replaces it. This midday sleepiness may be a problem at work. You would be able to accomplish more if you could squeeze at least *some* productivity out of those post noon hours. A tip? Eat a lighter lunch. If you stuff yourself at twelve, you are bound to feel sleepy till three. Unless you have nap after eating, light lunches will help keep your energy levels high. Avoiding meat while the sun is high in the sky. Around 4pm, grab a quick coffee or tea to pep you up.

Toward the middle of April, you might notice something crawling about your kitchen. Now, normally it takes a lot to scare such a fierce Tiger as yourself. But the sight of creepy, skittering cockroaches or scampering mice does daunt your fighting spirit. There is no time to waste. Look up the number of the local exterminator. You must get this problem cleared up ASAP. If your house has been rid of pests, perhaps another kind of pest has invaded your office. A pest of the human va- riety. A meddling middle manager is causing everyone grief. Unfor- tunately, this office scourge cannot be sprayed with RAID. You simply have to wait out the infestation!

A close acquaintance may be struggling with depression or another mild mental disorder (such as OCD or ADD). Of course, this problem has been around for years. But by the end of April they will have come to a crossroads they are torn between submitting to a full time diet of medication or simply toughing it out without chemical assistance. This individual does not want to face the stigma of relying on pills to feel normal. Counsel them. Explain that whatever their decision, you will certainly not judge them. Their personal happiness needs to come before the opinions of others. Without exception. If their friends cannot relate to that, then they are not true friends. This person will be forever grateful for your guidance.

TIGER May 2016

Unfortunately, our friend Mercury turns into his retrograde orbit on April 28. He remains there until May 22. During this period, be on the lookout for faulty communications. Mercury's influence makes it difficult for us to express ourselves clearly. You may have an important meeting approaching. Probably for your job. But it could be with a real estate agent, a lawyer, or an accountant. If the proposed date falls before the 22nd, postpone it. Otherwise, vital information could get lost in translation. Also, take this opportunity to back up your files. Computers have a way of crashing unexpectedly during Mercury retrograde.

A retreat beckons in mid-May. This event could be a yearly work outing. Or perhaps a family reunion. Ordinarily, such visits bore you. Luckily, this year ushers in a new destination. A city or campground that you have never before experienced. This fresh adventure should rev your engines. Unlike most retreats, this one offers a spree of activity. Sports during the day. Adult exploits at night. These changes should rejuvenate your vitality. Just remember: if you hit the town, do not overdo it with the booze. You might awaken to some embarrassing credit card purchases the next day. Or, even worse, a botched tattoo.

As May nears its end, you may be feeling some pain in your jaw. You are tempted to chalk it up to grinding your teeth at night. But if your discomfort persists, get your striped fanny to a dentist. If you still have your wisdom teeth, you might need to get one wrenched out. But in all likelihood, the ache stems from a simple cavity. Your dental professsional will able to patch things up with a simple filling. Just don't ignore the pain. If you take no action, the nerve might get infected. Does the term "root canal" sound enticing? Exactly. Your family will be impressed to see you being proactive with your health. With you leading by example, they will see that it's normal to seek help when one's body is sending out warning signs. In future, try to be more consistent about flossing and brushing your teeth at least twice a day.

TIGER June 2016

As April begins, the days alternate between sunshine and rainstorms. So keep an umbrella handy just in case. Speaking of storms—has your long-term relationship grown stale? You may have been pondering going back on the hunt for some time now. Events are soon to come to a head. The discord might be triggered by finances. Especially if your banking disagreements from March persist. Or something more innocuous could start the fireworks. A Freudian slip of the tongue. An undercooked dinner. Regardless of the impetus, you may want to seize this moment as an opportunity to slink out the back door. The thrill of chasing a new partner will be satisfying (at first). But you will find you miss the comforts of monotony. Try to maintain friendly relations with your ex. You may end up wishing you had never left.

Spend some time with your loved ones toward the middle of the month. Especially if you just went through a breakup. We all know you are a tough, courageous Tiger. Life's challenges faze you about as much as an ant crossing your path. But you may be suppressing some strong emotions about now. Even if you did not recently end a relationship, you would benefit from some family time. Go see aging parents. Return to your roots. If distance makes that impossible, get them to use Skype. At the very least, set aside some time on the weekend for your clan. Spend an energetic Saturday playing badminton in the yard. Reserve a night for a bowling expedition. You don't have to voice any of your feelings right now. You need to feel you belong somewhere. Spending time with the ones you love will recharge your battery and calm the anxiety you are feeling at this time.

Late April is a good time to invest in a low maintenance pet. A rabbit or cat would be ideal. If you are not ready an animal commitment, a hermit crab or frog might work. Especially if you have children. Kids always love having a little critter in the house. Delegate the responsibility of feeding and cleaning the animal to them as well. That experience will impart valuable life lessons to the young ones. Do however avoid getting a dog at this juncture. The canine's barking and constant need for attention is not in the cards for you at this testy time.

TIGER July 2016

A battle is approaching that will determine who is to be the alpha dog (cat?) at the office. It looks as though that the powers-that-be have hired a fresh face. This person is competitive, hard-working, and attractive. (Could be a Dragon Lady or a power mad Rat) You are natural rivals. You can deal with this hire in one of two ways. You can fight for your territory. You do love a challenge, after all. You know you will be able to continue your rise to power, regardless of the raw ambition of your new coworker. Or you can quit. The writing may already be on the wall. Perhaps your bosses want to go in a different direction. Maybe it's high time you had a change of scenery anyway. Open your mind to unusual job possibilities. You could transform from desk worker to physical trainer. Or you could found your own start-up where you would be the boss. Career changes such as these pique your interest. "New-ness" suits you. Why not shake things up a bit?

An unusual engagement in your social circle surprises you. Two friends may have been sleeping together behind everyone's back. Or a couple might decide to get hitched after a mere three months of dating. You have your doubts about the future of this union. But, unless one of the parties involved solicits your advice, keep them to yourself. You know very well that marriage is not a fairy tale. There will be plenty of room for I-told-you-so's if/when they split up.

Experiment with new music in late May. Ask your friends for recommendations to add to your listening rotation. If possible, catch a live act that you've never heard or heard of. Perhaps a concert at the stadium downtown. Or a simple performance at the local corner bar. If your time or resources are limited, download some tunes to jam to at your leisure. Who knows, you might discover a genre that you never knew existed. If you are a musician yourself, play around with different styles. Seek advice from fellow bards on which influences you can incorporate into your play. Perhaps an injection of variety could inspire some creativity in your own work.

TIGER August 2016

As August tips off, love is in the air. For my single Tigers my advice is to get out of the house! Hit the town. Crash a party not thrown by one of your close friends. Try a new bar or club. Stay out past your bedtime. Stretch your social boundaries. If you meet enough people, you *will* find a special someone. This is a numbers game. If you remain ensconced in your bedroom watching the telly every night, guess what? It ain't gonna happen. For paired-off Tigers, you too are feeling the stirrings of romance. Your partner may not be so quick on the trigger, however. So when you are feeling frisky, setting the mood is up to you. Light some candles. Burn some incense. Put on some Marvin Gaye. You know what style of romancing will light your partner's fire. Use it.

Business negotiations are nearing a critical point in August 2016. Your company is engaged in a series of harrowing negotiations. Jobs could be at stake. If yours is a self-run business, tread carefully during these meetings. It would be wise to bring in some outside assistance. You are a proud, independent creature. But negotiating with words is not your element. You risk being taken advantage of. Above all, do not let your Tigerish pride get in the way of your finances. Invite your lawyer or a diplomatic Libra or Rabbit friend to join you. And by all means, get everything wrapped up by August 30 when Mercury goes retrograde again. After that, until September 22 it will not be a good idea to sign on any dotted lines.

Toward the end of the month, be prepared to encounter a grisly scene. Especially if you reside in a city. One day, when you leave the house, you are likely to witness a nasty accident. Perhaps a bus will carom into a pedestrian. Or a motorcyclist will lose control of his bike. The sight will probably freeze you for a second or two, like a deer in the head-lights. But someone needs to take action. Call for an ambulance imme-diately. The rest of the crowd may assume that someone else has already done so. Beat that bystander mentality by being the person who acts ands asks no questions or nor seeks reward.

TIGER September 2016

September begins with Mercury firmly entrenched in his retrograde orbit. The trajectory does not stop until September 22. As always, be on the lookout for wonky communications. Mercury's interfering effects will impact your work life. You and your boss are not on the same page right now. You may not realize it. But you are not completing your tasks in the manner he or she envisioned. This is not the time for a powwow to patch things up, however. Since speech may be distorted, simply take a glance at some of your earlier projects. Compare them to your current work. You will probably notice some bad habits in your current files. And some better habits in the older selections. It is up to you to right the ship and return the quality of your output to its previous high level.

Someone in your nuclear family is struggling at work or school near the middle of the month. They are carrying these battles home with them, too. Maybe your better half is feeling the pressure of a new job. If the struggling person in question is a young student, phone the school to investigate. Perhaps they are being bullied. Or just slacking off in class. Ordinarily, a sit-down powwow would be the way to solve this pro-blem. But solving things might be difficult to pull off during Mercury retrograde. Instead, adopt a wait-and-see approach. The situation will probably rectify itself. Plus which, if the troubled individual can pull out of this tailspin without your assistance, their self-confidence will go through the roof.

As September fades away, you may be feeling burned out. Work has been stressful. Family life has been tense. Immerse yourself in an activity that you love. If you are a sporting Tiger, hit the links, field, or court. Ever made a beef stew? How about French onion soup? Enjoy cooking. Try a few new recipes. Or invent one of your own! Better still, find a new passion. Time to exercise that Tiger fondness for novel challenges! First time tennis player? Rookie at the gym? Better to attempt some changes now than to never try at all.

TIGER October 2016

As an independent soul, it is not your nature to hover over others. You may not always notice when a loved one's spirits are low. But lately tensions have been palpable. You can't help noticing that your relatives are anxious Because of work, relationships, school—the triggers are endless. So turn the first week of the month into family week. Plan a fun event each night. These do not have to be detailed, expensive outings. A simple movie evening would do wonders. If everyone's schedules are booked solid, even a quick meal of takeout food (Chinese? Pizza?) Can provide some glue for the family dynamic. A date on the town with your significant other? Just what the doctor ordered to spice your love life between the sheets.

Have you been eying a potential investment recently? The returns could be manifold. But do be careful. You risk heavy losses. Too leery to take the plunge? Fact is, there is no time like the present to take a gamble. Your finances are strong. Your income is stable. And the skies are in your favor. So see if you can flip that house. Take out a lease on a sparkling new car or a hefty 4x4. Invest a chunk of change in a fledgling company. If you choose your target wisely, you can easily recoup your capital while making a tidy profit at the same time! Remember, fortune rewards the bold

A priest or minister or some sort of clergy person is to figure prominently in your life in late October. Perhaps a family member or a close friend is suddenly contemplating joining the clergy. Their intentions may be honorable. But are they making this commitment for the right reasons? Reasons such as "my girlfriend/boyfriend broke up with me" or "I need some spiritual guidance." are not good reasons to join a ministry. Gently counsel this person to sleep on their hasty decision. Of course this be-frocked character could appear in another context. Maybe a clergyman will rear-end your car. Or you will be stirred by a rousing sermon to volunteer your services to a religious organization. Either way, at the end of October, a cleric is a harbinger of significant events to come.

TIGER November 2016

Your life has already experienced a plethora of changes in 2016. Since you revere such tests of your mettle, you have done your best to adapt on the fly. However, in the beginning of November, you need to reverse this trend of transition. Another enticing option has materiallized in front of you. Perhaps a stunning potential mate. A lucrative (but mysterious) job. Even something less significant, like the chance to escape on a road trip. Your instincts scream to jump ship. To leave behind your job, relationship, or family, and dive into the unknown. This choice represents the fulcrum of your entire year. And you must turn it down. You are better off where you are right now. Even Tigers need a modicum of stability. If you fly in the face of that truth, you run the risk of degenerating into a lonely vagabond. As appealing as the new opportunity may seem, a lonesome future is not what you desire.

Toward the middle of the month, invitations to social events flood your inbox. By all means, accept. Attend the parties. Be your charming, seductive self. But watch how often you tip the bottle. With so many celebrations, it would be easy to fall into a pattern of drunkenness. When trying to match the intake of the heavier drinkers, keep one thing in mind: not everyone has signed on for as many commitments as you this month. You are running a marathon, not a sprint. So pace yourself adequately. That way, you won't find yourself itching for a drink the week after your social schedule returns to normal!

As November draws to a close, you may feel the pull to make an impulse purchase. You would truly relish a brand-new fishing boat. Or a brand-name leather jacket. It seems natural to reward yourself for...well, being you. But such actions would leave your family in a jealous huff. So use your ingenuity to evade their disapproval. Go ahead. Make the acquisition. But be sure to keep the present in the family. Give official ownership to your spouse or a grown child. Don't worry. You will be still able to make use of it at your leisure. Yet you will appear benevolent for buying a surprise gift for a loved one. A true win-win!

TIGER December 2016

Be extra cautious with finances at the beginning of the month. Remember that banking is big business too. Though it doesn't show on the surface, your particular institution has fallen upon hard times. They may soon be bought out by a bigger company. If that comes to pass, put in an appearance at the financial institution that assumes control of their holdings. Meet with a banker. Discuss any policy changes in your accounts. If he or she starts blowing smoke about fees and extra costs, withdraw your funds. You are better off finding a different place to hold your money than dealing with a whole new set of rules and restrictions brought on by their mismanagement of your money.

The middle of December should be quiet. Work is chugging along steadily. Your relationships, the same. In fact, things are a little too quiet for your taste. You prefer a sizzling cycle of tension and release. Unfortunately, your employers and relatives do not share your proclivity for excitement in all area of life. So instead of doing something irrational and burning a bridge, lose yourself in athletics. The challenges and thrills of a competitive sport will sate your thirst for excitement. Be careful not to cause anyone to lose their job.

The holidays always have the potential to stir up drama. Put that many relatives in one room and add food and alcohol and trouble is around the corner. But not this December. The proceedings should flow smoothly. Family members will be more respectful. This surprising turn of events may have to do with how you handled the tensions in your love life earlier in the year. You might not have realized how much your ex grated on everyone's nerves. But with that individual out of the picture, everyone can breathe easier. Try not to take offense if your loved ones use their newfound freedom as an opening to vent about how much they hated your ex and why. Mercury turns retrograde on December 19 till January 8th. During Mercury Rx communication is muddled anyway. Take the family's nasty comments with a grain of salt.

TIGER January 2017

If you are not careful what you drink on New Year's Eve, the Gregorian New Year could start off with a nasty hangover. You are not alone in your weakened state, of course. Most of the western world's population overindulges during the holidays. Take it easy for the next couple of days. If you give 110% at work right away, you run the risk of falling ill. The same goes for workouts. While you are feeling wretched, avoid pushing yourself at the gym or in athletic matches. Over exertion will tax your immune system. On the plus side, your nausea may give you an aversion to alcohol for the foreseeable future and help you stay out of trouble. Since Mercury is still in retrograde until January 8, use this downtime as an opportunity to complete unfinished projects. If there is a half-written screenplay buried in your desk, polish it off now. If you have fallen behind on your correspondence with a faraway friend, put your thoughts to paper (or email).

Unfortunately, your pest problem from April may make a grand return in the middle of January. Again, phone the exterminator. Only this time, select another such specialist from the directory. The previous service was clearly ineffective. Or worse, they were trying to fleece you. If outside contractors at your place of work constitute the rejuvenated infestation, your company could be planning to lay workers off. Hold steady to your current course. Whether because your output is reliable or because you are a recent hire, you should survive this round of firings.

Ordinarily, I would counsel someone to reflect on their past year at this point, and to note the positives and the negatives. To apply the lessons learned to the coming year. But such nostalgia and misty-eyed recollections are not your style. Instead, simply look at the faces surrounding you. Some of them may have even lasted the whole year by your side! If they can survive that long with you and your ups and downs, it is safe to call them true friends. So let 2016 be a lesson in love. Jobs change. Homes change. You definitely change. But unless you want to grow old as a lonely Tiger, you will need some reliable companions on your path. So do everything in your power to keep these folks close forever.

YOUR MONTHLY FORECASTS FOR THE FIRE MONKEY YEAR

2016

CAT/RABBIT

Author's Note... Mercury Retrograde

Sometimes planets appear to be zooming backward through the zodiac. Of course this backward motion is only an illusion. The planet has not turned tail. But it appears to have. Astrologers call this apparent reversing: **"retrograde"**.

Any planet can be retrograde. But only Mercury's retrogrades cause communications to break down. Mercury has its retrograde period for a few weeks 3 or 4 times each year. Whilst Mercury is retrograde, we humans are encouraged to take stock, make plans and discuss different approaches to a variety of subjects. But because information is often muddled, promises broken and electronic devices on the blink during Mercury retrograde, we must remain flexible and open-minded. Advice? Always allow extra time for travel. Schedule changes are common. Do not sign any contracts or cement agreements during Mercury retrograde. Make no irreversible promises. Watch out for con artists. Make no final decisions, binding engagements or major purchases during a Mercury retrograde. You are allowed to have tantrums or rail against your fate. But Mercury will continue to be retrograde till it decides to go direct again.

Mercury Retrogrades
2016

January 5 thru January 25
April 28 thru May 22
August 30 thru September 22
December 19 thru January 8 2017

OVERVIEW OF 2016 THE YEAR OF THE MONKEY FOR THE CAT/RABBIT

Cautopus Cat/Rabbit

One of the most salient aspects of Monkeys (and hence of the years in which they govern us all) is that deep down; they really don't give a damn. You Cat/Rabbits give much more than a damn – about everything. So sometimes during Monkey years, you become frustrated. You wish people would DO something about the chaos, shore up the bridges, repair the roads, improve the schools and create some sort of public transport system that functions properly. As you are a bit of a fusspot when things don't work as they should, you are a sitting duck for living this Fire Monkey year in a state of agitation. This will be a year of social disruption for a medley of different reasons. One of those is the fact that Monkeys can solve most problems for others, but rarely for themselves. So when it's their turn to govern and the problems become theirs, they find it all a bit too complex.

Leading means visibility. Monkeys don't fancy being visible. They just want to be free to be entertaining and clever and solve lots of problems for others incognito. The Monkey wants no part of the notoriety and authority that come with reigning over millions of people. Needless to say, the Monkey's jaunty laissez-faire attitude toward governance irks you orderly Cat/Rabbits. You would prefer someone take action. Yet, because you never engage in conflict, you remain in the background, stewing. To palliate this general feeling of irritation, might I suggest twelve months of a duvet gentle life: hot water bottles, silken sheets and a soft loving companion will get you through admirably. sw

CAT/RABBIT January 2016

January is another excellent month for you, Rabbit. A powerful energy tingles in the air. Good luck springs up around you. Is someone is expecting a baby this month? Is it you? Do you have a new grandchild in the works? Or have you finally succumbed to your urges to coddle and cuddle and bought yourself a furry friend "baby?" There is no better way to ring in a new year than with the miraculous celebration of new life. Of course, you may have trouble remembering that fact when you're mopping up a leaky infant's messes in a few months time. But at the moment, everything is teacups and butterflies. And lots of tiny trinkets and outfits for the newborn.

That fertile wave of energy has a decidedly feminine touch to it this month. This is more than an urge to make babies. Your hobbies take a more tender tone. Gentle melodies and pastel colors will feel incredibly appealing all the way through the end of the Chinese year. You have an intense desire for everything floral and soft. Your *compadres* will notice this reflected in your clothing and your decor. Even our Mr. Rabbits may surprise their friends by buying pale mint green sheets for their bedroom or throwing a few flowery cushions on their old leather couch.

Water is another feminine element that will attract you in January. If you are a Southern Hemisphere Rabbit, you will be off to soak in the sun on hot summery beaches. Meanwhile, you Northern Rabbits will have to make do with the local indoor swimming pools. Or cave in and start planning a holiday somewhere with palm trees and tropical waters. If all of that is beyond your budget, or you simply cannot take enough time off work, put on some tropical music, light a few floral scented candles and go soak in your bathtub. Add a few delectable fragrant herbs to the water. Lie back and enjoy the sweet sensation of all remaining tension in your muscles seeping away.

CAT/RABBIT February 2016

Just like that, on February 8, 2016 the FIRE Monkey Year is upon us. This 12-month period will try your patience. Over and over again. February starts this pattern off. Events are spiraling out of control at your place of work. Did the office really need a manicured putting green? Of all people, why did the secretary get laid off? The higher-ups are certainly making some questionable decisions. Or perhaps the volume of work flooding your desk has become excessive. The clutter of papers or unread emails threaten to overload your order-loving brain. This discord is due to the influence of the devil-may-care Monkey. So take a deep breath. Personnel and structural changes at your job may be out of your control. But with a bit of mental elbow grease, you can begin to restore order to the small things in your life.

Toward the middle of the month, fears of an illness may leave you wracked with paranoia. Perhaps you notice an unexplained pain in your side. Or you might discover a newly-arrived mole on your leg. You are certain that these are signs of impending doom. But before your panic reaches its boiling point, take a step back. Examine the situation logically. That unpleasant sensation in your stomach probably stems from how much food you scarfed down at that feast you attended last night. And that skin growth? It was there the whole time. Turns out, you don't have a map of your moles memorized. Go figure! As a natural hypochondriac, you are probably overthinking this one. So give the Emergency Room a pass. If the symptoms persist, see a physician.

The year is young. But you could already use some R&R. As February comes to a close, see if you have any remaining personal days that you can take advantage of. If so, cash them out. What should you do for your grand vacation, you ask? It's simple: just vegetate at home. Curl up in bed with a big bowl of something delicious. And your favorite TV shows. Or a series of scrumptious novels. And don't vacate the premises until necessity demands it. This is the mental break you need. As the year progresses, indulge in a similar free day periodically. Doing so will help keep your battery running during the messy, Monkey-induced slog to come.

CAT/RABBIT March 2016

Early in March, a family member is due for some welcome news. An institution has recognized one of their achievements. And a tough-love boss could finally be rewarding your significant other with a promotion. Or an old-school coach may be getting ready to insert your son or daughter into the starting lineup. Either way, the honor will bring this person much-needed validation. Unbeknownst to you, your relative has been going through a crisis of self-confidence as of late. You are not exactly the pep talk type. As a consequence, you do not always provide a great pick-me-up in such situations. But do your best cheerleader impression now. Go ahead and celebrate this affirmation of their self-worth. A little bit of morale-boosting will go a long way. Plus, your aid will be remembered during your next argument.

Even as your job keeps you in the pressure cooker, hope flashes on the horizon. Could it be? Is that a new love interest? Perhaps the new barista at Starbucks has been aiming winks in your direction. Or that dreamy face in the accounting department has been steeling up the courage to ask you out. This connection is no sure thing, however. If you aren't paying attention, you might blink and miss it. My advice? Pull your head out of your down comforter. A cute lil' something is just what the doctor ordered to combat the Fire Monkey's confounding influence on you. So stop moping and meet this character halfway! For my paired-off Cat/Rabbits —seek out your partner for some quality alone time. A romp between the sheets will provide your mind - not to mention your nervous system - a pleasant distraction.

A gruesome news report may catch your eye in late March. You find yourself disturbed by the gory details. It seems impossible that such a crime could happen so close to home. This story really makes you ponder how vulnerable you are. So take the opportunity to beef up your home defenses. Installing a security system would be a great first step. For a quick fix to help you sleep at night, stick a baseball bat or knife next to your bed. Does that seem outrageous? It is. But you never know when you might need to defend yourself. In all likelihood, you will never even touch the weapon. But its mere presence will let you sleep on both ears.

CAT/RABBIT April 2016

Money is getting tight at the beginning of April. Your frayed nerves are once again put to the test as you gaze, open-mouthed, at your flimsy bank statement. This squeeze is a rare experience for you. Normally, you are adept at quietly earning your cash. And quietly stashing it away. But a series of unexpected expenditures have set you back. Before you sign up for a second job to bolster your income, look into the reasons behind your losses. Are you spending too much money on a special someone in your life? Were you dealing with a sick child or a personal health issue recently? As long as your earning is steady, your finances will stabilize. So do not make any rash decisions. Now is not the time to cash out your mutual funds. As difficult as it may be to stand pat, you just need to ride this one out.

Work conditions are slowly improving. Although you are perpetually under duress, you are gradually putting a dent in your workload. Your boss is dealing with his or her own pressures, however. He or she may not have noticed how much effort you've been putting in. Don't hold your breath waiting for acknowledgment. Let them know! Without being petulant, start mentioning how many tasks you have completed. Or how many hours of overtime you have worked. Before long, the overwrought manager will start cutting you some slack. Once he or she realizes how full your desk is, they can start redistributing projects to other colleagues. This respite may not last long. So enjoy it while you can.

A minor "pest" problem may disturb the end of April. Perhaps a flood of ants has taken over your kitchen floor. Or a cat unexpectedly produces a litter of kittens. Things could be worse. The ants could be cockroaches. And the kittens could be...well, something less cute. Use caulk to seal up the holes that the insects use to gain access to your house. That will save a call to the exterminator. And ask your friends if they or anyone they know wants to adopt a baby kitten. You will be surprised at how quickly those fuzzy little feline "pests" get snapped up.

CAT/RABBIT May 2016

Bad tidings for your fragile peace of mind as April gives way to May. Mercury dips back into his retrograde orbit on April 28. He does not right his trajectory until May 22. As always, this pattern in the sky creates faulty communication lines. Put off any important meetings, if possible. The tiny planet's confounding influence will jumble your words. Imparting meaning becomes nigh unto impossible. Luckily, you prefer to operate behind the scenes, rather than taking the verbal initiative. Chances are, your job does not require constant blabbing. If at all possible, lock yourself away with your work. You can use this Mercury retrograde as a chance to finish up old projects. With no one to distract you, you can be twice as productive. Go ahead. Take full advantage of this Mercury retrograde.

The middle of May sees an important invitation arrive in your inbox. It could be for a black-tie cocktail party. Or a powwow with some local politicians. Or even a dining experience with your in-laws. Being surrounded by this particular crowd ratchets up your insecurities. Perhaps you worry that the others have more accomplishments to their names. In their careers, their relationships—even in sculpting their bodies at the gym. Little do you realize that they are equally intimidated by your exploits. Your resume is not so paltry after all. So put on your game face. If you can hide your nerves, no one will sense your insecurities. And if it you play it cool here, the other guests will leave the event with an even higher opinion of you than before.

You are not traditionally a fan of impulse purchases. However, in late May, you might want to buck that trend. Your significant other is dying for a certain item. A flat screen TV, a videogame, a necklace. Something of that ilk. Honestly, they do not expect you to buy it for them.

They know your tendencies too well to hope for that. But that just means they will be all the more flabbergasted when you present them with the object of their desire. Doesn't it feel good to be generous sometimes? Plus, it never hurts to be in your lover's good graces!

CAT/RABBIT June 2016

Your finances threaten to give you heart failure as June takes over from May. Maybe your outlook is not quite as bleak as in April. Still, you fret over your bills. Will you be late on your rent this month? Are you falling behind on credit card payments? Maybe it is time to find another source of cash. In this case, family is more trustworthy than the bank. Your parents might be willing to help you out. Or a well-to-do sibling might lend a hand. But do be careful to take this loan seriously. Just because your creditors are your relatives does not mean that repayment is optional.

In mid-June, stress is wearing you down again. You need to brainstorm some ideas to get your mind off work and your finances. If you are in a relationship, it is high time for a date night. But a dinner reservation at that swanky new spot in town can wait. You do not need to break the bank here. Cheap ideas abound. How about a picnic in a nature preserve? A stroll through the local flora and fauna? Even just renting a movie and curling up on the couch together sounds exquisite. This simple outing will ease both of your anxiety levels. Sometimes, enjoying each other's company is more satisfying than indulging in fancy schmancy expensive luxuries.

As the month comes to a close, set aside a day solely for menial tasks. Catch up on all the duties you've been putting off. Do six loads of laundry. Wash every dish in the house. Does the yard need mowing? The garden weeding? Polish off that yardwork. It will be easier to attack everything at once than to hack away at a little bit each day. That kind of consistent, dull work is not your specialty. This catharsis of your chores will also help decrease your stress level. Having those obligations hanging over your head was not exactly improving your ability to concentrate on the things that matter.

CAT/RABBIT July 2016

Normally, you prefer to pull the strings from behind the scenes. You shun the spotlight like a vampire with stage fright. But at the beginning of July, prepare for a public evisceration. Maybe your boss will bawl you out in a crowded meeting. Or your spouse will start screaming at you in the middle of the supermarket. Ordinarily, this kind of unwelcome attention would make you cower for cover. But stand strong now.

Sure, they might have reason to be frustrated with you. But still. Their histrionics are a bit over the top. Defend yourself. Tell your boss or partner that you don't deserve this type of treatment. In the heat of the moment, they may not appreciate your feisty feedback. But your point will sink in eventually. After mounting your defense, feel free to slink back home. You will feel a bit less browbeaten than if you had kept silent and taken your licks.

Somebody's new boyfriend or girlfriend may throw a wrench in the family dynamic toward the middle of July. If you have children, try to keep tabs on their relationships. A seedy character has their eye on your offspring. Nothing bad will come of this. Not at this point, at least. But make sure you are reinforcing safe habits with your kids. And, without being too pushy, encouraging intelligent decisions. With any luck, your parenting skills will be enough to avert a future disaster. If an adult relative is the one dating the loose cannon, the situation is out of your hands. All you can do is sit back and enjoy the fireworks.

In late July, your hypochondriac tendencies may flare up again. Unlike in February, the problem is not a skin growth or stomach pang. It could be a nagging cough. Or a sore joint. Maybe you have been battling recurring back pain. This time, trust your instincts. This issue is not just in your head. Find help in alternative medicine. See a naturopath. Your GP would probably be at a loss for solutions anyway. Instead, make an appointment with an osteopath or a chiropractor. Or see your friendly Homeopath for just the right remedies to clear up what's bothering you.

CAT/RABBIT August 2016

As August begins, a friend is preparing to move. Probably to a far flung city. You are feeling wistful. As you come to terms with their departure, you will realize how far your social circle has spread. The members of your old crew all reside miles away now. Of course, drifting apart is inevitable. You cannot hope to maintain every friendship forever. Moves happen. Marriage happens. Children happen. Life happens. But, thank heavens, there are still a select few who are worth keeping in touch with. So use this moment of clarity as an impetus to get in touch with an old compatriot. Shoot an email to someone you have lost contact with. Discuss meeting up. You don't have to make concrete plans. Sometimes, just showing that you miss someone is enough to keep your bond alive.

Aggravating workplace experiences abound in the middle of August. You are not being treated with the respect that you deserve. Perhaps someone will blow off a meeting with you. Without any advance notice.

A simple email would have sufficed. Or maybe your coworkers are gossiping about you behind your back. These trials are gradually sending your blood pressure to record levels. You need an outlet for your frustrations. So get yourself to the gym. Burn off some steam. What could be a better motivation for a workout than being mistreated at the office? As you pump the weights, slog on the treadmill, or run around the field, you will be surprised at all the newfound energy. An elevated heart rate sometimes has hidden benefits!

The end of the month is sure to provide you with some learning opportunities. Breathe easy, all my school-hating Cat/Rabbits! Your August lessons will not come from a traditional academic source. Instead, pay close attention to the words of the elderly in your life. "Elderly" being relative, of course. Someone with more life experience than you has some valuable advice. It could be an aging parent. Perhaps a coach or teacher. Even the crazy-looking guy at the bus stop. Contrary to his outward appearance, he too has some valuable insights to share. This person can help you solve a major problem in your life. Such as how to handle your boss. Or how to break up with your girlfriend or boyfriend. Anyhow, the important thing here is to keep an open mind (and an open ear). If you are willing to tune in to a little-used frequency, you are already a step ahead of your peers. Use this advice to your advantage.

CAT/RABBIT September 2016

The beginning of September is quiet, at least in the workplace. Mercury once again reverts to retrograde orbit on August 30, and will remain that way until September 22. So a flurry of activity would not be to your advantage at this time. Curl up in bed or on the couch. If you have a significant other, recruit them to join you. Thanks to this momentary lull in your business life, you can catch up on your favorite TV shows. If you would rather do something active, avoid overexertion. Get thee to a secluded mini-golf course or take an easy hike in the woods. Revel in your leisure time. Fee free to hunker down until the retrograde passes.

The seedy character who began dating a family member in July? By mid-September, their relationship has soured. The honeymoon is on the rocks. If your son or daughter is the person in question, do not push them to break things off. That might create an "us versus them" mentality in the embattled lovers. Such behavior on your part may bond them all the more tightly. Instead, continue your gentle child-rearing style. Without the thrill of disobeying a parent, they may give up the unsuitable lover much sooner than anticipated. If this nefarious person is dating an adult relative, however, approach the situation differently. You actually fear for their well-being and can no longer ignore the situation. Give them a piece of your mind. As an adult, your relative or friend probably realizes that their partnership is an unhealthy one. But when you are madly in love, it's easy to be in denial. Take it slow. But speak your mind.

An errant Internet message will cause you problems toward the end of the month. Twenty years ago, no one could have foreseen the drama a text message could cause. Or a tweet. Or a Facebook status update. But these days, there is always someone watching you. The online "you," at least. So be careful of your phrasing. Remember that Mercury remains in retrograde until the 22nd. You would not want to post something that could sound racist. Or garble the punctuation in an email or text. A pro tip: avoid putting sarcasm into writing. You may end up offending the recipient instead of eliciting that sought-after chuckle.

CAT/RABBIT October 2015

Like it or not, religion is going to play a pivotal role in your life in October. Perhaps a religious dispute will embroil your family. Maybe spiritual differences of opinion will drive you and your romantic partner apart. Or a group of protestors might derail your morning com-mute. Try to keep your distance from the fray. Religion itself may not concern you overmuch. But nothing inflames certain people's passions as much as their beliefs. So maintain as much neutrality as possible. Being tolerant is easier than you think.

After some low points in the beginning of the year, your finances should have rebounded nicely. By mid October, you may even feel confident enough to go on a small shopping spree. If you have children, they would appreciate some spiffy clothes. If not...well, you could use some fancy duds yourself. Why not? If you can spare the capital, outfit yourself in something eye-catching. With any luck, the eyes you catch will belong to someone equally bedazzling. See? Sometimes, impulse purchases are not so wasteful as all that.

Your borderline obsessive-compulsive disorder is again rearing its head toward the end of the month. Your nerves have been tested throughout the year. Often by work-related problems. But this time, the triggers are seemingly innocent events. The neighbor's dog barking. A mosquito bite on your foot screaming to be scratched. The tag on your shirt rubbing against the back of your neck. All of these seemingly inno-cuous provocations are driving you up a wall. The solution? Get some exercise. Intense, heart-pounding exercise. The only way to get your mind to quiet down is to put your body in motion. Long walks or workouts will have the added effect of toning your muscles. If bodily activity doesn't tranquilize you, try meditation. There are many serious books and web sites which teach us to meditate. and be more mindful. If you can manage it, a combination of physical exertion and mental training will work wonders on your fragile nerves.

CAT/RABBIT November 2016

Up until this point, you have survived many trials and tribulations at your job. Murphy's Law - whatever could go wrong, did. - seemed to prevail. However, in early November, Mr. Murphy's trend should begin to reverse itself. Something is going to give. Maybe your company will hire someone to help shoulder your burden. Perhaps your supervisor will recognize your perseverance of late and recommend you for a promotion. On the other hand, the turning point may occur within *you*. Some small incident may be the last straw. After being served crappy sandwiches for so long, you might finally decide to throw down your pen and walk out. If quitting is a possibility, start discretely sending your CV to other places now. If you leave your current gig, it's vital that you have a backup plan in place.

Disorder and dysfunction may have you feeling down toward the middle of November. We all know that you like to be liked. Perhaps there is a lack of such admiration in your life. So throw a bash. Surround yourself with friendly faces. Reasons for celebration abound. Maybe your old friend from August is back in town. Or your significant other has achieved a long-term fitness goal. Or your son or daughter has won an academic honor. Whatever the excuse for the party, the important thing is that you invite some Cat/Rabbit groupies. Regale your guests with stories, intricate wordplay, or astute observations on various topics. As they delight in your intelligence, you will be lifted right out of the doldrums. No matter how strenuous things are in other realms of your life, you can count on harmonious social interaction to de-stress now.

Keep an eye out for phony financial come-ons in the last week of the month. You are positive that you have been paying your credit card bills punctually. So do not fall for the "ACT NOW before your credit rating plummets!" letter. And why would your bank ask you to confirm your online banking password in an unsolicited email? Take no further action until you speak with a live human from the call center. This message could be a phishing scam. A plot to steal your confidential information. Hit delete. As long as you relegate this phony message to the trash bin, you will be fine.

CAT/RABBIT December 2016

December tips off with an unexpected thrill. An old ex may pop back into your life. Things ended amicably between you too. Something superficial got in the way of your relationship. Perhaps a time-consuming job. Or a move to a faraway city. Or one of you was depressed and stopped participating. Now that circumstances have changed, the two of you might want to give your relationship another shot. If you are seeing someone else right now, stay in contact with the ex. Remain in touch.

Unfortunately, the holidays coincide with a retrograde period this year. Mercury's orbit reverses itself from December 19 through January 8. The prospect of family in-fighting is already spoiling your appetite. And that was before you could have anticipated all the misconstrued words and lack of clarity such a period heralds. So, if you can swing it financially, make this holiday season a "destination" event. Fly to an island for Christmas. Drive to the beach for Hanukkah. Only take along your immediate family. Hopefully, the distance you establish will weed out the troublemakers in your clan. The fire-starters should deem the trip too far or too last minute. Without the problem children, you can enjoy a peaceful celebration. If such an outing is too expensive, you can still take other measures to ensure calm proceedings. You could "accidentally" knock the booze off the counter while cooking. With no liquor around, you will be pleasantly surprised at how agreeable your thornier relatives become.

As the month comes to a close, pet problems are driving you insane. Maybe the neighbor's mutt refuses to shut up. I guess 3 AM is a logical time to start howling at the moon in dog-world? On the other hand, it could be your own animal that's giving you fits. A cat doing its business in all the wrong places. Aren't felines supposed to be the easy ones to potty-train? Handle these issues tactfully. Gently alert your neighbor that his or her pseudo-wolf is driving everyone nuts. Perhaps it is time for a return to obedience school. As for the kitty? Just keep tossing him or her into the litter box. He will get the picture eventually. Until then, keep cleaning fluid and rubber gloves on hand at all times.

CAT/RABBIT January 2017

As the New Year begins, the dentist's office beckons. You have an upcoming check-up. Do not cancel or avoid this visit. Remember, cavities start forming long before announcing their presence with a toothache. Just because your mouth feels fine now does not mean you are in the clear. Make the trip, fork over the cash, and go home with some peace of mind. In addition, if you are a single Cat/Rabbit, flash those pearly whites around the waiting room. Perhaps your winning smile will catch the eye of an attractive fellow patient.

For various reasons, work will return to its normal, ordered state by mid-January. Maybe your new colleague from November has restored your faith in humanity. With their assistance, you can finally compartmentalize your time again. Each hour has its own task. And nothing short of a fire in the break room can disturb that arrangement. If you left your job recently, the search for a new one should be heating up. It may not be hiring season. But a local company desperately needs to fill a newly vacated position. Cast your net as wide as possible. With any luck, you two will meet up and form the perfect match.

As you reflect on the FIRE Monkey Year, the stirrings of depression threaten to surface. There is no sugarcoating the situation. 2016 was a tough one. Disorder, unexpected challenges, family drama—all disturbed the clockwork of your neat little world. But there is always a silver lining waiting behind the thunderclouds. For one thing, the year is over! The Monkey has bounded back into the jungle, freeing you from his torments. Also, your struggles have revealed the true sources of strength in your life. Your gentle wit, of course. And your ties to family. And your friends who are your family of choice. Whoever composes it—your kin, your old friends, your significant other—keep them close. These people are your pillars. The ones who will be there for you when no one else is. Now, with your loved ones by your side, on to the FIRE Rooster Year!

YOUR MONTHLY FORECASTS FOR THE FIRE MONKEY YEAR

2016

DRAGON

Author's Note... Mercury Retrograde

Sometimes planets appear to be zooming backward through the zodiac. Of course this backward motion is only an illusion. The planet has not turned tail. But it appears to have. Astrologers call this apparent reversing: **"retrograde"**.

Any planet can be retrograde. But only Mercury's retrogrades cause communications to break down. Mercury has its retrograde period for a few weeks 3 or 4 times each year. Whilst Mercury is retrograde, we humans are encouraged to take stock, make plans and discuss different approaches to a variety of subjects. But because information is often muddled, promises broken and electronic devices on the blink during Mercury retrograde, we must remain flexible and open-minded. Advice? Always allow extra time for travel. Schedule changes are common. Do not sign any contracts or cement agreements during Mercury retrograde. Make no irreversible promises. Watch out for con artists. Make no final decisions, binding engagements or major purchases during a Mercury retrograde. You are allowed to have tantrums or rail against your fate. But Mercury will continue to be retrograde till it decides to go direct again.

Mercury Retrogrades
2016

January 5 thru January 25
April 28 thru May 22
August 30 thru September 22
December 19 thru January 8 2017

OVERVIEW OF 2016 THE YEAR OF THE MONKEY FOR THE DRAGON

Dauntless Dragon,

It's a well-known fact. Monkeys are some of the most unpredictable characters in the Chinese Zodiac. Hence, we are never very certain of outcomes in Monkey years. You Dragons don't usually resist change. Nor do you need to be reassured at every bump in the road. But the danger for Dragons in Monkey years is risk. As you know by now, your Dragon people rarely shrink from peril. You feel you know how to handle almost any and everything. If something goes wrong, you Dragons sincerely think you know how to finesse it. But in Monkey years, you cannot be so sure of yourselves. You may be inclined in these testy years to embark on one or two big, chancy ventures and then watch them slowly but surely disintegrate before your big, green eyeballs. So the message for Dragons in Monkey years is to hold off from embarking on gigantic, revolutionary projects. Remain in the realm of safe and sound investment. Put some money into further schooling or travel to places where you can learn something new that you will be able to use next year when the more predictable Rooster comes along and tries to hamper everybody's progress – except his own. sw

DRAGON January 2016

Just what you didn't need. Someone has confessed a dark secret to you. From the 5th to the 25th of January, Mercury retrograde returns. You may have trouble keeping confidential information confidential. Score some duct tape. Stretch it across your lips at your first urge to gab. Above all, do not share other peoples' deeply personal details with a soul. God forbid you become the one who blabs about your best friend's abortion. Or that you find yourself suddenly blurting that your immediate boss man gets a full body wax every month.

Halfway through January, your focus shifts. A person you love and admire is gravely ill. You long to be his or her savior. Leave that part to the doctors. Instead, think about what might cheer them up. Then bring them some food they particularly like or a few magazines on their favorite subjects. By the way, this person will recover. Just be there to listen and support them as they climb free of the malady which gripped them. Mercury retrograde begins to ease, but not without a few last gasps. Minor written mishaps. Typing errors that cause chuckles or start wars. Mixed-up texts. You phone to inquire about buying new software for your computer. Instead, you find yourself talking to a lingerie shop. No wonder they sounded perplexed when you said you needed a stronger firewall!

Near the end of January, you may have a chance to learn more about an unusual art form. A friend in the business needs help. Their partner is on holiday or on sick leave. Could you lend a hand? Why, you would be delighted! You have always wanted to know more about their particular discipline. It could be customizing cars. Or painting henna tattoos. The craft itself is what fascinates you. Though you may never become proficient enough to do it yourself, you will enjoy watching and being the artist's assistant. Such experimentation is a happy way to end the Sheep year. A welcome respite before the Monkey year grabs you by the tail and rattles your scales. Monkeys are imps. Monkey years are impetuous. You are in for an entertaining twelve months ahead.

DRAGON February 2016

On February 8th, the unpredictable Monkey Year gets started. Your career is proceeding satisfactorily. But slowly. Early in this month, you may receive an opportunity at another place of employment. Perhaps a job offer from a rival company. Maybe a chance to be your own boss. Or something quite outrageous, like dropping everything and becoming a ski instructor. If this opportunity sounds too good to be true, that's because it probably is. Stick to your current path. Although the lack of movement bores you, it would be unwise to change course now. This type of conundrum will be a recurring theme during the Monkey era—being tempted by risky changes. As frustrating as it may be, you must continue to make prudent decisions.

Dragons are born leaders. That characteristic often comes in handy in business negotiations. But it can also help you in other facets of life. In mid-February, your family will test the limits of your authority. If you have children, be prepared for a little in-house rebellion. Maybe a daughter will come home with a tattoo. Or a son will get caught smoking marijuana behind his school. Problems could also arise with your significant other. He or she may be wavering in their commitment to you. Or hinting that they are keeping their options open. Take any such defiance with a grain of salt. They are testing you to see if you will you snap. Do not lose your cool. The more you show that their actions don't ruffle your scales, the faster the insurrection will fizzle.

Toward the end of the month, you are searching for inspiration either in your own line of work or in the area of artistic creativity. You may even want to be assisted in making a crucial esthetic decision. Right now you feel as though your conscious mind is too preoccupied with daily banalities to come up with any suggestions. Use the fertile space just before you fall asleep to generate some ideas. As your mind and body relax, thoughts will float to the surface. Some are inane. But sometimes, a spark of brilliance will reveal itself just before you close your eyes. So keep pen and paper handy. You must jot down your musings before the clouds of slumber mask them.

DRAGON March 2016

Love is in the air during the first week of the month. If you are intimate with someone, passion may have been lacking of late. So plan a romantic date night. Pull out all the stops. Light scented candles. Spread flower petals on the bed. Have some smooth jazz or R&B playing softly. Remember to utter some extra sweet words of love. Your too-long lonesome bed sheets will quickly recede into the recesses of your memory. If you are single, early March is a good time to get set up on a blind date. Ask around. One of your friends of the opposite sex definitely has someone in mind. All you will need to do is firm up the plans. No one has ever accused you of being shy. You possess a thrilling ability to charm. Once your blind date meets you in person, they won't have a snowball chance in Hell of resisting.

Although 2016 is not a good year for Dragons to take risks, there is one type of investment you should definitely think about making. An investment in yourself. In furthering your education. Whether in the form of traditional schooling or in self-teaching, the middle of March should provide a first class opportunity to do so. Perhaps you will notice a flyer for business classes at your local community college. Or you'll pick up on a worn sign stapled to a telephone pole which promotes private computer science lessons. Though the advertising media may be humble, the classes could be top drawer. Don't turn up your fiery snout at anything. Sometimes, the best instruction comes from humble places. Conversely, the most expensive, name-brand schools do not always provide the instruction. Be sure to do some investigating before you fork over any cash.

During March's final days, avoid crossing through dangerous or down-on-their-luck neighborhoods. Obviously, steering clear of such areas is always a smart move. But your risk of getting held up is especially high during this period. If you absolutely must pass through a treacherous area, try not to come to a stop. Cruise through every traffic light. Don't get caught staring at the guys on the corner. And definitely do not fill up on gas in the ghetto. Fuel up before you leave the comfort of your precinct. These precautions may seem overblown. But in these troubled times, it truly is better to be safe than sorry.

DRAGON April 2016

In early April, a financial opportunity will tempt you. You may come across an article about a groundbreaking company that is developing some incredible technology. Could be something like a car that runs on recycled trash. Or a new-fangled smart phone that will unseat Apple's stranglehold on the market. Or perhaps a close friend is starting up his or her own business and wants you to back him. Again, as in February, resist the urge. Remember New Coke? Palm Pilots? The Aquacar? Not every scientific innovation is bound for success. If you pour capital into this venture, you may never see your money again. I know that advice gnaws at your pride. You Dragons always think you can deal with any challenge. In this case, your best bet is a simple "no thanks." It's that time of year again. Do not neglect to file your taxes. The last thing you need is the taxman breathing down your scaly neck.

A social gathering in mid-March places you firmly in your element. A born master of ceremonies, you immediately become the center of attention. Whether or not you will own up to the fact, the limelight is your preferred spot in any gathering. However, at this event, be careful whose toes you tread on. The host or hostess doesn't want to be upstaged. He or she will not appreciate your stealing the spotlight.

There can only be one prom king or queen. So if you wish to avoid creating an uncomfortable ambiance, restrain yourself. Be content to chat up your immediate neighbors. Although humility is not your strongest suit, it does suit you down to the ground.

Toward the end of the month, a new craze is likely to sweep your household. Especially if you have children. Do not be surprised if they come home from school begging to go shopping. For the newest card game. Or for a set of collectible stuffed animals. Maybe even for the skateboard or pair of rollerblades that all their friends are getting. Humor this fad. Allow them a small purchase at this time. Their obsession with trendy toys will soon go the way of the dodo.

DRAGON May 2016

I hope disaster did not befall you at the end of April. Or that maybe you peeked ahead to this section. Mercury went in his retrograde orbit on April 28. He remains there until May 22. As always, his skyward permutations will wreak havoc on our earthly communications. You may find it difficult to get your point across when conversing with others. Conversely, meetings and presentations seem to be in a foreign tongue as you try to follow along. Your concentration may seem fragmented. Because of Mercury's retrograde, now would be an inopportune time to put your signature to a fresh lease or mortgage. *Au contraire.* Postpone signing any important paperwork. It's always possible to stave off the inevitable. Instead, use these weeks to complete half-finished projects. Since your ideas have already germinated, the littlest planet's scrambling influence will not hinder your progress.

Of course even if backwards Mercury makes things a bit dicey for everyone, life does go on. In mid-May, you should receive a challenging assignment. It could come from your place of work. Or if you are enrolled in school, the challenge might come from a professor or teacher. Perhaps they want you to write a paper on quantum mechanics; or to prepare a presentation on minute variations in fashion since the 80's. In any case, the mission you are given threatens to be something you are not qualified for. This undertaking is daunting. So use the resources around you. Research the topic thoroughly. Start with Wikipedia or another type of encyclopedia. Then graduate to more thorough sources. Draw on previous studies or publications, then add your own inimitable style and the work will yield satisfactory results.

As May comes to a close, you may be experiencing some peculiar bodily sensations. A tremor in your hands. Or an inability to fall asleep at night. Your symptoms do not seem to be rooted in anxiety, however.

The cause is more simple. And so is the fix. Are you guzzling sugary sodas every day? Afraid to keep track of how many cups of coffee you average? Ditch the caffeine and 86 the sugar. Instead of sugary drinks and coffee, drink herb teas with a tiny bit of Stevia. There are a lot of interesting herbal flavors you can experiment with. If you take that advice, you can say bye bye to the jitters. If you absolutely cannot give up your precious mocha, refrain from drinking any after 3 PM. Cutting yourself off early in the day will ensure a more peaceful slumber.

DRAGON June 2016

Your personal health could become a problem in early June. One too many dinner parties have left you loosening your belt a notch or two. You are probably no stranger to such weight gains. Usually, you would just embark on a crash diet or rabid exercise routine to knock the pounds back off. However, this time around, do not make such a drastic lifestyle change. A trendy juice cleanse or Paleo diet is not the answer. Not in the long run, at least. Instead, build some healthy habits back into your life. Make eating two pieces of fruit every day a rule. Without exception. And eat dessert only at weekends. Coupled with regular exercise, these small dietary adjustments should soon help you return to your desired level of fitness.

Although your confidence is fairly unwavering now, toward the middle of June, someone close to you will be struggling with his or her own self-esteem. Anxiety or depression is threatening to overwhelm this person. Perhaps your partner is having trouble adjusting to a new job. Or your children are dealing with bullying or other schoolyard drama from their friends. Or worse, maybe they have trouble actually making friends. Everyone needs a mental break from time to time. Take your ailing friend or relative on long restorative walks in the woods. Go on lengthy drives and chat about what's on their mind. These cliché fixes do not really sound curative to you. But such exposure to nature and enclosure in a small space with nothing to do but talk will restore peace to their muddled mind. You will have to initiate the hike or the drive or the camping trip. And then suck it up and volunteer to accompany them.

Take a good look around your dwelling at the end of the month. Don't the decorations (or lack thereof) seem barren and devoid of comfort? Liven things up. Splurge on some cool new home accessories. Buy a couple of indoor plants for your living room. Spring for that colorful tapestry you've been eying at the local flea market. Splash one wall with bright paint. Spruce up your house and you will spice up your life. This remodeling effort will reap benefits when you bring visitors around.

They may not notice the new details. But they will notice the new feeling of cozy conviviality.

DRAGON July 2016

As July begins, you may receive an opportunity to travel. Perhaps on a business trip. Or to accompany your significant other on their own business trip. You may even be able to winkle out a short personal vacation. You can almost hear the nightlife calling your name as you touch down. By all means, wallow in the your luxury surrounds. But try as well to come away with something mentally beneficial. Investigate the museum scene. Soak up some of the native culture. You may not recognize the importance of learning about extinct plants right now. Or the use of gazing at exotic animals in a Panamanian zoo. Never mind. These intellectual memories will come in handy during long fallow periods when you have no holidays in view.

A relative is trying to kick a nasty habit. They have been doing so for a long time, in fact. But by the middle of July, they are truly motivated to sever their dependency. Perhaps you have an uncle with a gambling addiction. Or a sister who guzzles liquor like iced tea. Or maybe a friend is trying to quit smoking. A more serious problem, such as gambling or booze, will require outside help. A 12-step program works best. But whatever the addiction, the person must sincerely want to kick his or her habit. Ironically, casino ads often list a hotline for addicts. Next time you pass a billboard or hear a commercial about casinos, scribble the number down. As for the more minor obsessions, try to find a benign habit to replace the outgoing one - lollipops, for example, can help smokers stop puffing their lives away. Going to a gym can improve the shape of an overeater and thus inspire them to cut back on junk food. Giving up addiction is always a series of baby steps. You stop smoking ten times before you stop definitively. You may go to the gym regularly for a year before you feel the urge to maintain your progress by altering your diet. Give your pal or family member all the encouragement you can conjure.

Some trivial drama may seek to spoil the end of your month. Does a friend become standoffish because you forgot to wish them a happy birthday on Facebook? Or an acquaintance will take offense to a cryptic tweet. You Dragons can handle open confrontation. But this cowardly type of non- argument disgusts you. Before you blow your fiery top, try broaching the subject openly over a hearty breakfast or lunch. Wear a smile on your face. Turn on the charm. And remind those involved that words are only wind. I am sure they will agree that we should all focus our energy on more important matters.

DRAGON August 2016

Dragons love power. And power comes naturally to you. But in early August, that natural order is being threatened. A rival will attempt to endanger your spot in the workplace pecking order. Perhaps a new hire is assuming some of your duties. Or maybe a financial crunch means that your company must choose between retaining you or keeping your coworker around. The very idea of this competition might anger you. How can your bosses fail to see that you are clearly the more impressive candidate? You may even be considering barging in on a meeting to force them to decide on the spot. Resist this urge. A petulant tantrum will end up revealing your precarious temper. And that revelation would surely cause your stock to plummet in the eyes of the higher-ups.

Your relative who was struggling with a destructive habit in July has reappeared on the family radar. For all the wrong reasons. Unfortunately, he or she may have fallen off the wagon again. For all your faults, you are excellent when it comes to dealing with the emergencies of loved ones. This crisis should be no exception. Offer an ear to vent to. A shoulder to cry on. And try not to be judge mental. The afflicted individual hears enough disapprobation coming from within their own frazzled brain. Do watch out however not to get your fire too close to their fire. As you attempt to help this person with their demons, watch that you yourself are not led into temptation. It is never a good time to start (or re-start) smoking cigarettes. Or beginning play the slot machines or indulging in any other addiction. Keep the boundaries clear.

You are going to come into a bit of money toward the end of August. Perhaps a distant relative has died and left you a sum. Out of nowhere, your name surfaces in the will. Maybe it's not a legacy. Perhaps you will receive a bonus at work. Or your tax rebate will finally arrive. Handle your financial windfall wisely. Put at least half of it into savings right away quick. The other half? Splurge! Get a colorful tattoo. Buy a stylish pair of expensive Italian shoes. Take that special someone out to a big concert. Buy your sweetheart a new (used) car. Remember. You can't take it with you.

DRAGON September 2016

Extreme temperatures may start off your month of September. So, depending on where you live, check the air conditioner filter and/or confirm that you have enough fuel to face the coming winter. Short of a hurricane, you can handle weather fluctuations by taking simple precautions. To further clog the atmosphere, Mercury goes into another retrograde on August 30, and will remain in reverse orbit until September 22. As usual, all forms of exchanging information and ideas will be hampered. Trying to accomplish anything in the office or your personal business could be a bit more complex than usual. Why not make this Mercury Rx a down time? Catch up on your favorite TV series. Or binge-watch the classics by your favorite film director. Read all the books your favorite author ever wrote. Spend more time in the kitchen experimenting with new recipes.

A change is coming in your social circle. A mid-September rift will be influenced by the chaotic Monkey year. Perhaps a mutual love interest is at the core of the problem. Or maybe some of your comrades are jealous of another faction's career successes. When the dust clears, your group of close mates and pals may be divided down the middle. As a hardy soul, you excel at rolling with the punches. You will need those skills now. You occupy an interesting position. Since you were probably not one of the main combatants in the tussle, you should be able to remain on good terms with both parties. You might be hoping to inspire reconciliation. My advice? Save your breath. What's done is done. Your energy is best spent adjusting to the new situation. If you accept this new reality, through diplomacy, you can successfully maintain both sets of relationships.

Spend a family day out and about toward the end of September. Attend a sports match. Take your kids to an interesting museum. Take your significant other to an opera or musical. This excursion will be a bonding experience for everyone. If you have a teenager, getting him or her out of the house may feel like pulling hen's teeth. However, once you are all safely en route, your adolescent will decide that he or she is actually having a good time. They may even thank you later. But don't hold your breath.

DRAGON October 2016

As October begins, you sense a lack of purpose in your life. Luckily, this feeling is not hopeless ennui or depression. You can row yourself out of the doldrums. How, you ask? By running for some sort of leadership position. Is there is an opening in the local political sphere? Perhaps you could aim for a post in your workplace union. Taking a different tack, maybe you could found a charitable organization. Organize to supply clean drinking water to rural populations. Or bestow state-of-the-art textbooks or computers to inner-city schools. Spearheading such a cause would be a rewarding activity in its own right. But more importantly, on a personal level, this association will sate your current thirst for authority.

Office politics have you in a huff again toward the middle of the month. Your rival from August may draw public praise from your boss. Perhaps in a company-wide meeting. Or in a chain e-mail. You interpret these plaudits for your competitor as a direct insult to your own work. You could be about ready to burn the place to the ground with one great fiery Dragon snort. Or, since this is not a medieval legend, you might just be ready to quit your gig. However, stay your hand. Do not do anything rash. Perhaps you are a mite paranoid. Management will not think any less of you just because this other character is garnering so much attention. There is enough room for two success stories at your job. Slither along onward and upward with your usual aplomb.

Make sure you are sticking to your moderation mantra from the month of June. As October winds down, your proclivity for excess may once again rise to the surface. A delectable dinner sets off your basest dietary urges. After dining on saucy shrimp scampi or a rack of melt-in-your-mouth ribs, it will be difficult to return to eating healthy foods. And it could be especially difficult to return to normal portion sizes. To quell any bursts of hunger, stock up on yogurt. Make yourself a fruit smoothie or three. Healthier foods - even in quantity - will sate your gargantuan appetite and provide your body with vital nutrients.

DRAGON November 2016

November this year should begin with pleasant weather. Take full advantage. Spend more time outdoors. Go somewhere flat and fly a kite. Take a bike ride through the countryside. Enjoy this spell of clement weather while it lasts. In other news, you are likely to score a small workplace victory around now. Possibly a promotion. In name only, unfortunately. But still a win. Or you might come out on top during a set of negotiations. This success could even come at the expense of your rival, which would no doubt bring a smile to your lips. Be extra charming and willing to help out. Inflate your status in the eyes of your bosses. Just try to curb your bragging around the water cooler.

So far, 2016 may have been a quiet year between the sheets for single Dragons. That dry spell is set to change in mid-November. Keep an eye out for a fiendishly attractive person giving you the eye. This won't happen in any location or situation you might expect. Maybe you will be covered in dirt after gardening. Or wearing a smelly set of clothes as you run to the laundromat to catch up on your wash. Perhaps you will be drenched in sweat after an intense run or workout. You certainly don't look your best. Do not allow your lack of confidence to manifest in your body language. If you embrace the less-than-ideal circumstances with a friendly grin, your newfound love interest will find you all the more irresistible.

A new gadget is set to debut in the market toward the end of November. Somebody in your family wants it. Badly. If you have children, perhaps they are clamoring for the newest portable video game player. Maybe your better half is begging for the latest Apple knickknack. Or the gadget-hungry culprit could be...you! It has been a while since you updated your own phone. Or music player. The planets think it's high time you treated yourself. But take one precaution. If you intend to buy something for yourself and not for family members, be sure the gizmo is something you can all share.

DRAGON December 2016

This month starts off on a positive note. You will receive a compliment from someone whose opinion you hold in high regard. It's likely to be related to a project you've been working on for some time now. A plan you have been building toward very slowly. Something like a lengthy novel or a screenplay. It could also be a well-researched case study, or even an athletic move you've been practicing. Ordinarily, you do not exactly beg for recognition from your peers. But something about this person who compliments you -their status, their past accomplishments—inspires your belief in self. Take their praise to heart. You can always use their kind words for motivation later on.

In mid-December, Mercury turns retrograde. This retrograde lasts from the 19th until January 8th. Too bad. But it includes the holiday season. Ordinarily, such timing would be disastrous. But as you have already confirmed your plans for trips and visits this month, everything should go off without a hitch. It is in the workplace where problems might surface. You are likely to get your wires crossed when trying to schedule a meeting with someone. You show up an hour before your colleagues. And they pop their heads in just after you leave. So in this dicey retrograde time period, do not accuse anyone of deliberately avoiding you. Most errors of this kind are merely the result of miscommunication.

Late December is your chance to bask a little. Your family is in town (or you are in their town) for the holidays. At the dinner table, take some advantage of being the center of attention. Spin your yarns. Tell everyone about your latest business conquest. Your audience will be rapt. But do remember to give your other relatives their due. When someone else has the spotlight, resist the urge to upstage them. To help keep your mouth shut when others are speaking, stuff it full of humble pie.

DRAGON January 2017

As January begins, you are at odds with electronics. A dropped phone refuses to reboot. Your GPS system leads you on a wild goose chase through the middle of nowhere. Your blender laces your smoothie with shards of plastic instead of ice. Fret not. These are the last vestiges of Mercury's retrograde. Do take some preventative measures. Back up important files on an external hard drive. Or email them to yourself. That way, if your computer goes haywire, you will still be able to access what you need. And if something does break and is irreparable, do not lash out at the nearest target. It's not your spouse's fault that your music player is stuck on repeat. Nor is it your coworker's problem that your watch has definitively stopped running. If you have any pent-up frustration, take it out on your favorite form of exercise. Giving your pokey old heart rate a boost will be much more constructive than raising everyone else's.

Dragons must keep an eye on savings accounts toward the middle of January. Especially if you use online banking. A hacker may try to scam you out of your passwords. Or your bank may raise or lower its interest rates without alerting you. You can ward off scams if you use common sense. Better not to give information away over the Internet. And if you speak to a live banker, you can find out any policy changes ahead of time. Something less insidious might also happen to your funds. Maybe your savings will get rerouted to your checking account. If you do not notice, you may end up spending too much of your hard-earned spoils. So keep an eye on your balance.

At last, the unpredictable FIRE Monkey year is coming to an end. Use the final days of January to reflect on the past twelve months. See how the mischievous primate has affected you. Hopefully, you invested in yourself. In education and learning new skills. Also, think about what you learned about power dynamics. You had some battles in the workplace this year. But win or lose, you definitely benefited from your experiences. With your newly acquired competence and life lessons, you should be more than ready to take on the FIRE Rooster year on the 28th of January.

YOUR MONTHLY FORECASTS FOR THE FIRE MONKEY YEAR

2016

SNAKE

Author's Note... Mercury Retrograde

Sometimes planets appear to be zooming backward through the zodiac. Of course this backward motion is only an illusion. The planet has not turned tail. But it appears to have. Astrologers call this apparent reversing: **"retrograde"**.

Any planet can be retrograde. But only Mercury's retrogrades cause communications to break down. Mercury has its retrograde period for a few weeks 3 or 4 times each year. Whilst Mercury is retrograde, we humans are encouraged to take stock, make plans and discuss different approaches to a variety of subjects. But because information is often muddled, promises broken and electronic devices on the blink during Mercury retrograde, we must remain flexible and open-minded. Advice? Always allow extra time for travel. Schedule changes are common. Do not sign any contracts or cement agreements during Mercury retrograde. Make no irreversible promises. Watch out for con artists. Make no final decisions, binding engagements or major purchases during a Mercury retrograde. You are allowed to have tantrums or rail against your fate. But Mercury will continue to be retrograde till it decides to go direct again.

Mercury Retrogrades
2016

January 5 thru January 25
April 28 thru May 22
August 30 thru September 22
December 19 thru January 8 2017

OVERVIEW OF 2016 THE YEAR OF THE MONKEY FOR THE SNAKE

Bewitching Snake:

You will need all your indomitable strength this year to withstand the onslaught of the Monkey's outlandish antics. Monkeys need attention and will perform almost any type of outrageous act to get it. Perhaps you won't be drawn in by the Monkey's neurotic charm. But if you are – beware! You provide an excellent audience because you simply love spectacle. You are in no little danger in Monkey years because you find entertainment so attractive. If someone amuses you sufficiently, you can be duped and even diverted from your chosen path. Monkeys are tricksters who don't much care what audience they are playing to as long as the public applauds and throws coins their way. So in this year of the Monkey, Snakes must watch their wallets, tie their purse strings tightly and stay out of the way of temptation. Don't even THINK about entering a casino or going near a card game. Remain above it all by undertaking a major creative project that keeps you grounded and in one place. Your love life may also supply a safe haven – provided, of course, that you aren't married to a Monkey. Should this be the case, see a Dog or Ox psychiatrist or else – move to Tibet – alone! sw

SNAKE January 2016

January sees us in another Mercury retrograde. From the 5th to the 25th, your daily existence could be fraught with complications. Be particularly wary of come-ons from charities. The latest note will not seem out of the ordinary. After all, you are always giving money to this or sending indignant letters to defend that. This new organization seems perfectly genuine. But when they start pressing you for a donation, exercise caution. Do not hand over your bank details. The Sheep year's end is tricky. Keep your eye out for red flags.

In January you find yourself nostalgic. Perhaps this is because you have a school reunion planned for 2016. Is thinking about it making you relive the past? Or has an individual triggered these feelings in you? A man who was once of high importance in your life is due to return in late January. Maybe an old love, maybe an old friend. He is a strong-willed one. Intelligent and outspoken. Or at least he was when you last knew him. You will bump into this character in the least expected of places. He is older now, but just as charismatic. You have a lot of catching up to do. Retrograde effects be damned, you two always manage to understand each other. You might find, much to your surprise, that you end up asking his advice. And even though you have not spoken in ages, he will have the perfect wise man's answer to your problem.

At the culmination of this Sheep year, you are staring down a test of your commitment. Are you thinking of asking your new love to move in? Or has your old squeeze finally proposed? You are one part elated, two parts terrified. The trick is figuring out which reaction to heed. My advice? Wait until February. Then ask a Monkey person. Monkeys are notorious problem-solvers.

SNAKE February 2016

The FIRE Monkey Year wastes no time making its presence felt. Right away, you run the risk of getting pulled into a workplace squabble. Perhaps a group of mutineers are bad-mouthing a manager behind his or her back. Or a superior could be trying to turn you against your coworkers. This petty drama smacks of the mischievous Monkey's handiwork. Even if you are tempted to join the spectacle, your best bet is to keep your hands clean. Do not slap your signature on a petition to get your boss fired. And if someone asks you to rat out your colleagues for slacking on the job, think twice before acting. After all, your peers are the ones you have to face at the water cooler each morning.

Few can resist your allure. So when a loved one refuses to concede something to you toward the middle of February, your jaw unhinges and drops to the floor. Perhaps a girlfriend or boyfriend will kick you to the curb. Or maybe a friend will call you out on being a flake after you cancel some plans. This person's temerity stings. You are accustomed to getting what you want. Usually, a few bewitching words are all it takes for you to swing someone's opinion. But such schmoozing will get you nowhere this time. Your combatant sees right through you. So take your lumps. Besides, no one can resist your charm for long! Soon the law of averages will take over and you will be back in control.

By the final weekend of the month, you may be feeling a bit stir-crazy. Have you been glued to the couch recently? Binge-watching TV shows? Staring at your laptop screen, unable to start anything? Force yourself to get out of the house. If you work from home, set up shop in a cafe. If you want to relax, find a sports or coffee bar to kick back in. The change in scenery will alleviate your cabin fever. But if your goal is to be more productive, make sure you select a quiet spot. If fifty people are yammering away as you try to concentrate, your distracting excursion will not yield much of use.

SNAKE March 2016

As March begins, you notice a pattern in your life. People are not treating you as you think you should be treated. This lack of respect is wearing on you. It could be pushing you toward bad habits. Like draining a bottle of wine with dinner every night. Or gluing your eyes to an online gambling or drivel-packed website. You might even find yourself gnawing at your fingernails. Get a grip. No one ever said the world was a kind place. If you start relying on superficial solutions, you will grow into a lonely, bitter Snake. Instead, establish a concrete change in your own attitude. Pledge to put more effort into your work. To treat your significant other with more regard. To hit the gym more often. Your new attitude will force people to view you in a different light.

You may be feeling dissatisfied with your job toward the middle of March. Your occupation pays the bills. But it no longer inspires any passion in you. Instead of pondering a career change, use the wily spirit of the Monkey to begin a creative project on the side. If you like to write, start a novel. Or a series of short stories. If you prefer the visual arts, break ground on a new sculpture or painting. But take your time with this project. Rome wasn't built in a day. A couple hours per week will be enough. That way, you won't burn out. The idea is this. If you have a goal beyond merely punching the clock—a long-term venture to work toward—your life will feel more fulfilling. Plus, if your current gig ever falls through, you will have another set of skills to fall back on.

Nothing comforts you like being surrounded by familiar faces. So schedule a get-together with close friends toward the end of the month. Maybe a dinner out on the town. Or you could meet up for drinks during happy hour. Seeing the old crew always puts you in a state of bliss. There may also be some new faces present. Before you turn your back on them, make a mental note to be open to making new friends. Your comfort zone is mighty hospitable. But sometimes, it's healthy for your chilly Snake psyche to take baby steps beyond it.

SNAKE April 2016

As April takes the reins from March, the scent of love is in the air. Your flair for accessories is about to catch someone's eye. Someone who can appreciate a handbag that matches your jaunty scarf. Or a tie that dovetails perfectly with your dress socks. If you are a single Snake, let your natural allure take over from here. Your style got your toe in the door. But that charm will be what earns you a seat at the dining room table. On the other hand, if you are already ensconced with another lover, be upfront about your relationship status. The object of your desire will of course assume that they are the only such object. Be clear about your status. If you try to play two people at once, somebody is going to get burned. And it could be you.

A glittering item in a storefront window may sorely tempt you during the second week of April. Perhaps you catch a glimpse of the newest smartphone model. Or the hottest fashion trend out of Milan or Paris. Your finger feels magnetized by your credit card. But before you travel down that road, consider your recurring expenses. Do you have enough toilet paper for the month? Is your refrigerator bare? Have you paid your electric bill? When faced with shiny new toys, you have a tendency to forget about your basic needs. This is the 21st Century. That flashy phone won't do you any good if you don't have power to charge to with. Deal with the necessities before you make any impulse purchases.

Set aside time one night to watch one of your favorite movies. Who cares if you recite all the jokes before the characters even say them? That feeling of familiarity will put you in a fantastic mood. The experience will also energize you. Why not use that energy to fuel your creative project? Scribble the next chapter of your memoir. Lay the foundation for your art installation. Keep on embroidering that tapestry. The boost of mojo will help you resist the pull of shiftlessness, native to all Snake people.

SNAKE May 2016

The beginning of May could see you beset with some technical difficulties. Mercury enters the first retrograde period of the year on April 30. The planet will not revert to its normal orbit until May 22. In particular, the littlest planet's influence endangers the safety of your electronics. Vital calls may get dropped. Emails never appear in the inbox of the intended recipient. Old files disappear without warning. Some of this fallout is unavoidable. But if you back up important files, you can at least protect your most valuable information. An external hard drive would be a good investment. For now and the future. Just try not to spill a drink on it during a dinner party. Then all your information will go up in smoke. Literally.

Around the middle of May, the household goods you stocked up on last month should come in mighty handy. Mother Nature's fickle weather patterns threaten to sandwich you inside your house. Possibly even without power. This tempest will pass. Eventually. In the meantime, you (hopefully) have a supply of candles, water, and other necessities. You might as well have gone through a time machine. If modern distractions are unavailable, entertain yourself the old-fashioned way. Books, card games, Scrabble etc. You will have to admit that it's good for the soul to detach from the tube or computer for a while. On a more positive note, you are due a small piece of good fortune in the third week of May. Maybe you will happen upon some cash in the street. Or you might receive an inheritance from someone you least expected would leave you a dime.

Your social life has grown stale. Your weekends - too predictable. However, toward the end of the month, the cycle of tedium is due for a shake-up. A new friend is soon to waltz into your life. Someone with a different type of personality from yours. Perhaps an enthusiastic young student. Or a salt-of-the-earth bartender or barista. This relationship will shove you out of your comfort zone. Maybe this new crony will cajole you into attending a nude yoga class. Or browbeat you into frequenting a fine arts performance. At first, you will berate yourself for agreeing to such an adventure. But once you relax and go with the flow, you might actually catch yourself having a good time.

SNAKE June 2016

Your way with words will come in useful soon. Contrary to what the Bible says about Snakes, you are not the devil. Far from it. You love to help others do good deeds. Moreover, you possess the ability to work magic on the eyes and ears of an audience and to present an irresistible image of yourself. In the early days of June, an important meeting approaches. It could be a job interview. Or a meet-and-greet with the new owner or CEO of your company. Now is the time to work your magic. Charm the pants off this person. Beguile them with your gift of gab. You are so attractive that you can easily bewitch them into thinking you are the best possible candidate or worker. After you leave, they will be raving about you to anyone within earshot. Mission accomplished.

Luckily for you, your family gives you exactly the support you need. Unfortunately for them, you have been abusing your position of late. When surrounded by a loving cocoon, you tend to complacency. This probably entails a lot of lazing around on the couch while everyone else gets the chores done. So in the middle of the month, do something extra nice for your doting clan. If you have kids, treat them to a trip to a theme park. Promise your significant other a day where you handle all the busy work. And *they* get to lie on the sofa. Such an overture will restore their faith in you. Even better, your actions may earn you a couple more months of guilt-free lounging.

An attack of the sniffles threatens to spoil the end of June. Before you go running for the nearest cold remedy, think about your symptoms a little further. Could this be an allergy flare-up? Snakes are particularly susceptible to inflammatory problems and skin rashes. If you have a history of hay fever, your current troubles are probably seasonal. While you wait for the pollen or dander levels to recede, buy an over-the-counter medication that you can spray into your nostrils. Within minutes, your congestion will ease. After all, you never know when the ability to breathe through your nose will come in handy!

SNAKE July 2016

Unfortunately, your bugaboo rears its ugly head in early July. A rejection is heading your way. Probably in the realm of romance. When it comes to dating, you are accustomed to having your pick of the pack. Not for nothing is the Snake charm famous. But a plucky love interest is going to buck that trend. Maybe someone you've been seeing for a while will decide they are not getting enough out of your relationship. Or, more simply, an object of you affection might flat-out refuse your request to go to dinner with you. Before you slither back into your hole and throw a pity party for yourself, why not stick your neck out one more time? If your sweetheart has dismissed you, give them a second chance - a chance to come to their senses. If it's stranger who turned you down, be nice to yourself and ask someone else out. Even if it stings your pride, that mini experience of failure will make your next victory taste all the sweeter.

Amidst the turbulence in your social life, your bank accounts are steadily inflating. Although the occasional impulse purchase may tempt you, continue to allow your paychecks and other incomes to swell your nest egg. You will be needing extra capital toward the end of the year. Go ahead and ask your bank to funnel a chunk of your earnings straight into savings each month. That way, you won't even have to check your statement to know that you are stockpiling emergency cash.

Disaster is set to befall your residence toward the end of July. No, not a robbery. Nor a tree falling on the roof. Instead, your preferred method of warding off extreme temperatures may conk out. Perhaps the air conditioner will decide that it has had enough of being overworked. Or the furnace will emit the smell of burning hair. You have no option but to go back to basics. If you are too hit, break out the fans. Draw the blinds to keep the place dark. Or if it's cold where you live in July, dig up your old space heater. If you have a fireplace, start a big cozy fire. Although this setback is a nuisance, your clever self will see you through it.

SNAKE August 2016

Getting into gear in the morning is always a drag for you, and waking up is exceptionally rough at the beginning of August. Add a steaming cup of coffee or tea to your routine. The caffeine will soon remedy your sluggishness. You will need that hit of extra energy to ward off the lure of easy money. Among other come-ons, an acquaintance may offer you some part-time work around now. Probably in sales or freelance writing. Your duties seems simple enough. But beware. Any gig that does not pay you up front is suspect. Do you need to meet a quota of sales before your first paycheck? Or must your manuscripts pass muster with a complex algorithm before you are eligible draw your commission? This venture they are proffering sounds like a pyramid scheme. Decline politely. You work hard. Your future is assured now. Don't let the mirage of a quick buck distract you from your routine.

You are not the only snake in the grass at your place of business. Around the middle of August, another such sultry character is captivating bosses and colleagues alike. Perhaps they are talented for pleasant office banter. Or they give the impression they're plugging away, morning and evening, at a thankless position. This person's ingratiating personality raises your hackles. Could you have a rival? Not if you play this game close to your vest. Find a way to be on this person's list of friends, if you gain their confidence, you will soon see behind their facade. Maybe they enjoy talking trash in private on the same coworkers they flatter around the water cooler. Or they might be secretly trawling dating websites during their early mornings at the office. Armed with this backseat information, you can feel more secure in your position. If this competitor tries to undermine you in a meeting, whisper discreetly in their ear that you know about the hanky panky. They will capitulate.

Beware of being too enchanted by a street performer toward the end of the month. This person puts on quite the show. Crooning pitch-perfect tunes in a crowded subway car. Or crouching down on the street displaying an amputated limb. With your love of spectacle, you may buy right in to their show. Feel free to give them some cash. But not too much. You may feel betrayed when the afflicted individual unfolds a fully functional leg and ambles away under their own power. Or when the singer accidentally pauses the recording they are lip-syncing along to. Well, you have to admit—they earned their money.

SNAKE September 2016

Regrettably for your personal sanity, Mercury again decides to wreak havoc on all earthly plans on August 30. He will continue in his retrograde orbit until September 22. As usual, Mercury's influence will greatly impede verbal and written correspondence. So in this time of struggle, focus your attentions on past projects that you never completed. If you embarked on a creative endeavor in March, pick up where you left off. Follow your original idea to its logical conclusion. If you are writing, you will find it's bales of fun to express your original thoughts now. If your ambitions are musical, fine-tune the tunes you've already composed. Even though Mercury's power obstructs new undertakings, an artistic purpose will give you a tangible goal you can reach by staying out of Mercury's way.

A spot of indigestion is possible toward the middle of September. Luckily, you can take preventative measures. Eat more grains and avoid spicy foods for awhile. Drink gallons of water. And not only when your mouth is parched. A large glass every hour, on the hour. These extra fluids will keep everything flowing in your digestive system. Plus, gulping down more liquids has the added benefit of protecting against kidney problems. Problems, which Snakes are particularly susceptible to. Besides, more than half of our bodies are composed of H_2O that we need to replenish all day long.

Coupled with the retrograde, the cycle of temptation and resistance during the past month or so has left you drained of energy. Take refuge from the storm toward the middle of September. Swaddle yourself in romance. If you are seeing someone, it's their turn to love and comfort you. With breakfast in bed. And/or guilt-free foot massages. Maybe even a surprise gift. But be upfront about your neediness. If your partner understands your frustrations of late, they will be more likely to be sympathetic to your needs. If you are single, you must play your cards closer to your chest. It's doubtful anyone will start sleeping with you regularly or deciding on marriage after only a few dates. Go with the flow. Revel in the thrill of seduction.

SNAKE October 2016

Hopefully you set some money aside back in July for unforeseen expenses. Because in the beginning of October, that nebulous menace is about to become a reality. If you have children, you might need to come up with some cash to fund their latest hobby or sports interest. Perhaps some ill-timed mechanical troubles will land your car in the shop. Or maybe your own body will betray you. And these days, visits to a medical specialist rarely come cheap. Before your miser alarm starts sounding, take a step back and look at the big picture. Can you fix the problem yourself? If a broken machine is presenting the dilemma, research some do-it-yourself tips. But if your health is in question, fork over the cash for an expert. This type of situation is exactly why you stashed some cash in the first place.

As the second week of the month arrives, you are entering an important stretch in your job. Whether or not you realize it, the powers-that-be are scrutinizing your work closely. If you play your cards right, you could set yourself up for a promotion or cushy lateral move. If you are a freelance worker, your next project might lead to a long-term deal. So add some pizzazz to that article. Burn the midnight oil. Offer to take on more responsibility in the office. If you throw yourself into one of your workaholic furors, your efforts will reap tangible rewards. With a little push now, you can ensure to be sunning yourself on a tropical rock this time next year.

Your music selection has grown a little stale. So toward the end of October, solicit suggestions for new tunes from your friends. Then download their recommendations en masse. Refreshing your play lists will help you recharge your personal batteries. Also around this time, an inexplicable event may give you a scare. Perhaps a howling sound will emanate from your basement. Or a kitchen drawer will begin to open itself. Although you are a little spooked, do not panic. The noise was probably your radiator. And the drawer? Most likely opened because of faulty installation (Ikea?). Nothing to be afraid of. Sometimes resentments we harbor can cause poltergeists to invade our space.

SNAKE November 2016

The developments in your musical taste will pay dividends at the start of November. Especially in the realm of romance. Melodies and harmonies may provide single Snakes with an opening to chat up a ravishing potential paramour. Perhaps an attractive stranger will overhear a funky tune blaring from your headphones. Or maybe you will encounter an intriguing face while checking out a new band at the local cafe. Conversation about songs and singers can be a natural icebreaker. If you are a wedded Snake, look instead to the crooners of your early years. If you play an old favorite, you are guaranteed to put your partner in the mood. If that does not bring a sly smile to your face, I don't know what will.

By now, your finances should have stabilized after your October setback. No more living paycheck-to-paycheck for you! Celebrate by throwing a small dinner party. Invite a couple of close friends or nearby relatives. Ask someone you trust to bake something delicious. Let the wine flow. You deserve to relax. To surround yourself with loved ones. Avoid serving hard liquor with the meal, though. Although your mood is jovial, there is tension among some of your guests. Likely due to a love triangle. Wine is fine. But spirits always exacerbate problems. The last thing you need is a brawl in your dining room.

A family member is struggling with their self-image at the end of November. They have always been conscious of their appearance, refraining from sodas and fatty foods. Seeming to live at the gym. But now, an offhand comment from an outside source could actually drive them to do something rash. Like a starvation diet. Or running consecutive marathons. The crazy thing? This person is one of your better-looking relatives. So try to help them reconcile their actual physique with how they imagine they look. With your innate charm and guile, you may be the only one capable of convincing this individual of their attractiveness. However, if reasoning with your kinsperson fails, recommend they see a professional. That may be the only way to conquer their neurosis.

SNAKE December 2016

As December begins, you may realize that your creative project from earlier in the year is not turning out as you imagined it might. Perhaps your short story has morphed into a novel. Or your novel has shifted into a memoir. Maybe your kids have begun to treat your art installation like a jungle gym. Although it may irritate you now, this change in course is totally fine. Let your creation develop naturally. Although the finished product may differ from your original concept, the new result will end up being more useful or pleasing to the eye than what you visualized in the first place. Surprise yourself.

Our old pal Mercury return to retrograde orbit on December 19. This time around, his reversal lasts until January 8. As always, miscommunication runs rampant. And its teeth may bite you when you least expect it. Look for an old flame to reappear in your life around the middle of December. Someone you were once very passionate about. Of course, your relationship is totally platonic by now. But do not expect your significant other to understand that. Perhaps because of Mercury's obfuscating influence, he or she is likely to misinterpret your cozy attitude with your ex. Could be because of a flippant comment you made. Or a text message that he or she catches wind of. Unless you feel like fighting World War Three at home, stave off contacting the ex again until the middle of January.

In spite of Mercury retrograde, the holidays should proceed without a hitch. Your family may not always be the most affectionate at this time. They often resent reunions and gatherings. But this time around, make an effort to gather as many relatives as possible in one place. If people are reluctant to make the trip to your neck of the woods, offer to travel to them. Do whatever it takes to surround yourself with loved ones. Once you have taken care of that mission, grab a comfy seat and bask in the affection. The camaraderie and sense of stability will add a satisfying nightcap to the year.

SNAKE January 2017

As January begins, an illness leaves you feeling like you are knocking on death's door. You might develop a nasty fever or cough. Not quite how you envisioned ringing in the New Year. Rest as much as possible. Even when you are awake, confine yourself to the bedroom. Although your body feels ragged now, this sickness shall pass within a day or two. The timing of your recovery could not be better. You have an upcoming date. Probably with the former mister or missus. But perhaps with a more recent flame. You will need all your wits about you for this one. Spending the night with a self-pitying sick person will not exactly enthrall your companion. Keep that in mind when the bug hits you.

Unfortunately, another crisis may force you to draw on your savings. This time, a business dealing is at the root of the problem. Through no fault of your own, one of your investments may go into the red during the middle of January. Perhaps your accountant will make a mistake on your taxes. Or a stock index you thought stable will tank. Or maybe buying holiday gifts pushed you beyond your means. Again, there is no need to panic. As long as you have an emergency stash, you can afford to ride this crisis out. The economic tides will turn in your favor before long.

Toward the end of January, a neighbor's pet could drive you to the brink of insanity. Probably a barking dog. Or the culprit could be a squawking bird. Luckily, you should not have to wait very long for a resolution. The animal may be due for a return to the kennel. Or perhaps an eviction by the landlord will eliminate the problem altogether. On that pleasant note, take some time to reflect on the FIRE Monkey Year. During the past months, you experienced ups and downs. But you gained something from the process. Such as your creative undertaking. Or perhaps renewed confidence in your relationships. Keeping these lessons in mind, it's time to steel yourself for the trials of the FIRE Rooster era which begins early this year. Listen for the jaunty cock-a-doodle-doo on January 28.

YOUR MONTHLY FORECASTS FOR THE FIRE MONKEY YEAR

2016

HORSE

Author's Note... Mercury Retrograde

Sometimes planets appear to be zooming backward through the zodiac. Of course this backward motion is only an illusion. The planet has not turned tail. But it appears to have. Astrologers call this apparent reversing: **"retrograde"**.

Any planet can be retrograde. But only Mercury's retrogrades cause communications to break down. Mercury has its retrograde period for a few weeks 3 or 4 times each year. Whilst Mercury is retrograde, we humans are encouraged to take stock, make plans and discuss different approaches to a variety of subjects. But because information is often muddled, promises broken and electronic devices on the blink during Mercury retrograde, we must remain flexible and open-minded. Advice? Always allow extra time for travel. Schedule changes are common. Do not sign any contracts or cement agreements during Mercury retrograde. Make no irreversible promises. Watch out for con artists. Make no final decisions, binding engagements or major purchases during a Mercury retrograde. You are allowed to have tantrums or rail against your fate. But Mercury will continue to be retrograde till it decides to go direct again.

Mercury Retrogrades
2016

January 5 thru January 25
April 28 thru May 22
August 30 thru September 22
December 19 thru January 8 2017

OVERVIEW OF 2016 THE YEAR OF THE MONKEY FOR THE HORSE

Headstrong Horse,

Being of a pragmatic nature, you Horse people are not often drawn into shady schemes or led down sinuous paths where outcomes are not clearly defined. But Monkeys are agile folks. They are nimble of foot and mind. If you are ever tempted to get involved in anything that deviates from the straight and narrow, it is likely to happen this year. Watch your step. Horses need to work hard in order to make progress and earn success. You don't usually take shortcuts. You are anything but lazy and may even have to learn some things "the hard way". Therefore, should you be tempted away from your usual strict adherence to the rules of striving and toil, you may indeed fail – miserably. When presented with attractive "quick fix" plans to avoid taxes by sheltering your yacht in Panama or opening an offshore bank account, just say NO. This year there will be no free lunches for the hard driving Horse. Monkey years also threaten your waistline. Monkeys are nimble-minded creatures who cannot keep their hands off food. Don't follow their example. Be extra vigilant about watching your diet or this year can expand your girth and take a big bite out of your self-confidence. In fact, the general message for Horses in Monkey years is: Stick to routine. Keep your nose clean. And stay on the bus. sw

HORSE January 2016

I have a post holiday surprise for you. It is a big one. And boy, is it powerful. Yippee! A (nearly) full month of Mercury retrograde! That dastardly planet is in retrograde from the 5th until the 25th. As always, be prepared for communication problems and electronic breakdowns. Fortunately, this is a month of good fortune. Your health is excellent. So good in fact that you are tempted to begin a new energetic pastime. Martial arts, skydiving, maybe salsa dance classes? Something active and life-enhancing. A relative also has a new interest. Theirs relates to animals. Possibly horseback riding or obstacle course training for their very special dog. You might be asked to help with transportation. Especially if your kinsperson is older or does not drive.

Around the middle of January, an acquaintance is taking part in a talent competition. A relative who plays the trombone? A friend who pole dances? They want you to attend their event. You hesitate. You fear an evening of mediocre talents. But then your opinion of this person's actual skill level is irrelevant. You were invited for support. Not to criticize. Make the event about fun and enjoy the experience. No use obsessing over who's winning. Pay close attention to whom you meet there. Doubtless, you will be bumping into someone intriguing. Dazzling, charming and very interested in you. Single Horses, enjoy! For you bridled Horses, admire from afar. But do not touch.

A contract or bill of sale arrives this week. The document needs your signature. Set it aside until after the 25th when our friend Mercury goes direct. Make certain you read through it thoroughly before signing. The month ends on a mellow note. Romance is in the air and it just might be emanating from you and that delectable person you met at the talent show. Or perhaps a sexy movie or new song is stirring long-dormant recollections of your own passionate nuptials. Either way, you will be feeling lustful as well as loving. Time to dust off that bottle of vintage wine. Celebrate the arrival of the Monkey year on February 8th by cooking up a repast for two that you can be proud of.

HORSE February 2016

The Monkey Year starts off slowly. The mischievous primate seems to be biding his time. But do not be fooled—he will eventually try to wreak havoc on your best-laid plans. Work is trundling along. Your daily duties are filled with tedious tasks. If you work in an office, you may start having visions of incomplete paperwork in your sleep. If you are freelance or self-employed, your workload may be insufficient. Not enough upcoming projects. So use your free time now to plan your next move. How can you expand your business to attract more customers? Writers and teachers can advertise their skill packages on the web. Craft workers, or artists with economic aspirations, can also benefit from an online post. Just be careful not to overbook yourself. Knowing you and your diligent nature, your calendar will fill up again soon. Remember. Having too many clients lined up will prevent you from providing an adequate product to all.

Toward the middle of February, make an effort to invest some time in your parents. Especially if you left home at a young age, as wild Horses are wont to do. Your folks' empty nest syndrome is flaring up. Why not drop by for a surprise visit? Phone them up and ask how their day went. Maybe they will only say you won't believe what the neighbor said last night or complain of an ache or pain. Never mind. They need your love and attention. Refrain from wasting money on a gift. The best present you can give them is your time.

As February comes to a close, a flippant comment may ruin your mood. Maybe a stranger curses you out after you accidentally jostle them in the subway. Or you might overhear a coworker referring to you in less-than-flattering terms from the bathroom stall adjacent to yours. Perhaps an argument with a relative will go unresolved for a day too long. Put this reproach in perspective. Words are like the wind. They eventually blow themselves out. Don't take any passing indictments to heart. And most importantly, do not loose one of your legendary Horse outbursts on anyone now. Rein yourself in.

HORSE March 2016

As March begins, financial issues have you in a bind. Your situation is not desperate. Still, the dwindling numbers on your bank statement are not helping you sleep at night. Nothing seems to come cheap anymore. Perhaps your spending is outpacing your earning. Or some unforeseen expenses could have upended your budget. It seems as though in the nick of time, a quick fix comes along. Maybe an Internet query will lead to a seductive part-time job opportunity. Or an offshore company will offer you a chance to dodge those pesky taxes. Taking such a shortcut now may feel harmless. But your actions will produce a ripple effect down the road. At all costs, resist any dazzling lures. The promise of easy money is a staple of the devious Monkey's toolkit.

In spite of your independent spirit, you are exceedingly vulnerable to the throes of passion. Toward the middle of March, a member of the opposite sex threatens to upset your daily routine. Are you currently crushing on someone? Perhaps feelings of unrequited love are turning your mind to mush. You pine for an unattainable lover. The more unlikely the relationship, the stronger your emotions. But if mopey thoughts leave you unable to concentrate on the things you love, you can't be of use to anyone. Use some vigorous exercise to pull yourself together. Start a strenuous weightlifting regime. Or embark on a rugged all-day hike up a mountainside. Take walks in the forest. Nature and exertion can help take your mind off your aching heart.

Even under the Monkey's impish dominion, your health should be hardy as ever. Of course, your new exercise routine will help. However, a jolly dinner party will tempt you to overeat around the end of the month. Once you begin gorging yourself, you might not be able to stop. Gluttony is a slippery slope. Your increased level of physical activity does not give you license to shovel unlimited amounts of food down your gullet. Do take a hand in your destiny. Refuse that second helping of mashed potatoes. Resist the offer of cheesecake. A bit of self discipline around food is called for now.

HORSE April 2016

Sadly, a minor family incident spoils the mood in early April. Perhaps an elderly relative will pass away. An event not entirely unexpected, but painful nonetheless. Or it may be the death of a longtime pet that starts the waterworks. You are not known for your outward displays of emotion. In times of trouble, your facade is usually stoical. But this incident drives you to the breaking point. Try not to repress your feelings anymore or you will be risking an explosion. Release some steam from your pressure cooker now. Give a tender eulogy at the funeral. Tell stories about your pooch around the campfire. Talk things out. Ridding yourself of these pent-up passions will give you the best sleep of your life. Not to mention, that your loved ones will be ecstatic to see you finally baring your heart to them.

During the second week of April, you may feel inclined to take a hardworking youngster under your wing. Maybe a younger colleague is struggling to adapt to their workplace duties. Or a neighbor is way off target with their gardening habits. You know you can help. You are always happy to give a hand to a person in need. Especially if that person is goal-oriented and dedicated to the task at hand. But make sure you've judged this individual's character accurately. If they ask to borrow some money after a week of your tutelage, hide your checkbook from yourself. Smile indulgently. Then vacate the premises. There are a lot of seedy people out there looking for a handout. Don't let any one of them take advantage of your innocent idealism.

A stretch of pleasant weather casts a rosy tint on the third week of April. Get up off that couch! Use this period to enjoy the great outdoors. Basking in the sunlight (in moderation, of course) will blast your body with a healthy dose of vitamin D. Around month's end; an important sports match will temporarily inconvenience you. Maybe the flood of fans making their pilgrimage to the game will block your commute home. Or your significant other will cancel a hot date with you to watch the events unfold. Grit your teeth and take a deep breath. This obstacle is beyond your control.

HORSE May 2016

Time to batten the hatches. Mercury's first retrograde of the Monkey Year starts on April 28 and runs until May 22. As usual, person-to-person communication will be a choppy during this period. The littlest planet's obfuscating influence will garble your intentions at every turn. If possible, avoid embarking on new ventures. Asking that sexy neighbor out to dinner can wait. Accepting more responsibilities in the office might be risky too. Spend this time puttering at home, reading books you have meant to get to. Trying some exotic recipes and/or developing a plan you want to put in place after May 22. Keeping busy whilst waiting out the storm is your best course of action.

A paramour is going to throw your life into a tizzy toward the middle of May. Perhaps a new flame in your life is causing you to neglect your friendships. Or maybe you are pining for an ex who used and abused you. When a Horse's romantic passion awakens, he or she might as well have put on blinders for race day. Nothing else matters. Tread carefully with this situation. Old flames are likely to burn you again. They are not worth the investment. And reserve a weekend for relaxing with friends. Your pals like to feel as though they are important to you too.

At month's end, a mental block has you frustrated. Perhaps a creative project is stalled. Try as you might, you cannot compose the next sentence or visualize the next piece of the puzzle. A workplace obstacle could also be irritating you. You wonder why you keep on losing sales right before the close? Now's the time to break this cycle. Focus your mind on another task. Better yet, turn your brain off altogether. Go for a long hike in nature or indulge in a zippy sport. Join a theater group and lose yourself in a silly slapstick comedy. Sign up to be part of a choir. The message is "Change your goals. Have some fun." By the time you return to your original frustrating task, the stumbling block will have evaporated.

HORSE June 2016

You take pride in your self-sufficiency. *No one will ever tame this Horse!* But beneath that facade, you long to belong. So in early June, some kind of social banishment puts you in a deep funk. Perhaps you are asked to resign your post as treasurer of your children's Parent Teacher Association after an explosive tirade about taxes. Or maybe your favorite bar will ban you after you refuse to stop bragging about your darts championship. No one enjoys being rejected. But you will be taking this instance too much to heart. Chin up. Brooding won't help you solve problems. Pubs are a dime a dozen. You can easily find a new one. As for the PTA? A public apology should help you regain your seat. Do however examine the reasons behind your expulsion. Are you looking at a personality trait you could improve upon? Like angry outbursts? Or blatant hubris? If so, you have a new goal to work toward during the FIRE Monkey Year. Rein in the pride and soften your approach.

Toward the middle of the month, brace yourself. It is time to check your bank statement. Did you expect to see a couple more zeroes in that balance? Has your spending spiraled out of control? You should probably reexamine your budget. If you even created one in the first place. For starters, you never want to be stuck eating un-buttered pasta seven nights in a row before you get your paycheck. Always estimate high when it comes to food. Also, dig through your recent receipts. Did you really need a brand new spiffy toaster oven? Or two stone lions to flank the entrance to your tiny driveway? If you can consciously eliminate unnecessary expenditures, your finances will rebound quickly.

June ends in a haze of tranquility. For once, no duties are clamoring for your attention. For most people, this lack of responsibility would be heaven. But you crave activity and you love to work. So why don't you step into the time machine and reacquaint yourself with an old hobby? Break out that dusty basketball. Brush the cobwebs off your tennis racket. Phone your old bridge partner. You used to be obsessed with this pastime. The challenge of returning to your former level of proficiency will quickly eradicate your feeling of inertia.

HORSE July 2016

In the first week of July, a surprise weather incident may derail your plans. Perhaps lightning will rob your neighborhood of electricity. Or a blizzard will trap you on your property. Better start hunting for that deck of cards. You will need to think outside the box for activities to occupy your time. You could benefit from a lesson in patience. As if the cruel weather were not enough, a nasty cold may make the rounds through your family. Probably due to your current close proximity. Hot tea mixed with honey and lemon should alleviate the symptoms. And make sure that no one overextends their energy level. Otherwise, this illness could degenerate into something more serious.

Courage is your middle name. You had better double-check that quality, however. Because your job is going to require every iota of your valor toward the middle of July. Perhaps a round of layoffs will devastate the office atmosphere. Your job should survive the purge. But your bosses will certainly hand you new responsibilities. *You're trained as an accountant, huh? Of course. But I'm sure you can handle overseeing our marketing division.* No experience in finance? *No problem—we're being audited, so take a look through our records and see what you can do.* Try not to panic. You have overcome more difficult challenges than this. Take a deep breath. Start with baby steps. Research the field. Grill a colleague from your new department for advice. As usual you will gradually rise to top levels of success.

Toward the end of the month, relying on natural ability will finally burn you. Someone who puts in more practice time is going to embarrass you on the playing field. Or beat you out in an intellectual pursuit. Perhaps a younger opponent will juke you so badly that you twist an ankle. Or maybe you will be prattling on about the meaning of a classic rock song during a party, only to have a knowledgeable stranger correct your errors in front of everyone. Take this humbling experience as a sign. If you want to be considered an expert in any field, you must put in the grunt work. So start hitting the gym at the crack of dawn. Or reading up on recent studies over the weekend. God-given talent may no longer be able to carry the day for you. But with a little extra effort, you can still vanquish your opponents.

HORSE August 2016

As August takes the reins from July, a good deed of yours will be repaid in an unexpected manner. Perhaps the protégé that you took under your wing in April will return the favor. Maybe he or she will tip you off to a juicy job opportunity. Or lend you a chainsaw when a giant tree crashes down in your front lawn. Such a courtesy would have been impossible without your networking skills. So let your experience inspire you to help more aspiring youngsters. Sometimes, all it takes for a struggling person to break free of their cycle of negativity is a helping hand. Feel free to provide that leg up for more deserving people.

Toward the middle of August, you may be forced to rethink your budget from June. Your month-to-month estimates were fairly accurate.

But you forgot to account for seasonal fluctuations. For instance, December's holiday gift buying will increase your expenditures exponentially. Plus, an important celebration has slipped your mind. Is it a daughter's Sweet Sixteen party? Your wedding anniversary? A high school reunion that you offered to host ages ago? You know what they say. The best laid plans of mice and men (and Horses) often go awry. Scrap your old cost projections. You may need to avoid eating in restaurants for a couple of weeks. And that luxurious massage appointment may have to wait. But all those sacrifices pale in comparison to how embarrassed you would feel if you had to confessing your money struggles in front of your entourage. Bite the bullet. Temporarily going without frills is not the worst that can happen.

A superficial attraction threatens to divert your attention during the end of the month. Perhaps a coworker's dazzling smile has bewitched you. Of course, once those lips start to speak, you quickly realize that you two have nothing in common. Or you would realize that, if you weren't so smitten with the way they look or carry themselves or dress. On the other hand, maybe a friend's new wheels have turned your eyes green with envy. You feel you *need* that car. Driving that old hand-me-down sedan just isn't going to cut it anymore. Do hold off on making any snap judgments. Do not confess your secret feelings to your seductive colleague. And do not lease a mid-life crisis vehicle. This partial mind fog will lift from your vision soon enough.

HORSE September 2016

Just when you thought you had outfoxed the mischievous Monkey, that rascally primate does something to keep you on your toes. A scam is headed your way. Probably in the form of a predatory loan. Is your bank asking you to upgrade to a brand new remortgaging package? Maybe your credit card company is offering to double your monthly spending limit, no questions asked. Flip (or click) open your calendar. Mercury has reverted to retrograde and will muddy up our ears and eyes from August 30 until September 22. So put those tempting loan applications aside for now. If their prospects still intrigue you in a couple of weeks, have a lawyer read through the fine print. That way, you can be positive that no one is taking you for a ride.

A stretch of humdrum work approaches. In the middle of September, you are faced with a mountain of tasks. Perhaps your stack of paperwork has grown higher than your head. Or you are obliged to attend a series of meetings with your least favorite clients. Maybe you've been chosen to crunch the office budget. None of those duties sounds appealing. But there is no way around this rough patch. Fortunately, you are a natural heavy lifter in situations like these. Put that harness on and get to plowing. To make your daily grind more enjoyable, surround yourself with positivity. Listen to some tunes that take you to your happy place. Bring or buy a tasty grilled chicken sandwich for lunch. A nice dose of your favorite music and some healthy, filling food will reward you for putting up with the tedium.

As the month comes to a close, you are at risk for an accident. Be careful whenever you step into a vehicle. Especially if you are the driver. Maybe you've had a beer or a glass of wine with dinner. If you have consumed any alcohol at all, ask someone else to take the wheel. And make sure that your replacement is dead sober. If you take the proper precautions, you should escape this period unscathed. If you have children, use this time as an opportunity to drill the dangers of operating a vehicle while intoxicated into their heads. If they see you making responsible choices now, that positive image will stick with them into adulthood.

HORSE October 2016

You are a stickler for finishing the job. It takes a minor earthquake to break your concentration. But sometimes, that single-minded focus comes at the expense of your loved ones. Long nights at the office. Weekends spent glued to the phone. These things wear on your family. So as October begins, give yourself a night or two off. Close your laptop. Stop answering emails. Those annoyances can wait until the morning. Instead, crack a beer. Order a greasy pizza. Kick back and ditch your responsibilities. Your willpower is strong. A single night of fun will not send you spiraling into a rabbit hole of faulty decisions. If possible, spend some down time with your relatives. They will be overjoyed to see that you can prioritize them over the office and your incessant work for once.

Passion looms large. A close encounter of the romantic kind is within your grasp. But your paramour is not going to fall swooning into your arms. You need to put some effort into this one. If you are dating someone already, pull out all the stops. Candlelit dinners by the fire. A weekend tucked away in a cabin in the woods. Buying groceries, cooking a meal *and* washing the dishes together. If you play your cards right, you can look forward to an extended period of intimacy. To do this, single Horses must however leave their comfort zone. Terrified of dancing? Hit the club. Shy about approaching the opposite sex? Walk up and compliment a cute stranger. Fortune rewards the bold. Make a strong move, and you'll be surprised at the bevy of rewards.

As October wanes, you fell the house has sat silent for too long. Probably because a beloved family pet passed away in April. Never thought you would miss the dog's bark? Or finding cat hair ground into the fibers of the couch? Well surprise, surprise. Good and bad, you yearn for owning an animal again. So start perusing the market for a new furry friend. Something lovable. And with an unmistakable presence. Canine, feline, bovine or pig —avoid hermit crabs. You deserve to love a creature with a lifespan longer than the blink of an eye.

HORSE November 2016

During the early days of November, your stubborn streak may interfere with your personal relationships. Married Horses especially are at risk for petty bickering. Perhaps your spouse will ask you to wash the dishes or take the trash to the curb. A simple favor. But you refuse, or complain, and all of a sudden, World War Three hits your living room. Or maybe a friend will ask you for a ride to work. Or to borrow some cash to get through the month. Predictably, a fight results. No one can force you to do anything. Indeed, you are your own person. Why not pick your battles more wisely. Save your indignation for a more insidious situation. If you can't contain your rage, you may find yourself sleeping on the couch. Or sitting at home alone on Saturday night.

Work is also testing your patience. A public reprimand may humiliate you toward the middle of the month. Perhaps a boss will chew you out in a meeting for failing to meet a sales quota. Or you could get up-braided for forgetting to fill out some required paperwork. Do not swallow your natural reaction. If you take your dressing-down silently, it will reflect poorly on you. Whatever you do, don't start screaming and throwing staplers at the wall. Instead, excuse yourself. Go to the ladies or men's room and take five minutes to organize your thoughts. Then come back and present your defense. Let your voice reveal your inner emotions. Management will notice your passion for and devotion to your job. And, as unlikely as that may seem right now, they will reward you for it down the road.

Although you are a hardy soul, drama and infighting are wearing on your resolve. So toward the end of November, burn off some stress by switching up your exercise regimen. Sign up for boxing lessons. Join the AcroYoga group that practices in the park. Normally, such an activity is not your cup of tea. But a challenge is just what you need to kick start your engines. Just grit your teeth and go. The hardest part is the beginning. Once you get into the flow of the class, your competitive juices will take over. And when that happens? Everyone else had better watch out. There's a new sheriff in Yoga-Town.

HORSE December 2016

In the beginning of December, you may be hankering for a greasy cheeseburger. Or a cheesy, artery-clogging pizza. Even just a bowl full of candy. It sounds as though you are stress eating. You've experienced a testy couple of months. The upheaval in your life is probably pushing you toward what you think of as comfort foods. You must find a healthier outlet for these pressures. Exercise will be of assistance. But working up a good sweat is not enough. You need to find a listener person to vent to. Someone you can trust. Somebody who has been through some tough times of their own. It's never been easy for Horses to talk about feelings. But if you can teach yourself how to open up, you will become stronger. Once you've stopped searching for peace at the bottom of the potato chip bag, your can have "thank you" tattooed on your love handles.

On December 19, Mercury enters his fourth and final retrograde of the FIRE Monkey Year. This period will last until January 8. Unfortunately, Mercury's confounding presence coincides with an uptick in your work responsibilities. Especially if you are taking some time off for the holidays. Your boss is pressuring you to finish what feels like a thousand projects. But his or her expectations are unreasonable. Time is flitting by. What's the point of rushing to complete all these assignments if the results will be sub par? Instead, focus your concentration on one or two major tasks. Polish these off to the best of your abilities. Management might be bitter about your output now, but they cannot ignore the excellent quality of your output.

Mercury's fickle pull threatens to turn the holidays into a holi-daze. Mistakes abound. Relatives show up on your doorstep without so much as a phone call in advance. The meat catches fire in the oven. Gifts get mailed to the wrong recipients. At a certain point, you just have to laugh. Someone else is pulling the strings at this time. Embrace the mayhem with a smile and a bottle of eggnog. Gather everyone for a round of storytelling. Try to forget about the logistical problems. Just enjoy your moments together. By this time next year, this experience will just be another wacky family story.

HORSE January 2017

January begins with more minor mishaps. Maybe you will get ripped off or pickpocketed while trying to gain entrance to a New Year's party. Or you might tear open your pants while shopping at the mall.

Perhaps a child will stomp on your sparkling new shoes. You can avoid this irritant, but not without some planning. Stock up on groceries and hole up in your house. Plan a "weekend in" with your significant other. Try cooking some foreign recipes. Watch your favorite trilogy—back-to-back-to-back. Just stay on your own property for a couple days. That is the best way to keep the Monkey's Mercury-tinged hands off your peace of mind.

After some earlier struggles, you should end the year on a financial high note. Even after accounting for holiday spending, you may have some spare cash. You are tempted to invest it in something risky. To buy stock in a failing company. To put down a deposit on a timeshare vacation home. Resist any and all such schemes. Instead, turn to a safe, boring investment. Like a mutual fund. Or a retirement account. Of course, you have many years of work left in you. But it's never too early to start saving for the future. Would you rather be floating around the Caribbean on a yacht during your golden years? Or punching the clock until age seventy? The choice is up to you.

Set aside the last part of the month to plan for the FIRE Rooster Year which starts on February 8. Ask yourself which lessons can you draw from your FIRE Monkey experiences that will help you in the future? You have honed one particular skill this year. You have become an expert at resisting—or avoiding—temptation. But the Rooster will challenge you in a different way. He will try to restrain your freedom. And that does not sit well with your independent spirit. So keep in mind your December lesson about talking through your feelings. Instead of letting your frustrations mount up until your brain explodes, find a person who is willing to be your safety valve. Someone you can vent to and ask about solutions to thorny problems which stick inside your skull. This newfound pressure-release should steer you well through any rough seas that lie ahead.

YOUR MONTHLY FORECASTS FOR THE FIRE MONKEY YEAR

2016

GOAT/SHEEP

Author's Note... Mercury Retrograde

Sometimes planets appear to be zooming backward through the zodiac. Of course this backward motion is only an illusion. The planet has not turned tail. But it appears to have. Astrologers call this apparent reversing: **"retrograde"**.

Any planet can be retrograde. But only Mercury's retrogrades cause communications to break down. Mercury has its retrograde period for a few weeks 3 or 4 times each year. Whilst Mercury is retrograde, we humans are encouraged to take stock, make plans and discuss different approaches to a variety of subjects. But because information is often muddled, promises broken and electronic devices on the blink during Mercury retrograde, we must remain flexible and open-minded. Advice? Always allow extra time for travel. Schedule changes are common. Do not sign any contracts or cement agreements during Mercury retrograde. Make no irreversible promises. Watch out for con artists. Make no final decisions, binding engagements or major purchases during a Mercury retrograde. You are allowed to have tantrums or rail against your fate. But Mercury will continue to be retrograde till it decides to go direct again.

Mercury Retrogrades
2016

January 5 thru January 25
April 28 thru May 22
August 30 thru September 22
December 19 thru January 8 2017

OVERVIEW OF 2016 THE YEAR OF THE MONKEY
FOR THE GOAT/SHEEP

Good-natured Goat/Sheep,

The Fire Monkey year will be a bit on the chaotic side for your taste. Monkeys are forever dashing about hatching circuitous schemes and plotting ways to entertain the world whilst solving all of its problems. Fact is, Monkeys are rather discombobulated folks in the guise of orderly people. You Goats don't derive any rushes of security from Monkeys. And with good reason. They are neurotic as hell and are frequently imagining someone might be out to get them. They strategize and wangle. You prefer to see problems coming – even if you fail at sorting them out. The Monkey's planned chaos sets your teeth on edge and makes you doubt yourself. As you don't have all that much self-confidence to start with, this muddle-headed year makes you extra anxious, brings out your pessimistic side and more than once puts you in the corner with a dunce cap on. Why? Because you insist on being direct and open about what you are up to. Monkeys don't get that. They prefer labyrinths to freeways. If I were you in this Fire Monkey year, I would seriously consider a complete change of métier. Ask a rich friend to buy you a restaurant. Or get a lover to sponsor your career as an opera singer. Remember, you prefer security. And you prefer that said security come to you from outside. So do not self-finance. If you fail, let someone else take the fall. sw

GOAT/SHEEP January 2016

Thankfully, the Sheep that ate Christmas is dead. A new, brighter beast is ready to greet the New Year. Whatever got into you in December is history. You are now ready to return to a state of grace and accomplishment once more. A good thing, too. Because somewhere in the first part of 2016, you are going to be called upon to do a favor. More than a token deed: an act of pure charity and compassion. Someone needs your help. Most likely a younger person. This matter may be connected to a charity that serves children in need. The gruff Sheep of December would have yelled, "Baa humbug!" and slammed the door in charity's face. But now, you are in a better frame of mind. You are ready to be generous with your time and/or wallet.

By mid-January, you will probably find yourself heavily involved in this worthy new cause. You are beginning to make fast friends out of the new acquaintances you have met through this venture. In the third week, be vigilant for a stranger with a love of nature or languages. They might just turn out to be your new best friend. On the surface, you have nothing in common. But you share an unspoken bond that defies explanation.

The bad news is that as this new friendship blossoms, an older partnership withers. This loss will not hit home until the end of the month. It looks like a colleague or friend is bidding you farewell. A literal death could be separating you. But it is more likely that a second marriage or job relocation is driving a chasm through your relationship. Or perhaps this comrade is retiring and moving to a sunnier clime. This loss will distress you. You abhor farewells. But cut the other person some slack. They are truly pleased to be moving on. Stomach the goodbyes gracefully. Send them on their way with your blessing. The good times you shared will never be forgotten. When we truly love someone, we want them to be happy. No matter what that costs us emotionally.

GOAT/SHEEP February 2016

The FIRE Monkey Year gets off to a topsy-turvy start. Chaos reigns at your place of work. Normally, quality leadership is a must for your peace of mind. You prefer to follow a clear set of instructions. But toward the beginning of February, turnover in the management ranks may leave you hanging out to dry. Perhaps your favorite boss will get fired. Or maybe your company will get bought out by a different group, leaving everyone's job status up in the air. You might even—gasp—get promoted to a position of power yourself! While you wait for the dust to settle, look around for someone who can show you the ropes in this scary new world. A new mentor will ease your transition. The upheaval may inflict a wrench on your gut but you will soon get acclimated to your new situation.

Your family life is stable. Infighting is at a minimum. However, if you have children, they are likely to experience some growing pains soon. Perhaps an adolescent will sprout past your own height. Wasn't it just yesterday that they were crawling around on the carpet? Or maybe your son or daughter will have some trouble adjusting at school. Another student is picking on them, making their daily existence miserable. To combat this, teach them how to bully back. Everyone (except your innocent child) knows that if you bully a bully back, he or she will turn tail and move on to torment another victim.

An unexpected windfall brightens your day toward the end of the month. Maybe you will receive a surprise bonus from your job. Or a relative will drop by with a (possibly very) belated birthday present. So pay the good vibes forward. Help a stranger fish their credit card out of the dumpster. Buy a sandwich and a steaming coffee for a homeless person. Lend your neighbor a hand with their yard work. Your charitable deeds will bring a smile to someone else's face. Not to mention warming your heart with satisfaction. Selfless acts are beneficial for your soul. Give without expecting any return.

GOAT/SHEEP March 2016

Early March may see you perusing the romantic marketplace. In searching for a potential mate or lover, look for a person who can provide you security - both financial and moral support. Someone by whom you can set your clock. Preferably with a stable job. Don't fall for a transient individual. Avoid precarious writers, artists and musicians. Goats are happiest with a reliable down-to-earth partner. If you are already dating, take care that your *amour* not run roughshod over your own desires. Do you always eat out at *their* preferred restaurant? Has it been months since you've gone out with your own friends? You are naturally laid-back. But no one should confuse that trait with meekness. Sometimes, you need to put your foot down. Not to assert your dominance. But to assert your existence.

Unfortunately, the Monkey has a tight grip on your financial well-being. Or at least that's what he/she wants you to think. The truth is - your bank accounts will survive the year relatively unscathed. But now, in the middle of March, that does not seem a likely outcome. Maybe a change in tax structure will shrink your paycheck. Or a loved one's hospital bill will lighten your wallet. I know you detest budgeting. But before you panic and sell off all your assets, crunch some numbers. Think of this as a rough projection. Calculate how much money you absolutely need to survive the month. Fortunately, having accommodating acquaintances is one of the benefits of being a lovable Goat. So if you need some assistance, ask a wealthy friend for a small loan (or gift). Your connections will see you safely through.

As the month ends, investigate your household appliances. Is the cook stove leaking gas? Maybe the dishwasher is oozing water onto the floor. Or grease crumbs could be accumulating at the bottom of the broiler. These flaws present a hazard to you and your family. Spare no expense to patch them up. Better to reach for your checkbook than setting the kitchen on fire while trying to fry an egg.

GOAT/SHEEP April 2016

You have been considering launching your own commercial venture for a while now. Maybe you dream of opening a day-care center for the children of busy parents. Or you want to found an independent press to publish small works of poetry. The beginning of April presents an opportune starting point. But you should not be the one footing this bill. So before you put the figurative shovel to the metaphorical soil, find a financier. You are a master of manipulation and behind-the-scenes work. Use those wiles to select a business partner with deep pockets. Even though you are really serving your own interests, you should be able to convince him or her that they are the one in charge of the project. After they have signed on, you can proceed with minimal risk to your personal pocketbook.

You often have trouble discerning between being really ill versus just having a bad day. A cold appears to be developing in your chest toward the middle of April. Or is it an allergy flare-up? This time, take no chances. Call out of work or school. Prepare some hot tea with honey. Cocoon yourself in a blanket and unwind on the couch. Let the inertia wash over you. Even if your mystery virus passes quickly, (could be Spring or equinox fever) a day of relaxation would be good for all Goats right now. While you are lying there ruminating, develop a plan of attack for the coming months. You know that the Monkey is going to throw you some curve balls. Especially in the workplace. So set some goals that you would like to reach, irrespective of a certain inevitable turnover and mayhem among the staff.

The ability to laugh at yourself will come in handy at the end of the month. Perhaps you will shatter a jar of tomato paste just as you are berating your companion for not being careful with the groceries. Maybe you will dump a glass of red wine on your shirt at a black tie affair. Do not take your anger out on your surroundings. Nor should you turn your annoyance inward, toward yourself. Instead, be the first to smile at your mishap. That will be the cue for everyone else to start chuckling. Plus, now you have a funny story to tell at the next dinner party.

GOAT/SHEEP May 2016

Fasten your seatbelts. Monkey madness is about to take off full throttle. Mercury enters its first retrograde of the year on April 28 and does not revert to normal orbit until May 22. Within that time frame, you can anticipate both difficulties in communication and electronics. So avoid situations that rely on minute distinctions or nuances between words. Any discussion of your shared future with your significant other is a no-go. Such crucially important conversations with a lover or a business partner should be delayed until Mercury goes direct. Otherwise, you may end up with a shipment of ergonomic chairs that your company cannot afford. Or with a misunderstood spouse stomping back home to mother.

In mid-May, romantic frustrations may once again see you testing the waters of the single world. The game is easier these days. You don't even need to flip open a computer to get an online date. You can choose your pick of the "availables" directly from your cell phone. Such mobile applications are as ubiquitous as sandals in the summer. If you try a program like Tinder, you will be astonished at your initial success. Everyone wants to meet up with you! But be wary of exciting a surfeit of willing partners. After a couple of outings, you should trim your suitors to a manageable number. Otherwise, you run the risk of calling a date by the wrong name. Or showing up at the wrong apartment with a bouquet of flowers or a bottle of Bordeaux.

Toward the end of the month, workplace uncertainty is getting to you. Perhaps your managerial situation is still up in the air. Or are you questioning whether you've chosen the right line of work? Maybe you are having second thoughts about your boss' leadership abilities. To regroup, allow yourself a few private moments. Set aside an afternoon to read a book in the local park or arboretum. Or instead of hitting the clubs and doing up the town, spend a weekend catching up on old movies. Time alone will help you return to your job with a renewed focus.

GOAT/SHEEP June 2016

During the first days of June, a roommate or live-in lover is getting under your skin. No, they were not romancing your ex. Nor did they lift cash from your wallet. Nothing so extreme. Perhaps they are merely using your toothpaste without your permission. Not a huge issue, except they insist on losing the cap after each brushing. Or maybe your spouse keeps on forgetting to replace the toilet paper roll. Minor inconveniences like these may be forgiven once or twice. But every other day? Your close proximity is bringing such a seemingly insignificant issue to the forefront. Before you start putting itching powder in their deodorant or feeding laxatives to their pet rabbit, reconsider your plan of action. A simple sit-down should alleviate any problems. Granted, open confrontation is not your strong suit. But if you can get over that aversion now, you will avoid a bout of passive-aggression under your roof.

In contrast to how they function in your home life, your passive-aggressive skills may play to your advantage in the workplace. They may come in particularly handy around the middle of June. A standoff between labor and management threatens to halt business. Perhaps a local union is striking. Or a group of grumpy cubicle denizens have finally gotten fed up with being treated like hamsters on a treadmill. Enter the Goat. You have a subtle way of getting people to agree with you. Speak discreetly with both sides. Without the raised hackles of a public face-off, you may be able to worm out a compromise. This victory will make you a non-traditional kind of hero. But a hero nonetheless.

Toward the end of June, a new addition to your family brings joy to your dinner table. Perhaps a sibling is getting engaged. Or a cousin is going to pop out a baby. On a smaller scale, maybe your parents are adopting a friendly old dog or a long-in-the-tooth cat. Gather your loved ones to celebrate. Do not, however, expect the weather to comply. Choppy skies and dark clouds do not exactly reflect your festive mood.

GOAT/SHEEP July 2016

You have always been a dreamer. While others dove straight into nursing school or took trade apprenticeships at an early age, you preferred to imagine a more unique path for yourself. Now, a rare opportunity is triggering that inclination to be different. Perhaps your favorite athlete's game-worn jersey has just been placed on auction. Or maybe a chance to travel has opened up. Check your finances. Can they afford to take a temporary hit? If so, splurge on that piece of memorabilia; or spring for that vacation or overseas position. Working abroad especially would serve you well. Lest you worry about re-acclimating yourself to the domestic job market after a leave of absence, rest assured that having international experience will be a boon for you upon your return.

Goats often tend toward delicate constitutions and bizzaro eating habits. Such a combination does not bring to mind a chiseled body builder or toned acrobat. Luckily, there is a cure for this state of affairs. By building a strict routine and sticking to it, you can overcome many natural deficiencies. So toward the end of July, research some ideas for moderate exercise routines. Once you find a plan that tickles your fancy, look up the best kind of diet to pair with that particular brand of physical activity. A useful tip: slate your workout sessions for the morning. You are not the biggest fan of waking up early. But having a concrete reason to get out of bed every day will aid you in your quest to adhere to a firm schedule.

Keep an eye on your calendar or to-do list as July comes to a close. A relative's birthday is upon you. In the midst of rushing to buy him or her a celebratory card or gift, you may break a promise you made or neglect another commitment. You do not want to accidentally stand up your date. Or leave your son or daughter waiting for hours for their ride home from school. To avoid these slip-ups, make sure to enter all upcoming appointments in your mobile phone or laptop. Put that info somewhere safe where you will actually check them every morning (before your workout).

GOAT/SHEEP August 2016

A routine day at work could turn into a nightmare during the first half of August. One of your bosses has disappeared on vacation. The ship was running smoothly before he or she vamoosed. But now, anarchy reigns. Your colleagues are neglecting their duties. You operate most effectively under the pressure of a deadline. Without the normal chain of command to enforce such due dates, your own productivity is also in danger of falling into disarray. During this era of uncertainty, look to another source for inspiration. Dig up your list of personal goals from April. You should have some nuggets of wisdom tucked away in there. As advised above, read through your notes when you wake up each morning. This daily routine will reaffirm your purpose and help you chart your course for the day.

Your June arguments with your roommate have escalated. By mid-August, a change in your living situation may be in order. Perhaps you need some time apart from your spouse or housemate. While you are on hiatus, consider the virtues of your relationship. Is there a more compatible friend with whom you could share an apartment? Was your life more secure with your old romantic partner? After an appropriate cooling-off period, you should consider moving back in. Experimenting with living with strangers or with trying to support yourself alone can be enlightening. Nothing soothes a Goat more than stability. Plus, your temporary separation may have caused your partner to realize how much he or she needs you too. Once you have returned home, you may find yourself even more beloved than before!

Toward the end of the month, you may feel the urge to renege on a commitment. Perhaps you no longer want to attend a charity luncheon. Maybe grabbing dinner with your ex has lost its appeal. You would rather laze around the couch. Or revel in some quality alone time. But you should hold to your original promise. An unexpected bonus will materialize if you make it out of the house. You could end up making a new business connection. Or tripping over some cash in the street. Besides, if you flake too many times, the invitations will start drying up. Social interaction is the glue which holds our lives together.

GOAT/SHEEP September 2016

Mercury arcs into his second retrograde of the year on August 30. This one lasts until September 22. By this point, you know the drill. Put off signing important documents. Delay life-altering meetings. But an added wrinkle awaits you in early September. A technological mishap may take the wind out of your sails. Maybe a downed Internet connection will doom an attempted videoconference. Or a surprise rainstorm might destroy your cell phone. If possible, back up your data. Make a hard copy of your contact list. You don't want to be that person who emails everyone and their brother-in-law to ask for lost phone numbers. Maybe Mercury's influence will be less likely to ruin your devices if they are locked away in your house. During this retrograde, when at all possible leave expensive portable electronics at home.

A disrespectful relative puts a damper on the middle of your month. Perhaps a parent will disparage your career choice. Or ridicule your taste in the opposite sex. Maybe a cousin will taunt you at a reunion for your past athletic failures. Family disapproval always stings. But before you go running to the therapist's office, fire a salvo back. Just because this character birthed you or grew up with you does not put them beyond reproach. In fact, they may be denigrating your choices out of insecurity about some choices of their own. Ask them pointblank why they are throwing shade at you. Your reaction may startle them into actually revealing what they are upset about. Hash it out and before you know it, the two of you will be, once again, hand in glove.

Some issues with your pearly whites may crop up toward the end of September. Perhaps an ache in your mouth will leave you in agony. Or plaque buildup will force you to admit that you need a thorough cleaning. You have been neglecting your oral hygiene. Of course, all that talk about flossing daily sounds like a bunch of hot air. But investing some time in your habits could save you an emergency visit to the dentist. Why not start brushing your teeth after lunch? Buy a small bottle of mouthwash-to-go. Take your (dental) destiny into your own hands.

GOAT/SHEEP October 2016

Your efforts to improve your work life are paying off. In spite of fluctuations at the top of the office food chain, you have maintained your production levels. Early October should see you reaping the rewards of your stick-to-itiveness. Perhaps the CEO will take notice of your recent successes. Maybe your colleagues will nominate you for a regional award. On the other hand, another company might come calling with a job offer. This extra attention will reaffirm your self-worth. But do not let the flattery go to your head. That opportunity at the rival corporation may be more trouble than it's worth. Remember the factors that attracted you to your current gig in the first place. Is your situation uncomfortable enough to justify a big move? If the answer is no, you should probably consider sticking around.

Toward the middle of the month, devote some attention to the venture you undertook in April. Blogs and other independent projects are like flowers. They need a lot of watering and maintenance to truly flourish. Put some effort into the upkeep of your enterprise. Roll out some new articles or posts. Buy some space to advertise your business. Conversely, you could rent the sidebar of your webpage to an advertiser to generate some income. Turns out, starting up was the easy part. The grunt work of continuing once the initial thrill has faded is what truly separates the kids from the Goats.

In late October, you may feel like bailing on your fitness regime from July. All this waking up early and concentrating on your diet is boring your imaginative mind. You need a dose of motivation. But put down the self-help book. Don't bother with inspirational You Tube videos. Instead, peel your shirt or blouse off and grab a glance in the mirror. Who is that model person gazing back at you? Your profile certainly did not look that chiseled a few months ago. That realization alone should inject you with a shot of self-confidence. Use that self-esteem boost to spice up your love life. Hit the bar scene and flirt a bit. Your new glow and tighter muscles will make you irresistible.

GOAT/SHEEP November 2016

A small family success cuts through the monotony of early November.

Perhaps your significant other will receive a bonus or promotion in their line of work. Maybe one of your children will get the highest score in their basketball game. Or they'll ace a test in a brutal math course. Why not take the whole gang out to dinner? Celebrate the glad tidings appropriately. Once the festivities are over, offer some advice: don't take your foot off the gas. If your partner keeps pushing in his or her job, they have a chance to earn even more decorations. If your son or daughter fails to keep up with their studying, that A could degenerate into a C or D before you realize what is happening. This sage recommendation may not be what they want to hear right now. But your words will serve them well in the long run.

Mid-November takes a nastier turn. An economic downturn has destroyed your confidence in your finances. Perhaps layoffs at your place of work have you fretting over job security. Maybe a political tug-of-war is damaging commerce in your region. Or a money squabble with your lover might make you think twice about the wisdom of sharing a bank account. All of a sudden, uncertainty about the safety of your savings has you pulling your hair out. To combat these fears, stash some funds in a place where they cannot easily be withdrawn. They would be safe in a trust fund. Or in a 401k. Such measures will allow you to regain peace of mind. Regardless of whatever recessions are ravaging the rest of the population at least a fraction of your personal wealth is protected.

Your hippie tendencies rise to the forefront toward the end of the month. Maybe you will get the chance to catch a classic rock & roll show at a local festival. Or you might feel the urge to quit your job and start road tripping around the country. Don't go all delusional and try to dip back into the nastier habits of the free love era. Goats are particularly susceptible to the effects of drugs and alcohol. So if acute wanderlust is gripping your soul, take a vacation. If you choose the vagabond option, abandoning your earthly possessions will seem a lot less charming after a week of sleeping on the hard ground or in a drafty van.

GOAT/SHEEP December 2016

Your job may become hectic during the beginning of December. Everyone is rushing to polish off projects before the holidays bring everything to a screeching halt. But you thrive on pressure. Impending due dates inspire some of your best work. So by all means, put your axe to the grindstone. But do not expect your coworkers to maintain the same even-keeled disposition as you. Tempers may flare in the office.

If a colleague chews you out for forgetting to replace the paper in the printer, do not rise to the bait. Apologize, and then wipe the incident from your memory. Such heat-of-the-moment flare-ups are rarely personal. Take solace in the fact that you handle adversity better than your peers.

Watch out while rushing up and down staircases. A minor accident may leave you hobbling through the middle of the month. However, a limp could have some unexpected romantic benefits. Perhaps a kind angel will take pity on you. Next thing you know, you have a date booked for Saturday night. Looking forward to that outing should be enough to make you forget the pain. On the other hand, if you are already in a relationship, why not take advantage of your immobility to cash in on some alone time with your partner? After all, you are not exactly fit to run any errands in your current state. Instead, use your injury as an excuse to cuddle up next to your better half.

The Monkey's most devious doings take place at the end of December. Mercury's final retrograde of the year arrives just in time to blight your holidays. This retrograde begins on December 19 and stretches until January 8. Trying to coordinate family holiday plans could be a nightmare. Buying satisfactory gifts for your loved ones may become a labyrinth of futile indecision. The only way to outfox the Monkey's Mercury-induced madness is to firm up your arrangements before the 19th. As long as you get your presents early, no one will end up returning all your misfit gifts. And if you establish a meeting place pre-emptively (early on), no relatives will turn up on the wrong day on your doorstep.

GOAT/SHEEP January 2017

Careful about booze at the beginning of January. You might go overboard during New Year's Eve festivities. If you are an infrequent drinker, you run the risk of exceeding your limits. Remember. No one wants to get stuck holding your head over the basin during the height of the fun. Think about it. One evening of too much drink will ruin two days of your precious life. So go easy on the spirits. On the bright side, temperatures should be unseasonably mild for this time of year. Take advantage of your clarity of mind during this period by completing any outdoor chores that have been simmering on the back burner.

You set goals in April for how to handle Monkey-year uncertainty in the office. Keep this list of objectives handy. You are not out of the woods yet. Toward the middle of January, the impish primate throws you one last curveball. Maybe the topic of outsourcing your job will come up in a meeting. Or perhaps an injury will throw a spotlight on your workplace safety practices. You need to develop a plan of attack to respond to this criticism. Create a convincing presentation demonstrating why the quality of your company's product will diminish if your position is farmed out overseas. Or in the case of an accident, print out and implement the national guidelines for preventing accidents. If you can get in front of this crisis, you should be well able to spare your career.

As January comes to a close, you can finally breathe a sigh of relief. You have outlasted the Monkey's security-damaging influence. To celebrate, spend some time with your family. A movie night or day trip to a museum would fit the bill. Bask in the warm glow of your loved ones. And when you do get a moment to yourself, reflect on the events that transpired during the past year. What challenges presented themselves? How did you overcome them? In conquering your demons, what did you learn? It is vital that you avoid repeating mistakes. So scribble down your musings. When the going gets tough during the FIRE Rooster Year, you can flip back to these notes for a bit of hope and inspiration.

YOUR MONTHLY FORECASTS FOR THE FIRE MONKEY YEAR

2016

MONKEY

Author's Note... Mercury Retrograde

Sometimes planets appear to be zooming backward through the zodiac. Of course this backward motion is only an illusion. The planet has not turned tail. But it appears to have. Astrologers call this apparent reversing: **"retrograde"**.

Any planet can be retrograde. But only Mercury's retrogrades cause communications to break down. Mercury has its retrograde period for a few weeks 3 or 4 times each year. Whilst Mercury is retrograde, we humans are encouraged to take stock, make plans and discuss different approaches to a variety of subjects. But because information is often muddled, promises broken and electronic devices on the blink during Mercury retrograde, we must remain flexible and open-minded. Advice? Always allow extra time for travel. Schedule changes are common. Do not sign any contracts or cement agreements during Mercury retrograde. Make no irreversible promises. Watch out for con artists. Make no final decisions, binding engagements or major purchases during a Mercury retrograde. You are allowed to have tantrums or rail against your fate. But Mercury will continue to be retrograde till it decides to go direct again.

Mercury Retrogrades
2016

January 5 thru January 25
April 28 thru May 22
August 30 thru September 22
December 19 thru January 8 2017

OVERVIEW OF 2016 THE YEAR OF THE MONKEY
FOR THE MONKEY

Monkey Mine,

In your travels in this Fire Monkey year, you will meet someone who will have a profound influence on your career. It could be an older person who takes a shine to one of your brilliant ideas. Or it might be a contemporary who is willing to partner with you either in business or in love. Take notice of this person's Chinese astrological sign and compare it with yours for compatibility. If the match is harmonious, think seriously about pursuing a project or a building a serious couple. This is your year to shine and preen and prance and dance on the tables if you feel like it. But do climb back down to Earth once in awhile because this is also your year to plan your next dozen years. The Chinese don't have decades of ten years. Their calendar uses 12-year periods. Each year has a particular significance for each sign. When your own year rolls around, you are advised to sit down with pen and paper (or computer) and outline the next 12 years of your life. Where do you want to be in 2028? What can you see yourself doing? How might you plot the path to this goal, year by year, so you are more or less certain to attain that objective? Not an easy task? No. But a necessary exercise in order to build your own life - your way. Otherwise, you will not be using your time in this crucial year wisely. Take charge of your destiny in this propitious Monkey year. Live your Life proactively. Do not let your Life live you. sw

MONKEY January 2016

The first month of the New Year is spent almost entirely in the shadow of Mercury retrograde. From January 5th to the 25th, expect to find communication far more complicated than it should be. Do not be surprised if this confusion leads to cross-cultural horrors at your workplace. Perhaps the server will whimsically decide to translate all the email accounts into Arabic. Or maybe your company is sending its new Asian business partner a gift basket as a token of respect. Due to a clerical error, the package contains foods considered unclean in the local culture. Consequently, be prepared to beg pardon frequently in January. Soothe your nerves with a treat at home. Buy yourself that romantic new jazz album or action movie you have been wanting. Prop your feet up. And let your mind wander far away from your job.

Friends with children are due to visit mid-month. You love kids. Still, you prefer they keep their distance from your brocade curtains and priceless collectibles. Store any precious things in a secluded closet until the kiddies' visit is over. That way, you can avoid an awkward argument with your loved ones over their offspring's' savage behavior. See what your area has to offer in the way of family entertainment. But remember to lock up your house and car while out on the town. Unruly children can be very distracting. And your valuables are worth stealing.

A relative is currently researching the family tree. They might ask you to provide some historical information near the end of the month. While digging through old photos, you will come across other memories from your own past. Of the bittersweet variety. Old school friends and long-forgotten loves. But do not let the passage of time render you nostalgic or sad. You still have many memories to create in the future. As the month ends, the brand new Monkey year (starts Feb 8, 2016) beckons. This will be a memorable epoch for you. Full of thrilling possibilities. Embrace your future with arms open wide.

MONKEY February 2016

The FIRE Monkey Year is shaping up to be an era of lists. Ideally, where do you see yourself next year? Consider career possibilities, place of residence, love interests. The important things in life. Now how about in twelve years? During the coming months, compile your own personal 12-year plan. Write down all your goals, no matter how farfetched. Once these objectives are immortalized in pen and paper, attaining them will feel more realistic. By December, you should have something workable. But now, in early February, start with a more short-term to-do compilation. What chores do you need to polish off this month? What workplace projects would you like to complete? Do not forget to flip back to your index during the next few weeks. Doing so will help you focus on the things you actually want to accomplish.

The middle of the month sees you beset with a bit of bad luck. Maybe you splash into a muddy puddle while wearing your sparkly new shoes. Or a slip in the shower leaves a nasty bruise on your nether regions. These small inconveniences may leave you feeling like a hapless character in a slapstick comedy. But your fortunes will change for the better in the third week of February. A surprise encounter with an old friend or the discovery of some crumpled cash in your pocket will wipe any earlier tribulations from your memory.

At the end of February, something is throwing your sleep cycle out of whack. Perhaps roaring traffic outside your window has grown too loud to ignore. Maybe drinking too much coffee or tea is causing a bout of insomnia. Not getting a solid eight hours is bad news for jittery Monkeys. But conflicting internal forces might make snoozing difficult. Could your sleeplessness result from bouncing off the walls all day, all the while draining cup after cup of speed-inducing mocha. Replace coffee with mineral waters or make smoothies and pack them off to work with you in a thermos. You could soundproof your bedroom. Or start partaking of sleepy time tea or melatonin as the sun goes down. If you can broker a compromise between your boundless energy and getting adequate rest, you begin to wake up fully refreshed in the morning.

MONKEY March 2016

In early March, a romantic connection will befuddle your brain. Captivated by visions of your crush, the computer screen in front of you is a mere blur. Friends' phone calls fall on a deaf ear. Making plans is impossible. Concentrating at your place of work? Don't even try. My advice? Stop waiting around. If you are supposed to take your *amour* out on the town next week, reschedule the date for tomorrow night. The other party will be flattered by your sense of urgency. If you have been putting off chatting up the man or woman of your dreams, get a move on. The sooner you act on your carnal (and romantic) desires, the sooner you will be free to revert to your normal, productive self.

The middle of month presents a moneymaking opportunity. Perhaps you will have the option of buying up an old property at a dirt-cheap price. Or maybe you can parlay a series of penny stocks into a sizable return. The chances are not free handouts. You must use your wiles if you want to rake in some cash. Do you really have the spare time and desire to buy and then flip a house? Would you know an investment index from a phone book? If your answer is "No.", all is not lost. After all, you are a skilled researcher. If you study up on the intricacies of any business, it should not take you long to become proficient at anything from home repairs to financial finagling. Best of all? Your reputation as a newbie will precede you. People may think they can hornswoggle you. But we both know they can't.

Treat yourself to a present in the last week of the month. Is your significant other snickering at the holes in your socks? Are your ancient moth-eaten sweaters a running family joke? You really should hit the local shopping center. Invest in some fresh gear. Attractive new shorts will inspire you to exercise more. A classy T-shirt will give you some-thing less dorky to don for your next outing with friends. Just stay away from leather goods. A biker-gang jacket will only make you look like a wannabe. And upon further reflection, that new belt may end up being a little too tight around the waist.

MONKEY April 2016

At the beginning of April, you meet a person who is to play a vital role in your future. Or perhaps you are already acquainted with this character, but you are only now realizing their importance in your life. This person could be a wizened elder who takes a liking to your creative endeavors. Could you have found yourself a mentor? Or you might be growing closer with a colleague of the opposite sex. Could it be time to take your relationship to the next level? Play your cards right, and you may end up with a reliable partner. In business or in pleasure. Keep an eye on this individual as the year progresses. Make certain you have chosen an honorable cohort. But know this: if you do not stick your neck out, this tantalizing opportunity may slip out of your grasp. Making the first move is up to you.

A family squabble sours the middle of April. And the worst part? The blow-up is your fault. Maybe you will pick a fight with your spouse or partner over whose turn it is to wash the dishes. Or you might berate a child for neglecting his or her chores. You need to analyze your motives. Because right now, one of your worst characteristics—immaturity—is being brought to the forefront. What was at the root of your outburst? Are a significant other's nights out on the town stoking your jealousy? Are you having flashbacks to disobeying your own parents? Take some time to deal with your own issues. You must accept that your better half is needs to be independent. They are very probably not cheating on you. They have better things to do with their time. If you are jealous, that's your lookout. Resist taking out your frustrations on the kids or your work colleagues. Instead, let that natural Monkey generosity shine forth.

A stretch of beautiful weather provides April with a worthy send-off. Do not let this period elapse unappreciated, for storms may lie ahead. Live more outdoors. Plan a picnic. Take the whole family on an extensive hike. Do be careful not to upset a beehive or anthill. Stinging insects will quickly put a damper on the festive, cavorting-in-nature, mood. Just think. When thunder and lightning or torrential downpours have you barricaded inside your house in the coming weeks, you can look back fondly on memories of frolicking in meadows with loved ones.

MONKEY May 2016

Brace yourself. Mercury's first retrograde of the year begins on April 28 and lingers until May 22. Its fickle dalliances will cloud just about every possible method of communication. Luckily, seeing as we are currently embroiled in your namesake year, you should survive this period relatively unscathed. But all the same, do not tempt fate. Now would be a dangerous moment to embark on definitive ventures. Nor should you sign an apartment lease or refinance a mortgage at this time. Instead, go back and complete an unfinished project - that half-written screenplay you started in university? Dust off the manuscript. The garden you began to plant last spring? Hit the local store and buy some new perennials. Returning to tasks whose ideas have already germinated is the best way to circumvent the littlest planet's obfuscations.

Fall-out from your embarrassing outburst in April continues to irritate you. Perhaps your significant other has been giving you the cold shoulder after that ugly scene. Or maybe the children are spending more time alone in their bedrooms after you were so hard on them. Use a twofold method of making amends. First, sit down and talk with the aggrieved party. We all know you like to wax eloquent. So head to a local restaurant for a scrumptious meal with them. As the delicious food dilutes the tense atmosphere, explain (again) that you are sorry and that you will do your best to avoid such incidents in the future. The second way to heal these wounds should come naturally, as you are notoriously generous with presents. Buy the wounded party a necklace or new watch or a computer game or ticket to a concert. Combined with your honeyed words, such a blatant bribe will warm the frosty air.

Toward the end of the month, do something to hone your mind. Start learning a foreign language. Get hooked on playing Sudoku. Study an interesting tome on a subject which impassions you, but with which you have no experience. You are already sharp as a razor's edge. But even the sharpest of intellects needs practice to maintain its advantage. Your increased abilities will help you achieve some goals in the coming months. Plus which, you will know all the answers to the trivia questions at the bar or during the game show. Depending on who your companions are, that Monkey wit and knowledge may set a certain someone's heart a-racing.

MONKEY June 2016

A bout of heartburn or indigestion helps June get off to a horrid start. It probably feels as though knives are slowly traversing your alimentary canal. If this upset persists for more than a day, see a doctor. But if the pain is manageable, take matters into your own hands. Dietary choices are surely at the root of your tummy troubles. Begin to track your nutrition intake. Make sure to consume multiple helpings of fruit, vegetables and nuts every day. And eat at meals. Not catch-as-catch-can grab a bite here and there. Unless you are a confirmed vegetarian, you shouldn't neglect the lean meat section of the supermarket. A natural balance of different food groups is vital for the Monkey constitution. A word of advice? Tackle that plate of steamed carrots and peas by itself. Or eat a salad before your meal. Then let the vegetable *hors d'oeuvre* slowly drop into the machinery of your digestive tract. Eat slowly. Then wait five minutes before moving on to the brown rice. Conversation is a perfect aid to a good digestion. Handling each element of cuisine separately will ease the pressure. Both food preparation and its consumption take time. If you shirk that aspect of your life - your gut will let you know about it post haste.

Anticipate a modest workplace success around mid-June. Maybe a progress report of "exceeds expectations" will make the sun shine a little brighter. Or you might meet your monthly sales quota earlier than expected. Smile and allow yourself a celebratory pat on the back. But do not take your foot off the gas. Instead, use your victory as a stepping-stone to further triumphs. Read the specific comments in the evaluation to determine why you earned those high marks. Continue to chase new deals and contracts. Improving your output even more will lift you into high regard by the powers that be before year's end.

You may witness a stomach-turning scene near the end of June. Perhaps a store clerk is harassing someone of a different skin color for barely being able to speak the local language. Or maybe you will hear about a slumlord evicting some poor, vulnerable foreigners. Let people say what they want about your other characteristics, but you have zero tolerance for intolerance. So intervene. Tell that clerk or shopkeeper off for being a racist. In all likelihood, the other shoppers are wishing they had the courage to emulate you. As for the slumlord's shady housing practices, research lawyers or associations in the area who specialize in handling such cases. Hire them on to do their worst to the abuser. And don't forget that even an anonymous bit of gossip will go a long way toward improving that nasty landlord's behavior.

MONKEY July 2016

That possible advisor or partner you met in April is likely to resurface in early July. Perhaps you will be connected with a mandatory "mentor" due to workplace policy. Except instead of being an awkward, forced interchange, this meeting will blossom into a fruitful relationship. Or maybe that ravishing colleague is simply playing hard to get. Again, continue to put yourself out there. You may feel like a braggart as you ramble on about your accomplishments to your older tutor. But if you keep quiet, how is he or she supposed to accurately judge your capabilities? Talking about yourself will help this person see your potential. As for the flirtatious coworker? Avoid speaking with him or her for a day or two. Upon reassuming your entreaties, you will find your efforts much more successful. Absence really does make the heart grow fonder.

In mid-July, financial disputes with a roommate or live-in partner threaten to sour your good mood. Could be something simple such as splitting the price of a pizza among three people which somehow turned into you footing half the bill. It's a minor annoyance and can be forgiven. But perhaps a live-in partner will decide to go on a shopping spree. With your credit card. That kind of irresponsibility is harder to overlook. Before you blow your stack, think back to the genesis of your relationship. Has this type of mooching occurred before? Did you overlook some warning signs? If so, you are partially to blame. And if repeated offenses have demonstrated that your lover or crony cannot be trusted with your money, eliminate them from your life. Follow Paul Simon's instructions: "Skip out the back Jack. Make a new plan Stan. Don't need to be coy Roy - just set yourself free." The benefits of staying with this person do not outweigh the costs.

Discussions of furry creatures dominate the end of July. Perhaps a neighbor insists on letting their dog do his or her business in your yard. Maybe your children are clamoring for a new pet. If you have to hear about one more animal-related issue, you might go bonkers. In fact, you are on the precipice of banning the subject permanently. But before you do so, the problem needs a catharsis. Confront the culprit behind your soiled yard. Face-to-face. Or if he or she is elusive, hold your nose, scoop up the poop, put it in a zip-lock bag and then place it on the neighbor's front stoop or porch. Do this for a few days. They will get the point. As for the children, sit them down and tell them that buying a cat or hamster is not in the budget right now. This diplomatic exchange should buy you at least a month of peace and quiet.

MONKEY August 2016

As August begins, a certain experience is going to alter your dreams for the future. Perhaps you always thought engineering or law was the perfect career for you. But after attending a job skills workshop, you realize that your natural talents actually run in an entirely different direction. Or maybe you will happen upon the love of your life. An adoration so strong that it eclipses all other passions in your life. Remember that you are supposed to be compiling a twelve-year plan for the future? Well, if your notepad is still gathering dust, break it out now. This new *amour* or change in your career direction may steer your plans elsewhere. After adjusting for this epiphany, those planning scribbles may finally feel as though they are leading somewhere.

In mid-August, work demands your undivided attention. Have you been whiling the day away, musing on your next move? Perhaps unfinished projects are piling up. Or you might have to intervene in an international negotiation after a coworker unknowingly insults the culture of the competitors on the other side of the table. Use your natural perseverance and research skills to polish everything off or to soothe any ruffled feathers. Whether you are catching up on neglected duties or putting out someone else's fires, this challenge will inject some much-needed excitement into your workweek.

The month ends on a peaceful note. In fact, you might look into spending a weekend away from home. But avoid crowded beaches. Bustling city tours will also not jibe with your mood. Instead, search for a quiet getaway. Perhaps you could rent a cabin in a nearby mountain range. Or offer to housesit for an absent relative or neighbor. Pass the time fishing lazily or horsing around with the domestic pets. Catch up on your reading. If you insist on doing homework, sketch out a rough idea of how you will tackle September's dilemmas in the office. Another Mercury retrograde starts on the 30th of August. With it comes pressure, white noise and obscurity. So enjoy this serenity while it lasts. And plan while you still can.

MONKEY September 2016

As September opens, Mercury retrograde is in full swing. Until the 22nd, no systems of communication are foolproof. Routine meetings degenerate into shouting matches. Parent-teacher conferences turn into heated debates on the merits of the educational system. Thwart these negative influences by keeping yourself at home. Not chattering to anyone who will listen may drive you insane. But a temporary spell of madness is better than burning important bridges at work or in your personal life. Just take care that you do not knock over a computer or drop a smartphone into the Jacuzzi in a fit of stir-craziness. The littlest planet has a peculiar way of ruining electronic devices.

You have an abnormally sharp mind. To take advantage of such a wily creature as yourself is almost unheard of. But toward the middle of September, be on the lookout for a scam masquerading as a legitimate enterprise. Is a Nigerian prince emailing you with a tempting once-in-a-lifetime opportunity to invest in a diamond mine? Did your bank just send you an unsolicited e-mail asking for your online passwords? Trust no one. Click on nothing you are not completely sure of. Although you usually have a reliable nose for such things, err on the side of caution. Buying a stake in precious gems can wait. And if your banker really needs you to confirm important information, you can handle it in person. As long as you view any financial entreaties with a skeptical eye, you can survive this period unscathed.

Although we are finally out of the Mercury retrograde woods, an uninvited guest toward the end of the month may make you question whether the retrograde really ended on the 22nd. Perhaps a drunken uncle or loopy aunt will show up on your doorstep expecting to be fed and sheltered for a week. Or maybe your children will invite the whole neighborhood over for a sleepover without first asking your permission. Put your foot down. This is no time for subtleties. Kick all unwanted relatives and local kids out of your living room. Forcibly, if need be. After such a hectic a month as this, you deserve some peace and quiet.

MONKEY October 2016

Toward the beginning of October, something (or someone) is going to keep you up all night. Maybe a long evening at the office will lead into a wild night on the town with a cute stranger. Or your main squeeze might decide that the two of you need a marathon date to reignite waning passions. On a less steamy note, a new scientific revelation may have you burning the midnight oil to keep up with the latest advances. As I iterated earlier, a solid night's sleep is vital for the Monkey psyche. But in this case, throw out the rulebook. Embrace the wee-hours adventure. If you end up dancing with your crush until the sun rises, the sleep-deprived day will be worth it.

In mid-March, current events may spark some hostility within your family. Perhaps a racially tinged murder will dominate the dinner-table conversation. Or extremist activity in the Middle East will provoke mixed reactions. You are in your element here. As a natural teacher, you love to wax eloquent about the issues of the day. Dive right in. Stimulate the discussion. Do not worry about controversy or escalating tensions. A healthy debate may actually serve to unite points of view. If those of differing political opinions can learn to agree to disagree, you will have yourself a more resolute clan.

As the month ends, a doctor's visit brings glad tidings. Maybe a routine checkup will come back as a clean bill of health. Even your notoriously delicate stomach has healed. Or...the doctor's visit might reveal a pregnant sibling or a cousin's first ultrasound might reveal a healthy fetus kicking around. Such positive news is welcome. Do not, however, tempt fate by heading straight to the heartburn table at the next buffet. And avoid lifting weights with the mother-to-be. Putting an added strain on your digestive system or jeopardizing the baby's safety would be folly. Instead, enroll in a yoga class and eat more fruits and vegetables. Stick to low-risk activities.

MONKEY November 2016

An early November encounter with a rare problem you have trouble solving leaves you frustrated. Perhaps your company is moving to a different location after a corporate buyout. Or your employer might be folding entirely. On the other hand, maybe a relative's divorce has you wishing you could have done something to save the marriage. Is your mind replaying the same scenarios over and over again? Stuck in a rut of second-guessing yourself? Stop over thinking. Get some fresh air. Work up a sweat at the gym or the park. Anything to force your cerebrum to focus on something besides what is taunting you. If you want to avoid tossing and turning in bed all night, you must accept (for once) that you are/were powerless to prevent this chain of events.

Your investments are due for a modest gain during November. Maybe your monthly expenses will be less than you had anticipated, leaving a surplus to be spent on yourself. Or a stock portfolio might yield higher-than-expected returns. As a naturally generous individual, you immediately think of buying new cell phones or jewelry for your loved ones. But hold off. Although you may be flush with cash now, the holidays are rapidly approaching. Stash the leftover moolah away. It will come in handy at holiday time.

Exercise is important for everyone, regardless of sign. But Monkeys especially need to work up a frequent sweat. Bereft of a regular program, you risk developing brittle limbs. In late November, a fad workout may draw your attention. Perhaps the idea of signing up for a local Cross Fit course will beguile you. Or maybe a crush or live-in partner will inspire you to start training for a triathlon. I would caution you to sleep on this decision. Barbells threaten to snap your arms. Long runs put your kneecaps in danger of collapsing. Overly rigorous activity is dangerous for your constitution. Do not let the urge to show off to that special someone make you bite off more than you can chew. Instead, take up a more traditional sport. The physical benefits of playing tennis, badminton or swimming will make a decent consolation prize.

MONKEY December 2016

October saw your family learn how to amicably resolve a heated debate. Now, a December emergency puts those Monkey problem-solving skills to the test. Is the notorious black sheep up to his or her old tricks—dropping out of school or getting busted with drugs? Maybe a beloved aunt will ask her husband for a divorce out of the blue. Maybe the adults are experienced enough to sort out their own issues. But troubled teens need all the help they can get. Do not spring an intervention on the angry adolescent. Simply have a sympathetic character sit down with him or her, one-on-one. Feel free to offer your own services. Use those oratory and listening skills to decipher why this character is acting out. Problems with younger relatives can be gnarly. But if you demonstrate understanding and compassion, you might help the whole clan dodge years of heartache.

That important mentor or associate you met in April? By mid-December, your relationship has come to a crossroads. It could be that diverging career paths are pulling you in opposing directions. Or maybe a third wheel is competing for his or her romantic attentions. Regard-less, you must act now to salvage this connection. For prospective business partners, pitch an idea for a savvy cell phone app, an econo-mic think-tank, etc. Something that would involve the two of you teaming up. For the potential *amour*, take them out for a fancy dinner and confess your feelings. But be clear in your message - you need more reciprocal passion. Only by joining forces in business or by knowing what to ask for in your love life can you prevent a breakup.

Mercury's final retrograde of 2016 arrives just in time for the holidays. From December 19 until January 8, expect the usual hazards of faulty electronics and vague correspondence. The last thing you need is an uninvited guest showing up on your stoop this month. Make sure that no one gets their wires crossed about vacation plans. In fact, this might be a good year for a quiet in-house celebration. After all, without a houseful of guests, how much damage can Mercury's influence inflict?

MONKEY January 2017

You are an expert at flying under the radar. That is fortunate, because early January will require every ounce of those skills. Either an irate boss is terrorizing the employees or a coach or trainer who woke up on the wrong side of the bed seems to be trying to beat you to death. Who ever it is, an authority figure wants someone to pay the piper for a blown contract or an uninspired workout. You might want to make excuses and embark on a suddenly remembered important "doctor's appointment". Steer clear of this rampaging fellow or woman until he or she has calmed down. At that point, poke your head out of the rubble and proceed with business as usual.

Unfortunately, the FIRE Monkey Year refuses to quietly slip off into the sunset. Mid-January sees some romantic backlash thrown your way. Perhaps you will catch some flak for flirting with your lover's friend. Maybe after a request to buy him or her a drink, an attractive barfly will turn you down point-blank. Should you slink away after this rebuttal? No. Rise to the occasion. Do not take the rejection personally. Just cast another reel. You will eventually get a better bite. If bantering with his or her friends was causing your partner jealousy, put the spotlight firmly back on them. He or she was feeling left out. Take this as a challenge. Lavish your better half with honeyed words and appropriate presents. If you make them feel important again, they will not be able to maintain that sullen frown for long.

As the end of January and the final days of the Monkey Year approach, put the finishing touches on your twelve-year plan. What did 2016 teach you about yourself? Did you experience any epiphanies about where you see yourself down in 12 years? By this point, you should be fairly certain of your long-term goals. Keep your 12 year outlook in a safe place. If you are unsure of yourself as the months and years go by, get out the list and use it as a guideline to stick to your master plan.

YOUR MONTHLY FORECASTS FOR THE FIRE MONKEY YEAR

2016

ROOSTER

Author's Note... Mercury Retrograde

Sometimes planets appear to be zooming backward through the zodiac. Of course this backward motion is only an illusion. The planet has not turned tail. But it appears to have. Astrologers call this apparent reversing: **"retrograde"**.

Any planet can be retrograde. But only Mercury's retrogrades cause communications to break down. Mercury has its retrograde period for a few weeks 3 or 4 times each year. Whilst Mercury is retrograde, we humans are encouraged to take stock, make plans and discuss different approaches to a variety of subjects. But because information is often muddled, promises broken and electronic devices on the blink during Mercury retrograde, we must remain flexible and open-minded. Advice? Always allow extra time for travel. Schedule changes are common. Do not sign any contracts or cement agreements during Mercury retrograde. Make no irreversible promises. Watch out for con artists. Make no final decisions, binding engagements or major purchases during a Mercury retrograde. You are allowed to have tantrums or rail against your fate. But Mercury will continue to be retrograde till it decides to go direct again.

Mercury Retrogrades
2016

January 5 thru January 25
April 28 thru May 22
August 30 thru September 22
December 19 thru January 8 2017

OVERVIEW OF 2016 THE YEAR OF THE MONKEY FOR THE ROOSTER

Remarkable Rooster,

This Fire Monkey year may inflame your Roosterish temper even more than did the Goat. Monkeys can be clever tricksters. They sometimes manipulate events and people in order to get what they want. You Rooster people prefer direct, uncomplicated communication and action. You get things done by doing them yourself. Not the Monkey. The Monkey gets things done and solves problems by circuitous and not always truthful methods. Notwithstanding, Monkeys can solve problems. If you need a quick fix for a long overdue predicament, dial-a-Monkey. Parts of this year may find you griping. You won't be cranky because the trains don't run on time.. Monkeys are good at punctuality. You will simply deplore the fact that in order to understand what's going on in this tumultuous year, you have to read between the lines. No your strong suit. You are a straight shooter. The Monkey prefers to throw curve balls. Instead of being able to sit calmly down and hash out a budget for the year, you will be obliged to watch for ulterior motives in your associates and partners. Even your private life will be clouded by this sense that secrets are being kept. This mood of concealed chicanery gets on your nerves. Although your nerves were certainly run ragged last year, this year may be worse. You may feel somewhat lost "What is going on here?" You wonder. Keep on wondering. Or ask a Scorpio/Tiger pal to peek beneath the surface and uncover the plot. Next year is your year. Life will improve – vastly. sw

ROOSTER January 2016

Mercury is retrograde almost the entire this month. The zippy planet rides backwards between the 5th and the 25th. This planetary glitch could make this last month of the Sheep year into a bumpy ride. Try to avoid signing legal documents and beware of sending text messages. They will go astray. And documents are not the only thing being lost this month. You will misplace and then find some vital possession this month - your bank debit card or your wallet, your smart phone or your dog.

Someone has a proposal this month. It might be romantic, but it could as easily be a partnership of the business variety. Either way, a retrograde is not the best time to be making a decision. Tell them you need time. Be kind, but firm. Wait until after the 25th to be certain your mind and heart are in agreement. Watch out for a faulty electrical appliance mid-month. One of your items is about to die. You have already noticed a problem. Your hair drier crackles and turns on off when it gets too hot. Your electric razor is making a strange whining noise. Be prepared to buy a new one before the month is over.

A new friendship has you on edge around the 23rd this month. You argue constantly; but could that be part of the attraction? The very fact you are so different challenges you both to widen your vistas and see new perspectives. Challenging? Maybe, but with humor and mutual respect this relationship is well worth the effort. You are due to go on a short trip at the end of January. It's strictly business, not a holiday. You did not choose the accommodation, which is a pity. There is something decidedly off-putting about your room. Check the bed sheets and towels before you use them. If they are not satisfactory, ask to change rooms.

ROOSTER February 2016

As February opens, get ready to go back to school. Your first class? Patience 101. The Monkey is already beginning to infuriate you. Perhaps a significant other will ask you for an extra-special birthday or anniversary gift. But it's up to *you* to figure out exactly what will set their heart a-flutter. Or perhaps a boss insists on giving you intellectually inferior tasks with vague promises of a "future reward" or a "payoff down the line." You prefer clarity and transparency in life. But the need to speculate will be a recurring theme this year. Roll with it. To choose that special present, discreetly poll mutual friends on what would make a spectacular purchase. As for the job, drop some hints about your quandary to an executive. He or she should give you a straight answer about possibilities for career advancement. Although not your style, such a roundabout method of problem-solving should be successful in a Monkey year.

You are no stranger to financial pitfalls. So a mid-February dip in earnings should come as no surprise. Perhaps budget cuts will eliminate your bonus or shrink a monthly commission. Maybe the payments for that cushy new sofa have started catching up with you. Before your blood pressure begins to rise, look into alternative sources of cash. How about if your roommates paid for the groceries this week? Does a buddy owe you a favor after you footed the bill for dinner last month? Collect on all outstanding debts. It may take some weaseling (which you hate); but you need to pinch pennies until your balance sheet stabilizes.

Toward the end of the month, a structural problem at home requires immediate attention. Perhaps a gas leak threatens to engulf the place in flames right before a dinner party. Or maybe a washing machine is vibrating across the room, spewing water onto the kitchen floor. You need to act fast. Grab the toolbox and get busy. If you are unsure of your first move, a quick Internet search should point you in the right direction. With your street smarts and work ethic, you can save the evening (or the tiles) from certain disaster.

ROOSTER March 2016

Toward the beginning of March, your lucky number will be six and will feature prominently. Maybe you will stay in a hotel room with that number on a promising business trip. Or you might have a hot date scheduled for the 6th. This auspicious sign will keep on surprising you throughout March. It can help you to win a promotion or even to charm a potential *amour*. Do not get too full of yourself. This hot six streak will not last forever. If puff your chest out too far, envious colleagues might begin hiding important insider info from you. Or a shameless brag will send that romantic companion running for the door. Pride is your enemy this month. It could erase all the progress you've made, so make sure that when you're ahead, you keep your head.

As the month progresses, family strife is at an all-time low. Children are completing homework dutifully. Teenagers are staying in on the weekends. Voluntarily. Parents do not even bother to complain about how you never come to visit. Treasure this calm before the storm. The Monkey-era craziness will sink its fangs into your clan soon enough. In the meantime, take the youngsters out for pizza. Initiate an affectionate phone call to your mother or father. Surprise your sweetheart with breakfast in bed. Build up some familial goodwill. Boost your credibility and earn brownie points now by committing generous and unselfish acts. That way you might mitigate the ferocity of any future hostilities.

You are notoriously set in your habits. New ways of thinking may go in one ear and out the other. But in late March, a fresh set of ideas is the only thing that can save your fitness. Have you been jogging the same circuit for a decade now? Are you lifting the same weights or hitting the same yoga poses as you have been since university? Time to tweak your exercise routine. Start sprinting hills twice a week. Drag a partner to an AcroYoga class or start figure skating. When the same stress is repeated over and over, the body derives less advantage and simply adapts. But if you vary the type of stress, your muscles have no choice but to grow stronger. Need more motivation? Just think about how smashing you will look when you go out on the town! That image should get you through the blood, sweat and tears of those new exercise routines.

ROOSTER April 2016

As April begins, your topsy-turvy private life has you tearing at your own feathers. Is an ex phoning you every night as you try to rekindle a relationship? Is a dysfunctional relative embarrassing you? Keeping those skeletons hidden in your closet is growing more difficult than ever. Before anxiety rips you apart, you must find a way to balance the two facets of your life. If a family member is turning into the neighborhood drunk, stop pretending that you aren't related and host an intervention. And if a significant other is shooting suspicious glances at your cell phone, admit to having a crazy former flame who won't remit. Your lengthy late night phone conversations will make a lot more sense to your sweetheart now. If you are open about your hectic personal business, colleagues and companions alike will be a heap more understanding.

Aggravations at work spoil the mood toward the middle of the month. Perhaps the employees under you are spending more time on Facebook than on their jobs. Or maybe, after a series of missed deadlines, the laziness of your peers is making you look bad by association. Your organizational skills are legendary. So if you are the boss, reconfigure the office seating. Like children, if certain workers are separated, they will be much more productive. And if the problem is slacker cowor-kers, call a meeting. Light a fire under them by letting them know you know they have been goofing off. Embarrassed to be called out by an equal, their output should improve. Plus, if your methods provide noticeable progress, the powers-that-be might finally place you in the management position you were born to hold.

Late April sees you mired in the doldrums. Progress on work projects slows to a crawl. Schoolwork and jobs have your loved ones preoccupied. Since you have a bit of free time, focus on plans for the immediate future. What would you like to get done at the office? What chores or long-term ventures would you like to finish around the house? Detail the processes you will use to reach these objectives. Make lists. Be specific. Mercury enters its first retrograde of the year on April 28 and doesn't go direct till May 22. Mayhem is could follow. Develop a plan of attack for the coming month. Don't make snap decisions or sign your life away on the spur of an impulse. Minimize the fallout from future interrupted communications by reserving your judgment and/or signature till after May 22.

ROOSTER May 2016

As May takes the reins from April, Mercury retrograde is in full swing. Regular lines of communication may have broken down. Perhaps literally. A downed wire might cut off telephone or TV service from your home. Or the wireless network could crash, sending everyone in the office scrambling to find alternate methods of correspondence. Until the 22nd, when Mercury returns to its normal orbit, follow that late April plan of attack to the letter. If you implement the processes you've already outlined, you should be able to reach your goals in spite of the utter chaos around you.

Toward the middle of the month, more drama in your personal life will test that Rooster resilience. A long-term girlfriend or boyfriend might dump you unexpectedly. Perhaps two of your best friends are feuding. Or the problem could be something simpler, but still upsetting—like your favorite watering hole shutting down for good. Give that relationship a week before writing it off forever. If that union was meant to be, he or she will find their way back to you. If you are caught in the crossfire of two angry companions, remind them that they are behaving in an immature fashion. Brutal honesty will be the most effective method of repairing that connection. And if a bar shutting its doors has you that upset? Maybe you should take advantage of its closing and swear off social drinking for a bit.

Anxiety has been mounting in your chest for some time now. Personal pressures, normal workplace worries, and a stretch of humid weather make for a deadly cocktail. Around the end of May, the tension has reached a breaking point. You despise admitting weakness. Let alone asking for help. But you must find an outlet for these frustrations. Are slackers tempting you to blow your stack? Work off that frustration.

Try exercising during the lunch break. Are nighttime fights with a spouse or loved one starting to affect your office demeanor? Take a long, leisurely hike by yourself. There's no need to go sprinting off to a shrink just yet. Instead, find a passion or a physical challenge to take your mind off your personal nuisances. It's guaranteed; you will sleep much better at night.

ROOSTER June 2016

In early June, a long-buried issue will drive a wedge between you and your officemates or family members. Perhaps racial or ethnic violence will drive you to pick a side to defend. Or is it a political race that is polarizing the local community? You are staunchly in the camp of a particular group. But this is not a clear-cut struggle. Maybe no one knows who fired the first shot in this metaphorical gunfight. Or perhaps both candidates for office have inconsistent voting records on issues you deem crucial. You tend to see thing in black and white. Nuances escape your notice. You are sometimes simply unable to empathize with the other guy's point of view. My advice? Mind your tongue. Voicing uncompromising beliefs is not worth losing a friend or a job over.

A mid-June swoon in the economy has you nervous about the plunging numbers in your bank account. But for once, a bit of financial luck (or is it skill?) should save the day for you. Maybe a benefactor will offer to pay you handsomely for a freelance marketing or consulting job. Maybe the sector you work in will experience a boom while everything else is busting. Or a mail-in rebate you earned by buying a cell phone or computer will finally appear in the mailbox. Be thankful for this monetary boon. But don't let it lull you into complacency. Burn the midnight oil as you polish off independent projects. Continue to strive for excellence in the boardroom or office. If you keep busting your tail feathers, you can boost your profits in spite of the Monkey's mischievous spirit.

Toward the end of the month, take a look through your closet. Are those dress shirts looking a little threadbare? Have you been seen wearing that cocktail dress an embarrassing number of times? No Rooster worth his or her salt would be caught dead wearing mismatched colors or last season's styles. So treat yourself to a shopping spree. Pick up some fancy new duds. Spring for some sexy shoes. You deserve a treat. And once you've modernized your wardrobe, you might as well peacock around town. After all, the whole point of dressing to the nines is to get noticed. Go out and turn some heads.

ROOSTER July 2016

As July begins, backroom machinations are occupying your thoughts.

Perhaps muted whispers stop abruptly when you walk into a meeting. Or huddled family members start diversion conversations about the weather or what's for dinner whenever you enter the room. You detest subterfuge. But during the Monkey year, such deceptions are a fact of life. So assume the worst. Work associates are probably gossiping about your personal life. In all likelihood, the relatives are scheduling a vacation *sans*-Rooster. On the bright side, maintaining a trust-no-one mindset will make it easier to look out for number one. Start plotting your own private corporate takeover or tropical holiday. If everyone else is keeping secrets from you, they cannot expect you to sit idly by, twiddling your thumbs. Start scheming!

The middle of June presents a romantic opportunity. In the midst of the Monkey's obfuscation, your direct nature will serve you well with the opposite sex (or the same sex, if applicable). Stride on up to that cute face at the bar and ask for a date. Invite your partner on a sentimental vacation, just the two of you. Act boldly, and the world will be your oyster. But make sure to follow through on any promises. If you swear to take a lover to St. Tropez, you'd better start saving for the plane tickets now. And if you make plans for a riverboat tour for two on Saturday, make sure you show up. Don't leave your partner sobbing on the docks.

As July comes to an end, watch out for unsafe electrical appliances. Has the computer charger been sparking whenever you plug it in? Does the light switch threaten a shock when you flip it on? Don't try to fix it yourself. Best have a licensed electrician check out the wiring. Calling in an expensive professional to save the day may feel like a cop-out. But electricity is "iffy" and should never be relegated to an amateur handyman or woman. Safety first.

ROOSTER August 2016

In the beginning of August, you might get ditched by the family. Perhaps they will take a cruise with every last cousin and in-law in tow - except you. Or maybe your parents will decide to visit someone who is studying abroad and will claim they didn't know you might want to go along. Was your invitation was mysteriously lost in the mail? Probably not. In all likelihood, your relatives assumed you would be too busy to accompany them. In any case don't take it personally. You may be surprised when they announce a special holiday plan especially for them - and you!

Unfortunately, various events may force you to make a cold romantic calculation in mid-August. Maybe a casual girlfriend or boyfriend wants to spend more time together than you are comfortable with. Or it could be that a paramour's profession of love makes you realize that such feelings are not reciprocated in your own heart. Perhaps you are simply not in love with this person. If that is your conclusion, then you have no choice but to tell them the truth. The longer you wait to burst their bubble, they more attached they will grow. Of course no one doubts your ability to be straightforward. My advice? If you want to let this person down gently, wine and dine them first. Sharing a hearty meal together will help you break the news gently.

As the month comes to a close, look around your kitchen or dining room. Are the seat cushions slowly degenerating into a different color? Are the hinges on the collapsible dinner table rusted shut? It may be time for some new furniture. Start flipping through the IKEA selections. Or shop the equivalent inexpensive household goods distributor in your area. Keep an eye out for bargains. But do not rush any decisions. If you are patient with your search, the perfect set of chairs or nesting tables will come along and give your home the face lift it so badly needed.

ROOSTER September 2016

The early days of September are dominated by Mercury's disruptive forces. This retrograde lasts from August 30 to September 22. You know the drill. If possible, delay important conferences and the signing of life-changing documents. Focus on restarting old processes that you never quite completed. In particular, look into previous household projects. Did you begin to replace the gutters last May? Do the walls in the basement remain bare? Use this opportunity to finish what you started. Get out the ladder and nail in those new eaves. Dust off the brushes and get to painting that relaxation room. By the time Mercury's influence wanes, you will have an achievement you can be proud of.

A mid-September incident at the workplace will test your management skills. If you have people working under you, private problems are likely to get dragged into the light of day. Perhaps a workplace romance is interfering with productivity or making colleagues jealous. Or family strife is turning a certain cubicle dweller into a grouchy ogre. On the other hand, it could be that you yourself are having difficulty balancing a multitude of assignments. Put on your thinking cap. Would a refreshing bowling trip (in place of a normal workday) ease those tensions? How about transferring a headache-inducing employee to another department? If you act decisively, you can minimize any potential damage from an office drama. You may feel you are drowning in an excess of responsibilities. Only way out is to tackle projects one at a time. Checking items off your to-do list gradually is the only way to avoid losing your mind.

In late September, take some initiative with your personal hygiene. Have the bristles on your toothbrush gone horizontal? Are skin rashes or acne breakouts becoming too frequent to ignore? Hit the drug store or pharmacy. Look for state-of-the-art dental products. An ointment for those unsightly blemishes is also a must. If you are proactive in caring for your teeth and skin, you will save yourself a lot of heartache (and money) down the road. During the last week of the month, keep an eye out for an unexpected face. A former authority figure may make a welcome appearance in your life again. They will have changed - a lot! And for the better.

ROOSTER October 2016

In early October, a new character is moving into your neck of the woods. Sometimes a recent arrival to the area is desperate to make some connections. This person may be a stranger or the sibling of an acquaintance. They may keep coming round to your place seeking some connection and continually ask you to hang out or grab some dinner with them. Such forced interaction feels unnatural. But if you make an effort to take this person seriously, the acquaintance will benefit you in the long run. Luckily, you are a natural host. So dust off that charm. Invite neighbors and pals over for a homemade meal or a round of drinks. Introduce the newbie to any local contacts who might prove useful to him or her. It looks as though character may end up being a valuable business contact. Or a welcome romantic rebound. One thing that is certain. If you treat them poorly or seem standoffish, nothing positive will ever develop from your relationship.

Toward the middle of the month, inflation has you chewing your nails. Perhaps a devaluation of the local currency has you wondering when the cost of oranges will start to soar. Or maybe you are nervous about your company's annual cost-of-living raise. In light of rising prices, is a 2% salary bump really going to cut it anymore? Before you really start to panic, step back and examine the situation. Especially in Monkey years, certain events are simply out of your control. Make any (logical) fears about running out of money known to your employers. If they are reasonable, they might readjust your contract to account for fluctuations in commerce. Don't waste energy stressing over macroeconomic trends? Unless you are a politician, there is nothing you can do to affect change. Simply continue to work hard each day. These fiscal problems will sort themselves out. Eventually.

As October nears its end, watch your temper. A simple board game or lighthearted competition can inspire a tantrum. Infuriated by losing a silly game of Monopoly, you may feel like overturning the playing table. Or a backyard croquet defeat may tempt you to punt the wickets across the yard. Take a deep breath. If you feel an outburst coming on, count to ten before you open your mouth or move a muscle. Chances are, taking a minute to cool off will prevent your competitive juices from getting the best of you.

ROOSTER November 2016

Who can resist the lure of a fat raise? In early November, a job opportunity, a new role within your current organization or a chance at a generous freelance contract may open up. Perhaps a local business will offer you a well-compensated consultant position. Or a promotion will bump you into the next tax bracket. Weigh the options carefully. You need recognition, so if the offer will bury you in some cubical, don't bite. Although this advisory gig or career advancement places you in a position of power, you may no longer have anyone directly answering to you. You like to be in charge. So weigh the pros and cons. Does the income bump make up for the decrease in prestige within your current position? If so, snap this gig up. But expect a slight spike in blood pressure when you make the switch. Leaving one's comfort zone is never easy.

The Monkey Year has handed you no shortage of aggravation. Toward the middle of November, those frustrations are manifesting themselves in unexpected ways. Is motivation lacking? Are romantic urges waning? Do you find yourself barking at loved ones across the dinner table? You really need a day to reboot your hard drive. Take some time off work. Preferably during the middle of the week. Go out and connect with nature. A long hike or overnight camping trip will do the trick. The experience will help you twofold. The exposure to the earth and its itchy elements will make you thankful for the comforts of home and hearth. And the change of scenery will recharge your batteries. Upon returning, mojo rejuvenated, both grouchiness and depleted libido will have been forgotten.

As the month nears its end, aging relatives are dominating the dinner-table conversation. Perhaps your parents are discussing contemplating a move to a retirement community. Or an uncle is exposing the details of his liver troubles. Or a second cousin twice removed is visiting and wants to bunk in with you. By all means, discuss possible solutions. But do discreetly change the subject if talk of aches and pains and declining health stretches beyond fifteen minutes. Older people tend to waffle on about their illnesses which can put a damper on everyone's appetite.

ROOSTER December 2016

As December begins, a vision of beauty incarnate may make your reappraise your own appearance. Perhaps your significant other will introduce you to a stunning new work friend. Or a relative or friend will return from some time abroad with the body of an Olympic athlete. The sight of this human perfection is provoking a rare feeling of insecurity in you. Are you afraid you are not as attractive? Be rational. Comparisons of this nature are unreasonable. This flawless person's twin advantages of genetics and free time (to work out and cook healthy foods) make any analogy to you one of apples and oranges. A Greek god or goddess person, while attractive, is always intimidating. You would be surprised how few people actually ask them for a date.

The middle of December sees a lull in the office and the home. The bustle of gift shopping prevents you from spending much quality time with your loved ones. And with the holidays looming, your bosses have one foot out the door. But you know what else is looming? Another Mercury retrograde. The last such period of the year begins on December 19 and persists until January 8. Your blunt nature will serve you well here. Everyone else is passive/aggressively hiding their true opinions, making meetings and negotiations baffling. But you love to cut straight to the chase. So ask the CEO outright why the bonuses are being slashed. Clamor for a raise. Being direct with requests and criticism will help you cut a swath through Mercury's characteristic haze of confusion.

Toward the end of the month, whether you want to or not, you will be spending time with family. Try to make these moments count for something besides bickering. Make progress. Are any relatives feuding? Perhaps a dispute over money has driven a rift between two siblings or cousins. Or an annoying but well-meaning in-law is complaining about being treated like an outsider. Use the holidays as an excuse to broker a compromise. Invite both parties to a celebration. But warn neither that the other is coming. The situation will be dicey at first. But after the icebreaker of tasty food and the glow of a few drinks, you may be able to spark a reconciliation. Even if your attempts fail, at least you tried to do something positive for the clan. That intention alone has to count for something!

ROOSTER January 2017

The beginning of the month should see a swell in your bank account. Perhaps a generous holiday donation came your way. We are never too old to be excited about an envelope stuffed with cash. Or perhaps you were a savvy shopper and hit the bargain outlets instead of the department store while doing your own gift shopping. Now you have a bit of excess cash. Take advantage of this windfall. Buy yourself a jacket in a January sale or splurge on a piece of fine jewelry. Spruce up your appearance. Do avoid fur. No use angering local activists further.

You are in the midst of working toward a long-term objective. Perhaps your goal is to add a thousand words to your memoir every day. Or maybe to hit the gym every Monday, Thursday, and Saturday. Without exception. You deplore having to deviate from your schedule. But toward the middle of January, some unexpected occurrence is going to interfere with your plans. An accident might double the length of your commute, leaving you too exhausted to tackle any projects by the time you cross the threshold of your house. Or a loved one's illness could disrupt everything and absorb all your free time . Holding yourself to writing three pages after eight hours at the office or cranking out three workouts per week is a worthy goal. But if unpredictable events throw your routine off, do have the flexibility to compromise. Wake up early on a Saturday or Sunday to catch up on your scribbling. Such an abrupt change in routine may offend your well-developed sense of order. But making a gracious transition may just keep you from losing your mind.

As January ends, you can throw the damned fire Monkey out the window. As he or she soars away through the trees, ponder what you mastered during the primate's turn at the helm. Did you pick up any new negotiating skills? Have you learned to better navigate the waters of passive-aggressive business meetings? Store any newfound abilities in your bag of tricks. Of course you may not even need them during the fire Rooster year which starts on January 27, 2017. Triumphs and windfalls will come easier. Enjoy the reversal of fortune!

YOUR MONTHLY FORECASTS FOR THE FIRE MONKEY YEAR

2016

DOG

Author's Note... Mercury Retrograde

Sometimes planets appear to be zooming backward through the zodiac. Of course this backward motion is only an illusion. The planet has not turned tail. But it appears to have. Astrologers call this apparent reversing: **"retrograde"**.

Any planet can be retrograde. But only Mercury's retrogrades cause communications to break down. Mercury has its retrograde period for a few weeks 3 or 4 times each year. Whilst Mercury is retrograde, we humans are encouraged to take stock, make plans and discuss different approaches to a variety of subjects. But because information is often muddled, promises broken and electronic devices on the blink during Mercury retrograde, we must remain flexible and open-minded. Advice? Always allow extra time for travel. Schedule changes are common. Do not sign any contracts or cement agreements during Mercury retrograde. Make no irreversible promises. Watch out for con artists. Make no final decisions, binding engagements or major purchases during a Mercury retrograde. You are allowed to have tantrums or rail against your fate. But Mercury will continue to be retrograde till it decides to go direct again.

Mercury Retrogrades
2016

January 5 thru January 25
April 28 thru May 22
August 30 thru September 22
December 19 thru January 8 2017

OVERVIEW OF 2016 THE YEAR OF THE MONKEY
FOR THE DOG

Diligent Dog,

Monkey years can be way tricky. It doesn't look like this one will be an exception. Monkeys know all the ropes and will use cleverly them to climb up and over the rest of the world. As brilliant as you Dog people are, you are hardly ever guilty of hoodwinking merely for the sake of putting something over on someone. You want justice and mean to get things done right. But for once, in this complex year, you might just be obliged to take a big risk and start a new business or do something else quite daring. Why not try to strike it rich? Instead of remaining cozy in the back seat, you can use your wits to jump into in the driver's seat. It's about time you saw some extra financial gain. The family situation in the Monkey year will be happier than it has been in awhile. You may be more the center of attention than you like to be. Take it in stride. Invite your parents, your in-laws and your kids to share in the fun with picnics and barbecues, road trips and fun in the sun. You are always good to your family. But the reverse has not always been true. Enjoy this clement period while you can. While everything is moving so smoothly, you might want to have a few medical checkups. See your doctor for a general exam. Go to a specialist for specific symptoms and don't forget to visit the dentist every six months. You are cautious by nature. Nobody knows better than you that it's better to be safe than sorry. sw

DOG January 2016

The Dog warrior of December becomes the Dog worrier of January. The bills from the December shopping frenzy begin to arrive. You quake at the pallor of your bank balance. You realize now (in hindsight) that in December you were a bit drunk on your recent success and had a wad of extra cash in your paws. Not like you to go overboard. Okay you did it. You have run up some debt. But it can be whittled away with your dogged perseverance and determination. Have a chat with your bank manager. Bankers like honest straightforward people like you. They tend to prefer granting overdraft privileges to folks who confess to their excesses than with clients who come crying victim.

It's Mercury retrograde again. Starts January 5, 2016 and lasts till the 25th. Plunk in the Middle of January something goes wrong with the electricity at home. Could be caused by a storm or some kind of glitch in the central system. Fair warning. Do not tinker with electricity. You can be a competent mender of broken possessions and you are talented for building fires in the fireplace or chopping wood. But electrical matters are best left to the experts. Make sure your shoes have rubber soles when you plug in the iron or the electric saw. Call the central utility bureau to be sure it's not their fault. If it isn't, you better call in an electrician.

The last week of January (after the 25th when Mercury has gone direct) you will receive some paperwork about a certain project you had thought was defunct. But apparently it isn't. You initiated this innovative idea awhile back and fished around to get funding for its implementation. But at that moment nobody picked up the bait. These new documents put things in a new perspective. By the end of 2016 (Year of the Monkey) you might be running your own business selling a product of your own design.

DOG February 2016

As the Monkey's reign gets started, your legendary loyalty has you lodged between a rock and a hard place. After years of your faithful service, your employer might hire a younger worker to replace you. Or maybe a boss expects you to gloss over some accounting inconsistencies in a monthly report. You are torn. People whom you esteem and care about seem to be betraying you. Listen to your instincts. If the company is grooming your replacement, it could be time to look for a new job. If you are being asked to cover up money laundering or condoning tax evasion, you could be tempted to take the inside info higher up the chain of command. It will be difficult to keep any chicanery to yourself as you cannot abide treachery of any kind. But do be careful not to be charged as the whistle blower who can sometimes end up being the fall guy. If you alert the higher ups to this monkey business, your conscience will be clear. But your position may be in jeopardy.

In mid-February, long-dormant and thorny family relations are warming up. Perhaps two feuding siblings will be spotted grabbing a beer together. Or a divorced couple will be overheard chatting amicably on the phone. After the strife of the past year, this unexpected reconciliation is a welcome change. But you are not out of the woods yet. A single dinner or phone call cannot erase all those months of bickering. To nudge the healing process along, host a dinner party. Invite the afflicted characters. If you can get them seated next to each other at the feast, you can hasten their rapprochement. Just keep the spirits and wines to a minimum. The last thing you need is a drunken tongue regurgitating an ancient grudge.

You are the designated protector. Toward the end of the month, stock the larder with fruits and vegetables. A nasty cold or stomach bug is set to sweep through the local populace. If you buttress your immune system with healthy eats and natural vitamins, you can stave off symptoms, protecting both yourself and your loved ones. Plus, replacing salty snacks and sugary desserts with some nutritious apples or plums will help keep your waistline trim. If you want to get the whole family eating the safe way, institute a new house rule. No chips or junky snacks. Two servings of berries, apples or oranges. Every day. And if rebellious youngsters refuse to participate? Relieve them of their video games till they decide to come around.

DOG March 2016

Normally, you prefer a steady, secure income. But as long as the Monkey is in charge, such reliability is hard to come by. So in this year of chaos, why not try to strike it rich on your own? As March begins, take a financial risk. Perhaps you have been drafting a business plan in your head. Maybe you and your high school friends have been talking about opening up a restaurant together. Or you could be thinking about investing in a brand-new tech start-up. Before you do anything rash, crunch the numbers. Do you have enough cash saved up to make your dream a reality? If not, put those plans on hold. Take a couple of months to stockpile assets. Start asking people in the know whether they consider the venture viable. If so, what do they advise as a next move? Scribble notes on their recommendations. Around June, you should be ready to revisit the issue.

Flirting with strangers in a greasy dance hall? Not quite your cup of tea. Still, during the middle of March, heady romance is in the air. But it won't happen in the back of a dark bar or a singles' club. Instead, have a look at a preexisting friendship. Is there a confidant on whom you've always had a secret crush? Or a coworker with whom you exchange knowing glances at office parties? Ask them to lunch. Or out for coffee. Don't go so far as to lay on a fancy dinner. Not yet. If you get too fancy, the person might consider the outing as a date. Ease into this business gradually. If the air does start to heat up fast, watch out. As you already get along so well, you have a solid foundation for a successful long-term relationship. This person may figure prominently in your life from this point forward.

Toward the end of the month, a furry face may liven things up around your place. Perhaps a new pet will trot into your life. Or nursing a rescued squirrel or bird back to health will occupy both yours and the kids' attention for a jolly couple of weeks. Enjoy this newfound company. The pressure is set to rise at work in the coming months. You can use a non-judgmental companion to help get you through the stressful months ahead.

DOG April 2016

As forecast, things are heating up in the office in early April. Is a new boss breathing down your neck to work overtime? Or are you being forced to take on the responsibilities of an absent colleague? No commensurate increase in pay is in sight just now and you are fit to be tied. This situation offends your sense of justice. Doesn't that new manager realize that you have a life outside the office? Is the company is too stingy to pay you extra for assuming the job of a missing crony? It doesn't look like this is the time to make a stand. Stifle the urge to snap at supervisors. Hold the sarcasm too. Keep your head down and continue to grind. The right people will soon catch on and then you will see the fruits of your patient labors

In mid-April, a friend is planning a big move. Perhaps a job offer in another venue is too lucrative to refuse. Or a significant other could be carrying them off in a new direction. Despite the fact you will miss them tremendously, send them off with a bang. A roof-raising going-away party would be fun for all. But it may inspire unwanted emotion and nostalgia for times gone by. The geographical distance between you two may increase; but a true friendship can withstand the distance test. E-mail and free long distance phone services make staying in touch a cinch. If you are worried you might fall apart when the festivities are through, why not start planning your next reunion now? Looking forward to a get-together will put some starch back in your sails and set you to looking forward to a road trip or jolly long weekend meet-up.

Toward the end of April, friends and family alike are nagging you about your sporadic exercise habits. But should you really be staggering into the gym at 7 AM three times a week? Is it absolutely necessary to schedule a 40-kilometer bike ride every Saturday? Tune out the criticism. Continue playing tennis or swimming a few laps when the spirit moves you. Why should you obey detractors who keep hounding you to hit the weight room? You are not productive under rigid routine. You're better off working up a sweat when you feel like it. At the end of the day, the results will speak for themselves.

DOG May 2016

As May begins, we are caught the throes of our first Mercury retrograde of the year. From April 28 to May 22, moderate chaos is to be expected. The influence of the littlest planet blocks our ability to communicate clearly. Dealing with business meetings, legal documents and other forms of correspondence will be thorny, to say the least. If you have any such affairs on the docket, postpone them. During this iffy time, focus your energy on projects that you've already started but never completed. Slap that final coat of paint on the garage walls. Update your resume to include your latest accomplishments. Dust the cobwebs off those half-written memoirs. Your time is best employed on long-term work assignments, redecorating endeavors and creative efforts.

Toward the middle of May your productivity will start steadily declining. You may find yourself napping on your keyboard pillow. Or maybe it will take you forty-five minutes to analyze three lines of text. How much sleep have you been getting? I fear it has not been the recommended eight hours. Push through your fogginess until the weekend. Then take either Saturday or Sunday (or both) as a "me-day." Clear your schedule. Do not leave your bed until noon. Have steaming meals delivered to your door. Spend the remainder of your waking hours absorbing mindless TV shows or amusing movies, reading densely populated novels or lounging in the garden. A day of rest will make up for some of the slumber you've been missing. By the time you return to work, your energy levels should have regained their former exuberance.

The end of May has you worrying about the health of your family. A sick relative's condition could be worsening. Or a son or daughter might break a bone or strain a ligament while playing sports. Unfortunately, you lack the ability to heal a torn muscle or banish your mother's bronchitis. That realization may make you feel powerless. Be proactive. You can still help out - albeit in smaller ways. Do not let that sprained ankle or swollen wrist sit overnight without a hospital visit. Athletic injuries will worsen if left undiagnosed. To stem the progress of your relative's chronic illness, keep perusing the Internet for new treatment techniques. You never know when scientists will develop a more effective remedy for recurring back pain, diabetes or chronic bronchitis.

DOG June 2016

If you were planning to undertake a financial venture, early June is the time to take the plunge. Put down a deposit on the future location of your restaurant. Rent a place whence you can run that dreamed-of beauty salon or soup and salad bar. If you cannot afford your own space just yet, get creative. What better place to found a marketing agency or an innovative technology start-up than right in your own garage? This is the Monkey year. Be extra careful with whom you partner up. If you nominate a childhood companion or weekend acquaintance to work with you just because you like them, you run the risk of losing the entire investment. Take their past successes and failures into consideration. Ask for proof. Drinking buddies and gossipy friends do not necessarily make for great business allies. Trust your head, not your heart. A sensible, serious individual with experience in the field will make for a much better associate than your tenth-grade lunch buddy.

After all this time, you would think that your family would remember how much of a neat freak you are. Toward the middle of June, their messiness will test your patience. Maybe a toddler is painting the walls with spaghetti. Or a spouse insists on leaving empty snack wrappers in the car. Gather the offending parties. Without losing your temper, describe which of their habits are driving you nuts. Suggest an incentive program. Every time a child takes out the trash or empties the dishwasher, they receive a bit of cash. Every time your significant other cleans up the messy house, they get a special romantic surprise. The place will be spic and span before you can say "woof." Money and romance talk!

As June ends, bold moves will be rewarded. Petition your boss for a fat raise. Ask that pretty car saleswoman or that handsome hotel concierge for a date. Make sure you have a plan of attack. If you are requesting a salary bump, list the recent accomplishments that make you worthy of one and discuss it with the boss. And before you go a-wooing, brainstorm some fun date ideas. Your crush is much more likely to say yes if you outline a concrete proposal for an evening at a play or a concert or an afternoon paddling on the river.

DOG July 2016

You have always had a good nose for a conspiracy. In early July you appear to have sniffed out a juicy ruse at your place of work. Are your company's financial records showing mysterious deductions? Is a boss throwing an annual party where only certain ethnics or specific type sexuals are invited? Before you go accusing a superior of cooking the books or discriminating against any group, ask a colleague what they think. In all likelihood, a low-level accountant made a simple mistake. If you blow a false whistle, it might cost him or her a job. As far as the exclusive get-together? Do you really want your boss to be called on the carpet because of your own prejudices? Think about possible consequences before opening your trap.

During the middle of July, stay on the alert while commuting. Pick-pockets and purse-snatchers abound. You can easily protect yourself on the subway or bus by keeping your hands close to your pants and maintaining a tight grip on your bag. And if you drive to work? Make sure to lock up your car when it's parked. And don't leave anything visible inside. The last thing you need is to be relieved of your GPS unit or stereo system. If a nefarious character finds your vehicle sealed, he will prefer to search for an easier mark. If, however, you drive a Ferrari, the thief might want to work a bit hard to crack the locks.

Around the end of July, you should receive an opportunity to generate a secondary stream of revenue. Perhaps a part-time gig tending bar or tutoring rich children in a subject like foreign language or algebra will open up. This endeavor will require some effort. No one ever accused the service industry of providing us with easy work. If a colleague tips you off to a can't-miss mutual fund or other investment, check the market regularly to verify ups and downs. If you do your homework and get a little lucky, you should be able to develop a reliable source of income from investment.

DOG August 2016

In the beginning of August, a relative will triumph over a longstanding challenge. Did a fresh-faced university graduate finally land that first "real" job? Did a significant other score a coveted promotion? Perhaps a youngster will make the football team for the first time. After the stress of the last few months, this long-sought after success is exactly what the doctor ordered. Use this event to build on the family bonding that started in February. Reserve a big table at their favorite restaurant. Under the guise of celebrating the achievement, invite loved ones who may not otherwise dine with each other. Gathering everyone under the same roof will renew a sense of unity. But you will need to take the initiative - making calls and emailing invitations. Maintaining a close-knit clan is up to you.

Toward the middle of August, take advantage of a chance to work from home. Which sounds better: sitting with perfect posture, dressed to the nines, through a yawn-inducing PowerPoint presentation? Or lazing around in your dressing gown while tuning in to a teleconference? Bug your boss for the leeway to spend at least one day per week in the home office. However, if you are freelance you might want to, stop trying to write three articles in one day and be tired of editing manuscripts in the same room in which you eat and sleep? Too much working from home means you need to get of the house. Heading to a cafe or library to polish off your to-do list will breathe new life into your work and make you much more productive.

The seasons are not due to change for a couple of weeks yet. So a late August cold snap or heat wave may take you by surprise. Such a stretch of extreme temperatures threatens to throw your immune system into flux. My advice? Drink lots of tea. Try not to exert yourself. And do not be stubborn in your attire. If it's hot enough to give you armpit stains by the time you reach the office, pack the jeans and sweatshirts away. And if it's sufficiently frigid to kill all the local mosquitoes, break out the sweaters and knit caps. If you use common sense and dress appropriately, you can protect your body from developing a nasty cold.

DOG September 2016

As September begins, Mercury goes retrograde again. The usual mix-ups and breakdowns will occur. The current retrograde will stretch from August 30 to September 22. By this point, you know the drill. If possible, important meetings and discussions should be tabled under Mercury goes direct. During this particular wonky period be on the lookout for malfunctioning electronics. A sparking laptop charger might cut off your wifi connection. Or an unreliable cell phone will spontaneously send embarrassing photos to everyone in your contact list. To combat these baffling phenomena, handle business face-to-face. Scribble your parents a physical letter (gasp). The less you handle modern technology during this retrograde, the better.

The middle of the month may see an ultimatum from a significant other. Have you been ducking the marriage discussion? Or the eternal moving-in-together dialogue? Maybe your partner has yet to hear the words "I love you" pass from your lips. Or maybe you're feeling shy and are reluctant to ask out that cute crush. Your lover (or future lover) needs a sign of commitment. Some indication that you plan on sticking around for a while. But you are all heart. You cannot commit to just anybody. Be honest with yourself. Does your heart beat a little bit faster just hearing somebody's name? Are they worthy of your loyalty? If so, make a copy of your house keys. Buy an engagement ring. Beg the pleasure of their company full time. Once invested, no one makes a more faithful companion than you. Once the two of you are entwined in romantic bliss, all your uncertainties will be but distant memories.

As September comes to an end, creaky joints are complaining. Again. Is an arthritic elbow or knee flaring up? Did a simple game of basketball leave you moaning in agony? Do not dash for the bottle of painkillers just yet. And stay clear of the overcrowded emergency room. Could be moisture in the air is to blame for making those bones ache. At least wait for the current humidity or rain shower episode to dissipate before doing anything drastic.

DOG October 2016

By early October, you should be reaping the fruits of that June financial undertaking. Perhaps a big corporation will come calling with a lucrative offer for your little startup. Or maybe your do-it-yourself marketing agency will score a landmark contract. But just because you've netted a small profit, don't get lazy. It's imperative you continue putting in long hours and carefully overseeing day-to-day operations. A poorly run restaurant will soon be out of customer and luck. And even the most revolutionary mismanaged technology company risks getting eaten alive by larger competitors. As long as you maintain a healthy paranoia about failure and work longer hours than you ever have before, the venture should survive its infancy.

Around mid-October, look up a long-lost acquaintance. Perhaps you could reconnect with a former partner-in-crime from your university days. Or maybe it's time to reconcile with the ex who broke your heart. Embarking on a conversation out of the blue may feel awkward. But breathing new life into an old relationship could provide unexpected benefits. That crony from college could link you to some important business contacts. Or tip you off to a juicy job opening. And that bygone *amour*? Their emotions may have cooled long ago. But you want to remain friends and would rather the ugly breakup not be your last mutual memory. Phone them up. Chat about work, home, the weather. Steer clear of matters of the heart. Forge an amicable rapport. If you find yourself re-attracted the old flame, think twice before acting on the attraction. Remember why your relationship came apart in the first place. Put the heat on low under the friendship. But don't get carried away.

Have you been feeling lethargic of late? Stomach looking a bit doughy? Toward the end of October, do add some physical activity to your life. Perhaps CrossFit, with its combination of weightlifting and cardio. Or a mixture of calisthenics and resistance training. Varying the types of exercises is the best way to tone muscle and melt fat. Plus, having a new challenge to prepare for every day will help you remain motivated. Avoid grinding bodybuilder workouts and monotonous long-distance runs. Boring repetitive motions will only dull your initiative for getting back in shape.

DOG November 2016

Around the beginning of November, taking up a cause or joining a humanitarian movement may strike your fancy. Perhaps an upcoming election will inspire you to volunteer to hand out fliers for the Green Party candidate. Or noting all the garbage on the side of a local highway will spur you to join an environmental organization. Before you pledge your allegiance, run a background check on the organization. Has that so-called "Green" politician been accepting "donations" from oil companies? Is that "keep our forests green" group more of a gathering of superficial socialites than one of committed activists? It is your Dog-like instinct to fight for justice in all its forms. But it looks like this particular cause is not worthy of your loyalty. Reserve your efforts for a faction that's actually making a difference.

In the second week of November, you face pressure from an unex-pected source. Maybe a former peer will be elevated to a position of power at your place of work. And follow their promotion by insisting on micro-managing your day-to-day activities. Or perhaps a parent will phone you up to chastise you for certain of your life choices. Take these new developments with a grain of salt. That newly appointed boss? Their helicopter leadership style will not last long. He or she is trying to prove through excessive zeal that they deserve their new position. Once their insecurity wears off, things will return to normal. And if Mom or Dad voices a critique? Fill them in on your life plan and ambitions for the next few years. Hearing about those plans to go back to school or finally pop the question should mollify any concerns they may have about your future.

Toward the end of the month, take an umbrella when you leave the house. Sudden downpours threaten to ruin your ensemble and drown your *coiffure* to a flat top. A word of caution about whom you choose to brush lips with. A simple kiss may turn out to have far-reaching consequences. Perhaps a bout of mononucleosis will find you bedridden for weeks. Or that accidental smooch will turn out to have been accomplished with your boss's forbidden son or daughter. Think with your brain, not your libido. Give complications a wide berth at this stage. Sometimes going home alone is better than the alternative.

DOG December 2016

Hold onto your hat during the early days of December. Slow the pace. As everyone scrambles to complete projects before the holidays, your job may feel like it's drifting out of control. Is your superior sending out edgy mass emails? Is a colleague crying in the bathroom stall because he or she missed a deadline? Resist the urge to proofread thirty pages of financial data in twenty minutes. And skipping lunch to binge-write sports articles would be a bad idea too. Drastically speeding up your routine will result in below-par output. Instead, drop by the office on a Saturday. Or use a quiet Sunday to get some work done from the sanctuary of your bed. If you give up part of your weekend, you can maintain your normal speed during the week. Relaxing while at the computer will help you retain some semblance of personal sanity during the Monkey year's final push.

During the middle of the month, family drama sours the jovial mood. Perhaps the in-laws are upset that they were left out of vacation plans. Or cantankerous siblings are quibbling over who is the better cook. These arguments may seem trivial to you. But play the secret peacemaker. Privately urge both parties to be the first to extend the olive branch to the other. With any luck, at least one side will listen. And brokering a compromise now is of the utmost importance. If you do not act swiftly, late December's Mercury retrograde will upgrade this minor tiff to full-blown feud status. Luckily, if you can stem the bleeding before it really starts gushing, no relatives will stab each other over the eggnog or serve any poisoned fruitcakes for dessert.

From December 19 until January 8, Mercury retrograde dominates our lives. In particular, be wary of those ubiquitous anonymous gift-giving traditions. That bottle of wine you bought for the office Pollyanna could very well end up in the hands of the alcoholic. The automated whoopee cushion you were hoping your whippersnapper nephew would draw from the pile? It will most likely appear in the clutches of a most venerable (and huffy) aunt or grandparent. To keep things in perspective, dole out only the blandest of ties, socks or ultra plain placemats.

DOG January 2017

As January takes the reins from December, fallout from the last Mercury retrograde continues to cloud the air. But if you keep your lips zipped, you can avoid being affected. Perhaps a colleague will get tipsy at the annual office party and start flirting with the (married) boss. Or maybe a friend will accuse you of skimping out on the bill after an expensive dinner. Your best bet? Fly under the radar until the 8th. Do not participate in any water cooler gossip at your place of business. And take a rain check on that "Dutch treat" meal invitation. The less human interaction, the better. Dodge drama.

Toward the middle of January, take stock of your finances. Is the side business you started in June maintaining its profit margin? Did December gift shopping deplete your savings? If you are running low on cash or if that moneymaking scheme is floundering, do not panic. After the New Year's celebrations are over, this month's expenses will not be so taxing on your bank account. What about that lagging financial project? Try to dig up a contact that works in marketing. Finagle some free advertising for your product. The customers will materialize. You have already planted the seeds for future success. If you continue to water the sprouts, you should reap a handsome harvest!

Too often we plough ahead into the next challenge without pausing to absorb the lessons of the past. As we prepare to bid adieu to the mischievous Monkey, take some time to contemplate the events of the past year. What mistakes did you make? How can you prevent similar errors in the future? Perhaps a particular triumph really stands out in your memory. How can you put yourself in position to achieve similar successes? Scribble down all your ideas. Store the notes in a location you can't possibly forget about. Then, when and if the going gets tough during the FIRE Rooster Year, you will have a concrete list of resolutions to fall back on for guidance.

YOUR MONTHLY FORECASTS FOR THE FIRE MONKEY YEAR

2016

PIG

Author's Note... Mercury Retrograde

Sometimes planets appear to be zooming backward through the zodiac. Of course this backward motion is only an illusion. The planet has not turned tail. But it appears to have. Astrologers call this apparent reversing: **"retrograde"**.

Any planet can be retrograde. But only Mercury's retrogrades cause communications to break down. Mercury has its retrograde period for a few weeks 3 or 4 times each year. Whilst Mercury is retrograde, we humans are encouraged to take stock, make plans and discuss different approaches to a variety of subjects. But because information is often muddled, promises broken and electronic devices on the blink during Mercury retrograde, we must remain flexible and open-minded. Advice? Always allow extra time for travel. Schedule changes are common. Do not sign any contracts or cement agreements during Mercury retrograde. Make no irreversible promises. Watch out for con artists. Make no final decisions, binding engagements or major purchases during a Mercury retrograde. You are allowed to have tantrums or rail against your fate. But Mercury will continue to be retrograde till it decides to go direct again.

Mercury Retrogrades
2016

January 5 thru January 25
April 28 thru May 22
August 30 thru September 22
December 19 thru January 8 2017

OVERVIEW OF 2016 THE YEAR OF THE MONKEY FOR THE PIG

Pristine Piggy,

This is an excellent year for Pig born people. The Monkey is on your side. Monkeys are tricky critters and may manipulate others for their own ends. They are indeed far more guileful than Pigs and have a lot to teach you. But you have a nose for authenticity and if you get a whiff of chicanery, you quickly suss it out. You rarely get really angry and you hate to say "no". But if you sniff out any Monkey business, you will be the first to call the perpetrator to order. Someone who holds a higher rank will try to unseat you at work this year. Perhaps he or she wants to give your job to a niece or slot in a girl or boyfriend. Keep a weather eye out for this double crosser and nip him or her in the bud. No. Don't go trotting to the boss and rat on this person. This is a Monkey year. You must endeavor to be sly-er than usual. Find a chink in the double dealer's armor and subtly threaten to tell all if he or she persists in trying to get quits of you. Better to be tricky than sorry. Last year's love picture should go forward smoothly as well. The naughty Monkey encourages all manner of lecherous profligacy. I wouldn't advise you engage in downright lascivious behavior. But you Pigs do enjoy the game of sex. Why not take advantage of the sexy tone of this Monkey year and allow yourself a bit of sexual latitude? sw

PIG January 2016

January should carry a communications health warning. Not only is Mercury retrograde back, but it's back for almost the entire month. From the 5th to the 25th, it would be best to not try to accomplish much of anything. Oh yes. Do water those potted plants, listen to music and paint your fingernails. Apart from routine tasks, you might want to back up your computer's hard disk and ensure that the anti-virus software is up-to-date. Is there any good news to the coming Mercury retrograde? There is. Your intuition us in tiptop condition. When words make no sense, and incoming emails read like they were translated from some ancient form of Persian... trust your gut. No matter how good the figures look. No matter how many times you've checked the contract. Trust your inner compass. If something you read feels fishy – throw it back. Wait to make decisions until early February.

As if sensing the approaching Fire Monkey year, on February 8th, of 2016, the middle of this month is capricious. One moment - you are stuck in place. The next, you zoom forward at a dizzying pace. In your love life this tendency might show up as silly fights. Not to worry, they will be followed by steamy making-up sessions. At work, misunderstandings cause you to you grind your teeth. Then suddenly the boss or your disgruntled clients declare their love for you. Your friends seem tired and listless. Yet they want to arrange an all night card game at your house. Up – down. Stop – go. It makes you dizzy.

The upcoming Fire Monkey year (February 8, 2016) will rekindle the Christmas holiday warmth and help you forget about a dull January. Monkey years are full of mischief. You will be challenged. You'll need to keep your wits honed. But for you Pigs, the Monkey Year will prove to be a non-stop adventure.

2016, The FIRE Monkey Year: This year, the Monkey is on your side. Monkeys are tricky critters and may manipulate others for their own ends. They are indeed far more guileful than Pigs and have a lot to teach you. Watch for chicanery in the workplace this year. Someone who holds a higher rank will try to unseat you. Perhaps he or she wants to give your job to a niece or slot in a girl or boyfriend. Keep a weather eye out for this double crosser and nip him or her in the bud. No. Don't go trotting to the boss and rat on this person. This is a Monkey year. You must endeavor to be slyer than usual. Find a chink in the double dealer's armor and subtly threaten to tell all if he or she persists in trying to get rid of you. Better to be tricky than sorry. Last year's love picture should go forward smoothly as well. The naughty Monkey encourages all manner of lecherous profligacy. I wouldn't advise you engage in downright lascivious behavior. But you Pigs do enjoy the game of sex. Why not take advantage of the sexy tone of this Monkey year and allow yourself a bit of sexual latitude?

PIG February 2016

As the Monkey year takes over, temptation is the name of the game. Is a ravishing new coworker attempting to woo you away from your lover? Perhaps you are trying to balance the attentions of two suitors at once. I'm not going to lecture you on how to control your sexual impulses. Those are your decisions to make. My only advice? Be open and honest in everything you do. If you are gallivanting around behind your partner's back, break off that stale relationship. Trying to satisfy two mates at the same time? Tell both parties that you are keeping your options open. Have you ever seen a juggler trying to keep too many balls in the air? No matter their skill level, there is always a point where everything comes crashing down to Earth. That will be your love life if you try to balance multiple clandestine romances. Besides, Pigs do not deal well with recrimination. You don't often commit chicaneries. But when and if you do and you get caught, you are devastated.

Toward the middle of the month, incompetence at your place of work will see steam fuming out your ears. Maybe you will catch an employee mesmerized by a video game in his or her Web browser during business hours. Or a partner in a group project will go out drinking instead of completing their share of the workload. You have every reason to be angry. But before you unleash that famous temper, take a deep breath. There are other ways of handling the situation. Investigate methods of blocking certain websites on the office network. Perhaps you can nip those wandering eyeballs in the bud. And that unreliable workmate who drinks instead of working on your joint project puts your own reputation in jeopardy. So use diplomacy. Employ your native compromising abilities. Offer to help the shirker finish some tasks. Or email him or her every half hour for a progress report. Unfortunately, micromanagement is the only way to hammer in this particular bent nail.

During the final days of February, if you are leaving the house, grab a poncho, or raincoat. Stormy skies abound. But that slick umbrella with the oaken hilt? Save it for the next governor's ball or cocktail dinner. You are likely to forget it on the train. Or lose it to a wily pickpocket. In fact, keep an eye on all your accessories this month. State-of-the-art smartphones and diamond-encrusted wallets will only attract the wrong kind of attention. And the last thing you need is another trip to the electronics store or jewelry shop.

PIG March 2016

The beginning of March sees nothing but glad tidings on the horizon. A marriage or childbirth is likely to gather all the distant family members. Or perhaps a yearly reunion or nephew's academic success will be the reason for congregating. Either way, reconnect with a relative you don't chat with very often. This person can provide something of value to you. Maybe a distant aunt will offer some sage career advice. Or a blue-collar cousin will tip you off to a deal on a quality used car. But if you huddle in your usual corner, sipping wine with a brother or nibbling at shrimp with an in-law, you will miss the opportunity that was right under your nose all the time.

During the second week of March, pat your pockets. Double-check your bank balance. Scams and thievery are still in the air. In particular, watch out for online swindles. Did a Nigerian email you asking for a hefty donation to help feed their family? Is a pop-up advertisement preaching the astonishing weight-loss capabilities of some weirdo supplement? Take all of these come-ons with a grain of salt. All anonymous charity requests are cheap attempts to pick up your checking account number. You are much better off contributing to accredited organizations like the Red Cross or UNICEF. Or give money to someone who is down on their luck so they can pay the rent. And that miracle weight-loss pill? Unfortunately, there are no shortcuts to a flat stomach. If you truly want to trim fat, exercise and diet will get do the trick faster and more effectively than any mystery pills advertised on the Net.

Toward the end of March, another broken appliance may give you *another* headache. Perhaps a leaky dishwasher threatens to flood the kitchen floor. Or an inefficient refrigerator will let all those scrumptious groceries spoil. You don't like asking for help. But watching a "How To Fix My (Blank)" YouTube video does not make you a mechanical expert. Call in a professional. A plumber or electrician should have your wonky machinery up and running in no time. Although admitting defeat stings your ego, the dazzling dishes or freshly preserved meats will make the embarrassment well worth it.

PIG April 2016

In early April, education is becoming a thorny topic in your inner circle. Is a glass ceiling at your place of work making you consider a return to school? Is a child struggling with algebra or chemistry or another sticky subject? Do not overreact. Every kid goes through phases. Get some personalized tutoring to lift the child over this hump. And remember, a troubled third-grader can easily develop into a straight-A twelfth-grader. Just maintain a positive, reassuring influence to help him or her stay confident. And going after that masters degree or trade certification might be more hassle than its worth. Your failure to climb the ladder could be a consequence of the company's hiring policies, not your qualifications. If leadership is too shortsighted to see the value of promoting from within, regardless of scholastic accomplishments on your part; then it might be time to test the job market with a brand new CV.

The middle of April adds another layer of intrigue to the Monkey's hodge-podge of curveballs. Someone of a higher rank is trying to oust you from your job. In all likelihood, a boss is angling to fill your vacated position with a paramour or glassy-eyed relative. Or perhaps the brass is preparing for another round of layoffs. Before you trot into the CEO's office to complain or confront the conniver during a meeting, remember what year it is. Take a page from the impish primate's book. Is that manager trying to placate a mistress (or mastress) with a cushy gig to prevent any blabbing about their affair? Is the company secretly outsourcing work to an illegal overseas operation? Drop a subtle comment or raised eyebrow to the offender. Let on that you know everything. Using such sly subterfuge will be more effective than causing a big scene.

As April comes to an end, release your inner social butterfly. Accept all invitations. Did a colleague propose an evening of dancing at a reggae hall? Or maybe a cute friend of a friend offers to take you camping? Ignore any hesitations and dive in. Although unfamiliar social settings may feel awkward at first, by the end of the festivities you too will be boogying as though it were 1975. And jump at the chance to take that trip to the country? You are most comfortable when surrounded by nature. A night spent under the stars about now would do wonders for your constitution

PIG May 2016

In early May, a gastrointestinal problem has you clutching your gut. Illness rarely comes at an opportune moment. But this flare-up is particularly poorly timed. Our first Mercury retrograde of the Monkey Year begins on April 28. Until May 22, that planet's influence will tend to make all forms of communication blurry. Meetings and consultations may especially lead to inaccurate conclusions. Do not be surprised if a doctor misidentifies your innocuous stomach flu as a bleeding ulcer. Or insists that your chronic acid reflux is just a hypochondriacal delusion. Wait until after May 22nd to start on any powerful medications. Get a second opinion on the cause of that stomachache. If the original diagnosis was incorrect, you may avoid heavy medication altogether.

Around the middle of the month, the miscommunication carries over to hearth and home. If you do not tread carefully, a dinner table political discussion threatens to turn into a full-scale brawl. Or maybe a youngsters' dispute over whose toy or video game is whose will lead to tears. Remember: Mercury is still making it difficult to make things clear. A sit-down powwow will only exacerbate tensions right now. Instead of belaboring sore subjects, treat the family to a day of distraction. A trip to the local theme park or swimming pool will quickly raise everyone's spirits.

As May winds down, a recurring problem is gnawing at you. Has a blight of ants or cockroaches invaded your kitchen? Is a noisy pet driving all the neighbors crazy? Do not go phoning an exterminator or shipping the dog off to obedience school. A do-it-yourself solution is much more your style. For inspiration, turn to that great multipurpose tool of our era, the Internet. Asking for advice in a Facebook status or tweet is a great way to survey different methods of ridding an apartment of an ant or fruit fly infestation. Sometimes a simple search engine query could divulge a technique to discourage that pooch from barking at everything that moves. Use your favorite time-wasting social network for something constructive!

PIG June 2016

Your devotion to your loved ones is a constant. But toward the beginning of June, a friend's turncoat ways may lead to a cooling-off period with someone. Perhaps, after being invited for dinner, a colleague will openly criticize your significant other's cooking. Or they will drop a smart remark to your live-in lover about his or her choice of outfit. Could be a newly converted comrade will not stop blabbing about their passionate religious persuasion. This person's thoughtless actions have more than annoyed you. They have shaken your trust in their judgment. How dare that coworker come into your house and spew insults! And after being pleasantly non-denominational for so many years, why did your buddy choose this moment to start sermonizing? Give the person in question a wide berth. No need to write them off completely. Who knows? In a month or two, their dalliance with radical Islam or fervent Lutheranism could be a distant memory. And they might actually realize they were discourteous. If they wonder why you're being so cold, make it clear that good manners count for you. If they recognize their *faux pas* and apologize, there might be hope for a rekindling of affection between the two of you.

An economic triumph should brighten your day toward the middle of June. If you work in sales, you might be due for a hefty commission. Or maybe an investment will triple its value in the course of a single night. You are no stranger to financial success. So do what you do best. Flip this asset and double your money. Sell off fifty percent of that stock. Use the proceeds to buy cheap shares in a hit-or-miss technology startup. And instead of putting that bonus check straight into the bank, treat the new client to an expensive dinner. Build goodwill. Who knows? They may tip you off to another potential buyer. With even deeper pockets.

Be careful of over tippling at the end of the month. You are predisposed to indulgences as it is. And the pressures of a high-stakes job or squealing piglets at home are certainly not helping. Instead of seeking solace at the bottom of a bottle, surround yourself with close friends and delicious food. The more delectable, the better. Gorging on delicacies, while not ideal for the waistline, will soon displace your thirst for alcohol.

PIG July 2016

As July begins, a workplace scene threatens to upset your digestion. Again. Perhaps a rival is openly criticizing your decision-making abilities. Or a manager is constantly nagging you to pick up the pace. You are not one to seek an argument. But there is only so much abuse a person can handle. If you must lose your temper, try to contain the fallout to a confined area. Take your ire out on that competitive colleague or badgering boss in the fire exit staircase, where no one can overhear your shouts and blistering words. While not exactly healthy for your arteries, such an outburst should earn you some respect around the water cooler.

Around the second week of July, a roommate is starting to bring his or her own workplace troubles home with them. Listen and sympathize. But give sound advice and don't fawn over them. You are no stranger to conflict on the job and the anxieties it creates. Here is your chance to be the voice of reason. Your live-in person could be reticent to speak frankly about what's stressing them out. Don't stop trying to pry out the details. Persuade them to talk it through. If you can inveigle this person into examining and expressing their feelings, you can save them a lot of frustration.

As the month winds down, a stroke of excellent luck will smile upon you. Perhaps you will miss the bus to work only to see it crashed on the side of the highway on the news later on. Or maybe you will visit the ATM and find someone's forgotten wad of cash still in the tray. Since this boon came at the expense of other people, pay it forward. Buy a homeless man a meal. Send a grandparent or old friend a ticket to come visit you. Contribute to a worthy charity.

PIG August 2016

As August begins, that April office rival is at it again. Apparently, they are still hoping to get you fired. Or transferred to another location far away from their comfort zone. Although it might feel like the only option, avoid a direct confrontation. Instead, find a workplace ally or two. Befriend a superior. If you already have a mentor figure, turn to him or her for advice. Chances are, they will have encountered a similar bully on the way to the top. Their experience can be your guide. Of course you will *not* ask this adviser to intervene on your behalf. Carrying tales never serves one's purpose. Tattling on a cohort will only exacerbate the problem.

Quality family time is difficult to come by in this modern age. Especially if you have cell phone-addicted teenagers in the house. So toward the middle of the month, institute a mandatory clan bonding night. No phones allowed. How does pizza and a movie Tuesday sound? Or mini-golf Thursday? At first, the kids will whine about missing the party or wanting to see their girlfriend or boyfriend. So pick a flick that they will enjoy. Or sneak them a beer on the golf course. If you keep the event low-pressure and fun, even the surly adolescents will be smiling soon enough.

You have never been one to shy away from style and authenticity. So a late August auction or garage sale will sorely tempt you. Perhaps an alluring pair of antique pearl earrings will call out your name at flea market. Or maybe Louis XVI's personal armchair will appear for purchase on EBay. Never would I counsel you to skimp on fashion. But such baubles will take quite a bite out of your bank account. Is flaunting a fresh piece of jewelry or some antique furniture worth eating Ketchup sandwiches for a week? Probably not. Sashay right past the alluring merchandise. Don't even think about reaching for your wallet or scrabbling in your purse for your credit card. If necessary, calm your pressing desire for luxury by breathing several times into a paper bag. Your sensible self knows full well that you are better off saving that cash for practical purposes.

PIG September 2016

Alas, the planetary bugaboo returns. From August 30 to September 22, Mercury retrograde disrupts our best intentions. You know the drill. Postpone that meeting with the President. Cancel the lunch date with the Prime Minister. Delay the peace summit with North Korea. During this Mercury retrograde your words can be warped and meanings distorted. While your schedule is clear, reopen an old project that you never completed. Did you start paving the driveway before losing steam? Is half of a short story gathering dust on your desk? Since you've already formed the original idea, the littlest planet has nothing to obfuscate. Take advantage of this period of time to polish off suspended chores.

As we get into the thick of the month, you may sniff out some Monkey business in the workplace. Did an attractive colleague mysteriously receive a promotion? Did you overhear rumors about an office party that you were not invited to? Before you go accusing anyone of professional misconduct or of concealing plans from you, remember: Mercury is still in retrograde. Chances are, you are misreading the situation. Perhaps that coworker has been taking night classes in his or her spare time. They definitely earned that pay raise. As for the fiesta? It's probably a surprise party—for you!

Around the end of September, a bout of insomnia has you struggling to keep your eyelids open during the day. You are tempted to turn to booze or prescription medication to knock yourself out. But relying on liquor or pills to fall asleep may lead to a host of other problems. Instead, take a holistic approach. Have you been living a too sedentary lifestyle? Start getting more daily exercise. Also, force yourself to wake up earlier. If you tire your body out and stop sleeping in mornings, you will find yourself snoozing like a baby when the sun goes down. Avoid the perils of self-medication at all costs.

PIG October 2016

In the beginning of October, watch your temper in public places. An upsetting text message may send you into a rage while you're at the movie theater. Or a family squabble in a shopping mall will cause your blood pressure to spike. Before you start throwing popcorn at innocent film patrons or grabbing a whiny kid by the ear for the entire world to see, remember where you are. Stay your hand and still your tongue. By the time you are safely ensconced back at home, your ire will have cooled. That bad news text you received will seem a lot less disturbing. Process the unfortunate information and move on.

As for the whiny children, don't initiate a screaming match. Try a stern talking to instead. Things are starting to look up by the middle of the month. Mostly thanks to another financial success. Is that stock portfolio continuing to churn out windfalls? Did you recently back into a hefty inheritance? Use this boon to do something nice for your family. Buy the kids a long-desired game or toy. Or surprise your significant other with a fine leather jacket or a shimmering necklace. If you outfit them in style, that lover will be less likely to quarrel with you over who will take care of washing the dishes. If there's any cash left over, think of a way to improve your house. If you replace that sagging sofa or invest in a hammock for the porch, everybody wins

Toward the end of October, a friend or family member is developing a nasty habit. Could be a live-in partner or a colleague who starts to chew tobacco or drink whisky whilst staring at the computer screen. Or is a younger sibling sneaking cigarettes in the backyard? This pattern is disturbing. Mention it once. Too many remarks will be interpreted as meddling. No matter how much you want to intervene, there is only so much you can do. Let your disapproval be known. After you've spoken your peace, ignore their behavior. As I said earlier, there is really nothing one can do to discourage a nascent addiction.

PIG November 2016

Toward the beginning of November, your good looks are going to land you in some trouble. Prepare to fend off the advances of an undesirable lover. Perhaps an innocuous smile from you will earn you the attentions of that horny neighbor you love to hate. Or your brother's wife or your sister's husband will pat your rear end at a family reunion. This is a potentially toxic situation. Although it may run contrary to your "never say no" personality, do say a resounding NO this time. If a simple NO doesn't work, sit the individual down and explain in no uncertain terms that you are annoyed by their assumptions. Tell them outright that you are simply not attracted to them. Sometimes, no matter how much we don't want to hurt feelings, we have to get nasty.

In the middle of the month, a family emergency may force you to scale back your standard of living. Perhaps an economic downturn will force you to auction off the name-brand purses or the exotic car. Or maybe the firing of a significant other will signal the end of those weekend beach trips with your friends. Do keep in mind the reason for your sacrifice. If there are kids in the picture, they need healthy food and new clothes much more than you do. And if your companion or spouse has lost their job, they may have to cut back (but not give up) on weekly massages or sessions with the shrink. Seeing your loved ones comfortable and thriving has always put a smile on your face.

That friend or relative who started a nasty habit last month? By the end of November, their addiction may actually be interfering with their work. Perhaps a cigarette-smoking nurse is about to lose his or her health insurance. Or a boss is complaining about the chewed tobacco remnants scattered around the colleague's desk. Could be the youngster who was sneak-smoking out back is now smoking full time. It's a shame and it cuts into your rescuer streak not to say or do something. But for people to put a stop to a dangerous habit, they have to want to give it up. Nothing we say or do will change that fact.

PIG December 2016

December begins with a flurry of activity. Long-lost relatives want to schedule a visit for the holidays. Stressed-out superiors are cracking the whip to make sure yearly goals are met. Before you have a Piggy panic attack, indulge in a guilty pleasure. Ironically, a double dose of greasy cheeseburgers may be the best salve for your (mental) health. Or perhaps an extra glass of wine at dinner will steady your nerves. Although comfort food and an uncorked bottle can help you survive these few weeks, by no means are they a permanent solution. But vacation looms. Once you can string together a couple of free days, you will find you care less about the unwanted guests and/or the whip-cracking supervisor.

Toward the middle of the month, a significant other's social exploration may put your jealousy to the test. Perhaps a lover will turn a few too many heads at the annual office party. Or you might spot the object of your desire on a dinner date with another man or woman. You are a purist at heart. You did not sign up to be part of a timeshare. So make your disgruntled feelings known. Instead of pretending you aren't upset, politely explain that their wardrobe choice for the social event in question did not leave enough to the imagination and that dating outside the relationship is not on the menu. If this relationship is meant to be, once you make your rules clear, your main squeeze will settle down. If they don't, they are not your type to begin with.

Tread carefully during the holiday season. From December 19 to January 8, our old friend Mercury is back in the spotlight. As always, communication will be impaired. So this may be the year to leave the drunken aunt or the terminally angry cousin out of any vacation plans. They will surely end up running their mouths and sparking a family feud. In addition, be careful of malfunctioning technology. Faulty

Christmas tree lights risk starting a house fire. Tiny electronic toy parts present a choking hazard for the little ones. But if you are extra vigilant in your search for broken bulbs or miniscule LEGO batteries, you can avoid most of the retrograde fallout.

PIG January 2017

Just when you thought you were free of the Monkey's mischievous clutches, he lands one final gut punch. As January begins, a mysterious illness invades your body. Perhaps a mild flu will linger in your system for a suspicious amount of time. Or a sharp pain will start lancing through your spine. Avoid reading medical journals or WebMD-ing the symptoms. Studies say that cancerous tumors begin with discomfort in the spine. That nagging cough has you convinced you have lung cancer. Self-diagnosing with too much information from the Web will only serve to terrify you. Swallow your pride. Bite the bullet and see a doctor. Nothing makes us feel better than a visit with a professional who can put our mind to rest.

In the middle of the month, good news abounds in the workplace. Has your office nemesis been fired? Did the CEO send you a congratulatory email after you landed a big sale? Allow yourself to feel proud. But do not go bragging about this success at the dinner table. A loved one has not been so fortunate. Perhaps a spouse recently received a public dressing-down after a clerical error. Or a friend has just been notified that his or her contract will not be renewed next year. Offer to buy the dejected soul a round of drinks. Or come home with a surprise bouquet of flowers. Right now, consoling this person is more important than giving yourself a pat on the back.

During January's final days, reflect on the outgoing Monkey year. What transpired in your career? How did your personal life change? Grab a notebook and pen. In a pinch, a computer document will also suffice. Divide the major events of the past twelve months into categories of good and not-so-good. How can you ensure that the coming FIRE Rooster Year has more of the positive and less of the negative? Scribble down some ideas on how to improve relationships, business dealings and your standing in the community. In future, when the going gets rough, refer to this list to help you right the ship.

Books by Suzanne White

CHINESE ASTROLOGY PLAIN AND SIMPLE

THE NEW ASTROLOGY™

THE NEW CHINESE ASTROLOGY

THE ASTROLOGY OF LOVE

THE NEW ASTROLOGY BY SUN SIGN SERIES

THE NEW ASTROLOGY POCKET GUIDE

Download an e-book at: http://suzannewhite.com
Available in paperback from Amazon.com.

Visit http://suzannewhite.com for Books, Personal Chart Readings,
Horoscopes & Lifestyle Advice

ABOUT THE AUTHOR

Best-Selling author Suzanne White is American. She lives in France. In Provence. Suzanne speaks and writes in both French and English. She has been a college professor, a fashion model, a journalist, an interpreter, a novelist, a fireworks salesperson, director of a Parisian Couture boutique, an elevator operator, a shoe salesperson, a single mother and a simultaneous translator. She came to writing late at age 33. By age 38, she had written her first best seller. THE NEW ASTROLOGY™, a savvy fusion of Chinese and Western astrological signs creating 144 NEW SIGNS. Suzanne White's fans and readers have dubbed her: "The High Priestess" of Chinese and Western Astrologies. Suzanne's books are on every best seller list worldwide. She does Private Chart Readings http://www.suzannewhite.com

And Suzanne answers all e-mail personally. suzanwhite@aol.com

51536138R00200

Made in the USA
Lexington, KY
26 April 2016